Guilty Acts, Guilty Minds

OXFORD
UNIVERSITY PRESS

Oxford University Press is a department of the University of Oxford. It furthers the University's objective of excellence in research, scholarship, and education by publishing worldwide. Oxford is a registered trade mark of Oxford University Press in the UK and certain other countries.

Published in the United States of America by Oxford University Press
198 Madison Avenue, New York, NY 10016, United States of America.

Library of Congress Cataloging-in-Publication Data
Names: Garvey, Stephen P., 1965–, author.
Title: Guilty acts, guilty minds / Stephen P. Garvey.
Description: New York : Oxford University Press, 2020. |
Series: Studies in penal theory and philosophy |
Includes bibliographical references and index.
Identifiers: LCCN 2019053400 (print) | LCCN 2019053401 (ebook) |
ISBN 9780190924324 (hardback) | ISBN 9780190924348 (epub) | ISBN 9780190924355
Subjects: LCSH: Criminal law—Philosophy. |
Criminal justice, Administration of—United States.
Classification: LCC K5018 .G374 2020 (print) | LCC K5018 (ebook) | DDC 345.01—dc23
LC record available at https://lccn.loc.gov/2019053400
LC ebook record available at https://lccn.loc.gov/2019053401

1 3 5 7 9 8 6 4 2

Printed by Integrated Books International, United States of America

Joseph P. Garvey, Jr. (1932–2017), father, for industria

Joseph Wagner (1945–2016), teacher, for philosophia

Contents

Introduction	1
1. Authority	20
Anarchism—Rex's Dilemma	24
Criminalization	26
Culpability	29
Punishment	30
Statism—Leviathan's Peace	35
Social Peace	36
Political Peace	40
Democratic Authority	46
A State's Right to Conformity	47
A Democratic State's Authority	50
Rights	60
Criminalization	62
Punishment	65
Culpability	70
2. Rights	72
Actus Reus	77
The Conventional Theory	78
The Rights Theory	87
Knowledge	87
Ignorance	90
Mens Rea	94
The Conventional Theory	94
The Rights Theory	95
Knowledge	97
Ignorance	103
The Jekyll Test	108
Boundaries of the Will	113
3. Knowledge	118
Actus Reus	121
The Capacity to Choose Otherwise	121
The Stephen Test	127
Insanity	132

Mens Rea 135
Duress Two Ways 135
Sacrificial Duress 135
Dysphoric Duress 140
Provocation 149
The Willing Addict 153
Tracing 157

4. Ignorance 162
Ignorantia Juris 166
The Maxim's Scope 166
Defending the Maxim 170
"Ignorance" of "Law" Defined 173
"Ignorance" 174
"Law" 178
Actus Reus 180
The Lex Test 181
Insanity 183
Mens Rea 186
The Jekyll Test 186
Putting Jekyll to Work 191
Forgetting 191
Lookin' for a Loophole 194
Imaginary Crimes 196
Stand Your Ground 199
Tracing 202

5. Agency 207
Tradition 210
Irrationality 222
Unintelligibility 224
Delusion 228
Lost Agency 233
The Demon Within 236
Defects of Consciousness 247
Hypnosis 247
Sleepwalking 250
Multiple Personality Disorder 252
Authority 256

6. Injustice 260
Revolution 263
The Revolutionary Road 263
Stop One 264
Stop Two 266

Stop Three 268
Stop Four 270
After the Revolution 270
Resistance 274
Soft Resistance 275
Hard Resistance 277
Reform 279
Culpability 281
Standing 286
Hypocrisy 288
Complicity 291
Authority 295
The State of Exclusion 297
Core Crimes 299
Non-Core Crimes 301
Conclusion 304
Index 311

Introduction

The criminal justice system has few friends these days. The allegations against it are legion, coming from all directions, aimed at features of the system from beginning to end, from policing to punishment. Yet when all's said and done, the allegations boil down, mostly, to the system punishing when, as a matter of justice, it shouldn't punish at all, or punishing too much when, as a matter of justice, it should punish less. The justice system teeters on oxymoron: It unjustly punishes the innocent, unjustly over-criminalizes, unjustly over-punishes, and unjustly mass incarcerates, which is no way to run a justice system of any sort. Indeed, the system has even been characterized as "evil."[1]

In the face of all this injustice, the system's critics want more or better justice.[2] That seems reasonable. But is justice the only measure or metric we have to judge state punishment? What, in particular, about legitimacy?[3] Does it make sense to ask if a person's punishment was legitimate, even if you firmly believe it was unjust? That would depend on your theory of the state, and here you have two basic options: philosophical anarchism or statism.

[1] Andrew Koppelman, *American Evil: A Response to Kleinfeld on Punishment*, 50 Ariz. St. L.J. 179, 179 (2018).

[2] *See, e.g.*, Sharon Dolovich & Alexandra Natapoff, *Introduction*, *in* The New Criminal Justice Thinking 1, 27 (Sharon Dolovitch & Alexandra Natapoff eds., 2017) ("[T]he criminal justice system of the 21st-century has become a primary battleground for civil rights and social justice."). We're now even beginning to see meta-critiques. *See, e.g.*, Benjamin Levin, *The Consensus Myth in Criminal Justice Reform*, 117 Mich. L. Rev. 259 (2018) (critiquing the thesis that critiques of the criminal justice system reflect a consensus).

[3] Political philosophers have lately taken renewed interest in the concept of legitimacy. For three recent additions to the literature, with an express focus on legitimacy, see Arthur Isak Applbaum, Legitimacy: The Right to Govern in a Wanton World (2019); Legitimacy: The State and Beyond (Wojciech Sadurski et al. eds., 2019); Political Legitimacy: NOMOS LXI (Jack Knight & Melissa Schwartzberg eds., 2019). For an earlier collection, see Legitimacy and the State (William Connolly ed., 1984).

Shifting from a focus on justice to a focus on legitimacy is, according to some commentators, "a move . . . characteristic of realist political theory more generally." Manon Westphal, *Theorising Modus Vivendi*, *in* The Political Theory of Modus Vivendi 1, 11 (John Horton et al. eds., 2019). Realists, or at least some of them, "assert the primacy of legitimacy by stressing the extent to which reason does not lead to unanimity in moral or political matters and hence the creation and maintenance of a legitimate authority that can make binding collective decisions on such issues becomes of paramount concern. Politics must settle through authority and law what cannot be settled through reason or morality." Enzo Rossi & Matt Sleat, *Realism in Normative Political Theory*, 9 Phil. Compass 689, 692 (2014).

Guilty Acts, Guilty Minds. Stephen P. Garvey, Oxford University Press (2020). © Oxford University Press.
DOI: 10.1093/oso/9780190924324.001.0001

Describing a state's action as legitimate means different things to different people. For our purposes, a state's action is legitimate if the state has authority, and a state has authority insofar as it has a moral power: the power to impose a moral obligation, on its citizens and officials, to conform to the law.[4] Philosophical anarchists believe no state action is legitimate, because no state can ever have what it would take to be vested with the power in which authority consists. Anarchists believe morality is the only authority we have: It alone has the power to impose moral obligations. If no state action is legitimate, then perhaps the anarchist should, if only for the sake of conceptual clarity, avoid talk of legitimacy altogether. If an anarchist nonetheless chooses to use the language of legitimacy, that's harmless enough, so long as we keep in mind that he draws no real distinction between justice and legitimacy.

Anarchists might, for example, say a state's laws are legitimate, and punishments imposed in conformity with those laws are legitimate, provided the laws and the punishments themselves conform to morality, and thereby to the demands of justice. When the state punishes, it punishes legitimately, for an anarchist, only insofar as its officials conform to the laws authorizing punishment, and only insofar as those laws themselves conform to justice. If its laws don't conform, the state punishes unjustly, and so illegitimately. That's not incoherent, but it removes any conceptual space between justice and legitimacy. At the end of the day, the only metric against which an anarchist has to judge state punishment is justice.

Enter the statist, with a stubborn fact: People disagree about what justice requires. These disagreements are, moreover, persistent and, it seems, often reasonable. What to do? We presumably need some practical way to carry on, to reach some resolution, and to keep the peace, however provisional,

[4] *See, e.g.*, Stephen Perry, *Political Authority and Political Obligation*, *in* 2 Oxford Studies in Philosophy of Law 1, 5 (Leslie Green & Brian Leiter eds., 2013) (observing that the "term 'political legitimacy' . . . [has] been accorded many meanings in the literature," but arguing that "a Hohfeldian power—the ability of a state to intentionally change the normative status of its subjects—is, both morally and conceptually, the core understanding of political legitimacy"). Although we'll continue to describe the relevant obligation as an obligation to conform one's conduct to the law, it would probably be more precise to describe it disjunctively, as an obligation to conform to the law, or if one chooses not to conform, then as an obligation not to protest one's conviction and punishment, insofar as one failed to conform to an obligation to which that state has assigned punishment as a sanction. *See, e.g.*, David Lefkowitz, *On a Moral Right to Civil Disobedience*, 117 Ethics 202, 202 (2007) (arguing that the "duty correlative to a liberal-democratic state's justified claim to political authority is in fact a disjunctive one: either citizens of such a state must obey the law or they must publicly disobey it"); Philip Petit, *The Control Theory of Legitimacy*, *in* Legitimacy: The State and Beyond, *supra* note 3, at 7, 11–12.

in the face of different beliefs about, and reasonable disagreements over, the obligations justice places on us. That job goes, as a matter of practical necessity, to the state. In the end, the state decides whose vision of justice prevails, and whose vision of justice gets embodied in law. Here's where the statist's path diverges from the anarchist's.

Unlike the anarchist, who believes no state action is legitimate, the statist believes democratic states do act legitimately, because they have authority, and with it, the power to impose a moral obligation to conform to democratically enacted law. When a democratic state resolves through law reasonable disagreements among its citizens about justice, it does so authoritatively, and as such, its citizens and officials are morally obligated to conform. When a democratic state punishes, when its officials conform to democratically enacted law authorizing punishment, the statist believes the punishment imposed is, all else being equal, legitimate, even if some (or many) of its citizens, whose visions of justice lost out in the arena of democratic politics, firmly believe otherwise. Legitimacy, for the statist, doesn't reduce to justice. Justice is one metric against which to judge state punishment, and legitimacy is another.[5]

An example might help sharpen the differences between the anarchist and the statist. Suppose John lives in a state in which the unauthorized use of Woodsy Owl's image is a crime. In fact, 18 U.S.C. § 771a does exactly that: "Whoever, except as authorized under rules and regulations issued by the Secretary, knowingly and for profit manufactures, reproduces, or uses the character 'Woodsy Owl,' the name 'Woodsy Owl,' or the slogan 'Give a Hoot, Don't Pollute' shall be fined under this title or imprisoned for not more than six months, or both."[6] A forest ranger friend of John told him § 771a made it a crime to use Woodsy's image without the Secretary's permission,

[5] *See, e.g.*, Matt Sleat, *Justice and Legitimacy in Contemporary Liberal Thought: A Critique*, 41 Soc. Theory & Prac. 230, 231 (2015) ("[S]urely the justice of a state is one thing (the extent to which its basic social, political, and economic institutions are in line with the demands of justice), while its legitimacy (the state's right to rule over those subject to it) is quite another."). Once justice and legitimacy are distinguished, they can combine in two ways (just and legitimate social order, unjust and illegitimate social order) and come apart in two ways (unjust but legitimate social order, just but illegitimate social order). *See* Philip Pettit, On the People's Terms: A Republican Theory and Model of Democracy 140 tbl.3.1 (2012).

[6] If over-criminalization had a poster child (or animal), Woodsy Owl would be it. For just a few examples presenting Woodsy as over-criminalization's Exhibit A, see Erik Luna, *The Overcriminalization Phenomenon*, 51 Am. U.L. Rev. 703, 704 (2005); Julie R. O'Sullivan, *The Federal Criminal "Code" Is a Disgrace: Obstruction Statutes as a Case Study*, 96 J. Crim. L. & Criminology 643, 652 (2006); William J. Stuntz, *The Pathological Politics of Criminal Law*, 100 Mich. L. Rev. 505, 517 (2001).

but John didn't care (or didn't care enough). His job paid minimum wage, and he wanted some extra cash. So off he went, selling T-shirts emblazoned with Woodsy.

A philosophical anarchist doesn't believe the state has authority, and suppose neither does he believe the state has any business criminalizing, as a matter of justice, the use, authorized or not, of Woodsy's picture. When the state punishes John for violating § 771a, hauling him off to jail for a month, the anarchist believes the state has punished John unjustly. He might also say John has been punished illegitimately, because, and only because, he believes his punishment was unjust.

It doesn't matter for now why the anarchist believes criminalizing the use of Woodsy's image is unjust. Maybe he has a well-articulated theory of justice in criminalization to back up his belief. Maybe he just feels it in his bones. Either way, when John heads to jail, the anarchist will see injustice being done. Indeed, if he believes the state unjustly punishes too many people for too many crimes for too long, he'll see injustice on a grand scale. He'll see a crisis of over-criminalization and mass incarceration, where criminalization is "over,"[7] and incarceration is "mass," compared to some baseline he's drawn

[7] Criminal law theorists have developed any number of normative theories of criminalization, which can then be deployed to identify crimes no just criminal code should include. The number of crimes thereby excluded would constitute one measure of "over"-criminalization. Most, if not all, theories of criminalization out there would, one can safely say, diagnose the U.S. Code, and probably all state codes, to be suffering from a bad case of over-criminalization. *See, e.g.*, Douglas Husak, Overcriminalization: The Limits of the Criminal Law (2008). We also have positive theories of over-criminalization, which try to explain why penal codes in the United States contain, according to some normative theories, too many crimes. *See, e.g.*, Luna, *supra* note 6; Stuntz, *supra* note 6.

Theorists have done less to develop normative theories according to which we can judge if and when a state suffers from "mass" incarceration, but that's beginning to change. *See, e.g.*, Richard Dagger, *Playing Fair with Imprisonment*, 23 The Good Soc'y 30 (2014); Hamish Stewart, *The Wrong of Mass Incarceration*, 12 Crim. L. & Phil. 45 (2018). For example, according to Vincent Chiao, "punishment theorists face a choice: either they can endorse the claim that the United States unjustly incarcerates too many people, or they can endorse a strictly deontological theory of punishment. What they cannot do is endorse both." Vincent Chiao, Criminal Law in the Age of the Administrative State 130 (2019).

If we're short on good normative theories telling us when incarceration becomes "mass" incarceration, we're not short on positive theories, which try to explain how our prison populations grew so much over the last forty-five years or so. According to one prominent account, our prisons are bulging because the war on drugs put too many people away for too long. *See* Michelle Alexander, The New Jim Crow: Mass Incarceration in the Age of Colorblindness (rev. ed. 2012). That account is familiar, but it probably explains only a small part of the increase in prison population. Our prisons are bulging, according to an alternative story, not so much because we imprison too many drug offenders for too long, but because, among a declining percentage of arrestees, more were charged with felonies, when in the past they would have been charged with some lesser offense, or not at all. *See* John F. Pfaff, Locked In: The True Causes of Mass Incarceration and How To Achieve Reform 6 (2017) ("The primary driver of incarceration is increased prosecutorial toughness when it comes to charging people, not longer sentences."). According to this alternative account, "[a]ny significant reduction in the US prison population is going to require states and counties to

(or tacitly assumed), based on some theory of justice, however inchoate, he believes to be true.

The statist approaches John's punishment from a different angle, with a different concern. When the state punishes John for selling his Woodsy T-shirts, it may or may not, according to the statist, be guilty of injustice. That would depend (in part) on one's theory of justice in criminalization. The statist knows a lot of people who, when they ask what justice requires, see § 771a as an obvious injustice. All he did, after all, was sell some T-shirts. It's not like he killed anyone. On the other hand, he knows other people who don't really see what the fuss is all about: Woodsy's image wasn't John's to profit from, and he knew it.[8] He basically stole something, knowing the law didn't permit him to steal it, and now he has to pay the price.

The statist has his own beliefs about what justice requires when it comes to punishing Woodsy T-shirt sellers, and he voices them in the arena of democratic politics, which is where disputes about justice get resolved in democratic states. Maybe he believes § 771a is unjust. Maybe not. Either way, he hopes his side wins and gets reflected in law, in which case justice, as he sees it, will be done. But justice isn't his first priority. His first priority is legitimacy, as a virtue of social institutions distinct from justice.

Again, unlike the anarchist, the statist believes the actions of democratic states are, or at least can be, legitimate, insofar as democratic states have authority. A democratic state's authority, consisting in the power to impose on citizens and officials a moral obligation to conform to the law, doesn't cease to

rethink how they punish people convicted of violent crimes, where 'rethink' means 'think about how to punish less.'" PFAFF, *supra*, at 185. Why more people were charged with felonies is harder to explain. *See, e.g.*, John Pfaff, *Decarceration's Blindspots*, 16 OHIO ST. J. CRIM. L. 253, 259–61 (2019) (exploring possible explanations, including as "[p]erhaps the most important," an increase in the number of prosecutors); Ryan D. King, *Cumulative Impact: Why Prison Sentences Have Increased*, 57 CRIMINOLOGY 157, 174 (2019) (prosecutors may have started to charge more people with felonies because a "larger proportion of arrestees had criminal records").

[8] Despite the apparent consensus banishing § 771a from any self-respecting penal code, one wonders if § 771a has been falsely accused. The bill (S. 1585) making Woodsy's unauthorized use a misdemeanor passed the House of Representatives on April 2, 1974, and the Senate on June 18. *See* 120 CONG. REC. 9308-10 (Apr. 2, 1974) (House); 120 CONG. REC. 19562 (June 18, 1974) (Senate). According to the House Report on the bill, the Department of Agriculture licensed the use of Woodsy's image and his slogan in exchange for royalties, which it used to further its environmental protection efforts. H. REP. NO. 93-948, at 2 (1974). At the time, another part of the Federal Code provided criminal sanctions to protect against infringing privately held copyrights for profit. Section 771a extended the same courtesy to Woodsy. 120 CONG REC. 9308 (Apr. 2, 1974) (statement of Rep. Edwards) (referencing 17 U.S.C. § 104). Today, punishment for infringing privately held copyrights is provided for in 17 U.S.C. § 506, but no one seems to complain about § 506. One wonders what makes Woodsy so different.

exist even when the law is unjust.[9] Some statists believe democratic authority knows no bounds. Nothing a democratic state does can be illegitimate, on this view, as long as the officials through whom the state acts conform their conduct to laws enacted through the democratic process. More cautious statists don't go that far, believing that democratic authority is limited authority, such that some state actions are illegitimate, even when democratically enacted law would otherwise permit them. Citizens of democratic states have, they believe, immunity rights, disabling the state's authority within the domain the right encompasses. When state action infringes those rights, the state acts *ultra vires*, beyond the scope of its authority, and therefore illegitimately.

When the statist sees John being jailed for selling his T-shirts, he wants to know, of course, if John has been treated unjustly. If he has, the statist will protest and petition to change the law. At the same time, he also wants to know if the United States has punished John illegitimately. He wants to know if the United States had authority, and if so, if it exceeded its authority, when it enacted § 771a, because and insofar as John had a right disabling it from enacting that section. When asking these questions, the statist brackets questions about the justice of § 771a, inasmuch as his fellow citizens disagree on the answers to those questions, and the state, democratically and for the time being, has resolved those disagreements in favor of § 771a. What remains is the question of legitimacy.

It takes three sets of rules to get to punishment. One set defines crimes. Another defines the conditions under which the state will ascribe culpability or guilt. A final set prescribes punishments. Citizens of democratic states have, according to statists who countenance limits on state authority, rights circumscribing the state's authority over each set.

Rights limiting the first and third sets are familiar, insofar as our constitutional tradition happens to recognize such rights. We have, for example, rights against the state criminalizing free speech or the free exercise of religion. Likewise, we have rights against the state imposing cruel and unusual punishments, including a right limiting the state's authority to impose grossly disproportionate terms of imprisonment. Rights limiting the state's authority over the second set of rules, the set of rules defining culpability, are less familiar, perhaps because such rights aren't part of our constitutional law,

9 "Legitimacy allows for an indeterminate range of injustice that justice does not." John Rawls, *Political Liberalism: Reply to Habermas*, 32 J. PHIL. 132, 176 (1995).

or at least not a very big or prominent part. Nonetheless, these rights exist, and deserve recognition. If so, what, in particular, are these rights?

This book offers an answer to that question, building on two ideas familiar to criminal lawyers, usually expressed in Latin as *actus reus* and *mens rea*, typically translated as "guilty act" and "guilty mind." When it comes to *actus reus* and *mens rea*, criminal lawyers profess a common creed.[10] As Justice Jackson put it over sixty-five years ago, "[C]rime . . . [is] a compound concept[] . . . constituted only from a concurrence of an evil-meaning mind with an evil-doing hand."[11] If that's right, if a crime is constituted from a concurrence of an evil-meaning mind (*mens rea*), and an evil-doing hand (*actus reus*), then presumably no one can (in some sense) be found guilty of a crime—the state can't (in some sense) ascribe guilt to a defendant's choice to commit a crime—without *actus reus* and *mens rea*. Unfortunately, the lawyer's creed is ambiguous.[12]

On one side of the ambiguity is the conventional theory, according to which lawyers, when they talk about *mens rea* and *actus reus*, always do so in reference to a statute defining a crime. *Actus reus* refers to the circumstance and result elements of an offense, together with some voluntary action, all of which can be found in the language of a statute. *Mens rea* refers to mental states, like intent or knowledge, likewise found in the language of a statute.[13]

Consider the crime of murder, defined as intentionally causing the death of another human being. Murder's *actus reus* is some voluntary act the result of which is the death of a human being other than the accused. Murder's *mens rea* is intent. At the time the accused voluntarily acted so as to cause the

[10] The *actus reus–mens rea* distinction is deeply entrenched in the way criminal lawyers think about and describe the criminal law, but fair questions can and have been raised about the usefulness of that distinction, as well as the usefulness of the concepts themselves. *See, e.g.*, Paul Robinson, *Should the Criminal Law Abandon the Actus Reus-Mens Rea Distinction?*, *in* Action and Value in Criminal Law 185, 189–90 (Stephen Shute et al. eds., 1993) ("What we refer to as *actus reus* requirements or as *mens rea* requirements are in fact a collection of entirely distinct doctrines," and the "[c]riminal law would be better off if we abandoned the [*actus reus–mens rea*] distinction and referred instead only to the individual underlying doctrines.").

[11] Morissette v. United States, 342 U.S. 246, 251 (1952).

[12] Distinguishing two different senses or conceptions of *mens rea* isn't new. Criminal lawyers commonly distinguish, for example, between a narrow, elemental sense of *mens rea* and a broader, culpability sense of *mens rea*. *See infra* Chapter 2, p. 94 n.54. The conventional theory of *mens rea*, discussed in the text, is equivalent to the narrow, elemental sense. The rights theory, also discussed in the text, is related to the broader, culpability sense of *mens rea*, albeit situated more precisely within an account of moral responsibility associated with "quality of will" theories, and conceptualized as a limit on state authority.

[13] Sometimes judicial interpretation results in additional elements being announced or discovered, but these additional elements are, officially at least, grounded in an interpretation of the language of the statute itself.

death of another human being, he must have intended thereby to cause another human being's death.

According to the conventional theory, *mens rea* and *actus reus* have no meaning or significance apart from the statute they reference. Moreover, the elements of any criminal statute are, nowadays at least, products of legislatures. Legislatures decide what elements make up this or that crime. *Actus reus* and *mens rea* are thus really nothing more, on the conventional theory, than labels lawyers use to describe a legislature's work product. The conventional theory allows lawyers to say things like, "The *actus reus* of section thus-and-so is such-and-such," or "The *mens rea* of section so-and-so is thus-and-such."

All that's helpful, but if the only purpose *actus reus* and *mens rea* serve is analytical, enabling lawyers to more easily organize and talk about the various bits and pieces of criminal statutes, then they're probably not worth getting too worked up about. Yet lawyers do sometimes seem to get worked up about *actus reus* and *mens rea.* Moreover, their angst appears based on the belief that it would, in some sense, be wrong for the state to convict and punish someone without *actus reus* or *mens rea*, even if he's patently guilty as charged under a statute.

The conventional theory of *actus reus* and *mens rea* isn't the only one around or imaginable. According to the rights theory, *actus reus* and *mens rea* are more than tools used to categorize the words used in statutes defining crimes. Understood as the conventional theory understands them, a*ctus reus* and *mens rea* are handy labels for classifying and organizing a crime's elements, but the conventional theory's rendering robs them of any independent moral force or significance. The conventional theory doesn't explain any sense in which it would be wrong to punish absent a guilty act or mind. *Actus reus* and *mens rea*, on the conventional theory, describe what a legislature has done in the exercise of its authority to define the elements of crimes. They don't in any way limit the exercise of that authority, or stand for any rights against its exercise.

On the rights theory, that's precisely what they do. *Actus reus* and *mens rea*, on this alternative account, mark boundaries on a democratic state's authority to define culpability. A democratic state has the authority to define the conditions under which it will ascribe culpability, just as it has authority to define crimes and prescribe punishments, but its authority to do so is limited, just as its authority to define crimes and prescribe punishments is limited. The requirements of a guilty act and a guilty mind impose substantive limits on the state authority's to define and ascribe culpability or guilt, and thus to render a person liable to punishment. If a democratic state ascribes culpability beyond those limits, it exceeds its authority. If it punishes a citizen who committed a crime but whose act or mind bore no guilt, the punishment it imposes isn't simply unjust; it's illegitimate.

Generalizations are generally risky, especially when dealing with fine-tuned arguments and ideas, which are often laced with fine-tuned caveats. Having said that, those who write about the criminal law appear, by and large, either to openly embrace philosophical anarchism, or if not, to remain silent, noncommittal or vague on the existence, nature, and source of a state's authority, understood as the power to bind conformity, even to unjust laws. The primary purpose of a criminal law theory, according to many writers, if not most, is to explain under what conditions state punishment is just, and to describe the rules comprising a just regime's criminal law. The central question is the justice of state action, not its legitimacy.[14]

Anarchical theorists of the criminal law can, of course, believe citizens have a moral obligation to conform to the law, but the existence of any such obligation would depend on the law's conformity to justice. Some writers, attempting to describe the rules of a just system of criminal law, tend to draw inspiration mostly or firstly from the resources of moral theory; others tend to draw mostly or firstly from political theory, although some theorists, perhaps even many, see themselves as drawing on both.[15]

On the one hand, criminal law theory appears for some to be, in the main, a species of theory beginning with, emphasizing, or located in, moral theory, where moral theory is understood as a normative theory governing the relations between and among individual moral agents.[16] On this account, the

[14] We'll continue to speak about the moral permissibility of state action in terms of justice or injustice, such that a particular rule, or action in conformity with that rule, is morally permissible insofar as it conforms to the requirements of justice. One could substitute or emphasize some other concept, like the "common good," as the relevant benchmark, such that a rule, or action in conformity with that rule, is morally permissible insofar as it conforms to the "common good." Any such substitution or change in emphasis shouldn't alter the general point made in the text, insofar as reasonable "people like us" disagree about the rules that "shape the life of [our] political association," whether we disagree over those rules because we disagree about the "right" or the "good" or whatnot. *See* Charles Larmore, *What Is Political Philosophy?*, 10 J. Moral Phil. 276, 306, 292 (2013).

[15] As George Fletcher put it many years ago in the opening line of *Rethinking Criminal Law*: "Criminal law is a species of political and moral philosophy." George P. Fletcher, Rethinking Criminal Law xix (1978).

[16] With apologies for any misunderstanding, we'd include, in the moral theory camp: Larry Alexander & Kimberly Kessler Ferzan with Stephen Morse, Crime and Culpability: A Theory of Criminal Law (2009); Larry Alexander & Kimberly Kessler Ferzan, Reflections on Crime and Culpability: Problems and Puzzles (2018); Douglas Husak, The Philosophy

theorist's goal is to develop a moral theory and use it to derive first-order rules for the criminal law, including rules implementing a theory of punishment. The theory, whatever its details, is then deployed to evaluate and pass judgment on the justice of the actual rules through which state actors decide what to punish, whom to punish, why to punish, and how much to punish. Reforms are then recommended where and when positive law and theory diverge.

On the other hand, criminal law theory appears for others, in the main, to be a species of theory beginning with, emphasizing, or properly located in, political theory, where political theory is understood as a normative theory governing the relations, not between and among individual moral agents, but between the state and the individual.[17] Nonetheless, the goal remains the same: to develop a normative theory and use it to derive first-order rules for the criminal law, including rules implementing a theory of punishment. Once again, the theory, whatever its details, is then deployed to evaluate and pass judgment on the justice of the actual rules through which state actors decide what to punish, whom to punish, why to punish, and how much to punish. Reforms are then recommend where and when positive law and theory diverge.

Whether insight and guidance come from moral theory or political theory, the overall project is to give answers to first-order questions about the requirements of justice: Should a state, as a matter of justice, follow this or that theory of punishment? Should its penal code include, as a matter of

of Criminal Law: Selected Essays (2010); Michael S. Moore, Placing Blame (1997); Victor Tadros, The Ends of Harm: The Moral Foundations of Criminal Law (2011).

[17] Again, with apologies for any misunderstanding, we'd include, in the political theory camp: John Braithwaite & Philip Pettit, Not Just Deserts: A Republican Theory of Criminal Justice (1990); Chiao, *supra* note 7; R.A. Duff, The Realm of Criminal Law (2018); Matt Matravers, Justice and Punishment: The Rationale of Coercion (2000); Guyora Binder, *Punishment Theory: Moral or Political?*, 5 Buff. Crim. L. Rev. 321 (2002); Chad Flanders, *Punishment, Liberalism, and Public Reason*, 36 Crim. Just. Ethics 61 (2017); Ekow N. Yankah, *Republican Responsibility in Criminal Law*, 9 Crim. L. & Phil. 457 (2015). Alan Brudner offers his "liberal theory of penal law" as an interpretive theory, in contrast to a prescriptive theory, "about when it is permissible for the state to coerce a free agent." Alan Brudner, Punishment and Freedom: A Liberal Theory of Penal Justice 326–27 (2009). He reserves for another day whether the theory he describes should be constitutionalized and its norms made enforceable through judicial review. *See id.* at 328.

In a recent contribution, Christopher Bennett starts with a theory of punishment (a communicative theory) and then asks what implications accepting such a theory would have for a theory of legitimate state authority. *See* Christopher Bennett, *The Authority of Moral Oversight: On the Legitimacy of Criminal Law*, 25 Legal Theory 153 (2019). In contrast, the present project starts with a theory of legitimate state authority and then asks what implications such an account has for the criminal law, and in particular, for the state's authority to prescribe conditions under which a person is liable to punishment (under any theory of punishment).

justice, this or that crime? Should it include, as a matter of justice, this or that justification defense or excuse defense, and if so, what should be its elements? Concerns about reasonable disagreement over what justice requires, based on different beliefs about what justice requires; questions about legitimacy (as a virtue distinct from justice); and sustained inquiries into the nature and grounds of, and potential limits on, democratic authority tend not, so far as one can tell, to frame the theoretical project.[18]

The present effort puts democratic authority and its limits front and center.[19] It asks not if the rules comprising the criminal law—rules criminalizing conduct, providing affirmative defenses, and authorizing types and degrees of punishment—are just. Instead, it zeros in on legitimacy. It first offers reasons to believe a democratic state is (or can be) legitimate, with the power to morally obligate conformity to its rules. It then tries to identify limits, captured in the twin requirements of *actus reus* and *mens rea*, on a democratic state's authority to ascribe culpability to a citizen who's chosen

[18] Another way to try to make the point might be to say the current project adopts a "conception of political philosophy [or theory] centered on the problems of conflict and authority . . . [rather than on one] that regards [political philosophy] as principally engaged in mapping out the structure of the ideal society." Larmore, *supra* note 14, at 289. Yet another way might be to say that most criminal law theorists appear to agree with Rawls insofar as they take justice to be the first virtue of social institutions, including the institutions of the criminal justice system, whereas the current project, in sympathy with recent work associated with "realism" in political theory, *see* William A. Galston, *Realism in Political Theory*, 9 European J. Pol. Theory 385 (2010), takes legitimacy to be the first virtue, even while justice remains the supreme virtue. *See* Charles Larmore, *The Truth in Political Realism*, *in* Politics Recovered: Realist Thought in Theory and Practice 27, 32 (Matt Sleat ed., 2018).

[19] Among the work of which I'm aware, that of Malcolm Thorburn, on authority, and Dan Markel, on specifically democratic authority, are probably most congenial to the analysis offered in Chapter 1. Thorburn, for example, emphasizes punishment as a practice that must be available to "vindicate" a state's authority. Malcolm Thorburn, *Punishment and Public Authority*, *in* Criminal Law and the Authority of the State 7 (Antje du Bois-Pedain et al. eds., 2017). Markel, meanwhile, argues that a "liberal democratic polity has a weighty and always available rationale for imposing [political] retribution, against competent offenders who violate a wide range of criminal laws, without justification or excuse, so long as those laws are otherwise consistent with a certain kind of liberalism and are products of liberal democratic authority," where "political retribution" functions to "vindicate" values to which liberal democracies are "committed." *See* Dan Markel, *Retributive Justice and the Demands of Democratic Citizenship*, 1 Va. J. Crim. L. 1, 6 (2012).

Thorburn and Markel focus on punishment. Their project is to explain how punishment, or at least the availability of punishment, is needed to "vindicate" the authority of a state (Thorburn), or more narrowly, the authority of a liberal democratic state (Markel). Chapter 1 ends up endorsing a similar conclusion, but the book's principal task, taken up in the remaining chapters, is to show how the requirements of *actus reus* and *mens rea* can be rendered as limits on the authority of a democratic state to assign culpability. As Thorburn insightfully says, once one sees the connection between "authority and the operations of criminal justice," two tasks remain: one, which he says is a "matter of constitutional theory, broadly understood," is to identify limits or constraints on the authority's jurisdiction; and two, to "contribute to substantive political debate about how the public authority ought to exercise its legitimate powers in the operation of criminal justice institutions today." Thorburn, *supra*, at 31. The present project is dedicated to the first task. Much criminal law theory, drawing inspiration from moral theory or political theory, appears dedicated to the second.

to do something the state has declared to be a crime. The focus is thus on one second-order moral constraint on a democracy's authority, to which a democratic state must adhere if the punishments it imposes are to be legitimate.

Chapter 1 opens with Ellen Campbell, who in a 1992 case captioned *United States v. Campbell*,[20] from the U.S. Court of Appeals for the Eleventh Circuit, challenged her conviction for money laundering. It brackets Campbell's legal challenges, and imagines she had instead claimed it was unjust for the United States to punish her for money laundering, as the law defined it, because she believed it was unjust, among other things, for the government to define her conduct as criminal in the first place. Chapter 1 uses Campbell's case, and the disagreement over the justice of criminalizing money laundering, to segue into a discussion contrasting philosophical anarchism and statism.

Chapter 1 tells two light-hearted stories. The first is about an imaginary monarch, an anarchist king named Rex. The story is meant to illustrate the anarchist philosophy, and especially the problems anarchism faces when citizens disagree about the rules justice requires. The second story is about a character named Leviathan, and his life on an island named Anarchia. Leviathan's story is offered in an effort to explain why any state, democratic or not, is morally permitted to punish those who commit what are called core crimes, like murder and theft, and why democratic states are (within limits) morally permitted to punish any crime pursuant to morally binding rules constituting the substantive criminal law.

Chapter 1 then goes on to explain why democratic authority is limited authority, affirming that citizens of democratic states have immunity rights circumscribing the state's authority and disabling its authority whenever its exercise would encroach on those rights. These include rights limiting the state's authority to define crimes and prescribe punishments, together with rights, which the remainder of the book identifies and describes, limiting its authority to define and ascribe culpability.

Chapter 2 introduces *actus reus* and *mens rea*, understood as immunity rights limiting a democratic state's authority to define culpability. It opens with two venerable cases from the United States Supreme Court. The defendant in *Powell v. Texas*,[21] decided in 1968, was convicted of being drunk in public, but insisted he was a chronic alcoholic who couldn't have chosen otherwise. The defendant in *Morissette v. United States*,[22] decided in 1952, was

[20] 977 F.2d 854 (4th Cir. 1992).
[21] 89 U.S. 65 (1968).
[22] 342 U.S. 246 (1952).

a World War II vet charged with stealing government property, but insisted he thought the property was abandoned, and so presumably didn't realize he was committing a crime when he took it.

If Leroy Powell, being an alcoholic, truly lacked the power to avoid being drunk in public, did Texas have the authority to enact rules allowing a jury to convict him? If Joseph Morissette, thinking the property he took was abandoned, truly didn't realize he was committing a crime, did the United States have the authority to enact rules likewise allowing a jury to convict?

Chapter 2 begins the effort, not completed until Chapter 4, to answer these questions. It distinguishes between the conventional theory of *actus reus* and *mens rea*, mentioned above, according to which *actus reus* and *mens rea* are labels used to categorize and describe the elements of criminal statutes, and the *rights theory*, also mentioned above, according to which *actus reus* and *mens rea* impose normative limits on the exercise of a democratic state's authority to define the conditions under which the state can legitimately permit itself to ascribe culpability to an accused's choice to commit a crime.

Under the rights theory, as we'll see, a defendant's choice to commit the crime charged doesn't satisfy the *actus reus* requirement if he lacks the capacity to conform his conduct to the demands of law, assuming he knows what they are; or, if he doesn't know what they are, lacks the capacity to know what they are. Likewise, his choice to commit the crime charged doesn't satisfy the *mens rea* requirement if his choice to commit it, or the ignorance in which he commits it, doesn't reveal an ill or indifferent will. A defendant's mind is guilty only if his choice or ignorance reveals a will worthy of blame, and a will is worthy of blame only if it manifests insufficient concern, compared to the will of a law-abiding citizen, for the law and its ends. Chapter 2 introduces a test, called the Jekyll test, for sorting ill and indifferent wills from law-abiding ones.

The next two chapters dig deeper, adding detail to the basic ideas introduced in Chapter 2. *Actus reus* and *mens rea*, as limits on a democratic state's authority, play out in one way when the accused realizes he's committing a crime, and in another when he doesn't. Chapter 3 looks more closely at *actus reus* and *mens rea* in the first scenario, when the accused realized he was committing a crime. Chapter 4 looks more closely at *actus reus* and *mens rea* in the second scenario, when the accused didn't realize he was committing crime.

United States v. Moore,[23] a well-known case from the U.S. Court of Appeals for the District of Columbia, decided in 1973, frames Chapter 3. Like Leroy

[23] 486 F.2d 1139 (D.C. Cir. 1973) (en banc).

Powell, Raymond Moore was an addict, only Moore was addicted to heroin, not alcohol. Charged with heroin possession, Moore insisted he lacked the capacity to choose not to possess heroin. He was, he said, compelled to use, and in order to use, he had to possess. Chapter 3 explains in greater detail the conditions under which the requirements of *actus reus* and *mens rea* limit the state's authority to ascribe culpability to someone who, like Moore, realized his conduct was criminal, but claimed his choice to commit the crime wasn't freely made, because it was either compelled or coerced.

When someone realizes he's committing a crime, but chooses to commit it anyway, a democratic state has the authority, most of the time, to declare him culpable, and to punish him accordingly. But not always. Its authority runs out if the accused lacked sufficient capacity to choose not to commit the crime charged (thereby failing the *actus reus* requirement, such that his choice was compelled); or, if he could've chosen not to commit it, if his choice to commit it, despite being a choice to commit what he realized was a crime, nonetheless revealed no ill will or indifference toward the law and its ends (thereby failing the *mens rea* requirement, such that his choice was coerced).

Chapter 3 introduces a test, called the Stephen test, for separating those who couldn't have chosen otherwise from those who could (and thus those who satisfy the *actus reus* requirement from those who don't). It also illustrates in more detail how the Jekyll test, introduced in Chapter 2 as a tool for sorting ill and indifferent wills from law-abiding ones (and thus those who satisfy the *mens rea* requirement from those who don't), would work when the accused realized he was committing a crime.

Chapter 4 opens with *Lambert v. California*,[24] a well-known but enigmatic case from the United States Supreme Court, decided in 1957. Virginia Lambert was a legal secretary, and also an ex-convict. Her status as an ex-con meant she was required, pursuant to the Los Angeles Municipal Code, to register with the Chief of Police. She never did, and was prosecuted. Like Joseph Morissette, Lambert said she didn't realize she was committing a crime. Morissette said he didn't realize because he thought the property he took had been abandoned. Lambert said she didn't realize because she had no idea Los Angeles required ex-cons to register. Chapter 4 explains in greater detail how *actus reus* and *mens rea* limit the state's authority to ascribe culpability to those who, like Morissette and Lambert, didn't realize they were doing anything criminal.

[24] 355 U.S. 225 (1957).

When someone chooses to do something amounting to a crime, but doesn't realize it amounts to a crime, a democratic state has no authority, as Chapter 4 argues, to punish him. That's the general rule, but it has a two-part exception. The state retains the authority to punish someone who didn't realize he was committing a crime, but only if he had sufficient capacity to realize he was committing a crime (thereby satisfying the *actus reus* requirement), and only if his failure to realize he was committing a crime was itself the product of an ill or indifferent will (thereby satisfying the *mens rea* requirement).

Chapter 4 introduces yet another test, called the Lex test, for separating those who could have realized they were committing a crime from those who couldn't. It also details how the Jekyll test, as the tool for sorting ill and indifferent wills from law-abiding ones (and thus those who satisfy the *mens rea* requirement from those who don't), would work when the accused unwittingly committed a crime. Along the way, it offers a brief in favor of retiring the venerable maxim *ignorantia juris neminem excusat* (ignorance of the law is no excuse).

Chapter 5 gets off the ground with a famous English case, decided in 1843, known as *M'Naghten's Case*.[25] Daniel M'Naghten killed Edmund Drummond, the prime minister's private secretary, mistakenly thinking he'd killed the prime minister himself. M'Naghten suffered from delusions of persecution. The Tories, he thought, were out to get him. The verdict at trial was not guilty "on the ground of insanity." Traditional doctrine nowadays says the insane shouldn't be punished because, as a result of mental disease or defect, they're incapacitated: They couldn't know or conform to the law. A prominent alternative, found in the academic literature though not reflected (at least not explicitly) in law, says the insane shouldn't be punished because they're hopelessly irrational. Chapter 5 spends most of its time casting doubt on these two approaches.

With the traditional doctrine and the irrationality alternative put aside, if not to rest, Chapter 5 soldiers on, describing and defending an unorthodox theory of insanity, according to which the insane are insane, not because they're incapacitated or irrational, but because they lack a sense of agency. On this theory, called the lost-agency theory, the minds and bodies of the insane move, and commit crimes, but the accused doesn't experience himself as the author of those movements. The *actus reus* and *mens rea* requirements,

[25] M'Naghten's Case, (1843) 8 Eng. Rep. 718.

as discussed in the preceding chapters, presuppose the accused experienced himself as an agent when his mind and body chose to commit the crime. Insofar as the insane don't experience themselves as agents, neither *their* act nor *their* mind is guilty, which places them beyond the state's authority to fasten culpability to their choices.

Chapter 6 returns to the disagreement, discussed in Chapter 1, between philosophical anarchism and statism. It begins with *United States v. Alexander*,[26] another well-known case, which the U.S. Court of Appeals for the District of Columbia decided in 1973. Benjamin Murdock, a defendant in the case, was convicted of murdering a Marine lieutenant named William King. Murdock's background, as his lawyer put it, was "rotten," because Murdock grew up impoverished in the Watts neighborhood of Los Angeles. Does the fact that Murdock's background was rotten, together perhaps with the fact that the state bore some responsibility for its being rotten, render it unjust or illegitimate for the state to punish Murdock for King's murder?

As one might expect, anarchists and statists approach Murdock's case in different ways. Some anarchists believe the state isn't morally permitted to punish citizens like Murdock, not because the state failed to lift them from unjust poverty, but because morality doesn't permit the state to punish *anyone*, whether advantaged or disadvantaged. Other anarchists don't go so far. They believe morality permits the state to punish disadvantaged defendants like Murdock, but nonetheless insist the state should punish the disadvantaged less, perhaps much less, than the advantaged. Still other anarchists believe morality permits the state to punish disadvantaged defendants like Murdock, but only if the state has standing to punish them, which it may not have, given how miserably it's treated them.

Statists tackle the problem differently. When anarchists say, as they sometimes do, that the state has treated some of its citizens so poorly as to exclude them from the life of the polity, or that it's treated them like second-class citizens, or that the disadvantaged aren't really members of the political community, what they seem to mean, so far as one can tell, is that the state has lost its authority over them. It no longer has the moral power, in which its authority consists, to bind them to conform to democratically promulgated rules. If so, then the statist can offer one of two replies to this challenge, depending on the nature of the crime charged. Returning to a distinction made in Chapter 1, between core and non-core crimes, if the offender's crime

[26] 471 F.2d 923 (D.C. Cir. 1973) (per curiam).

was a core crime, then the state can legitimately punish him, even if it lacks democratic authority over him, because any state, democratic or not, has the authority to punish non-core crimes; if the crime was a non-core crime, however, then the state can legitimately punish the offender only if the rules permitting such punishment, including the rule making the non-core crime with which he's been charged a crime in the first place, themselves conform to the demands of justice.

The book's rhetorical style and tone is meant to make it broadly accessible. It avoids jargon, where possible, and uses analogies and examples, real and hypothetical, in an effort to make things more entertaining and reader-friendly. Discussions of, and citations to, the relevant literatures are, as a rule, limited to footnotes. Unfortunately, what's "entertaining and reader-friendly" to some might (in the words of one reviewer) be "cutesy" and "off-putting" to others, especially to a specialist who prefers a more conventional and somber style befitting the serious nature of the subject. At the same time, some of the ideas are presented in a technical fashion, bordering on the quai-mathematical, to make them as precise as possible, which might put the non-expert off. All of which means everyone has a fair opportunity to find something they dislike. The expert is apt to find some parts not to his liking, and the non-expert is apt to find other parts not to his. For the specialist, *caveat emptor*; for the non-specialist, buyer beware.

The book doesn't engage directly with the work of other scholars. Doing that would have required close attention to specific authors and specific texts, along with detailed exegesis, with the ever-present risk of misunderstanding what any particular author was trying to say. It would also make the book less digestible to the laity. The ideas in the text are thus presented without much, if any, such author-specific engagement, which of course runs the risk that any imagined interlocutor or stand-in for a particular view or theory will be dismissed a strawman. But that's the risk we take. Moreover, just because specific authors aren't directly engaged doesn't mean debts aren't owed to others or their work. On the contrary, the debts are considerable. Indeed, I sometimes think all I've done is take others' ideas, pick the ones most sensible me, and arrange them in ways I find appealing. Still, one likes to believe the whole is greater than the sum of its parts, with the resulting arrangement saying something different from what's been said before. At any rate, I hope the full measure of my many debts is adequately acknowledged and registered in the footnotes.

About those footnotes. Most of the writing I've done has been for publication in American law reviews, and in that forum, for better or worse, lengthy footnotes, sometimes taking up more room on a page than the text itself, are not unknown. Old habits die hard, and some of the footnotes herein are guilty of that sin. The material in some of the lengthier notes was consigned there at least partly on the thought that including it in the text would be unnecessary to the overall thrust of what was being said in the text. The footnote material tends to be material thought to be of more interest to specialists than to non-specialists. The especially long notes often collect and reference the relevant literature, so those looking for the literature on which the ideas in the text draw inspiration and support will hopefully find what they're looking for at the bottom of the page.

With one exception, most of the chapters haven't been previously published, at least not in anything like their current form. The exception is Chapter 5. Revised here to fit within the book's larger argument, that chapter originally appeared as *Agency and Insanity*, 66 Buff. L. Rev. 123 (2018). Glimpses, though probably not much more than that, of Chapters 1, 4, and 6 can be seen in, respectively, *Was Ellen Wronged?*, 7 Crim. L. & Phil. 185 (2013), *Authority, Ignorance, and the Guilty Mind*, 67 SMU L. Rev. 545 (2014), and *Injustice, Authority, and the Criminal Law, in* The Punitive Imagination: Law, Justice and Responsibility 42 (Austin Sarat ed., 2014). Differences will be found, reflecting evolution of thought and sometimes outright change of mind, between what was said in those early incarnations and what's said here.

Chapter 1 was presented at the University of Toronto Law School in 2017, and a much earlier version at the University of Sterling in 2011. An inchoate version of Chapter 4 was presented at SMU Dedman School of Law and the SUNY Buffalo Law School in 2014. Chapter 5 was presented at the Cleveland-Marshall School of Law and to a small get-together of criminal law scholars at Northwestern University School of Law in 2017, and a nascent version of Chapter 6 was presented at the University of Alabama School of Law in 2012. Thanks to all those who organized those gatherings, as well as to everyone who participated in them.

Thanks also go to all the Cornell Law School students who participated in seminars on the manuscript during the Fall 2016, Spring 2018, Spring 2019, and Spring 2020 semesters. Their thoughtful criticisms and feedback are much appreciated. Neil Gulyako (Cornell '16) provided excellent help with research, together with good-humored criticism and insight. A special word of thanks goes to Jill Flohil, for her careful copyediting of the draft submitted to the press, and to Salvadore Diaz (Cornell '21), Zora Franicevic (Cornell '21), Lauren Kloss (Cornell '20), Michael Mills (Cornell '21), Ashley Mullen (Cornell '20), Emily Szopinski (Cornell '20), Taylor Woelcke (Cornell '20), and Michelle Zhu (Cornell '21), for all their hard work editing the proofs and saving me from error. Last but not least, thanks to Antony Duff, prolific scholar and friend, not to mention downright decent human being, without whose help the book's publication would not have been possible. Antony graciously read and commented on the penultimate draft of the manuscript, and then later on the final version submitted to the press.

I dedicate this book to two Joes. The first, my father, passed away in 2017. A proud man, and good Irish Roman Catholic, he worked hard, loved his family, laughed whenever he could, and always provided, not without some cost to his pride. The second, a great teacher among many great teachers, passed away in 2016. An inspiration to generations of undergraduate students at Colgate University, he pushed every one of them, always with a gentle and loving hand, to think hard, and especially, self-critically. He was, indeed, a Renaissance man and true lover of knowledge: a philosopher. I'm guessing he would've disagreed with much of what follows, especially the bit about authority. I wish he were here to show me the errors of my ways. Both are dearly missed.

Last but not least, I'd like to thank my wife, Carolyn, my two boys, Liam and Amon, and our two Basenjis, Annabelle and Gamer. I've searched for words to express to them my love and gratitude. The search failed. The search itself will need to suffice.

1
Authority

Ellen Campbell was a real estate broker, doing business in posh Lake Norman, North Carolina. Mark Lawing was a drug dealer. He wanted to buy a house, and contacted Campbell for help. Lawing eventually settled on a house for $182,500, but told Campbell he could only secure a mortgage for $122,500. To get around the shortfall, he offered the sellers $60,000, in cash, under the table, in exchange for a renegotiated purchase agreement for $122,500. They agreed, and the house was his. The $60,000 came from selling drugs. The money changed hands, the closing documents were signed and sealed, and Lawing had successfully concealed $60,000 worth of dirty drug money in a piece of nice, clean real estate.[1]

Campbell, the broker, was charged under 18 U.S.C. § 1957(a) with "knowingly engag[ing] . . . in a monetary transaction in criminally derived property of a value greater than $10,000 . . . and derived from specified unlawful activity,"[2] otherwise known as money laundering. The jury convicted: Campbell had "engage[d] in a monetary transaction" (the transfer of the $60,000) in "criminally derived property of a value greater than $10,000" (the $60,000 came from drug dealing), and she knew the $60,000 came from a "specified unlawful activity" (drug dealing).[3] Lawing never told her, not in so many words, that the money was drug money. Campbell figured it out anyway (or so the jury believed). Again, Campbell was a real estate broker, not a drug dealer. All she did was sell a house, realizing dirty money was involved in the sale. Yet that's all it took to make her a money launderer under § 1957(a).

[1] United States v. Campbell, 977 F.2d 854 (4th Cir. 1992).

[2] 18 U.S.C. § 1957(a). Federal law contains two money laundering offenses: § 1957(a), usually described as a "trafficking" offense, and § 1956, usually described as a "transaction" offense (under § 1956(a)(1)), or as a "transportation" offense (under § 1956(a)(2)). Campbell was charged under both § 1957(a) and § 1956(a)(1). The case against her, under each provision, turned on proving she knew the $60,000 was dirty money, i.e., money derived from specified unlawful activity.

[3] A "monetary transaction" means (among other things) the "transfer, or exchange in or affecting interstate . . . commerce, of funds . . . by, through, or to a financial institution," 18 U.S.C. § 1957(f)(1), and a "financial institution" means (among other things) "persons involved in real estate closings and settlements," 31 U.S.C. § 5312(a)(2)(U).

Guilty Acts, Guilty Minds. Stephen P. Garvey, Oxford University Press (2020). © Oxford University Press.
DOI: 10.1093/oso/9780190924324.001.0001

Campbell faced ten years, a fair amount of time for selling a house involving dirty money. She appealed her conviction, and was granted a new trial. After that, the trail gets cold. Chances are she worked out a deal to avoid a retrial.[4] For present purposes, imagine she was retried and convicted once again. Following the Federal Sentencing Guidelines, the trial judge sentenced her to two years in prison.[5] She appealed, on a number of legal grounds, all of which were rejected. She now petitions some higher authority, one in which the rules of justice, not law, are followed. Her ultimate plea is based on a simple, albeit abstract, claim: putting her away for two years for what she did would be unjust. Backing up that basic claim, her petition makes three supporting ones:

1.

It was unjust for the United States to imprison Campbell for two years, because it was unjust for the United States to criminalize "money laundering" in the first place, either because criminalizing anything not itself a moral wrong is unjust, and money laundering isn't itself a moral wrong; or, if money laundering is itself a moral wrong, it's nonetheless unjust to criminalize it.

2.

It was unjust for the United States to imprison Campbell for two years, because, even if criminalizing money laundering isn't unjust, her conviction was unjust, because she didn't realize she was committing a crime, and convicting someone of a crime when she didn't realize she was committing one is unjust.

3.

It was unjust for the United States to imprison Campbell for two years, because, even if criminalizing money laundering isn't unjust, and even if her

[4] The trial court, unlike the jury, didn't believe the government had proven beyond reasonable doubt that Campbell knew the $60,000 was derived from criminal activity. *See* United States v. Campbell, 777 F. Supp. 1259, 1268 (W.D.N.C. 1991) ("[N]o rational jury could have found from the evidence offered at trial that Ellen Campbell knew Mark Lawing was paying for real estate with drug proceeds."). The trial court therefore entered a judgment of acquittal on the money laundering counts, and conditionally granted Campbell's motion for a new trial on them, in the event its judgment of acquittal was reversed on appeal. The Court of Appeals for the Fourth Circuit reversed the trial court's judgment of acquittal, but affirmed its grant of a new trial. *See Campbell*, 977 F.2d at 860.

[5] Based on facts in the reported cases, Campbell's conviction on one count of violating § 1957 would presumably have resulted, under the Federal Sentencing Guidelines, in an offense level somewhere in the neighborhood of 15. Assuming a criminal history category of I, the resulting guidelines range, advisory under United States v. Booker, 543 U.S. 220 (2005), would be 18–24 months.

conviction wasn't unjust, it was unjust to sentence her to two years because two years in prison is an unjust punishment for money laundering.

One's response to Campbell's claims will naturally depend on what one believes about justice. It will also depend on what one believes about state legitimacy, and the nature and grounds of state authority. On the question of state authority, and at the risk of over-simplification, suppose we have two options: anarchism and statism.

A statist believes a state can be legitimate, a legitimate state has authority, and a state has authority if it has an extraordinary moral power (or capacity), namely, the power to intentionally change the "normative status" or "situation" of anyone subject to its authority.[6] One way for a state to use its authority, and change a citizen's normative status, is to create and place them under a moral obligation not existing, or not owing to the state, before the state exercised its authority.[7]

The statist label shouldn't mislead. It might conjure up images of dictators and servile subjects, not to mention authoritarians and their followers, but it shouldn't. A statist might, along the contemporary political spectrum, lean left or right. One's politics don't make someone a statist or an anarchist. All it takes to be a statist is to believe a state can have the power to obligate its subjects or citizens to conform to its laws. A statist believes states can have authority, but nothing stops him from objecting, in the name of justice, to how the state uses the power in which its authority consists.

An anarchist, in contrast, doesn't believe any state is legitimate, which means no state has authority, which means no state has the power to change the normative status of its citizens. Like the statist label, the anarchist label shouldn't mislead. It might conjure up images of rampart-manning

[6] *See, e.g.*, Stephen Perry, *Political Authority and Political Obligation*, *in* 2 OXFORD STUDIES IN PHILOSOPHY OF LAW 1, 5 (Leslie Green & Brian Leiter eds., 2013) (observing that the "term 'political legitimacy' . . . [has] been accorded many meanings in the literature," but arguing that "a Hohfeldian power—the ability of a state to intentionally change the normative status of its subjects—is, both morally and conceptually, the core understanding of political legitimacy"). *But see* Richard Dagger, *Authority, Legitimacy, and the Obligation to Obey the Law*, 24 LEGAL THEORY 77, 86–89 (2018) (critiquing Perry's conception of authority as a moral power in favor of authority as a claim right). For a helpful overview of the philosophical literature on authority, see Thomas Christiano, *Authority*, STAN. ENCYCLOPEDIA PHIL. §§ 3–4 (2013), and for related entries, see Richard Dagger & David Lefkowitz, *Political Obligation*, STAN. ENCYCLOPEDIA PHIL. (2014); Leslie Green, *Legal Obligation and Authority*, STAN. ENCYCLOPEDIA PHIL. (2012); Fabienne Peter, *Political Legitimacy*, STAN. ENCYCLOPEDIA PHIL. (2016).

[7] The state can change a citizen's normative status in other ways, besides imposing obligations, like giving them permission to do something they'd otherwise have been prohibited from doing, or bestowing on them moral powers of their own.

revolutionaries, but it shouldn't. Those are political anarchists, dedicated to overthrowing the state. In contrast, philosophical anarchists,[8] those in mind here, are just as likely as statists to conform to the law,[9] but when anarchists conform, their conformity has nothing to do with abiding any duty owed to the state. One can't tell a statist from a philosophical anarchist by what they do. One needs to ask what they believe. Statists believe some states are legitimate (or can be). Anarchists don't.

That may not be entirely fair to the anarchist. An anarchist might insist that he too is entitled to use the language of legitimacy. True, but the sense in which he believes a state can be legitimate isn't the same sense in which the statist believes a state can be legitimate. When an anarchist uses the word "legitimate" and its cognates to describe a state, he has in mind a state with authority, but its authority isn't a moral power. It's instead a moral permission,[10] in particular a permission to make laws, issue threats to coerce conformity to those laws, and deploy coercion against those who don't conform.[11] A state

[8] On philosophical anarchism generally, see A. JOHN SIMMONS, *Philosophical Anarchism*, *in* JUSTIFICATION AND LEGITIMACY 102 (2001).

[9] *See, e.g.*, Heidi M. Hurd, *Why You Should Be a Law-Abiding Anarchist (Except When You Shouldn't)*, 42 SAN DIEGO L. REV. 75 (2005) ("[T]he fear of error and the values that lie behind the rule of law and the protection of democracy conspire to demand a pretty law-abiding life . . . [b]ut . . . [n]one of these considerations, nor any set together, justifies blind obedience to law or unthinking social conformity.").

[10] In Hohfeldian terminology, a moral permission is the same thing as a privilege, liberty (or liberty-right), or justification-right.

[11] *See, e.g.*, Allen Buchanan, *Political Legitimacy and Democracy*, 112 ETHICS 689 (2002); David Copp, *The Idea of a Legitimate State*, 28 PHIL. & PUB. AFF. 3 (1999); William A. Edmundson, *Legitimate Authority without Political Obligation*, 17 LAW & PHIL. 43 (1998); Robert Ladenson, *In Defense of a Hobbesian Conception of Law*, 9 PHIL. & PUB. AFF. 134 (1980); Christopher Heath Wellman, *Toward a Liberal Theory of Political Obligation*, 111 ETHICS 735 (2001). *See generally* Christiano, *supra* note 6, at § 1.1 (discussing the distinction between authority as a moral power to change the normative status of those subject to it and authority as a moral permission to coerce).

A number of political philosophers and criminal law theorists use legitimacy and authority in this way: to mark out states whose use of coercion is morally permissible. For an example from political philosophy, take the work of John Rawls. A. John Simmons concludes, in his analysis of Rawls's writings, that "it seems likely that Rawlsian legitimacy is only a liberty (or justification) right [to coerce]." *See* A. JOHN SIMMONS, *Justification and Legitimacy*, *in* JUSTIFICATION AND LEGITIMACY: ESSAYS ON RIGHTS AND OBLIGATIONS 122, 145 n.48 (2001). John Perry appears to draw the same conclusion. *See* Perry, *supra* note 6, at 6 n.11. For an example from the criminal theory literature, in which a state's moral permission to use coercion is said to depend on morality having granted it that permission, or what seems very close to the same thing, in which the legitimacy of a state's punishment is said to depend on the substantive justice of its laws, see Alice Ristroph, *Conditions of Legitimate Punishment*, *in* THE NEW PHILOSOPHY OF CRIMINAL LAW 79, 81 (Chad Flanders & Zachary Hoskins eds., 2016) ("Legitimate punishment depends on fair substantive laws.").

The statist's theory of state legitimacy (authority as a moral power) and the anarchist's theory of state legitimacy (authority as a moral permission) are the two most common theories. For an "independent third conception," see Arthur Isak Applbaum, *Legitimacy without the Duty to Obey*, 38 PHIL. & PUB. AFF. 215, 227 (2010), according to which state legitimacy is a "kind of *moral* power, the power to create and enforce *nonmoral* (or perhaps . . . not yet moral) prescriptions and social facts." *Id.* at 221.

is morally permitted to do all those things, but only if morality gives it permission, which it will, but only if the state's laws, threats, and use of coercion are just. So, when the dust clears, and an anarchist says a state is legitimate, he means its laws (or enough of them) conform to the requirements of justice (or conform enough). For an anarchist, state legitimacy is a matter of more or less. The more a state's laws conform to justice, the more legitimate the state; the less they conform, the less legitimate.

In order to contrast how an anarchist, compared to a statist, would go about responding to the claims in Campbell's petition, I present two stories. The goal of the first story is to illustrate the extent to which criminal law theorists disagree about what justice requires across a range of rules governing the imposition of state punishment. The goal of the second is to illustrate how state authority provides an important good—authoritatively resolving reasonable disagreements among democratic citizens about the requirements of justice—and why those subject to a democratic state's authority are morally bound to conform their conduct to the law resolving those disagreements.

Some readers won't care for these stories. Indeed, some might find them (as one reviewer did) "condescending and tedious." That, it should go without saying, isn't the intent. The intent, once again, is to illustrate, in a lighthearted way, the wide range of issues on which anarchical criminal law theorists reasonably disagree about the requirements of justice, and to make plausible, in an accessible way, the claim that democratic citizens are obligated to subject their individual wills, but not their reason, to the collective will, determined through a democratic process. Those who prefer a more formal style of presentation should skip ahead two sections, where they can find an effort to summarize, using more general and abstract language, the lessons the stories are meant to illustrate.

Anarchism—Rex's Dilemma

Imagine Campbell was prosecuted for money laundering, not in the United States, but in the Kingdom of Rex. Rex's kingdom is much like the United States. The kingdom is large, with an economy based more or less on the free market. Rex's subjects enjoy a range of civil rights. The laws Rex declares are enforced in courts with judges independent of Rex's influence, and so on. The rule of law is honored and observed.[12] Of course, unlike the United States, the Kingdom of Rex has a king. He's a good king, but a king all the same. He loves his people, but they don't elect him. They don't elect anyone.

Unlike some kings, Rex doesn't believe in divine right. On the contrary, he's a committed philosophical anarchist. As such, he doesn't believe his subjects are morally obligated to conform to the laws he promulgates just because he promulgated them. He believes he's morally permitted to coerce his subjects to conform to his laws, but only insofar as his laws conform to the requirements of justice. Rex's moral permission to coerce his subjects thus depends entirely on the moral content of his laws, which is why Rex needs to know if his laws are just.

The Campbell case has become a *cause célèbre*. The people are divided, with half believing Campbell has been punished unjustly, and the other half believing justice was served. The legal proceedings in Campbell's case ended when the Kingdom's Supreme Court declined to hear her appeal. Campbell has now petitioned Rex to let her go, or reduce her sentence, all in the name of justice. Rex therefore needs to decide if the laws through which Campbell ended up sentenced to two years in prison were just. If not, Rex will grant her petition, because Rex, as an anarchist, believes the legitimacy of his regime depends on how well its laws approximate justice.[13]

Rex has established the Office of Moral Counsel. The office is big, with folks who deal with foreign relations, commerce, labor, housing, agriculture, civil rights, taxes, and so on. The office dealing with criminal law, with all the rules defining criminal conduct, establishing excuses, prescribing punishments, and so on, is small. It has two members, Hercules and Athena, each a prominent criminal law theorist in the kingdom. Both have devoted their careers to figuring out what justice requires when it comes to the criminal law and its rules. They rightly consider themselves experts on the justice and morality of the criminal law.[14]

[12] Harvard Law professor Lon Fuller long ago chronicled the story of another king, also called Rex, who failed to follow the rule of law, or what Fuller called the "inner morality of law." It ended badly, such that Rex, according to Fuller, didn't manage to create anything worthy of being called "law" at all. *See* LON L. FULLER, THE MORALITY OF LAW 33–38 (rev. ed. 1964).

[13] Rex is sometimes asked to grant petitions, not to correct an injustice, but to show mercy. Adding mercy to Rex's deliberations would raise additional questions, involving the relationship between justice and mercy, which we set aside for now. *See generally* Stephen P. Garvey, *Questions of Mercy*, 4 OHIO ST. J. CRIM. L. 321 (2007) (identifying a range of questions about the relationship between justice and mercy).

[14] Criminal law theorists typically consult their own intuitions when trying to figure out what rules, as a matter of justice or morality, should make up a criminal code. In contrast, Paul Robinson has long argued that the criminal law's rules should be based, not on any philosopher's intuitions of justice, but on the intuitions of the laity. Relying on lay intuitions wouldn't make the rules any more

Rex asks Hercules and Athena each to write a memo addressing Campbell's moral claims, which are, once again: *Claim 1* ~ Punishing someone for money laundering (as defined in 18 U.S.C. § 1957(a)) is unjust, because justice wouldn't permit money laundering (so defined) to be criminalized. *Claim 2* ~ Even if criminalizing money laundering is just, punishing someone who didn't realize she was committing a crime is unjust, and Campbell (she claims) didn't realize she was committing a crime. *Claim 3* ~ Even if criminalizing money laundering isn't unjust, and even if punishing someone who didn't realize she was committing a crime isn't unjust, two years in prison for money laundering is an unjust punishment.

Hercules and Athena are, like Rex, committed philosophical anarchists, believing, as does Rex, that any authority Rex's laws enjoy depends on how well they approximate justice.

Criminalization

Campbell's first claim involves criminalization. No one, she avers, should be punished for money laundering because money laundering should not, as a matter of justice, be a crime.

Hercules and Athena happen to agree that Rex, as a matter of justice, should only criminalize moral wrongs. They also agree that crimes like murder, mayhem, and so on are moral wrongs: They are wrong in and of themselves, whatever the law says about them or anything else. That makes them *malum in se*, at least on some accounts of what it means to call a crime *malum in se*. But Hercules doesn't believe money laundering is like murder. Money laundering is nothing more than using dirty money in an otherwise morally permissible way, knowing the money used is dirty. If so, and if money laundering is a moral wrong, its wrongfulness must, according to Hercules, depend in some way or another on the fact that the law prohibits using dirty money in an otherwise morally permissible way, knowing the money is dirty. In other words, if money laundering is *malum* (wrong) it must be because the law has declared it *prohibitum*.

Hercules believes the law, when it prohibits otherwise non-wrongful conduct, can sometimes thereby transform it into wrongful conduct. Take the

likely to reflect moral truth, but it would, he argues, enhance the criminal law's "moral credibility" with the people, and having a criminal law with moral credibility is the optimal way to control crime. *See* Paul H. Robinson, Intuitions of Justice and the Utility of Desert (2013).

rules of the road. Driving on the left isn't morally wrong all by itself. Yet once Rex tells everyone to drive on the right, it becomes morally wrong to drive on the left. Rex's rule solves what economists call a coordination problem. Rex could've told everyone to drive on the left, but he didn't. Having arbitrarily opted for the right, everyone is thereafter obligated, morally, to stay to the right. Going left, when everyone else is going right, is now dangerous.[15] As Hercules sees it, money laundering doesn't, at least not in any straightforward way, fit this theory. Making it a crime to use dirty money doesn't solve any coordination problem. Hercules therefore concludes that money laundering, despite being prohibited, isn't a moral wrong and thus shouldn't, as a matter of justice, be criminalized.[16]

Athena disagrees. Money laundering involves dirty money changing hands, knowing its dirty. All by itself, that's harmless enough. Still, harmless or not, it facilitates all kinds of other activities, some of which plainly cause harm and are, for that reason, morally wrong. If drug dealers couldn't wash their ill-gotten gains, they'd have a hard time spending it, and if they couldn't spend it, drug dealing would be less attractive. If drug money couldn't be laundered, the lives of drug dealers, racketeers, and so forth would become more difficult, and drug dealing, racketeering, and so forth, along with all the harm those activities cause, would diminish. Prohibiting money laundering thus sensibly helps discourage or preempt all manner of upstream and downstream harm, thereby serving the cause of justice. So, as Athena sees it, money laundering is a moral wrong, inasmuch as it facilitates harmful conduct.[17]

Hercules and Athena agree, as a matter of justice, that nothing should be a crime unless it constitutes a moral wrong, but disagree on the moral status of money laundering. Hercules believes it isn't a moral wrong; Athena believes it is. They also happen to agree that justice permits Rex to criminalize some moral wrongs, but not all moral wrongs.[18] They disagree, however, about

[15] For more on this account of the conditions under which enacting a law can transform otherwise morally permissible conduct into morally wrongful conduct, see, for example, R.A. Duff, Answering for Crime: Responsibility and Liability in the Criminal Law 166–74 (2007); Douglas Husak, Overcriminalization: The Limits of the Criminal Law 103–19 (2008).

[16] *See, e.g.*, Husak, *supra* note 15, at 119 (examining a variety of attempts to explain "why the punishment of persons who commit *mala prohibitum* offenses might conform to the wrongfulness constraint" and concluding that none of them "provide[s] a persuasive rationale for punishing persons convicted of money laundering").

[17] *See, e.g.*, Robert Young, *Douglas Husak on Dispensing With the* Malum Prohibitum *Offense of Money Laundering*, 28 Crim. Just. Ethics 108, 113 (2009) ("[T]he wrongfulness of money laundering . . . [is] a function of the harmful economic effects it is apt to have.").

[18] Penal codes in the United States suffer, according to most theorists, from over-criminalization, containing too many crimes compared to what justice says they should contain. Sometimes, but

which moral wrongs justice permits Rex to criminalize and which ones it prohibits him from criminalizing.

Hercules adheres to a theory of criminalization dating back to John Stuart Mill, a nineteenth-century English philosopher, according to which harm to others, either risked or caused, was the only good reason to criminalize acts causing or risking it.[19] Under Mill's much-debated harm principle, a person can harm himself, or offend others, as much as he likes. Just don't harm others. That's when the criminal law should intervene. Of course, because Hercules doesn't believe money laundering is morally wrong in the first place, he doesn't need to ask if it should be criminalized. He would therefore grant Campbell's first claim: It would be unjust to punish Campbell for money laundering because, as a matter of justice, money laundering should not be a crime.

Athena adheres to a different theory of criminalization, known as legal moralism, according to which justice requires Rex to criminalize and punish all moral wrongs, subject to important and substantial caveats.[20] These caveats, themselves grounded in competing principles of justice, place limits on the theory's standing injunction to criminalize all moral wrongs. Moreover, according to Athena's account of legal moralism, moral wrongs shouldn't be confused with vice. Morality, for example, doesn't care what Rex's subjects do in the privacy of their bedrooms. Some of the kingdom's subjects might want Rex to punish some of the sexual practices in which some of his other subjects engage, but Rex should not, as a matter of justice, do as they want. Morality gives the state permission to punish moral wrongs, but no consensual sexual practice is a moral wrong.[21]

much less often, they're said to suffer from the opposite problem, failing to include a crime justice says they should include. For example, criminal codes commonly make it a crime to obtain property through extortion or blackmail, but less commonly make it a crime to obtain sex in the same way. For an argument in favor of criminalizing sexual coercion, see STEPHEN SCHULHOFER, UNWANTED SEX: THE CULTURE OF INTIMIDATION AND THE FAILURE OF LAW 114–67 (1998).

[19] J.S. MILL, ON LIBERTY 13 (C.V. Shields ed., 1956) (1859). For a Mill-inspired theory on the moral limits of the criminal law, see 1 JOEL FEINBERG, HARM TO OTHERS: THE MORAL LIMITS OF THE CRIMINAL LAW (1984).

[20] Michael S. Moore, *A Tale of Two Theories*, 28 CRIM. JUST. ETHICS 27, 31 (2009) ("[P]rima facie, *all* moral wrongs culpably done should be criminalized."). For other theories of criminalization, which are but a sample of the many on offer, see HUSAK, *supra* note 15; DENNIS J. BAKER, THE RIGHT NOT TO BE CRIMINALIZED: DEMARCATING THE CRIMINAL LAW'S AUTHORITY (2011); A.P. SIMESTER & ANDREAS VON HIRSCH, CRIMES, HARMS, AND WRONGS: ON THE PRINCIPLES OF CRIMINALIZATION (2011); VICTOR TADROS, WRONGS AND CRIMES 159–72 (2016).

[21] *See, e.g.*, MICHAEL MOORE, PLACING BLAME 662 (1997) ("[M]orality is indifferent to sexual practices, and . . . much else in the way of conventionally regarded 'vice' is only supererogatory but not obligatory.").

According to Athena, money laundering is indeed a moral wrong, not just a vice. Moreover, she concludes that none of the usual caveats against criminalizing it apply. Athena would therefore deny Campbell's first claim: It would not be unjust to punish Campbell for money laundering inasmuch as money laundering is a moral wrong and Rex is, as a matter of justice, permitted to prohibit it as a crime.

Culpability

Campbell's second claim involves ignorance. Even if her conduct amounted to a moral wrong; and even if that wrong was, as a matter of justice, properly criminalized, she claims no one should be found criminally culpable for doing something she had no idea was wrong, let alone criminal. Ignorance of the law should, as a matter of justice, excuse.

Athena makes quick work of Campbell's second claim. *Ignorantia juris neminem excusat*: Ignorance of the law does not excuse, Campbell's claim to the contrary notwithstanding. The *ignorantia* maxim is deeply rooted in the criminal law, and Athena believes its deep roots are grounded in justice. Campbell knew what she was doing, even if she didn't know it was a crime. She knew she was closing on a house, and she knew dirty money changed hands in the process. She doesn't, thanks to the *ignorantia* maxim, need to know, in addition, that closing on a house using dirty money is a crime, nor does justice require her to know it amounts to a crime in order for her to be culpable for its commission.[22] Athena would therefore reject Campbell's second claim.

Hercules disagrees. The *ignorantia* maxim has a long history, but just because a rule has a long history doesn't guarantee that it comports with justice. As Oliver Wendell Holmes famously observed: "It is revolting to have no better reason for a rule of law than that so it was laid down in the time of Henry IV. It is still more revolting if the grounds upon which it was laid down have vanished long since, and the rule simply persists from blind imitation of the past."[23] Sure, when Rex's Penal Code was limited to crimes like

[22] Failure to provide notice and estoppel are the two most common exceptions to the maxim. *See, e.g.*, Model Penal Code § 2.04(3)(a) & (b) (Am. Law Inst. 1985).
[23] Oliver Wendell Holmes, Jr., *The Path of the Law*, 10 Harv. L. Rev. 457, 469 (1897).

murder, rape, and robbery, anyone not insane would have realized, when he murdered, raped, or robbed, that he was committing a crime.

But that was then. Things are different now. When a criminal code includes crimes like money laundering, not to mention all manner of regulatory or public welfare offenses, even a law-abiding subject might, innocently and unwittingly, find himself on the criminal law's bad side. Having already found in her favor on the first claim, Hercules would find in favor of Campbell on her second claim as well: Justice requires Campbell be given a fair opportunity to prove that she reasonably failed to realize she was committing a crime.[24] If she carries her burden, justice requires an acquittal.

Punishment

Campbell's third claim involves punishment. Even if her conduct amounted to a moral wrong; even if that wrong was, as a matter of justice, properly criminalized; and even if her alleged ignorance didn't, as a matter of justice, excuse her crime, two years in prison is, she claims, a disproportionate, and therefore unjust, punishment.

In order to assess Campbell's third claim, Hercules and Athena begin from the same premise. They agree morality gives each of Rex's subjects a standing claim right not to be punished, unless he culpably commits a crime, in which case he forfeits his right. That means morality obligates Rex not to punish anyone, unless and until he culpably commits a crime.[25] Anyone who culpably commits a crime, thereby forfeiting his right not to be punished, and transforming it into a no-right not to be punished, confers on Rex a moral right to punish him. This right is a liberty right or permission. It permits Rex to punish culpable crime-doers, but doesn't obligate him to punish them.

[24] *See, e.g.*, Douglas Husak, Ignorance of Law: A Philosophical Inquiry 1 (2016) ("[A]n ideal penal code should explicitly allow far more exculpatory significance to ignorance of law than is presently granted in existing Anglo-American criminal justice."); Ronald A. Cass, *Ignorance of the Law: A Maxim Reexamined*, 17 Wm. & Mary L. Rev. 671, 699 (1976) ("*Ignorantia legis* . . . should be set aside by the courts as a quaint relic of the times when neighbors knew each other, citizens were familiar with the criminal laws, and crimes required criminal intent.").

[25] In other words, Rex gives each of his subjects a moral power to change his normative status. When a subject culpably commits a crime he exercises that power: He transforms his Rex-given right not to be punished (corresponding to Rex's duty not to punish) into a no-right not to be punished (corresponding to Rex's permission (or privilege or liberty-right) to punish). For a defense of the thesis that state punishment is permissible when and because criminal wrongdoers forfeit their right not to be punished, see Christopher Heath Wellman, *The Rights Forfeiture Theory of Punishment*, 122 Ethics 371 (2012).

Even if Rex is permitted to punish Campbell, insofar as she culpably committed a crime, Hercules and Athena agree that he still needs a good reason to exercise his permission. They disagree, however, on what counts, as a matter of justice, as a good reason.

Hercules adheres to a philosophy of retribution, according to which Rex always has a good reason to punish someone who's culpably committed a crime. The suffering of culpable criminals isn't just an instrumental good, something that's good only insofar as it's a means to something else that's good; it's also an intrinsic good, good in and of itself.[26] The guilty deserve to suffer, deserved suffering is an intrinsic good, and thus giving the guilty what they deserve is always a good reason to punish them.[27] Criminal wrongdoers, according to Hercules' brand of retributivism, should suffer as much as they deserve, but no more than they deserve.

Although Hercules doesn't believe Rex can, as a matter of justice, criminalize money laundering, nor that he can, as a matter of justice, reject reasonable ignorance of the law an excuse, Hercules is willing to bracket those conclusions in order to reach the question of Campbell's punishment. Assuming Campbell culpably committed the crime of money laundering, Hercules needs to decide if two years in prison is the amount of suffering she deserves for her crime. Unfortunately, making the punishment fit the crimes is probably the greatest problem and puzzle for Hercules' retributive theory.[28] Alas, Hercules finds that he can't pinpoint the exact number of years Campbell deserves. The best he can do is come up with a range, but when Rex

[26] Mitchell N. Berman, *The Justification of Punishment*, *in* THE ROUTLEDGE COMPANION TO PHILOSOPHY OF LAW 141, 147–48 (Andrei Marmor ed., 2012) (discussing "teleological retributivism" or "consequentialist retributivism," according to which punishment is a "means to bring about the good of deserved suffering."). For a recent review of retributive justice, see Alec Walen, *Retributive Justice*, STAN. ENCYCLOPEDIA PHIL. (2016), and for an insightful effort to explain why deserved punishment is intrinsically good, see LEO ZAIBERT, RETHINKING PUNISHMENT 43 (2018) ("The reason . . . deserved punishment can, other things being equal, be better than impunity is because desert gives a certain *order*—a certain meaning—to the whole in which it appears, and this in turn generates intrinsic, non-medicinal value.").

[27] Philosophers have of course developed any number of theories, besides the retributivist and consequentialist theories discussed in the text, attempting to explain when morality permits, or even obligates, a state to punish, and the number continues to grow. Among those many theories, two of the more influential have been R.A. DUFF, PUNISHMENT, COMMUNICATION, AND COMMUNITY (2001) (punishment permissible as a form of "secular penance"), and VICTOR TADROS, THE ENDS OF HARM: THE MORAL FOUNDATIONS OF CRIMINAL LAW (2011) (punishment permissible as a form of societal "self-defense"). For my own contribution to the ongoing debate (from a much-younger me), see Stephen P. Garvey, *Punishment as Atonement*, 46 UCLA L. REV. 1801 (1999).

[28] Heidi M. Hurd, *Expressing Doubts About Expressivism*, 2005 U. CHI. LEG. F. 405, 415 (Retributivism's "greatest [puzzle] is the question of whether it can defend, in any principled way, claims about the proportionality of particular punishments to the particular harms culpably caused by particular offenders.").

asks if two years is within the range, Hercules doesn't know what to think, so he defers judgment on Campbell's final claim.

When Athena turns to Campbell's third claim, she can't fathom how Hercules can believe suffering can be intrinsically good. Unlike Hercules, she believes punishment's suffering is intrinsically bad. She therefore rejects retribution in favor of consequentialism. At the same time, she nonetheless believes that punishment's intrinsic badness can produce good consequences, which can sometimes outweigh its intrinsic badness. Rex's use of punishment to pursue such good consequences, she further believes, must proceed within some non-consequentialist metes or bounds. Justice permits punishment if and when the good consequences outweigh the bad, but it nonetheless prohibits punishing the known innocent, as well as imposing undeserved punishment on the guilty, even when one believes the good consequences of doing so would outweigh the bad.[29]

Foremost among the possible good consequences is less crime. For example, once people see what happens to convicted money launderers, they'll be less likely to follow suit, which means less money laundering overall, which means less of the harm money-laundering engenders. For another, an offender, like Campbell, having been punished, might conclude the crime wasn't worth the time, and so won't do it again; or even better, having come to see the error of her ways, might not even want to do it again, even if she could get away with it. At the least, if an offender is incarcerated, he won't have much opportunity to engage in more crime. The question for Athena is whether these hoped-for goods outweigh the certain two years of Campbell's suffering. The calculations are complicated. Athena doesn't know what to think, so she too defers judgment on Campbell's final claim.

After receiving their memos, Rex has another question for Hercules and Athena. How is it that he, as a matter of justice, has a right to punish anyone? A culpable criminal wrongdoer, according to Athena and Hercules, forfeits his right not to be punished, but who gains the permission to punish him? Suppose, rather than launder dirty money, Campbell had punched John in the nose for no good reason. Why doesn't justice give John permission to punish Campbell? Why should Rex think he gets permission?

[29] *See, e.g.*, H.L.A. HART, *Prolegomenon to the Principles of Punishment*, *in* PUNISHMENT AND RESPONSIBILITY: ESSAYS IN THE PHILOSOPHY OF LAW 1 (2d ed., 2008); NORVAL MORRIS, THE FUTURE OF IMPRISONMENT (1974). Morris's theory, known as limiting retributivism, is now reflected in the Model Penal Code. MODEL PENAL: SENTENCING § 1.02(2)(a)(i) (AM. LAW INST., Proposed Final Draft 2017). For a detailed defense of limiting retributivism, see RICHARD S. FRASE, SENTENCING: PRINCIPLES AND PROCEDURES FOR A WORKABLE SYSTEM (2013).

As an anarchist, Rex doesn't believe he has the power to obligate anyone to conform to his laws. When someone commits a crime, he doesn't violate any obligation owing to Rex, which means he does Rex no wrong. When Campbell punches John, Campbell morally wrongs John. That, of course, would be true even if assault wasn't a crime. Punching someone in the nose for no good reason is a moral wrong, whether or not Rex has made it a crime. Campbell also wrongs morality, because morality, unlike Rex, does have the power to obligate conformity to its rules. Morality obligated Campbell not to assault anyone, but she violated that obligation, thus defying morality's authority, and in that sense she wronged morality, as well as John.[30]

When Rex's agents prosecuted Campbell, the case was captioned, in accordance with long-standing custom, *Rex v. Campbell*, as if Rex had been the one on the receiving end of Campbell's right cross. But he wasn't. John was. Campbell wronged John, as well as morality and the justice it demands, but she didn't wrong Rex. Why, then, isn't the case against Campbell captioned *John v. Campbell* or *Justice v. Campbell*?

It's true, Hercules concedes, that Campbell hasn't wronged Rex. That doesn't mean, however, that Rex lacks standing to call Campbell to account for wronging John. On the contrary, morality confers on Rex the standing he needs. Morality permits Rex to punish Campbell, and at the same time prohibits John from punishing her, even though Campbell never wronged Rex. As Hercules sees it, someone has to punish Campbell, if she's to be punished at all, at least if one sets aside the possibility of leaving her punishment to the hereafter. The question is a practical one: who's the best person for the job?

It doesn't make sense to let John do it. If morality gave him the job, he'd be apt, being the victim and only human, to go overboard, punishing Campbell more than justice would allow. Being more dispassionate, Rex is more likely

[30] It may sound odd to speak of "morality" being "wronged," insofar as that's not how we usually speak, but the proposition doesn't seem incoherent. Kenneth Himma writes, for example, that "[i]f morality is objective and manufactured by a personal God, then the norms of morality are authoritative in virtue of being issued by a divine authority. Arguably, objective moral norms are no less plausibly characterized as 'authoritative' if a personal God does not exist." Kenneth Einar Himma, *Authority*, *in* Handbook of Legal Reasoning and Legal Argumentation 194–95 (Giorgio Bongiovanni et al. eds., 2018). If it makes sense to speak of morality as an authority, similar to the way we speak, without any apparent hesitation, of law as an authority, and if one can defy the law qua authority, then it would seem to follow that one can defy morality qua authority. And, if defying is a form of wronging, then it should make sense to speak of wronging morality. *See* Jean Hampton, *The Nature of Immorality*, Soc. Phil. & Pol'y, Autumn 1989, at 22, 41 (offering an account of the "nature of immorality" according to which moral wrongdoers "are rebelling against the moral authority of morality").

to get the job done right, and to punish Campbell only so far as justice permits him to be punished. Morality therefore enlists Rex as its agent, giving him the task of punishing. It permits Rex to punish Campbell, not because she wronged Rex when she punched John, but because, as between Rex and any other plausible candidate, Rex happens to have the comparative advantage.[31] If someone better at doing justice came along, then morality would give them the job. But, so far, no one has.

Athena offers a different answer to the hypothetical in which Campbell punishes John in the nose. She believes Campbell has, in an extended sense at least, wronged Rex when she punched John, though not because she owes and violated any duty to Rex to conform to his laws. Instead, Campbell's attack on John is a wrong against Rex, as well as John, because Rex and John are like family. Rex cares about John, as he does all his subjects. When his subjects suffer, Rex suffers, albeit vicariously. Of course, Rex doesn't always suffer when his subjects suffer. His sympathy and compassion have limits. He suffers only when morality tells him he should suffer, and morality tells him he should suffer only when one of his subjects has been the victim of a "public wrong," which is a wrong Rex can properly make his business.[32]

Again, morality can't punish all by itself. Like the Supreme Court, morality has no sword, only judgment. When morality permits punishment, it needs someone in the real world to do the punishing it permits. On Athena's theory, morality gives Rex permission to punish, not so much because Rex is better at punishing, but because Rex, insofar as he properly identifies with the John, has himself been wronged, at least in a vicarious sense, based on his having properly identified himself with John.

Still, Rex feels dishonest punishing in his name. Wouldn't it be more forthright and straightforward to caption the case against Campbell *Rex ex rel. John v. Campbell* or *Rex ex rel. Justice v. Campbell?* The phrase "*ex rel.*"—meaning "on the relation of" or "on behalf of"—would at least make explicit

[31] *See* MOORE, *supra* note 21, at 152 ("Retributive punishment is dangerous for individual persons to carry out . . . But implicit in the Biblical injunction [that 'Vengeance is mine, saith the Lord'] is a promise that retribution will be exacted. For those like myself who are not theists, that cleansing function must be performed by the state, not God.").

[32] For thoughts along these lines, see S.E. Marshall & R.A. Duff, *Criminalization and Sharing Wrongs*, 11 CAN. J. L. & JURIS. 7, 19 (1998) (arguing that "public wrongs," which are the only wrongs the state should criminalize, don't cease to be the victim's wrong, but that a "public wrong" is also "'our' wrong insofar as we identify ourselves" with the victim: a public wrong committed against "this individual victim is itself also an attack on us—on her as a member of the group and on us as fellow members"); R.A. Duff, *Relational Reasons and the Criminal Law*, *in* 2 OXFORD STUDIES IN PHILOSOPHY OF LAW 175, 206 (Leslie Green & Brian Leiter eds., 2013) ("An offender must answer for her criminal wrongs to her fellow citizens, whose business those wrongs are as public wrongs.").

the fact that Rex is punishing, not in his own name, but in the name of, or on behalf of, John or morality. Captioning the case *Rex v. Campbell* looks, on its face, like deceptive advertising.

In the end, Rex decides to deny Campbell's petition. Of course, when Rex tells Campbell the bad news, she takes little solace when he assures her she hasn't been treated unjustly. Like Rex, Campbell is a philosophical anarchist, who believes, as does Rex, that the legitimacy of his rule depends on making sure his laws conform to justice. Rex believes, in utmost good faith, that he's doing morality's will when he denies Campbell's petition, but Campbell believes Rex is wrong. He's misunderstood what justice really requires.

Rex's story is meant to make a simple, if not obvious, point. Experts and non-experts alike disagree about what justice requires when it comes to the many legal rules governing the decisions and choices that a range of state actors must make before someone is, in the state's name, subject to the censure and hardship we call punishment. The fact that people of good faith reasonably disagree over what, as a matter of justice, those rules should be puts the anarchist in a difficult position. Because the anarchist makes no distinction between justice and legitimacy, the criminal law's rules can only be defended in the name of justice. Defending them as legitimate, even when others might reasonably believe them to be unjust, isn't an option.

We can reframe the problem if we distinguish between justice and legitimacy. That move is one a philosophical anarchist can't make, but a statist can. In an effort to make the case for statism, and more specifically, the case for the legitimacy and authority of a democratic state, we'll tell another tale. Again, if you prefer a general and abstract mode of presentation, skip ahead to the next section.

Statism—Leviathan's Peace

This is the story of Leviathan. It comes in two parts. The first part, preliminary to the second, explains why any state (democratic or not) is morally permitted to punish, in its own name, violations of the criminal law's core prohibitions. The second part explains why democratic states, and only democratic states, have authority over, and thus the power to impose a moral obligation on, all those subject to the state's jurisdiction to conform to all the criminal law's rules, inside the core and out. How to distinguish between rules inside the core and those outside it will be explained in due course.

The first part begins as follows.

Social Peace

Thomas, John, and Jean-Jacques are passengers on the *S.S. Commonwealth I*. The ship sinks, and they alone make it to a nearby island, which they call Anarchia. The men, comparable in raw physical strength, don't get along. Fights break out over who's in charge. Thomas steals fish and pineapples from John, John steals from Jean-Jacques, Jean-Jacques steals from Thomas, and so on. None is particularly happy about the prevailing state of affairs. Life isn't exactly solitary, nasty, brutish, or short, but it comes close. The trio believe they'd all, individually and collectively, be better off, on balance, with some simple ground rules, but no such rules exist. Life goes on, disordered.

When the *S.S. Commonwealth II* sails past Anarchia, its captain, named Leviathan, decides to stop. Leviathan is much stronger than Thomas, John, and Jean-Jacques, alone or combined. Leviathan is appalled at the disorder, and decides to do something about it, as only he can. He sets down a simple set of rules, which he expects everyone to follow. The rules, known as the Code, are simple. Don't physically harm anyone else, let alone kill, and don't steal either. (Leviathan includes another rule, according to which everyone gets to keep what he captures. If you get your hands on a pineapple or fish first, it's yours. No one can take it unless you agree to trade or give it away).

Leviathan coerces anyone who fails to conform to the rules with the threat of confinement in the Cage, which is, as the name implies, a cage made from bamboo. The islanders weren't motivated to cooperate before, but Leviathan's threats make cooperation, through obedience to the Code, the prudent course of action. The Code isn't hard to follow. The rules are understandable. They are stable over time. They don't contradict each other. They're not enforced retroactively, and so on. All the islanders know the rules, as well as the consequences for failing to conform to them. Leviathan is a potentate, but a benevolent one. He does only what's necessary to secure social order, enforces the rules consistently and fairly, and subjects himself to the same rules as everyone else.

On the day after Leviathan promulgates his Code, Jean-Jacques steps over the line. He steals a pineapple from Thomas. Not because he was starving, but just because he was covetous and the opportunity presented itself. Once the Code is in place, Jean-Jacques can no longer act with impunity, as he more or less could before. Insofar as coercion is the only way to bring about the good of social peace, from which each of the islanders realizes he benefits, Leviathan is morally permitted to use the Cage to coerce conformity to the Code. The islanders, if they break a rule, have no right not to be coerced (since Leviathan is permitted to coerce them), but they don't owe Leviathan any duty to conform to the Code's rules.

When Jean-Jacques steals Thomas's pineapple, he wrongs Thomas, morally speaking. Once a system of property rules is in place, stealing is morally wrong. The Code prohibits stealing, but stealing is morally wrong independent of the Code's prohibition. Having been morally wronged, Thomas is apt to be angry with Jean-Jacques, resenting how Jean-Jacques treated him. He might express his anger in words, telling Jean-Jacques what he thinks of him. He might also avoid contact and dealings with Jean-Jacques, to the extent he can, at least for some period of time. Of course, Thomas might want to go further. He might want to express his anger, not only in words, but with the back of his hand. That, however, would be prohibited under the Code, which permits Leviathan alone to use physical force against another islander.

Having stolen Thomas's pineapple, Jean-Jacques morally wrongs Thomas. He hasn't, however, morally wronged Leviathan. He didn't steal anything from him, and Leviathan doesn't have the power to impose on anyone a duty, owed to him, to conform to the Code. Because Jean-Jacques didn't morally wrong him, Leviathan has no reason to be angry with Jean-Jacques. He might vicariously share Thomas's anger, as might John, but neither John nor Leviathan have themselves been wronged. Accordingly, when Leviathan confines Jean-Jacques in the Cage, he doesn't thereby intend to express anger, or otherwise condemn or censure. Being confined to the Cage thus doesn't amount to punishment, not if punishing means condemning. Instead, time in the Cage is a penalty, which is like punishment, but without the condemnation.[33] The

[33] The distinction between penalties (coercion without censure) and punishment (coercion with censure) is common in the literature, going back at least to Joel Feinberg's essay on punishment's "expressive dimension." *See* FEINBERG, *supra* note 19, at 98 ("[P]unishment is a conventional device for the expression of attitudes of resentment and indignation, and of judgments of disapproval and reprobation, on the part either of the punishing authority himself or of those 'in whose name' the punishment is inflicted. Punishment, in short, has a symbolic significance largely missing from other kinds of penalties."). Feinberg's discussion begins with Henry Hart's well-known observation:

> [A crime] is not simply anything which a legislature chooses to call a "crime." It is not simply antisocial conduct which public officers are given a responsibility to suppress. It is not simply any conduct to which a legislature chooses to attach a "criminal" penalty. It is conduct which, if duly shown to have taken place, will incur a formal and solemn pronouncement of the moral condemnation of the community.

Cage is like civil contempt, where coercion is intended simply to force compliance, and not like criminal contempt, where coercion is intended to condemn as well (and thereby vindicate the court's authority).

Over time the islanders begin getting along. Thanks to the Code, with backup from Leviathan, the islanders are no longer in their own micro-state of nature. They're cooperating with each another, inasmuch as everyone is following the Code's rules. Each refrains from violating the rules, and they call the resulting social peace the *Pax Levum*, the Peace of Leviathan.[34]

The *Pax Levum* creates a new relationship among the islanders, and between the islanders and Leviathan as the author of the Code. The islanders sustain the *Pax Levum* insofar as they conform to the Code. Out of respect for those who conform to the Code, which they all do, at least enough to preserve the peace, everyone subject to the Code becomes morally obligated likewise to conform. Respect for those who are following the rules, thereby upholding the *Pax Levum*, obligates each islander to subordinate his will to the rules. This duty to conform runs to every other islander individually, and it also runs to Leviathan, not just in his capacity as another islander, but in his capacity as the author of the Code. Correlative to this duty, each islander has a right to the conformity of every other islander, as does Leviathan in his capacity as the Code's author.

The islanders' duty to conform, and Leviathan's right to their conformity as author of the Code, is limited. The islanders aren't Leviathan's vassals, duty-bound to do anything and everything Leviathan says to do, just because he says it. They're bound to Leviathan as the Code's author, and as such, their fidelity extends only to the rules necessary to maintain the *Pax Levum*. If, for example, Leviathan added a provision to the Code requiring Thomas to fetch him breakfast each morning, Thomas wouldn't be bound to conform. He's

Henry M. Hart, Jr. *The Aims of the Criminal Law*, 23 LAW & CONTEMP. PROBS. 401, 405 (1958).

Some authors have nonetheless rejected Feinberg's analysis of punishment insofar as it includes an "expressive function." *See, e.g.*, Ambrose Y. K. Lee, *Arguing Against the Expressive Function of Punishment: Is the Standard Account that Insufficient?*, 38 LAW & PHIL. 359, 383 (2019) (denying that an expressive function "is either a necessary, an essential or a defining feature of punishment"). Other authors stipulate a definition of punishment ostensibly excluding an expressive dimension. For example, according to one author: "I will count as punishment any court ordered sanctions that depend on criminal conviction." ERIN I. KELLY, THE LIMITS OF BLAME: RETHINKING PUNISHMENT AND RESPONSIBILITY 122 (2018). But does this definition introduce an expressive dimension *sub silentio* when it speaks of "*criminal* conviction," insofar as a criminal conviction just is a "formal and solemn pronouncement of the moral condemnation of the community"?

[34] Compare the "king's peace" of medieval England, on which for more, see Malcolm Thorburn, *Punishment and Public Authority*, *in* CRIMINAL LAW AND THE AUTHORITY OF THE STATE 7, 23–25 (Antje du Bois-Pedain et al. eds., 2017).

only bound to conform to those rules necessary to secure and sustain the *Pax Levum*. Disobedience to a breakfast provision might risk Leviathan's wrath, but it wouldn't jeopardize the social order in which the *Pax Levum* consists.

With the *Pax Levum* established, and with the islanders cooperating with one another through conformity to the Code's rules, all goes well, for the most part. Alas, in time, Jean-Jacques returns to his old tricks. Once again, when the opportunity presents itself, and with larceny in his heart, he steals one of Thomas's pineapples. Once again, Leviathan apprehends him, and confines him to the Cage. It all looks, superficially at least, like it did before, prior to the *Pax Levum*. But looks can be deceiving, and the post-*Pax Levum* world is not the same as the pre-*Pax Levum* world. Before the *Pax Levum*, Jean-Jacques wasn't obligated to conform to Leviathan's Code; after, he is so obligated. That change brings more changes in its wake.

Prior to the *Pax Levum*, Jean-Jacques's theft was a moral wrong (stealing) against Thomas, but only Thomas. This time around, however, Jean-Jacques hasn't just stolen from and thus wronged Thomas. He's also wronged his fellow islanders and Leviathan (in his capacity as another islander), not by stealing from them, but by failing to conform to the Code. He wrongs the other islanders, because they, unlike Jean-Jacques, at least in this instance, do conform to the Code. Moreover, he wrongs Leviathan, not just in his capacity as an islander, but in his capacity as the Code's author. Both the Code and conformity to it are needed to secure the *Pax Levum*. If Leviathan leaves, taking his Code with him, and if the islanders, with Leviathan no longer around, cease to conform, the *Pax Levum* will collapse. The state of nature will return.

If actions speak louder than words, Jean-Jacques's theft says more after the *Pax Levum* than it said before. Before the *Pax Levum*, Thomas had a moral right to his pineapple, which Jean-Jacques failed to respect. Through his theft he declared himself superior to Thomas, free from the limits Thomas's moral rights imposed on him. After the *Pax Levum*, each islander has a right to every other islander's conformity to the Code. Jean-Jacques's theft declares him free from those rights as well. Once an insult only to Thomas, Jean-Jacques's theft, post-*Pax Levum*, constitutes an insult to all the islanders, including Leviathan. It also constitutes an insult to Leviathan in his capacity as Code author. Jean-Jacques's sin against the other islanders and Leviathan isn't really greed or avarice, it's pride—as in arrogance, arrogating to himself the freedom not to conform, when everyone else is conforming.

Prior to the *Pax Levum*, only Thomas had cause to be angry with Jean-Jacques, because Thomas was the only one he wronged. After the *Pax Levum*, Jean-Jacques has wronged the other islanders (including Leviathan in his capacity as an islander), and he's wronged Leviathan in his capacity as the Code's author. He wrongs them insofar as he fails to discharge his obligation to conform to the Code, which is an obligation he owes to each islander and to Leviathan as the Code's author. That means Thomas isn't the only one entitled to be angry. The other islanders are also entitled, as is Leviathan qua Code author. Moreover, because the Code permits only Leviathan, as the Code's author, to express his anger using physical force, and prohibits anyone else from doing so, Leviathan qua Code author can alone condemn Jean-Jacques for his failure to conform and confine him to the Cage. The time Jean-Jacques spends in the Cage, once the *Pax Levum* is in place, is therefore more than a penalty for a violation. After the *Pax Levum* is secured, it becomes a punishment for a crime.[35]

That brings us to the second part of the story.

Political Peace

Life on Anarchia has been much more peaceful since Leviathan promulgated the Code. Because the islanders generally conform to the Code (except sometimes Jean-Jacques), Leviathan hasn't had much occasion to coerce conformity to the rules. He spends his spare time at the lagoon, watching the fish. He's become particularly fond of an abundant species of beautiful yellow fish, which the islanders call Lemon Fish. In order to preserve the natural beauty of the lagoon, including its resplendent Lemon Fish, Leviathan decides to add a provision to the Code. Section 10 of the amended Code reads: "No one shall remove Lemon Fish from the lagoon."

Jean-Jacques thinks Lemon Fish are beautiful too. He also thinks they're delicious. He's fully aware of Leviathan's new prohibition, but doesn't care. He was morally bound to conform to the original Code, because conformity secured social peace, and respect for the forbearance of his fellow islanders obligated him to do likewise. Lemon Fish are another matter. Things won't fall apart if the islanders are permitted to catch and eat a Lemon Fish from time to time, so he can't see how he's morally obligated to conform to §

35 For a qualification to this claim, see *infra* note 45.

10's ban. He therefore goes to the lagoon, catches a Lemon Fish, and has a lovely meal.

When summoned before Leviathan for violating § 10, Jean-Jacques protests, claiming Leviathan isn't permitted to punish him for removing Lemon Fish from the lagoon. The islanders are duty-bound to conform to the Code, insofar as conformity was necessary for social peace, and insofar as respect for all the other islanders who conformed generated an obligation to conform, chargeable to each and every one of them. But § 10 isn't necessary for social peace. Leviathan could, of course, still enforce his will, and protect the Lemon Fish, but the islanders would have no duty to conform to § 10, and Leviathan would have no right to their conformity. If Leviathan confined Jean-Jacques to the Cage anyway, his coercion would be morally impermissible.

The islanders have a problem. No one really disagreed when the Code was limited to its original set of basic rules. No murder. No mayhem. No larceny. And so on. Following those rules, they realized, made them all better off. Social peace, secured through the basic rules, was a good everyone wanted. The same doesn't go for § 10. Thomas and John, it turns out, endorse § 10. They too want to preserve the lagoon's beauty, including its Lemon Fish. Jean-Jacques disagrees. He prefers eating Lemon Fish to watching them, and so far as he can tell, Leviathan isn't permitted to punish anyone unless the rule he violates is necessary to secure rudimentary social order.

Leviathan believes all the islanders are entitled to an equal say in determining what rules, beyond the basic ones, will govern their life together on Anarchia. They're the ones who have to live with each other, after all. Imagine how insulting it would be to Jean-Jacques, for example, if Leviathan decided Thomas and John could have a say, but not Jean-Jacques. Leviathan might think Jean-Jacques shouldn't have a say, because, for example, he believes Jean-Jacques isn't very bright or well-educated, and indeed, maybe Jean-Jacques isn't very bright or well-educated. But how shabby would it nonetheless be to exclude him? The only plausible way Leviathan can imagine to give each islander an equal say on what the rules, beyond the basic ones, will be, and so to treat them all as equals, is to give each an equal vote.[36]

[36] As Jeremy Waldron writes:

> One line of reasoning in support of democratic decision-making in the face of disagreement is simple respect for the capacity of ordinary men and women to form reasonable and considered views on matters of public importance. To assign decisions to an expert or committee of experts would be to act as though individuals' views did not matter; it would be an insult to them, and it would mean slighting rather than respecting

Leviathan promulgates yet another new rule. When the islanders disagree about how things should be done, the matter will, according to this new rule, be put to a vote. Each islander will have a full and fair opportunity to persuade his fellow islanders that his way of resolving the disagreement is the right way, but at the end of the day, a vote will resolve whatever disagreement remains. Each islander is entitled to one vote, and a proposed rule will become part of the Code if it gets a majority. Disagreements will, in other words, be resolved democratically.

Jean-Jacques doesn't like Lev's new rule instituting democracy on Anarchia. Contrary to what Leviathan thinks, Jean-Jacques thinks he knows better than the rest when it comes to questions about how, as a matter of justice, life should be arranged on Anarchia. His moral insight, he believes, is superior to the rest, and indeed, his insight truly may be superior. But imagine if Leviathan had said that he and Jean-Jacques would thereafter make all the rules, with Thomas and John having no say whatsoever. So long as Thomas and John refused to believe that Leviathan and Jean-Jacques were moral authorities, with superior insight into the demands of justice, they'd have no reason to defer to their judgments about what justice required. Besides, even if Thomas and John did believe Leviathan and Jean-Jacques had greater moral insight, they could always decide to cast their votes in line with however Leviathan and Jean-Jacques voted. Recognizing all this, Leviathan believes democracy is the only way to respect the fact that all the islanders are equal to one another, with no one's moral judgment superior to anyone else's.

With democracy in place, § 10 is put to a vote. The conclusion is foregone. Three in favor. One opposed. Section 10 becomes part of the Code. Section 10-1 is also put to a vote. According to proposed § 10-1, Leviathan shall publicly declare "guilty" anyone he finds has, in violation of § 10, removed Lemon Fish from the lagoon. Section 10-1 also provides that Leviathan shall, upon

> the capacities involved in their formation. Of course, empowering ordinary individuals might involve greater risk of wrong or inappropriate answers than empowering a committee of experts, but the case for democracy is that it is worth accepting this risk for the sake of the opinions of ordinary people.

Jeremy Waldron, *Democracy*, *in* The Oxford Handbook of Political Philosophy 187, 194 (David Estlund ed., 2012).

Resolving disagreements by drawing lots or flipping coins can also "avoid unequal rule," but democracy has additional virtues drawn lots and flipped coins lack, like allowing citizens to "exercise . . . political agency" through deliberation and voting. *See* Daniel Viehoff, *Democratic Equality and Political Authority*, 42 Phil. & Pub. Aff. 337, 375 (2014). *But see* Alexander A. Guerro, *Against Elections: The Lottocratic Alternative*, 42 Phil. & Pub. Aff. 135 (2014) (defending a "lottocratic" system of elections).

such a finding, be permitted to put anyone guilty of violating § 10 in the Cage for a week. Section 10-1, by the same 3–1 vote, carries. Of course, neither § 10, nor § 10-1, is set in stone. Jean-Jacques, who lost on each vote, is free to propose rescinding the ban, doing his best to persuade the others to change their minds, in the hope they'll come to see the moral light as he sees it.

Conforming to the original Code, with its basic rules, allowed the islanders to secure the good of social peace. Leviathan's simple democratic process allows them to secure another good. It enables them to secure agreement in the face of disagreement. Conforming to rules like § 10 enables them to secure political peace, bringing to a close, at least provisionally, what would otherwise be ongoing and debilitating disagreements. Conforming to the original Code made it possible to live together without being in constant fear. Conforming to the new Code, which includes democratically enacted provisions, like § 10 and § 10-1, makes it possible to live together without being in constant disagreement over the demands of justice.

Jean-Jacques disagrees with § 10 and § 10-1, believing that punishing Lemon Fish fishing is unjust. Nonetheless, as a citizen of Anarchia, he's morally bound to conform, even if he's right about the justice of Lemon Fish fishing.[37] The democratic process respects each islander as an equal, giving each an equal chance to influence the rules governing their collective coexistence. Because each islander is morally obligated to respect his fellow islanders as equals, each is also morally obligated to conform to the rules the democratic process produces. Although no islander is obligated to submit his reason to others, insofar as each is entitled to believe the others have misunderstood what justice requires, each is nonetheless obligated to submit his will to the general will, for the sake of political peace. This obligation runs from each islander to each of his fellow islanders, and from each islander to Leviathan, in his capacity as the Code's author. Of course, Leviathan's authorship is now nominal. The Code's true authors are the Islanders themselves, as a collective or corporate body.

Everyone recognized the need for conformity to some basic rules, embodied in the original Code, for the sake of peaceful coexistence. Once those rules were in place, and once everyone (or most everyone) was conforming to them, each islander's obligation to respect his conforming

[37] *See* Scott J. Shapiro, *Authority*, *in* The Oxford Handbook of Jurisprudence and Philosophy of Law 382, 437 (Jules Coleman & Scott Shapiro eds., 2002) ("It is no defence for the rebel to point out that the procedure produced an incorrect result—for whether it did or not, it is not 'up to him' to impose his own judgment on others.").

fellow islanders generated a moral obligation, incumbent on each islander, and running to all the other islanders and to Leviathan, to conform to the original Code's basic rules. Leviathan thereby gained a right to conformity, and along with it permission to punish anyone who failed to conform. Nonetheless, Leviathan still lacked authority: He had no moral power to change the islanders' normative situation. His right to conformity was grounded in the fact that the islanders were all conforming to the basic rules, which he was morally permitted to promulgate, but he had no authority to promulgate them.

The birth of democracy on Anarchia changes things. It gives the Islanders, collectively, the moral power associated with authority. With the coming of democracy, the Islanders, collectively, acquire the moral power to impose on themselves a moral obligation to conform to any rule they together agree upon through majority vote. This obligation binds them all, even those who believe this or that particular rule is unjust. Democracy gives the Islanders, collectively, the moral power to impose on themselves a moral obligation to conform to the rules they together decide will govern their coexistence on Anarchia.

Jean-Jacques is unimpressed. He heads once again for the lagoon, takes out his fishing pole, and catches a Lemon Fish. When he's brought before Leviathan, he can no longer claim Leviathan isn't morally permitted to punish him. Jean-Jacques's choice to violate § 10—taking a single fish—doesn't, in and of itself, wrong anyone. Removing one fish from the lagoon isn't like stealing Thomas's pineapples. The democratic enactment of § 10 nonetheless puts Jean-Jacques, along with all the other islanders, under a moral obligation to conform to § 10. When Jean-Jacques violates § 10, he thereby wrongs his fellow islanders, as well as Leviathan (as the Code's nominal author). Moreover, violating § 10 is a crime, not only a wrong, inasmuch as § 10-1 obligates Leviathan to condemn § 10 violations, and permits him to send violators to the Cage. Confinement in the Cage for § 10 violations is therefore a punishment, which makes § 10 a crime.

When Jean-Jacques removes a Lemon Fish from the lagoon, after the democratic enactment of § 10, he implicitly asserts a claim of superiority. He declares himself free from, and so above, the rules to which everyone is morally bound to conform, and thus above all the "little people"—to quote Leona Helmsley—who honor their obligation to conform.[38] He arrogates to himself

[38] Elizabeth Baum, Helmsley's housekeeper, testified during Helmsley's trial on fraud and extortion charges that Helmsley hold her, "We don't pay taxes. Only the little people pay taxes." Helmsley

the authority to decide which rules he'll follow and which he won't, which is to (try to) install himself as an authority in place of the islanders' democratic authority. His claim is bound to misfire because he lacks such authority. His claim is false. He's not above the rules everyone else is bound to follow. He's not, in short, above the law.[39]

The story has one more twist. Suppose when Jean-Jacques is called to account for his illicit fishing, he doesn't claim that § 10 is unjust and thus that he's not obligated to conform to it, although he believes that's true. Instead, he claims he had no choice. He claims the thought of eating Lemon Fish overcame him, rendering him powerless to resist picking up his pole, heading for the lagoon, and removing a Lemon Fish. He couldn't help himself. Or so he claims. Leviathan doesn't know what to say. Is he, under the circumstances, still permitted under § 10-1 to confine Jean-Jacques in the Cage? Has Jean-Jacques, under the circumstances, really forfeited his default right not to be punished for violating § 10?

On reflection, Leviathan believes he has. It doesn't matter, Leviathan thinks, if Jean-Jacques lacked the capacity to choose otherwise or not. He consults with Thomas and John, who disagree. Unlike Leviathan, they believe that if someone couldn't choose otherwise than to violate § 10, he shouldn't be punished. Leviathan puts the matter to a vote. The question is on proposed § 11, which reads: "No one shall be punished for violating any provision of the Code if, through no fault of his own, he lacked the capacity to conform his conduct to the requirements of the provision he is charged with violating." The vote is 3-1, with Thomas, John and Jean-Jacques voting yes, and Leviathan voting no.

Section 11 is unlike § 10. Section 10, which forbids removing Lemon Fish, applies to all the islanders. Section 10 is a primary rule or rule of conduct. It governs all the islanders as they go about their lives, and everyone

always denied making the statement. *See Maid Testifies Helmsley Denied Paying Taxes*, N.Y. TIMES, July 12, 1989, at B2.

[39] For similar thoughts, see Thomas Christiano, *The Authority of Democracy*, 12 J. POL. PHIL. 266, 286 (2004) ("Citizens who skirt democratically made law . . . when there is substantial and informed disagreement . . . on the grounds that these are unjust are simply affirming a superior right to that of others in determining how the shared aspects of social life ought to be arranged."); Shapiro, *supra* note 37, at 437 ("[O]ne who disagrees with the outcomes of a socially necessary, empowering, and fair procedure, and thus disregards it, acts, we might say, like a dictator: he unilaterally 'dictates' the terms of social interactions to others and thereby exercises inappropriate control over the lives of his fellow citizens."); *id.* ("The conclusion I would like to draw is that disobedience to the democratic will, at least under certain circumstances, amounts to an unreasonable arrogation of power.").

is morally obligated to conform to it. Section 11 is different. It applies only to those tasked with deciding if someone else, who's been charged with violating a primary rule, should nonetheless not be punished. Section 11 is a rule of decision or principle of adjudication, governing the decision-making of anyone assigned or selected to decide if someone else has no right not to be punished. Anyone assigned the burden of decision is morally obligated to conform to § 11. Upon finding that someone charged with violating a primary rule couldn't have chosen otherwise, § 11 obligates them to further find that the person charged retains his right not to be punished.[40]

With that, the second part of the story comes to an end.

Democratic Authority

Life on a four-man island is one thing. Life in a large-scale, complex, modern-day state is another.[41] The task we now embark upon is to derive from Leviathan's story a more abstract and general account explaining, first, why any state (democratic or not) is morally permitted to punish those who commit wrongs constituting core crimes, and second, why a democratic state is a legitimate state, and why it therefore has the authority, within limits, to grant itself moral permission to punish anyone who commits any act it declares to be a crime.

[40] For more on the distinction between these two types of rules, see, for example, Meir Dan-Cohen, *Decision Rules and Conduct Rules: On Acoustic Separation in Criminal Law*, *in* Harmful Thoughts: Essays on Law, Self, and Morality 37 (2002); Paul H. Robinson, *Rules of Conduct and Principles of Adjudication*, 57 U. Chi. L. Rev. 729 (1990). The distinction between conduct rules and decision rules is useful, but applying it to real-world criminal codes isn't always easy. One state might, for example, intend a rule to be a conduct rule, while another might intend the same rule to be a decision rule. For more on this problem, see Mitchell N. Berman, *Justification and Excuse, Law and Morality*, 53 Duke L.J. 1, 68 (2003).

Applying decision rules like § 11, which provide what would typically be called an excuse, is in many countries the job of a jury, at least when the defendant hasn't waived his right to a jury. Jurors take an oath to follow the law, as federal judges do to "perform all the duties incumbent" upon them "under the Constitution and laws of the United States," 28 U.S.C. § 453, and the oath they take reinforces their moral obligation to conform to the applicable decision rules, but even if they never took an oath to follow the law, they'd nonetheless be morally bound to follow it anyway. As citizens of a democracy, they're morally bound in that role to follow every law applying to them.

[41] One obvious difference between Leviathan and the state is that Leviathan is a real person, whereas the state is an abstraction, or at best a corporate person.

A State's Right to Conformity

When a state first comes on the scene, establishing rules to govern the conduct of those within its jurisdiction, it acquires a moral permission (or liberty right) to coerce conformity to its rules, provided such coercion is necessary to assure conformity to its rules; conformity is necessary to achieve some good for all those subject to its coercion; and the good is one everyone, or most everyone, recognizes and wants but isn't able to secure without general conformity. One such good is social peace, stability, order, and so on, without which everyone within the state's jurisdiction would continue to languish in a state of nature, and without which they'd be unable to pursue their own ends, at least not with anything resembling peace of mind.

Once those subject to state coercion begin to cooperate with one another, conforming to a set of basic rules needed to secure social peace, thereby bringing social peace into existence, the moral landscape changes.[42] Respect for those conforming to the rules places everyone, conforming or not, under a moral obligation to conform, like it or not. No one gets a free ride. Once cooperation, in the form of conformity to the rules, takes hold, everyone benefitting from such conformity, as everyone does, becomes duty-bound to conform. This duty runs not only to everyone who likewise conforms, but also to the state in its role as author of the rules. Because the state's subjects have a duty to conform, limited to the rules needed to secure social peace, the state has a corresponding right to conformity. Failure to conform violates one's moral obligation to the state and thus constitutes a moral wrong against the state.[43] Moreover, the state's right to conformity with the basic rules needed to establish social peace, and duty of its

[42] According to John Perry, what matters for the argument from fair play, as an argument designed to establish the existence of an obligation to conform to the law, is "not the fact that the relevant directives were issued by a legitimate moral power . . . , but rather the fact that other people have obeyed the directives (*however they came into existence*) and one has, under certain circumstances, a duty to reciprocate." Perry, *supra* note 6, at 30 (emphasis added).

[43] Political theorists and criminal law theorists alike make use of stories about schemes of cooperation, about those who accept or receive the benefits of such schemes, and about the changes such schemes make to the relationship between cooperators and defectors. Political theorists typically use these stories to explain why citizens owe a moral obligation to the state to conform to the law, and thus tend to talk about fair play theories of *political obligation*. Criminal law theorists typically use them to explain why punishment is permissible, or why it amounts to something good, when imposed on defectors or free riders, and thus tend to talk about fair play theories of *punishment*. For a recent effort to bring these two literatures together, see RICHARD DAGGER, PLAYING FAIR: POLITICAL OBLIGATION AND THE PROBLEMS OF PUNISHMENT (2018).

Among political theorists, appeals to fair play began with H.L.A. Hart and John Rawls. *See* H.L.A. Hart, *Are There Any Natural Rights?*, 64 PHIL. REV. 175 (1955); John Rawls, *Legal Obligation and the Duty of Fair Play*, *in* LAW AND PHILOSOPHY 3 (Sidney Hook ed., 1964). The subsequent literature

subjects to conform to those rules, doesn't depend on its being a democratic state. As long as the state, democratic or not, promulgates the basic rules needed to secure social peace, and as long as its subjects generally conform to those rules, thereby realizing social peace, the state's subjects come under a duty to conform, and the state gains a right to their conformity.

Imagine Peter robs Paul. He uses force to steal Paul's wallet. Assuming Peter lives in a state in which social peace has been secured, because everyone, or most everyone, is more or less conforming to the rule against robbery, along with all the other basic rules, he commits three moral wrongs, not just one, when he robs Paul. First, he wrongs Paul. Once a regime of property rights is in place, robbery is wrong in and of itself, independent of any legal rule proscribing it. Second, he wrongs everyone else who's conforming to the rule against robbery and who aren't robbing. His wrong here consists in his failure to conform to the law prohibiting robbery, from which everyone benefits if everyone, or most everyone, conforms. Third, he wrongs the state. His wrong here is, again, his failure to conform to the law prohibiting robbery, which the state has promulgated to secure social peace.[44]

on the fair play theory of political obligation is enormous. *See generally* Dagger & Lefkowitz, *supra* note 6, at § 4.3 (discussing literature). Perhaps the most prominent defense is George Klosko, The Principle of Fairness and Political Obligation (1992). If fair play can successfully account for a moral obligation to conform to the law, the duty it generates is probably limited in scope, extending no farther than the state's "*core* functions," like securing social peace. *See* George Klosko, Political Obligations 8–9 (2005) ("[S]erious problems with the [fairness] argument . . . are encountered as we attempt to move beyond the government's core functions."). Justin Tosi has recently emphasized that the fair play theory of political obligation requires the existence of some set of rules. *See* Justin Tosi, *Rethinking the Principle of Fair Play*, 99 Pac. Phil. Q. 612, 616 (2018) ("To play fair with others is to treat oneself as equally subject to the same set of *rules* as them.") (emphasis added).

Among criminal law theorists, appeals to fairness and fair play began with Herbert Morris. *See* Herbert Morris, *Persons and Punishment*, *in* On Guilt and Innocence: Essays in Legal Philosophy and Moral Psychology 31 (1976). The rules of the system Morris imagined were limited to what he called "primary" rules, which, he said, "closely resemble the *core* rules of our criminal law." *Id.* at 33 (emphasis added). The subsequent literature on the fair play theory of punishment is also enormous. *See, e.g.*, Richard Dagger, *Playing Fair with Punishment*, 103 Ethics 473 (1993); Zachary Hoskins, *Fair Play, Political Obligation, and Punishment*, 5 Crim. L. & Phil. 53 (2011); Göran Duus-Otterström, *Fairness-Based Retributivism Reconsidered*, 11 Crim. L. & Phil. 481 (2017); Matt K. Stichter, *Rescuing Fair-Play as a Justification for Punishment*, 16 Res Publica 73 (2010); Peter Westen, *Retributive Desert as Fair Play*, *in* Legal, Moral, and Metaphysical Truths: The Philosophy of Michael S. Moore 63 (Kimberly Kessler Ferzan & Stephen J. Morse eds., 2016).

[44] Three wrongs seems right, but others see only two. For example, according to one theorist, "Should the subject disobey the authority, he will have committed two offences: he will have performed an action that, independent of the directive, he should not have performed *and* will have violated his moral obligation to obey." Shapiro, *supra* note 37, at 435. That way of looking at it, however, doesn't tell us to whom or what the "moral obligation to obey" is owed. If that duty runs to both one's fellow citizens and to the state, that would make three wrongs: 1) the "action that, independent of the directive, he should not have performed"; 2) the violation of his moral obligation to obey, owed to his fellow citizens; and 3) the violation of his moral obligation to obey, owed to the state.

Peter's triple-headed moral wrong makes him a sitting duck for anger and resentment. Everyone Peter wronged is entitled to be angry with him, and to express it. Paul's entitled: He was the one Peter robbed. Peter's fellow subjects are entitled: They conformed, but he didn't. The state's entitled: It had a right to Peter's conformity, but he violated it. The state typically reserves, but in principle needn't reserve, one mode of expressing anger, the forcible imposition of material burdens, for its exclusive use. Everyone who Peter wronged is permitted to censure and condemn him, but the state typically doesn't permit them to do anything more, like take money from him or lock him away, or otherwise coerce him to do things he'd rather not do. In other words, the state typically permits itself, but no one else, to punish Peter, and attaching punishment to violations of the rule prohibiting robbery makes robbery a crime.[45]

[45] This claim needs, in response to two possible objections, qualification and elaboration. First, the qualification responds to the following objection. If punishment conceptually requires a relationship of authority qua moral power between the state as the one doing the punishing and the person being punished, and if the state lacked authority, then the state, conceptually speaking, can't punish anyone. In response, we should concede the point. If the burden a state without authority imposes is nonetheless called punishment, it must be understood as punishment in a non-paradigmatic or non-central sense.

Second, the elaboration responds to the following objection, which might be called the one-punishment-fits-all objection. When someone commits a crime, the wrong he commits, as a wrong against the state, consists in his failure to conform to the law. But any crime, from murder to the unauthorized sale of Woodsy Owl T-shirts, consist in the accused's failure to conform to the law qua wrong against the state. If so, it would seem to follow that all crimes, from murder to the unauthorized sale of Woodsy Owl T-shirts, should get the same punishment, inasmuch as they consist in the same wrong, but that, so the objection goes, would amount to a *reductio ad absurdum*.

In response, I'd suggest that most crimes are compounds. They're wrongs made up of one fixed or constant wrong (a content-*independent* wrong against the state) and a variable wrong (a content-*dependent* wrong, usually against someone other than the state). When the state punishes, it gives itself permission to punish both. Because it was the victim of the fixed wrong, it makes sense for the state to give itself permission to punish that wrong. It also makes sense for the state to give itself permission to punish the variable wrong, even though the state isn't usually the victim of that wrong (except, perhaps, when the crime is plausibly understood as a crime against the state, like treason, or the administration of justice, like perjury or obstruction of justice). It makes sense for the state to assign itself permission to punish the fixed wrong, and at the same time to obligate the victim of that wrong not to take matters into his own hands, because doing so helps to secure social peace and order, and helps to prevent vigilantism, which is the opposite of peace and social order. Of course, the state does permit other authorities—parents, social organizations, schools, universities—to punish those subject to their authority, but it typically limits the kind of burdens they can impose. A university, for example, isn't permitted to send a student to jail for violating a provision of the university's code of conduct. A state might allow a parent or teacher to resort to corporal punishments, but if it does, its permission is limited in scope. Parents who exceed the scope of the permission would themselves likely be guilty of a crime, like child abuse.

The one-punishment-fits-all objection has also been directed at fair-play theories of punishment. For responses to this objection, see, for example, Dagger, *supra* note 43 at 265 ("One can hold . . . that the state's right to punish is grounded in fair play without concluding that the agents of the state can consider nothing but unfair benefits when deciding how or how much to punish offenders."); Hoskins, *supra* note 43, at 54 (interpreting the fair play theory of punishment, according

Once the rules necessary for social peace are in place, and once everyone, or most everyone, is conforming to them, thereby securing social peace, the state's permission to coerce compliance is transformed into a permission to punish noncompliance, for violating the duty to conform. Still, the state isn't yet an authority. It has yet to go from having a right to conformity, and a moral permission to punish nonconformity, to having a moral power intentionally to change the normative status of those within its jurisdiction.[46] That transformation—moving from a right to conformity, coupled with a moral permission to punish, to a moral power to change its subjects' normative status—doesn't happen unless and until the state makes the turn to democracy.

A Democratic State's Authority

The rules necessary to move from a state of nature to civil society constitute what we might call the criminal law's core crimes. A lawyer might loosely describe them as *malum in se*.[47] Again, the duty to conform to the rules defining core crimes doesn't depend on how those rules became law. The process might have been democratic, or it might not have been.

Malum in se crimes form the core of the criminal law, but the criminal law doesn't live on *malum in se* alone.[48] Crimes outside the core, those not needed

to which the theory is intended to explain why the state is permitted to punish, not why it should exercise that permission, nor how much it should punish when it exercises it); Stichter, *supra* note 43, at 74 (The one-size-fits-all objection fails "to distinguish between what justifies punishment as a response to crime (which necessarily requires pointing out a common element to all crime) and what justifies attaching particular penalties to specific crimes (which necessarily requires making distinctions in the seriousness of various crimes).").

[46] Assuming the principle of fair play can explain when a subject is morally obligated to conform to the state's laws, any such obligation will entail only the state's right to the subject's conformity. It will not entail the state's moral power to change the normative situation of its subjects. In other words, you can go from a moral power (in the state) to a moral obligation (in the subject), but you can't go in the reverse direction, from a moral obligation (in the subject) to a moral power (in the state). *See* Perry, *supra* note 6, at 35 ("The argument from fair play depends on the acceptance of benefits associated with a certain state of affairs, namely, the compliance of other persons with the rules, that normally can only come into existence, where it does come into existence at all, at a time *after* the rules have been enacted. Because this is so, the argument cannot plausibly be regarded as justifying the existence of a moral power to issue binding rules in the first place."). For an effort to show fair play *can* generate a moral power (in the state), see Justin Tosi, *A Fair Play Account of Legitimate Political Authority*, 23 Legal Theory 55, 65 (2017); Justin Tosi, *The Possibility of a Fair Play Account of Legitimacy*, 30 Ratio 88, 95 (2015).

[47] If the phrase *malum in se* is used to identify moral wrongs whose wrongfulness doesn't depend on the existence of any law, then the set of what's here called core crimes would constitute a subset of *malum in se* crimes; namely, those *malum in se* crimes without which social peace would be insecure.

[48] Even if the criminal law tried to live on *malum in se* alone, such that the specific part of its penal code was limited to core crimes, democratic authority would still be needed to resolve disagreements

to secure social peace, crimes like money laundering, are common. Indeed, according to many, they're too common. Nor can the criminal law live on crimes alone. Aside from conduct rules defining crimes, the criminal law needs decision rules, which obligate juries and judges to acquit those who, for example, commit a crime but who aren't culpable or worthy of blame. Excuses fall into this category. Likewise, it needs decision rules obligating or permitting judges (or sometimes juries) to obligate others to punish those found to have no right against such treatment. If a state has authority over these non-core rules, the good that grounds its authority isn't social peace. The state of nature won't reemerge if, for example, a state decides not to criminalize money laundering.

Authorities exist to secure some good.[49] A state's authority to promulgate the criminal law's non-core rules delivers what can be called, over that domain, the good of political peace. Once we step outside the criminal law's core, we're apt to encounter disagreement over what those rules should be, as a matter of justice, because different people believe justice requires different things. What acts or omissions should be subject to punishment? Indeed, should crimes be limited to acts and omissions? When should a jury or judge excuse someone who'd otherwise be criminally liable? When should a judge order someone, like a prison official, to punish someone else who's been found to have no right against punishment? We need some way to settle these disagreements, and the only way we can realistically settle them so as to beget a moral obligation to conform to the rules settled upon is to settle them democratically.

When disagreement over the just terms of collective coexistence, including the terms of the criminal law, is settled in a way giving everyone an equal say over those terms, everyone, having had their equal say, is morally obligated to conform to the resulting rules. A democratic citizen is morally obligated to respect each of his fellow citizens as an equal to himself, endowed with the same freedom to form beliefs about what justice requires when it comes to the rules governing his relations with his fellow citizens.

arising over the specific elements defining those core crimes, not to mention disagreements over the specific elements defining the various rules comprising the general part. For example, should the crime of "murder" be defined such that someone is guilty of "murder" only if he intentionally causes the death of another, or will other mental states, like knowledge or extreme recklessness, suffice?

[49] *See, e.g.*, Perry, *supra* note 6, at 26 ("Legitimate moral authority can only exist if there is something sufficiently good or valuable about one person being able intentionally to change the normative situation of another person.").

That cornerstone obligation generates another: the obligation to conform his conduct to the rules resulting from the only real mechanism available to resolve their disagreements consistent with the status of each as equally free. That mechanism is democracy. When a state resolves disagreements over justice (and thereby secures political peace) in a democratic way, thus respecting everyone's bedrock status as equally free, it resolves them in an authoritative way, and resolving them in an authoritative way means everyone is obligated to conform to the collectively agreed-upon rules.[50]

[50] More philosophically rigorous efforts to vindicate democratic authority, though in ways different from the way offered in the text, can be found in, for example, THOMAS CHRISTIANO, THE CONSTITUTION OF EQUALITY: DEMOCRATIC AUTHORITY AND ITS LIMITS 235 (2008) ("[S]omeone who proposes standards for the evaluation of political institutions and expects them to be implemented without regard for the judgment of others is somehow placing himself and his judgment above that of others in a way that a parent places her judgment above that of an infant or a god places its judgment over that of a human being."); JEREMY WALDRON, LAW AND DISAGREEMENT 114–15 (1999) ("[A]ccording equal weight or equal potential decisiveness to individual votes is a way of respecting persons. In this sense, majority-decision is a respectful procedure—not just an admirable device for securing action-in-concert in the circumstances of politics."); Christiano, *supra* note 39, at 287 ("[T]he democratic assembly has a right to rule . . . since one treats its members unjustly if one ignores or skirts its decisions. Each citizen has a right to one's obedience and therefore the assembly as a whole has a right to one's obedience."); Scott Hershovitz, *Legitimacy, Democracy, and Razian Authority*, 9 LEGAL THEORY 201, 214 (2003) ("Democratically enacted law demands our respect because it stands for the time in the name of the whole community and represents how we have bound ourselves through fair procedures in the face of disagreement.") (internal citations omitted); Niko Kolodny, *Rule Over None II: Social Equality and the Justification of Democracy*, 42 PHIL. & PUB. AFF. 287, 315 (2014) ("Insofar as relations of social equality are partly constituted by . . . [an] equal opportunity for influence," disregarding a democratic decision "depriv[es] others of that equal influence, relating to them as a social superior, at least in that instance."); David Lefkowitz, *A Contractualist Defense of Democratic Authority*, 18 RATIO 346, 364 (2005) ("Morality itself . . . requires a citizen of a liberal democratic state to treat the directives that state issues as authoritative reasons for action."); Shapiro, *supra* note 37, at 437 ("[D]isobedience to the democratic will . . . den[ies] the majority the respect due them as equal participants in a fair power-sharing arrangement."); Viehoff, *supra* note 36, at 352 ("[U]nless we accept as binding the directives of an authority whose decisions have not been shaped by unequal power advantages, it is often impossible for us to achieve certain ends (in particular, ends that require co-ordination among people who disagree about which co-ordination solution is best) without violating the demands the equalitarian ideal makes on us."). Such arguments haven't persuaded everyone. According to Harrison Frye and George Klosko, for example, the "democratic provenance" of law "grounds . . . requirements to *respect*" the law, but doesn't "establish[] moral requirements to *obey* it." Harrison Frye & George Klosko, *Democratic Authority and Respect for the Law*, 36 LAW & PHIL. 1, 1 (2017).

These efforts ground democratic authority in the importance or value of relating to one's fellow citizens as, in some sense, equals. If you step off that ground, and try to say instead that democratic states have authority because their laws are more likely, compared to non-democratic states, to be just, you'll quickly encounter the disagreement between those who believe democratic states are indeed more likely to be just, *see, e.g.*, DAVID M. ESTLUND, DEMOCRATIC AUTHORITY: A PHILOSOPHICAL FRAMEWORK 1 (2008) ("My goal is to show how a concern for the quality of political decisions, properly constrained by other principles, supports democratic political arrangements."); HÉLÈNE LANDEMORE, DEMOCRATIC REASON: POLITICS, COGNITIVE INTELLIGENCE, AND THE RULE OF THE MANY 1–2 (2013) (arguing that "democracy is a smart collective decision-making procedure that taps into the intelligence of the people as a group in ways that can even, under the right conditions, make it smarter than alternative regimes such as the rule of one or the rule of the few"), and Plato's heirs, who believe democracies should be replaced with epistocracies (rule of the knowledgeable). *See, e.g.*, JASON BRENNAN, AGAINST DEMOCRACY 15 (2016) ("In recent years, Plato has made a

The obligation to conform runs in two directions. It runs, first, to one's fellow citizens individually. Each citizen is obligated to conform and each citizen has a right to the conformity of every other citizen. It runs, second, to the state, as nominal author of the rules, and thus collectively to the People, as their true author. For within a democratic state, any line between the People and the state is ideally a matter of form, not substance. In democratic states, the People are self-governing: the authors of their own laws. When someone is punished for a crime, whether inside or outside the core, he's punished, in part, because he wronged the state so conceived. He violated his obligation to the state to conform to a democratically enacted rule defining a crime, and thus his failure to conform wronged the state.

When a state transitions to democracy, it transitions to authority. It moves from having a right to conformity, and the moral permission to punish core crimes, to having the moral power to change the normative status of its citizens, including its officials. Democratic states acquire this power because without it citizens would live in a perpetual state of disagreement, resulting from incompatible beliefs about the requirements of justice, making cooperation and coordination impossible. Democratic citizens are liable to the exercise of this power, and obligated to subordinate their will to the collective will, expressed in the form of law. They're obligated to conform to the law because no other way exists to resolve disagreements among equal citizens about what justice requires of them.

The force of this obligation can be seen if you imagine being at a stoplight on a deserted stretch of road.[51] You're traveling on a road in, say, Alaska. You come to an intersection with a stoplight. The light is red. You stop, probably on instinct. You look around. You can see for miles and miles, and you see nothing—no cars, no people, no bikes, no trains, no nothing—coming your way. What do you do? Do you wait the light out, or do you run it? It seems silly to just sit there, doesn't it?

If you ignore the light, you'd be committing a crime, albeit a tiny one, and you know it. You're also a citizen of Alaska, bound to conform to Alaskan law. The law, we're supposing, carves out no exception, even in the present circumstances, allowing you to run the red. The law might make an exception.

comeback. In political philosophy, epistocracy has emerged as the main challenger to democracy's throne.").

51 The example is usually attributed to M.B.E Smith, *Is There a Prima Facie Obligation to Obey the Law?*, 82 YALE L.J. 950, 971 (1973).

Current Alaska law, for example, recognizes a defense of necessity, which allows you, roughly speaking, to commit a crime if a greater evil was your only other choice,[52] and maybe just sitting there, under the circumstances, is a greater evil than running the red. That's highly doubtful, but just to be safe, assume Alaska law doesn't recognize necessity, and you believe, if you run the red, that you'd be committing an offense denominated as a crime under Alaska law.

There you sit. On the one hand, your inner philosophical anarchist tells you: Go ahead. Run the red. Running the red isn't morally wrong, all things considered, at least not under the circumstances. Morality, your inner anarchist tells you, says go, and for now, let's stipulate your inner anarchist is right. Running the red wouldn't be morally wrong, all things considered, with or without the law requiring you to stop at red lights. Nor will your running the red lead through any causal chain to the collapse of the social order. You believe morality, had it not conferred authority on the state, would permit you to run the light.[53]

On the other hand, your inner law-abiding citizen tells you: Yes, morality is one authority to which you owe allegiance, and yes, morality, you believe, would permit you to run the light. Nonetheless, you realize that morality has conferred authority on the democratic state of which you're a citizen to impose on you moral obligations that morality itself would not, and as such, you owe allegiance to the law, which embodies the collective judgment of your fellow citizens, as well as to morality. As a citizen of a democratic state, you believe you're morally obligated to conform to its laws, including the law prohibiting running the red, even if you also believe morality itself would otherwise permit you to run the red.

You struggle between your allegiance to morality, as a moral agent whose reason is unbound to any authority other than the authority of morality, and

[52] *See* ALASKA STAT. § 11.81.320(a) ("Conduct which would otherwise be an offense is justified by reason of necessity to the extent permitted by common law."). On the general contours of the common law defense of necessity, see JOSHUA DRESSLER, UNDERSTANDING CRIMINAL LAW § 22.02, at 273–75 (8th ed. 2018).

[53] William Edmundson asks: "What, other than fetishism, an abject, abstract *sycophancy*, could compel anyone to say that in these circumstances I nevertheless have a prima facie moral duty to come to a full stop?" Edmundson, *supra* note 11, at 45–46 (emphasis added). If morality's your only authority, that's probably how it looks. If you see yourself as a law-abiding citizen, however, it looks different. As he sits at the light, Edmundson imagines thinking: "My well-entrenched habit is to come to a full stop before proceeding; but I want to know *what it is like* to disobey the law." *Id.* at 45. All of which makes one wonder: What, other than an abject, abstract *defiance*, could compel anyone to fail to conform to the law just to "know know what it is like to disobey the law"?

your allegiance to the democratic state, as a law-abiding citizen. What do you do?

Nothing stops you from running the light. Perhaps you see yourself as a rebel. You know the difference between right and wrong; running the light isn't wrong, and no one can tell you otherwise. Or perhaps you see yourself as a gambler. Running the light risks a fine, but it's a risk worth taking to get where you're going a few seconds faster. Or perhaps you see yourself as a conscientious objector. You're not just running a red light. You're planting a flag for moral truth.

What you can't do, if you run the red, is see yourself as a law-abiding citizen, unless, as we'll see, you truly and firmly believe beyond reasonable doubt that the rule against running red lights was beyond the state's authority to enact in the first place. You might generally be law-abiding. You might possess the virtue of law-abidance, but you're not law-abiding at the moment you press the accelerator. So, if you speed through, and the hidden camera catches you, you have no reason to complain, as a citizen, when the state issues its rebuke and forces you to pay a small fine for your failure to conform. You violated your moral duty to conform, and you knew it. As a law-abiding citizen, you should accept the consequences of your choice without protest.

A democratic state has the authority to impose on its citizens, through the exercise of its authority, a duty to conform to its laws. The state doesn't care why you conform.[54] Maybe you conform because you believe you're morally bound to conform, as you are. Indeed, maybe you believe your duty to conform preempts all other moral considerations. Or maybe you believe it just carries a certain amount of weight.[55] Or maybe you conform out of

[54] *See, e.g.*, Scott Hershovitz, *The Authority of Law*, *in* THE ROUTLEDGE COMPANION TO PHILOSOPHY OF LAW 65, 66–67 (Andrei Marmor ed., 2012) (distinguishing between obedience to authority as compliance and as conformity and arguing "in the normal case one does all the law requires if one acts as it demands, whatever one reasons"); Perry, *supra* note 6, at 14 ("[T]he law, for the most part, does not care why we do as it requires, so long as we do it."). *But see* Michael Sevel, *Obeying the Law*, 24 LEGAL THEORY 191, 200 (2018) ("[O]bedience as mere conformity to the reasons the law provides is deeply implausible."). Although the state usually doesn't care why we conform, it does often care why we don't conform. Our reasons for failing to conform can, as explained more fully in Chapter 3, make us more or less culpable, or even not culpable at all.

[55] If we have a moral obligation to obey the law, is that obligation preemptive or *pro tanto*? That question has been much debated, although some philosophers say that, at the end of the day, not much difference exists between the two. *See, e.g.*, Matthew H. Kramer, *Legal and Moral Obligation*, *in* THE BLACKWELL GUIDE TO THE PHILOSOPHY OF LAW AND LEGAL THEORY 179, 188 (Martin P. Golding & William A. Edmundson et al. eds., 2005) ("[T]he two perspectives are by no means as clearly divergent as they might at first seem to be."). Alternatively, as suggested in the text, perhaps the answer is both. In one's role as a law-abiding citizen of a democratic state, the obligation to conform will be experienced as preemptive. In one's role as a subject of the moral law, whose only loyalty is to morality, the obligation to conform to the law, if it amounts to an obligation at all, will be experienced as at most *pro tanto*. On the more general idea that being an authority, and being subject to

prudence, because you don't want to risk the fine. A democratic state needn't care. When it comes to conforming, it cares about what you do, not why you do it. It commands your will, not your reason. You're free to think what you like. Affix a bumper sticker advertising that you "Defy Authority." Express indignation at what you believe to be the law's injustice or stupidity. You're free to do all that, and more, but as a citizen, Jeremy Bentham said it well: "Under a government of laws what is the motto of the good citizen? . . . To obey punctually; to censure freely."[56]

Not everyone will accept the idea that a democratic state is vested with authority, or that citizens of a democratic state are morally bound to conform to its laws. A democratic skeptic doubts the existence of democratic authority, not because he believes democracies can't have authority, but because he believes no democratic state has so far managed to have the democratic bona fides it takes to earn authority. The skeptic believes all democratic states alive today fall short of his democratic ideal, and neither has history known a democracy capable of making the grade. According to the democratic skeptic, no state is, nor has any state ever been, democratic enough, because none has managed to structure itself so as to earn the authority a true democracy would have earned.[57]

Point well taken. Nothing has been said here about the details, where the devil is forever found. Nothing has been said amounting to a theory of democracy—a theory about how democratic a state must be (along some continuum of "democraticness"),[58] or how it must be arranged, or how it must

authority, attaches to roles, see Scott Hershovitz, *The Role of Authority*, 11 Philosophers' Imprint 11, 18 (2011) ("Recognizing that authority attaches to roles allows us to appreciate that one might obey a parent, chef, or conductor because one *is* a daughter, cook, or cellist.").

[56] Jeremy Bentham, A Comment on the Commentaries and a Fragment on Government 377 (J.H. Burns & H.L.A. Hart eds., 1977) (1776).

[57] *See, e.g.*, James Lindley Wilson, Democratic Equality 9 (2019) (offering a "conception of political equality" to "help organize and resolve controversies about the proper design of democratic institutions"); Samuel Issacharoff, *Democracy's Deficits*, 85 U. Chi. L. Rev. 485 (2018) (describing four causes of the "current democratic malaise").

[58] *See, e.g.*, Alvin I Goldman, *What Is Democracy (and What Is Its Raison D'Etre)?*, 1 J. Am. Phil. Ass'n 233, 253 (2015) (suggesting that "democraticness comes in degrees and that higher levels of democraticness are associated with greater equality of (positive) political power"). Perhaps democratic states gain authority only if citizens, when they vote, do so only with some specified motivation, like achieving the common good, and not out of self-interest, for example. *See, e.g.*, Viehoff, *supra* note 36, at 374 ("[W]here citizens vote solely to advance their own interest and without an eye toward how their vote contributes to the common good, the distinctive authority of egalitarian political procedures is undermined."). Or perhaps democratic states gain authority only if everyone has "equal availability of resources, such as wealth and leisure, to apply to the legal or procedural structure to acquire information and influence the votes of others (or the decisions of delegates)." Kolodny, *supra* note 50, at 332.

work, and so on—before it can be rewarded with authority. Must a democracy be "deliberative" before it can acquire authority, or can a "competitive" democracy qualify too?[59] What about the electoral system, assuming direct democracy isn't required? Is proportional representation needed for authority, or will first-past-the-post fill the bill?[60] Is a Westminster parliamentary system needed, or will a Washington presidential checks-and-balances system do the trick?[61] Can legislatures include chambers, like the U.S. Senate, with debatable democratic bona fides?[62] Is the filibuster tolerable?[63] Nothing has been said about questions of that sort. Nor has anything been said about the corrupting influence of money in politics,[64] gerrymandered voting districts,[65] limits on access to the franchise (including the much-discussed disenfranchisement of felons),[66] the allegation of an uninformed (or worse) electorate,[67] nor any other malady from which you might believe modern democracies suffer.

Alternatively, the democratic skeptic's skepticism might be more circumscribed. Democracy, on this view, works well enough most of the time to endow it with authority, but not when it comes to the criminal law. When it comes to the criminal law, the democratic process is broken. Maybe the People make the law most of the time, but when it comes to the criminal law, that's not how it works. Instead, police, prosecutors, and politicians really make the law, not the People. That makes the politics of the criminal law, as some say, pathological. In order to see why that's so, one needs to appreciate the political economy of the criminal law, or at least the political economy of the criminal law in the United States.[68]

59 *See, e.g.*, DAVID HELD, MODELS OF DEMOCRACY (3d ed. 2006).

60 *See, e.g.*, THE OXFORD HANDBOOK OF ELECTORAL SYSTEMS (Erik S. Herron et al. eds., 2018).

61 *See, e.g.*, AREND LIJPHART, PATTERNS OF DEMOCRACY: GOVERNMENT FORMS AND PERFORMANCE IN THIRTY-SIX COUNTRIES (2d ed. 2012).

62 *See, e.g.*, ROBERT A. DAHL, HOW DEMOCRATIC IS THE AMERICAN CONSTITUTION? 144–45 (2001).

63 *See, e.g.*, RICHARD A. ARENBERG & ROBERT B. DOVE, DEFENDING THE FILIBUSTER: THE SOUL OF THE SENATE (rev. ed. 2014).

64 *See, e.g.*, ZEPHYR TEACHOUT, CORRUPTION IN AMERICA (2014).

65 *See, e.g.*, Charles R. Beitz, *How Is Partisan Gerrymandering Unfair?*, 46 PHIL. & PUB. AFF. 323 (2019).

66 *See, e.g.*, MILENA TRIPKOVIC, PUNISHMENT AND CITIZENSHIP: A THEORY OF CRIMINAL DISENFRANCHISEMENT (2018).

67 *See, e.g.*, ARTHUR LUPIA, UNINFORMED: WHY PEOPLE KNOW SO LITTLE ABOUT POLITICS AND WHAT WE CAN DO ABOUT IT (2016).

68 *See, e.g.*, RACHEL ELISE BARKOW, PRISONERS OF POLITICS: BREAKING THE CYCLE OF MASS INCARCERATION 105–24 (2019); William J. Stuntz, *The Pathological Politics of Criminal Law*, 100 MICH. L. REV. 505 (2001); Richard H. McAdams, *The Political Economy of Criminal Law and Procedure: The Pessimists' View*, *in* CRIMINAL LAW CONVERSATIONS 517, 517–21 (Paul H. Robinson et al. eds., 2009). On this account, democratic politics, and the criminal laws it yields, is presumably

The full story is complicated, but the gist is this. When it comes to the criminal law, the People care about crime rates. Meanwhile, police and prosecutors care about arrest rates and conviction rates, respectively, and more criminal law (more crimes on the books) makes it easier for the police to arrest and for prosecutors to convict. Politicians can satisfy both at the same time. All they have to do is make more criminal law. That makes police and prosecutors happy, because it allows them to keep their rates up. It makes the People happy, because they'll think all that can be done to reduce crime is being done. The result is more and more criminal law, which police, prosecutors, and politicians want, but which maybe the People don't, or at least wouldn't, if only they were to realize that more law, the argument goes, doesn't necessarily mean greater safety.[69]

A full-dress theory of democracy tells us what a democratic state must look like in order for it to have authority. Some such theory is needed,[70] but no such theory will be offered in the pages to follow. You'll need to decide for yourself what it takes for morality to invest a democracy with authority, either in general or limited to the criminal law.[71] You can, for now, assume the democratic state discussed hereafter satisfies all the minimal system requirements you have in mind. Of course, that would mean the democracy

pathological, at least in part, because it fails to reflect the "will" of the People, or what the People "really" want. Of course, that claim makes sense only if we have some other way, apart from an existing democratic process, to determine what the People's will "really" is.

[69] A democratic skeptic might offer another, still more limited, objection, focused on regulatory crimes, which arise when an administrative agency promulgates a regulation, and the legislature attaches punishment to acts or omissions violating it. Administrative agencies, the skeptic might say, lack the democratic bona fides necessary for their regulations to be legitimate. The fact that a legislature has delegated rule-making authority to the unelected members of an administrative agency, and has attached punishment to violations of the resulting regulations, just isn't democratic enough to support the legitimacy of regulatory offenses. Thus, criminal laws as such don't necessarily lack legitimacy, but regulatory offenses do. *Cf.* Whitman v. United States, 135 S. Ct. 352, 353 (2014) (Scalia, J., dissenting from the denial of certiorari) (observing in a different context the "norm that legislatures, not executive officers, define crimes").

[70] As Laura Valentini has said: A "theory of justice designed for . . . conditions [of reasonable disagreement] should be primarily a theory about the external limits, *and internal constitution*, of democracy." *See* Laura Valentini, *Justice, Disagreement and Democracy*, 43 Brit. J. Pol. Sci. 177, 199 (2013) (emphasis added).

[71] Among those who spend time thinking about crime and punishment, and its relationship to "democracy," a dichotomy has emerged. Both sides agree that something called the "criminal justice system" is in a state called a "crisis," but beyond that, one side tends to believes the solution to the crisis is more democracy (where "more democracy" commonly means more local and lay involvement in policing practices, charging decisions, and sentencing decisions), while the other side believes the solution is less democracy (where "less democracy" commonly means less local and lay involvement). *See, e.g.*, Joshua Kleinfeld, *Manifesto of Democratic Criminal Justice*, 111 Nw. U.L. Rev. 1367, 1397–1401 (2017) (describing these two camps, respectively, as "democratizers" and "bureaucratic professionalizers").

you conjure would have authority. It wouldn't necessarily mean the democracy we're presently stuck with has authority, since the democracy we now have might fall short of any threshold conditions you require. The democracy we have, you might think, has no authority at all, in which case you will, with the anarchist, believe its laws are binding only insofar as they conform to justice.

Speaking of the philosophical anarchist, neither will he be persuaded about the authority of democracy. The democratic skeptic can at least entertain the thought that some democracy, someday, will make the cut, and achieve authority. The anarchist, in contrast, is apt to believe authority is not to be had in this world, whatever shape the state takes. For the anarchist, only morality has authority, and the anarchist might believe morality would never give a state authority over anyone unless he consented—really, not just hypothetically—to its authority.[72] Yet few people actually give consent, or at least global consent, to having their moral situation changed at the state's command. Anarchists prize autonomy and lend their obedience to the moral law, and the moral law alone.[73]

The following chapters are written for democratic statists. They won't hold much appeal for democratic skeptics or anarchists, or at least not for skeptics or anarchists unprepared to suspend their doubts about democratic authority. Where a democratic citizen sees a state with authority, the skeptic and anarchist will see a gunman writ large. The gunman might be morally permitted to coerce conformity to his rules, for the sake of social peace, but those rules will lack the force of moral obligation. For the skeptic and the anarchist, the extent to which positive law has the force of moral obligation is entirely parasitic, extending only so far as the positive law conforms to the moral law.

72 *See, e.g.*, A. John Simmons, Political Philosophy 112–17 (2008) (arguing that the only way to be morally obligated to conform to the output of a democratic process is to consent to be bound to it); Michael Huemer, The Problem of Political Authority: An Examination of the Right to Coerce and the Duty to Obey § 4.4, at 79 (2013) ("The fact that a majority of persons favor some rule does not justify imposing that rule by force on those who do not agree to it nor coercively punishing those who disobey the rule."); A. John Simmons, *Democratic Authority and the Boundary Problem*, 26 Ratio Juris 326, 346 (2013) (proponents of democratic authority can't accuse those who don't conform of being arrogant unless they explain why the non-conformer is "legitimately subjected" to the state's democratic process for resolving reasonable disagreements in the first place). *But cf.* Eric Nelson, The Theology of Liberalism: Political Philosophy and the Justice of God 158–65 (2019) (suggesting that legitimate political authority rests on "tacit consent," and that whether or not a person or a people have given "tacit consent" depends on the "presence or absence of a realistic option of popular non-cooperation," not on the "presence or absence of elections").

73 *See* Simmons, *supra* note 72, at 114 ("[W]e must not let such rhetoric [i.e., the rhetoric of democratic politics] uncritically guide our thinking.").

Rights

If a democratic state can have authority, maybe its authority is unlimited. Insofar as democratic authority exists to authoritatively settle disagreements about the rules of collective co-existence, maybe it exists to settle disagreements about all the rules, not just disagreements over first-order rules, but also disagreements over any proposed second-order right purporting to limit the scope of democratic authority. If so, then democratic authority would know no bounds. No rights could be said to exist disabling a democratic state from enacting authoritative rules inconsistent with any right this or that citizen believes to exist as a moral barrier to state action, save perhaps for those rights needed to create and maintain a democracy's authority in the first place.[74] That's one path on the question of rights.

It's not the path taken here. Democratic authority begins from the commitment that everyone subject to its authority is free and equal. Free, insofar as we are all endowed with the capacity to be self-governing, with the capacity, through the exercise of reason, to discover the demands morality places on our choices.[75] Equal, insofar as we are each, all of us, endowed with this capacity. The need for democratic authority arises from the fact that we disagree when we deploy our capacity to discover what morality requires, combined with the realization that those we call our fellow citizens sometimes disagree with our discoveries, arising from the further realization that our own moral insight is limited. No one speaks *ex cathedra*.

Having said that, recognizing the limits of our moral insight needn't lead us to doubt all our moral convictions, lest we descend into nihilism. Even if we can't with confidence say what the state must do to achieve justice, perhaps we can at least say with some measure of confidence what it must do to avoid injustice. Perhaps we can forge a set of principles, formulated at some level of abstraction, describing limits beyond which the state cannot act without being guilty of manifest injustice. If so, then these principles would express rights we believe we have, as equally free citizens, against the

[74] WALDRON, *supra* note 50, at 282 ("The idea of democracy is not incompatible with the idea of individual rights. On the contrary, there cannot be a democracy unless individuals possess and regularly exercise . . . 'the right of rights'—the right to participate in the making of the laws.").

[75] Locke writes: "The natural liberty of man is to be free from any superior power on earth, and not to be under the will or legislative authority of man, but to have only the law of nature for his rule." JOHN LOCKE, THE SECOND TREATISE OF GOVERNMENT § 22 (Thomas P. Peardon ed., 1952) (1690). For more on this way of conceptualizing the "equal freedom" of moral persons, see GERALD GAUS, THE ORDER OF PUBLIC REASON: A THEORY OF FREEDOM AND MORALITY IN A DIVERSE AND BOUNDED WORLD 14–20 (2011).

otherwise legitimate exercise of democratic state authority. If a democratic state were to permit its agents, through the exercise of its otherwise legitimate authority, to act in ways inconsistent with what we believe these rights to be, it would act *ultra vires.*

Faith in democratic authority involves humility, because it involves recognizing and accepting the proposition that our individual moral discernment is limited and fallible. Conversely, believing in rights against the exercise of democratic authority involves a measure of hubris and an ever-present risk of dogmatism. Declaring the existence of a right disabling democratic authority is in effect an expression of bewilderment as to how anyone could believe morality grants the state the power to permit its agents to act inconsistent with the right declared. It involves a declaration to the effect that, if you fail to acknowledge the right declared, your reason has, at least on this occasion, failed you, leading you to mistakenly believe justice permits the state to treat a citizen in ways in which, in fact, it does not. Rights against democratic authority are proposed, one might say, as self-evident truths, and so shouldn't be proposed lightly.[76]

A card-carrying democrat needn't be a rights skeptic, for whom morality imposes no limits, expressed as rights, on a democratic state's authority to settle disagreements among its citizens. A committed democrat can consistently believe in democracy and in the existence of rights limiting democratic authority. He might nonetheless be skeptical, not about the existence of rights against democratic authority, but with how they become institutionally recognized, interpreted, and enforced. He can believe rights exist, without believing they should necessarily be canonized in a constitution, or if they are, without believing they should be enforced through some form of judicial review, especially in its strong form, in which a court (or majority of its members) decides what a constitutional provision means, with its interpretation being "authoritative and binding on the other branches, at least in the short to medium run."[77]

At any rate, the task at hand isn't to catalogue all the rights we believe democratic citizens have disabling otherwise legitimate exercises of democratic authority, nor to advance anything like a theory of judicial review. Our less ambitious task, though still ambitious enough, is to state, in an abstract

[76] Chapter 2 attempts to formulate a test one can use to judge for oneself whether or not to agree with any rule proposed to function as an immunity right against the exercise of otherwise legitimate democratic authority. *See* Chapter 2, pp. 81–82.

[77] Mark Tushnet, *Alternative Forms of Judicial Review*, 101 MICH. L. REV. 2781, 2784 (2003).

and general way, the rights we believe citizens have limiting democratic authority over the rules comprising the criminal law. Those rules come in three sets—rules defining crimes, rules ascribing culpability, and rules prescribing punishments—and democratic citizens have, we believe, rights associated with each set.

Criminalization

The first set includes all the rules defining acts (or omissions) subject to punishment, otherwise known as crimes. Crimes are conduct rules, addressed to everyone, telling us what we can and can't do, on pain of punishment. What criminal lawyers call "justification defenses," like self-defense and defense of others and property, are also rules of conduct. They allow someone, under the circumstances spelled out in the defense, to commit what would otherwise be a crime. They make otherwise impermissible conduct permissible. One such defense, usually called "necessity" or "lesser evils," is a justification of last resort, permitting an accused to commit a crime if necessary to avert an evil greater than the evil the crime he committed was intended to avoid.[78]

When anarchists debate this first set of rules, they commonly urge the state to follow, in the name of justice, a principle or set of principles limiting what it criminalizes. An anarchist might, for example, urge the state to embrace Mill's principle: harm, or the risk of it, is the only good reason to criminalize. Alternatively, he might urge legal moralism, pursuant to which the state should, as a matter of justice, criminalize all moral wrongs, harm or no harm, unless doing so would conflict with a list of other, superseding moral requirements. Another, less-discussed proposal is the dignity principle: The law should criminalize only those acts or omissions necessary to defend and uphold human dignity.[79] The list of possible limiting principles is long, with new contenders entering the ring with some regularity.[80]

[78] *See, e.g.*, Model Penal Code § 3.02 (Am. Law Inst. 1985).

[79] *See* Meir Dan-Cohen, *Defending Dignity*, *in* Harmful Thoughts: Essays on Law, Self, and Morality 150, 150 (2002) (The dignity principle is the "view that the main goal of the criminal law is to defend the unique moral worth of every human being."); Meir Dan-Cohen, *Dignity, Crime and Punishment: A Kantian Perspective*, *in* Foundational Texts in Modern Criminal Law 101, 104 (Marcus D. Dubber ed., 2014) (developing a "conception of criminal law according to which its main mission is to uphold dignity, that is to uphold the equal moral worth of human beings").

[80] *See, e.g.*, Joshua Kleinfeld, *Three Principles of Democratic Criminal Justice*, 111 Nw. U.L. Rev. 1455, 1476–79 (2017) (proposing the "moral culture principle of criminalization").

As this anarchist debate marches on, the statist takes a different tack. An anarchist believes a state shouldn't criminalize an act or omission unless his preferred principle or principles permit criminalization. A statist believes a democratic state has the authority to criminalize whatever it wants, provided it violates no right he believes citizens have disabling the state's authority. The anarchist looks for moral principles permitting criminalization. The statist looks for rights disabling state authority. As long as the state respects the limits those rights impose, it can legitimately criminalize whatever the People decide to criminalize, so long as they have some rational reason for their decision, which isn't a high bar.

Without at this point developing an account of what makes a proposed limit on legitimate democratic authority itself legitimate (more will be said in Chapter 2), here are some intuitively plausible candidates for the job, albeit formulated at an unhelpfully high and gauzy level of generality. We can start with rights defining freedoms traditionally associated with what we know as "liberal democracies," i.e., freedom of speech, press, and peaceable assembly, at least insofar as those freedoms safeguard meaningful participation in democratic politics.[81] The right to the free exercise of religion should probably be included as well, together with some right to private property.[82] Added to these might be a right to protect oneself, and maybe one's property, when necessary, against the use of private force.[83] With considerably less confidence one might include a right to make "self-defining choices,"[84] which travels in the United States under the guise of a right to privacy.

The important point is the difference. The anarchist tries to state some general moral principle or set of principles, understood as a deliverance

[81] *Cf.* John Hart Ely, Democracy and Distrust: A Theory of Judicial Review 93–94 (1980) ("The expression-related provisions of the First Amendment . . . were centrally intended to help make our governmental processes work, to ensure the open and informed discussion of political issues, and to check our government when it gets out of bounds.").

[82] Theorists disagree on the scope and status of a right to private property, with modern or high liberalism placing it low on the hierarchy of rights, and libertarian and classical liberalism placing it on par with them. *See, e.g.*, John Tomasi, Free Market Fairness xxvi (2012) (distinguishing classical liberals who affirm a "thick" conception of economic liberty and high liberals who affirm a "thin" conception).

[83] See Claire Finkelstein, *On the Obligation of the State to Extend a Right of Self-Defense to Its Citizens*, 147 U. Pa. L. Rev. 1361, 1397–38 (1999) ("A [state] prohibition that significantly impaired each citizen's ability to defend his own life without a strong, principled basis for its adoption would lack normative authority for those who must live by its rules."); Dennis Klimchuk, *Excuses and Excusing Conditions*, *in* Rethinking Criminal Law Theory 161, 168 (François Tanguay-Renaud & James Stribopoulos eds., 2012) ("Subjecting to punishment" someone who "kill[s] another to save [himself] when circumstances force the choice" is "beyond the state's authority."). We should probably add some right against the state criminalizing something for no intelligible or rational reason.

[84] *See, e.g.*, Moore, *supra* note 21, at 772.

of justice, to circumscribe the criminal law's domain. Yet insofar as other theorists believe justice demands something else, the existence of their disagreement suggests the proposed principle shouldn't serve as a limit on democratic authority, but should instead enter the arena of democratic politics to compete with other principles for the People's approval. A democratic statist, in contrast, tries to identify a set of abstract rights limiting democratic authority.[85] Because these rights place boundaries on the scope of democratic authority, one needs to believe their status as moral truths is somehow more secure compared to other proposals to limit the scope of the criminal law; otherwise, rather than placing limits on democratic authority, their recognition would instead be subject to its exercise.

Take money laundering, the crime Ellen Campbell was alleged to have committed. The anarchist looks at the statute defining money laundering and subjects it to his preferred principle or principles. Does it pass muster? If you defend the harm principle, for example, you'd first need some account of what qualifies as a relevant harm. Among other things, do remote harms count?[86] You'd then need to ask: Does money laundering cause or risk harm so defined? If it does, that's a reason, perhaps among others, to criminalize it. Or, if you're a legal moralist: Is money laundering a moral wrong? If not, end of story. If so, that gives a reason to criminalize it, unless some other moral principle nonetheless precludes criminalization.

In contrast, a statist would ask: Does criminalizing money laundering infringe any right citizens possess against the exercise of democratic authority? None comes immediately to mind. Indeed, for what it's worth, the money laundering statute under which Campbell was convicted remains on the books, thus presumably having survived judicial scrutiny under the rights enumerated in the federal Constitution's Bill of Rights. In any event, if no right to engage in the conduct defined as money laundering exists, then any

[85] A passage from one of Justice Scalia's judicial opinions reflects a statist approach to finding limits on the state's authority to criminalize:

> [I]n our democratic system, how much harmless conduct to proscribe is not a judgment to be made by the courts. So long as constitutionally guaranteed rights are not affected, and so long as the proscription has a rational basis, all sorts of perfectly harmless activity by millions of perfectly innocent people can be forbidden—riding a motorcycle without a safety helmet, for example, starting a campfire in a national forest, or selling a safe and effective drug not yet approved by the Food and Drug Administration.

City of Chicago v. Morales, 527 U.S. 41, 97–98 (1999) (Scalia, J., dissenting).

[86] *See, e.g.*, SIMESTER & VON HIRSCH, *supra* note 20, at 53–88 (discussing the need for an extended harm principle to deal with the problem of remote harms).

disagreement as to the justice of criminalizing money laundering should be authoritatively settled in the messy forum of democratic politics.

Punishment

Skip to the third set of rules, those prescribing punishment. These rules, unlike those defining crimes, aren't conduct rules addressed to everyone. They're decision rules, usually addressed to judges. They're composed of obligations and permissions through which judges decide what can be done to an accused once he's convicted. The rules derive from whatever theory of just punishment, if any, the state has embraced. Today, it might be rehabilitation; tomorrow, retribution; the next day, consequentialism, perhaps with retributive limits of some sort; and so on.[87]

Alternatively, the theory behind the rules might not be a theory at all: It might be a hodgepodge. The relevant rule or rules might list a wide range of plausible purposes or reasons to punish, and then obligate judges to impose a "sentence sufficient, but not greater than necessary, to comply with those purposes."[88] That, for instance, is the basic rule federal judges are bound to follow. Another currently popular option is to create a sentencing commission, tasked with constructing a more or less elaborate code of sentencing. The code might give judges a lot of discretion, or very little, with critics commonly claiming the current balance, whatever it is, goes too far in one direction or the other, thereby failing to do justice.

When anarchists argue over theories of punishment, the aim is to identify the theory justice requires. The statist, once again, takes a different approach. He doesn't defend one theory over another. The theories over which anarchists argue identify reasons supporting the state's decision to exercise its permission to punish, when the defendant, having culpably committed a crime, forfeits his right not to be punished. When it comes to that debate, the statist remains mostly on the sidelines. The one true theory of justice in punishment might well exist, but the statist recognizes his fellow citizens disagree on what it is. Instead, the statist looks for some limit on the state's authority

[87] *See* Model Penal Code: Sentencing § 1.02(2) (2017) (Am. Law Inst., Proposed Final Draft 2017).

[88] 18 U.S.C. § 3553(a).

to impose punishment, under whatever theory. Any punishment beyond the limit renders the surplus not merely unjust, but illegitimate.

As just mentioned, the statist remains mostly agnostic on the reasons to which a democratic state appeals when it exercises its permission to punish, but he's not entirely agnostic. Among the ends punishment serves, and thus among the reasons a state might give to exercise its permission to punish, one, for a statist, is *sui generis*: vindicating the state's authority. We can imagine a state deciding not to punish some crimes some of the time, but can we imagine a state, or at least a state claiming authority, deciding never to punish anyone for any crime? If the state is in charge of settling the rules governing how its citizens relate to one another, but then never punished anyone, or at least never publicly censured anyone, for violating any of those rules, we'd begin to wonder who's really in charge. Vindicating its authority is thus always a sufficient reason, according to the statist, for the state to exercise its permission to punish.[89]

Returning to the question of limits, when the state, for whatever reason, exercises its permission to punish, the language of proportionality is a standard and common way to articulate a limit on state punishment. The state ought not, the thought goes, impose a punishment disproportionate to the crime. Construed as a limit on democratic authority, the proposed limit would thus be stated: A democratic state lacks the authority to impose (because an offender has an immunity right against) any punishment

[89] Thanks to Malcolm Thorburn for pressing this point. As Thorburn puts it:

> [W]hen the state threatens criminal offenders with deterrent sanctions, it claims not only the power to impose costs on those who would violate its laws. It also claims the last word over the normative position of the offender. The offender tried to take on decision-making authority over how he shall relate to others (by acting on his own view of the matter rather than according to the state's law). If he were to evade punishment, then his decision would in fact be the last word on his normative relations with others. But where he is subject to criminal punishment, the state reasserts it authority over him (and everyone else in the jurisdiction).

Thorburn, *supra* note 34, at 9.

Thorburn adds that the "pedigree of this account of punishment is . . . long and distinguished, stretching centuries through the natural law tradition, from Thomas Aquinas and Francisco Suárez through Jean-Jacques Rousseau and Immanuel Kant and dominating nineteenth century German criminal law theory." Malcolm Thorburn, *Criminal Punishment and the Right to Rule*, 70 U. Toronto L.J. 45, 49 n.15 (Supp. 1 2020). Joel Feinberg made a similar point many years ago: "A statute honored mainly in the breach begins to lose its character as law, unless, as we say, it is *vindicated* (emphatically reaffirmed); and clearly the way to do this (indeed the *only* way) is to punish those who violate it." Feinberg, *supra* note 19, at 104 (emphasis added). So, too, more recently, has Alan Brudner: "[B]y visiting the self-destructive consequence of the wrongdoer's principle upon him, punishment removes the appearance of its worldly validity and vindicates the worldly authority of Law." Alan Brudner, Punishment and Freedom: A Liberal Theory of Penal Justice 47 (2009).

disproportionate to the seriousness of the crime and the culpability with which the offender committed it.

That formulation faces the following objection. The language of proportionality is most naturally associated with a retributive theory of punishment. A disproportionate punishment is an undeserved punishment, and the language of desert is the language of retribution. So proportionality as a moral limit on state punishment is fine for a retributivist, but the statist can't help himself to retribution. He needs to remain agnostic on which theory of punishment a democratic state adopts, insofar as democratic citizens disagree about which theory best comports with justice. If so, then the statist can't, consistent with his agnosticism, deploy to the language of proportionality as a limit on state authority, not if doing so implies a prior commitment to retribution as a theory of punishment.

Imagine that the shopkeepers in a small town experience a rash of shoplifting. The things stolen are trivial. Still, it all adds up. The local kids are taking candy and gum left and right, and the storekeepers want it stopped. The duly elected members of the city council agree. They enact new penalties for shoplifting, hoping to deter the delinquents. Before the new ordinance, first-time shoplifters got a nominal fine. That, let's stipulate, was precisely what they deserved, no more, no less.[90]

After the ordinance, first-time shoplifters get a week in jail, no exceptions, for the sake of deterrence. If the pre-ordinance nominal fine was the perfect retributive punishment, then the post-ordinance jail time is necessarily disproportionate, retributively speaking. Nonetheless, the city council decided, all things considered, that the anticipated crime-reduction benefits were worth the (modest) retributive injustice. Has the city council overstepped its authority, such that any punishment imposed on shoplifters beyond a nominal fine is illegitimate? When the city court judge sends Butch to jail for a week for stealing a Snickers, has he violated Butch's rights?

If the state could never punish culpable offenders out of precise retributive proportion, its authority to use the criminal law for consequentialist ends would forever be subject to a strict retributive cap. Nonetheless, the town's citizens believe justice permits them, from time to time, to exceed the cap,

[90] This assumes we can identify, with some precision, the punishment an actor deserves. That assumption, though heroic, is necessary to make the conceptual point the hypothetical tries to make. If you believe the punishment someone deserves can't be pinpointed, if the best we can do is to identify a range of deserved punishments, then any punishment extending some way above the top of the range would presumably qualify as grossly disproportionate.

and to authorize disproportionate punishments, because they're collectively convinced the non-retributive good it aims to produce is worth a measure of retributive injustice.[91] Inasmuch as that judgment isn't patently wrong, then a strict proportionality limit doesn't adequately capture the nature of the limit on a democratic state's authority to punish.

Still, at some point one wants to be able to say the state has gone too far, with all due deference to what the People's elected representatives say or believe. At some point, disproportion for the sake of consequentialist ends has, one wants to be able to say, gone too far, bearing in mind as best one can the contrary good faith beliefs of others. The problem is how to express this limit. One proposal is to say the state lacks authority to impose *grossly* disproportionate punishments.[92] That's probably as good a way as any to convey, in the abstract, the limit we're after. The claim, then, would be that insofar as a state authorizes the imposition of grossly disproportionate punishments, any such punishment would not only be unjust, but illegitimate. A grossly disproportionate punishment is *ultra vires*, an exercise of state authority beyond its legitimate bounds.[93]

[91] *See* Sharon Dolovich, *Legitimate Punishment in Liberal Democracy,* 7 Buff. Crim. L. Rev. 307, 385–04 (2004) (using Rawls's idea of the original position to support the claim that disproportionate punishments can sometimes be legitimate punishments for a liberal democratic state to impose).

[92] "Gross disproportionality" is the general principle the Supreme Court uses to determine when a term of incarceration violates the Eighth Amendment's prohibition on the imposition of "cruel and unusual punishments." *See* Ewing v. California, 538 U.S. 11, 23 (2003) (opinion of O'Connor, J., joined by Rehnquist, C.J. & Kennedy, J.); *id.* at 36 (Breyer, J., dissenting, joined by Stevens, Souter, & Ginsburg, JJ.). One can endorse "gross disproportionality" as the correct formulation, in the abstract, of the principle limiting the extent to which a democratic state can legitimately incarcerate a person for the commission of a crime, without endorsing how any one court, including the U.S. Supreme Court, has in fact applied that standard to the facts of any specific case.

[93] Based on press reports, one might imagine the problem of mass incarceration results in part from people being sent to prison for grossly disproportionate terms of incarceration. But John Pfaff, having looked at the numbers, writes:

> Stunningly long prison sentences make the news. . . . One prominent criminologist has argued that since the 1990s, punishment in the United States seems to have focused on "throwing away the key." Indeed, after the "war on drugs," the most prominent part of the Standard Story [offered to explain mass incarceration] has been its emphasis on the amount of time people serve in prison. . . . [But] [t]he impact of time served is not really as important as the Standard Story claims. It's true that by international standards US sentences are long, both nominally and in practice. The amount of time people spend in prison, however, is surprisingly short, and there's no real evidence that it grew much as prison populations soared. In fact, recent evidence suggests that time behind bars may even have decreased over the past few years.

John Pfaff, Locked In: The True Causes of Mass Incarceration and How to Achieve Real Reform 51–52 (2017). Pfaff reiterates: "[W]hile it is true that . . . *official* sanctions may have gotten tougher over time, the amount of time *actually spent* in prison has remained fairly constant . . . [w]ith one important exception: murder." John Pfaff, *Decarceration's Blindspots*, 16 Ohio St. J. Crim. L. 253, 258 (2019).

If we can affirm any rights with thoroughgoing conviction, such that violations of those rights would offend our abiding sense of justice, the right to speak freely, to a free press, to practice one's religion, to be free from grossly disproportionate punishment, and so on, are among the most plausible candidates. Unfortunately, the conviction with which these rights can be held and asserted is due in large part to the vague and abstract language in which they're framed. Abstraction is one tried and true way to secure confidence in a moral proposition, but that doesn't mean disagreement goes away. Instead, it gets redirected, resurfacing when abstract rights, confidently affirmed, are relied on to adjudicate real-world disputes. Once again, the devil hides, as ever, in the details.[94]

Even if we confidently assert a right to free speech against any contrary exercise of state authority, does that include the right to speak hatefully?[95] Even if we confidently assert a right to a free press, does that include the right to libel a whole group of people?[96] Even if we confidently assert a right to practice one's religion, does that mean communicants are entitled to use controlled substances?[97] Even if we confidently assert a right to privacy, does that include the right to a second-trimester abortion,[98] or a doctor's help to commit suicide?[99] Even if we confidently assert a right to self-defense, does that include a right to keep a handgun in your house?[100] Even if we confidently assert a right against grossly disproportionate punishment, is a mandatory sentence of life imprisonment, without any chance of parole, grossly disproportionate for knowingly possessing a pound and a half of cocaine?[101] And so on.

Rights don't apply themselves. If our convictions about the rights we have against democratic authority are described at a high level of generality, the rights we have against democratic authority are bound to be indeterminate. Our confidence will begin to falter when we turn to those abstract rights, which all to often conflict with one another, to resolve concrete cases and controversies. Doubt in the application of confidently affirmed rights is, it

94 Gaus, *supra* note 75, at 355 ("The strength and weakness of arguments from abstraction is that they focus our attention on general ideas with which we agree, but they mask the disagreement that erupts when we turn to specific interpretations.").

95 *See* R.A.V. v. City of St. Paul, 505 U.S. 337 (1992).

96 *See* Beauharnais v. Illinois, 343 U.S. 250 (1952).

97 *See* Employment Div. v. Smith, 494 U.S. 872 (1990).

98 *See* Roe v. Wade, 410 U.S. 113 (1973).

99 *See* Washington v. Glucksberg, 521 U.S. 702 (1997).

100 *See* District of Columbia v. Heller, 554 U.S. 570 (2008).

101 *See* Harmelin v. Michigan, 501 U.S. 957 (1991).

would seem, the piper's price for asserting the existence of any rights against democratic authority. Doubt in the application of abstract rights in whose existence we have little doubt appears baked into the structure of limited democratic authority.[102]

Culpability

So much for the first and third sets of rules, on crimes and punishments, and their limits. That leaves the second set, whose rules govern the ascription of culpability. Like the rules of the third set, which tell judges when to punish, the rules of the second set speak to a limited audience: to judges and juries tasked with deciding if and when someone was culpable at the time of the crime. These rules, like the rest, are determined in the first instance through the democratic process. One citizen might believe, for example, that, as a matter of justice, ignorance of the law is no excuse. It's been that way for a long time. Another citizen might believe otherwise: How can anyone reasonably be expected to conform to a law about which, through no fault of his own, he had no idea his conduct ran afoul? The democratic process authoritatively settles whose beliefs get reflected in law.

[102] If immunity rights limiting democratic state authority are enforced through the work of non-democratic institutions, like constitutional courts, some mechanisms for enforcing those rights might be more respectful of democratic authority than others. One needn't be an alarmist to have fair-minded worries that, for example, the way in which constitutional judicial review now works in the United States is unhealthy for a political system wanting to see itself as a democracy. *See* David A. Kaplan, The Most Dangerous Branch: Inside the Supreme Court's Assault on the Constitution (2018).

Democracy and judicial review can doubtless be defined so as to define away any contradiction, tension, difficulty, and so on between them. Absent such legerdemain, the best resolution to whatever difficulty exists between the two probably won't be found in any theory of constitutional interpretation. The proliferation nowadays of so many theories of constitutional interpretation, from originalism to living constitutionalism and beyond, all of which are meant to lead judges to the right answer, reminds one of a line from the 1983 movie *WarGames*: "The only winning move is not to play." WarGames (MGM 1983). A satisfying resolution, or at least truce, can perhaps only be found in the minds of judges, and in the attitude with which they approach their difficult task. They should start, not with "What do I decide?," but with "May I in fact decide?" *See* J. Harvie Wilkinson III, Cosmic Constitutional Theory: Why Americans Are Losing Their Inalienable Right to Self-Governance 60–61 (2012). Deference to democratic institutions should be a matter of principle, not expediency. *See* Larry Kramer, *Judicial Supremacy and the End of Judicial Restraint*, 100 Calif. L. Rev. 621, 633 (2012). For some of the literature along these lines, see generally Sanford Byron Gabin, Judicial Review and the Reasonable Doubt Test (1980); Larry Kramer, The People Themselves: Popular Constitutionalism and Judicial Review (2004); Mark Tushnet, Taking the Constitutional Away from the Courts (2000); Adrian Vermeule, Judging Under Uncertainty: An Institutional Theory of Legal Interpretation (2006).

When anarchists turn their attention to culpability, they purport to explain what justice truly requires.[103] What, as a matter of justice, makes someone culpable for committing a crime, and what excuses its commission? One popular answer locates culpability, as a matter of justice, in free choice, and excuse in its opposite. If you freely choose to commit a crime, you're culpable; if not, then no blame should come your way. Another locates culpability, as a matter of justice, in character. If your crime manifests vice, or perhaps some limited range of vices, you're culpable; if not, then you're free to go. Whatever the theory, its success and authority, for an anarchist, depend on the extent to which it truly reflects what justice requires when it comes to ascribing culpability.

The statist sets himself a different task. He needn't doubt that justice picks out some particular theory of culpability, but the task isn't to say what it is. Instead, the task is to locate limits on a democratic state's authority to promulgate rules through which it ascribes culpability. Success in this task needs to be judged against a different test. As we'll see in Chapter 2, one possible test invites those to whom any proposed limit is offered to ask themselves, not what they believe justice requires, but whether they believe it would be unjust beyond a reasonable doubt for a democratic state to ascribe culpability to someone who failed to satisfy the conditions set forth in the proposed limit. In line with that suggestion, the following chapters should be seen as proposing principles I believe, beyond reasonable doubt, establish limits beyond which it would be unjust for a democratic state to ascribe culpability.

I'll use two Latin expressions, *actus reus* and *mens rea*, to broadly capture the proposed limits. No one is guilty, and so culpability cannot legitimately be ascribed to him, unless his act and mind were guilty. Guilt assigned without *actus reus* or *mens rea* has been assigned illegitimately. What comes next is a portrait of *actus reus* and *mens rea*, offered as limits on, and expressed as immunity rights against, a democratic state's otherwise legitimate authority to ascribe culpability to a citizen accused of a crime.

[103] These theories of culpability or excuse usually start with some inventory of statutory rules pre-theoretically assumed to be excuses. The search is then on for some deeper moral principle hidden beneath the statutory noise. Once that principle is found, a theory is born. In contrast, this book begins, not from an inventory of existing statutory excuses, but from *actus reus* and *mens rea*, construed as principles setting limits on the state's authority to define culpability, whatever moral principle or principles hide behind the existing statutory curtain.

2
Rights

Leroy Powell, a resident of Houston, Texas, was a chronic alcoholic. On December 19, 1966, like many days before, Powell got drunk (we don't know where) and was found wandering along the 2000 block of Hamilton Street.[1] At the time, Texas Penal Code article 477 made it a crime to "get drunk or be found in a state of intoxication in any public place, or at any private house except his own."[2] Powell was arrested and charged with violating article 477, as he had been over one hundred times before. Tried without a jury, he was convicted and fined $20.[3] Powell worked at a tavern shining shoes, but since he made only about $12 a week, he usually worked in jail (at $5 a day) to pay off his fines.[4]

Powell appealed his conviction, eventually to the Supreme Court. Was it "cruel and unusual" to punish Powell for violating article 477?[5] That was the legal question. Powell argued it was. As a chronic alcoholic, the "power of his will to resist the constant, excessive consumption of alcohol" had been, he said, "destroyed," and punishing someone whose will to resist had been destroyed would, he claimed, be "cruel and unusual."[6] A divided Court let Powell's conviction stand. Lawyers today still wonder what constitutional rule or doctrine, if any, the Court's opinion in *Powell* stands for.[7] All one can

[1] Powell v. Texas, 392 U.S. 514, 555 (1968) (Fortas, J., dissenting).

[2] *Id.* at 517 (quoting Tex. Penal Code art. 477).

[3] Statutes like article 477, which criminalize being "found" somewhere, are usually construed to require the state to prove the accused voluntarily acted to cause himself to be found in the place described, or voluntarily failed to act to remove himself from the place described. An often-cited exception to this general rule is an older and much-maligned English case, *R. v. Larsonneur*, (1933) 24 Cr. App. R. 74. *See* A.P. Simester et al., Simester and Sullivan's Criminal Law: Theory and Doctrine § 4.1(ii)(a), at 78–79 (discussing *Larsonneur*).

[4] *See Powell*, 392 U.S. at 555 (Fortas, J., dissenting).

[5] "Excessive bail shall not be required, nor excessive fines imposed, nor cruel and unusual punishments inflicted." U.S. Const. amend. VIII. How these words should be interpreted has been much debated. For a recent effort to explain their "original meaning," see John F. Stinneford, *The Original Meaning of "Unusual": The Eighth Amendment as a Bar to Cruel Innovation*, 102 Nw. U.L. Rev. 1739 (2008); John F. Stinneford, *The Original Meaning of "Cruel,"* 105 Geo. L.J. 441 (2017).

[6] *Powell*, 392 U.S. at 554.

[7] The enduring question *Powell* raises, together with an earlier case, *Robinson v. California*, 370 U.S. 660 (1962), is the extent to which the Eighth Amendment limits the state's power to punish. For a recent discussion, see Ian P. Farrell & Justin F. Marceau, *Taking Voluntariness Seriously*, 54 B.C. L. Rev.

Guilty Acts, Guilty Minds. Stephen P. Garvey, Oxford University Press (2020). © Oxford University Press.
DOI: 10.1093/oso/9780190924324.001.0001

say for sure is that punishing Powell with a $20 fine didn't, on the facts of the case, amount to a cruel and unusual punishment.

In order to advance the ball, enter the following stipulations, which admittedly rest on an account of the nature of voluntary action with which not everyone will agree. First, a bodily movement resulting from a mental state called a volition makes that movement "voluntary." Second, a "voluntary" bodily movement is a "voluntary act." Third, Powell's bodily movements causing him to become "drunk" and causing him to appear in a "public place" resulted from a volition, thus making them "voluntary acts." Fourth, Powell couldn't have acted otherwise than to drink (and thereby become drunk), nor could he have acted otherwise than to appear in public (while drunk). Those acts were, in other words, compelled. Fifth, those acts were nonetheless voluntary, having resulted from a volition.[8] Sixth, Powell was in no way to blame for lacking the capacity to have chosen otherwise. Those are big stipulations, especially the fourth one. We make them, not because they reflect the truth about Powell, but because they advance the discussion.

Assume Powell is charged and convicted, as he was, with violating article 477. When he hears the verdict, he's shocked. His lawyers assured him he couldn't be convicted and punished unless his acts were guilty—unless he satisfied the *actus reus* requirement. The *actus reus* requirement was, they said, a bedrock requirement for criminal liability. How, Powell wonders, can the acts for which he was convicted have been guilty—how can he bear guilt for them—when (as stipulated) he was powerless to have acted otherwise?

Seventeen years before Powell tried to make his case before the Supreme Court, twenty-seven-year-old Joseph Morissette tried to make his. Morissette,

1545, 1611 (2013) ("It is fair to say that all nine of the Supreme Court justices in *Powell*... endorse the view that voluntariness is a constitutional requirement for criminal conviction for punishment. The Justices merely disagreed about whether the appellant or other alcoholics voluntarily complete the *actus reus* of public drunkenness."). When Farrell and Marceau refer to "voluntariness," they mean the ability to do otherwise. *See id.* at 1579. ("It is this ability to do otherwise... that we take as the sine qua non of voluntariness.") Thus, as they read *Powell* and *Robinson*, the Eighth Amendment prohibits the state from punishing anyone for an act when he lacked the ability or capacity to have acted otherwise (and presumably wasn't at fault for lacking that capacity).

[8] Justice White, who concurred in the result, thus providing the fifth vote needed to affirm Powell's conviction, believed, based on the record, that Powell was compelled to drink, but not to appear in public. *See Powell*, 392 U.S. at 552–53 (White, J., concurring) ("Whether or not Powell established that he could not have resisted becoming drunk... nothing in the record indicates that he could not have done his drinking in private or that he was so inebriated at the time that he lost control of his movements and wandered into the public street.").

an honorably discharged veteran of World War II,[9] went deer hunting in December 1948. His trip took him, along with his brother-in-law, to the Oscoda Air Base, a "large tract of uninhabited and untilled land in a wooded and sparsely populated area of Michigan."[10] The federal government owned the land, which it used for practice bombing. "[K]nown as good deer country and . . . extensively hunted,"[11] it was littered with three-and-a-half-foot spent bomb casings. Signs reading, "Danger—Keep Out—Bombing Range" were scattered about, as were rusted casings, "not stacked or piled in any order."[12] Morissette didn't get a deer, but he took a few tons of casings to meet the trip's expenses, making no effort to conceal what he was doing. He crushed the casings, sold them to a coal and iron company,[13] and made $84. A state police officer saw Morissette transporting the casings and inquired. Morissette replied that he didn't think "anybody would care if he took them."[14] The state police officer apparently called the FBI, which came knocking.

Morissette was charged with violating 18 U.S.C. § 641, which made it a crime to "embezzle[], steal[], purloin[] or knowingly convert[]" government property.[15] According to the indictment, Morissette "did unlawfully, wilfully and knowingly steal and convert" property of the United States.[16] At trial, Morissette apparently didn't contest that the casings were government property. Instead, he said he thought the casings had been abandoned, and so didn't realize they were government property (or anyone's property). Consequently, he doubtless neither realized he was doing anything wrong, let alone anything that would get him in trouble with the law. According to the trial court, however, Morrisette's ignorance didn't matter. Section 641 didn't require the prosecution to prove Morissette realized the casings were government property, only that they were property.[17] Any belief about the

[9] Morissette v. United States, 187 F.2d 427, 431 (6th Cir. 1951) (McAllister, J., dissenting).
[10] Morissette v. United States, 342 U.S. 246, 247–48 (1952).
[11] *Id.*
[12] *Id.*
[13] 187 F.2d at 428.
[14] *Id.* at 432 (McAllister, J., dissenting).
[15] 342 U.S. at 242 & n.2.
[16] *Id.* at 242.
[17] The trial court also told the jury: "[I]f you believe the testimony of the government in this case, he intended to take it. . . . He had no right to take this property. . . . [A]nd it is no defense to claim that it was abandoned, because it was on private property." *Id.* at 249. In other words, even if the government was required to prove Morissette realized he was taking government property, the trial court told the jury to conclusively presume Morissette did so realize because, as Morissette admitted, he

status of the casings as government property was, on the court's reading of the statute, irrelevant. Morissette was convicted, and sentenced to two months in prison or a fine of $200.

Like Powell, Morissette appealed his conviction, also making it ultimately to the Supreme Court. The narrow question before the Court was how to read § 641. Did it require the government to prove Morissette realized the casings were government property, or not? Morissette said it did. The government said it didn't. Which side was right depended on what Congress intended when it enacted § 641. The Court agreed with Morissette: Congress, without expressly saying so, never intended to punish anyone for violating § 641 if he believed the thing he took was abandoned, and thus not anyone's property, let alone the government's property.[18]

Once again, in order to advance the discussion, suppose the Court, in a different case decided before Morissette took the casings, had agreed with the trial court in the actual case. When Congress enacted § 641, the Court said in this imagined earlier case, it did indeed intend to criminalize taking government property, whether or not the accused realized the property taken was government property. With this earlier decision on the books, Morissette is again charged with violating § 641. Not surprisingly, he's convicted: The property he took was government property, and that, after the Court's imagined earlier decision, is all it took to violate § 641, whatever Morissette believed.

Like Powell, Morissette is shocked. His lawyers assured him he couldn't be convicted unless his mind was guilty—unless he satisfied the *mens rea* requirement. The *mens rea* requirement was, they said, a bedrock requirement for criminal liability. How, Morissette wonders, can his mind have been guilty when (as we'll assume) he had no idea he was doing anything wrong, not to mention criminal?

Before we can give Powell and Morissette answers to their questions, we need some account of *actus reus* and *mens rea*. What do those Latin phrases mean? A natural place to begin is with Saint Augustine, who in a sermon

took the property from land he realized was government land. *See id.* at 273–76. These instructions too, the Supreme Court said, were "in error." *Id.* at 274.

[18] *Id.* at 273. One might wonder if Morissette's mistake was a mistake of fact, or a mistake of some law other than the criminal law: here, the civil law of property. The answer didn't matter to the Court. As one thoughtful commentator has said, the distinction between mistakes of fact and mistakes of noncriminal law is "irrelevant under the prevailing approach to mistakes as to property law in theft offenses." Kenneth W. Simons, *Ignorance and Mistake of Criminal Law, Noncriminal Law, and Fact*, 9 Ohio St. J. Crim. L. 487, 505 (2012).

some scholars believed was preached around the year 415, famously declared "*actus reus non facit reum nisi mens sit rea*,"[19] which can be translated as "an act is not guilty unless the mind is guilty." According to Augustine's maxim, the guilt of an act is thus based on, or results from, the guilt of the mind. Acts, according to Augustine's maxim, aren't guilty all by themselves. Their guilt depends on the mind's guilt. With all due respect for Augustine, we decline any invitation to reduce *actus reus* to *mens rea*. Instead, we want to keep the two ideas separate. Calling an act guilty is one thing, calling a mind guilty is something else. Neither reduces to the other. We begin with two theories of *actus reus* and *mens rea*, both of which portray them as separate and distinct.

The *conventional theory* reflects what lawyers usually have in mind when they talk about *actus reus* and *mens rea*. The conventional theory, as we'll see, would say that Powell's acts, drinking and appearing drunk in public, were indeed guilty. The conventional theory would likewise say that Morissette's mind, when he took the casings, was indeed guilty. On the conventional theory, Powell and Morissette have no good reason to complain when they're punished, at least not on the ground that Texas violated the *actus reus* requirement when it punished Powell, or on the ground that the United States violated the *mens rea* requirement when it punished Morissette.

The other account is the *rights theory*. The rights theory, as we'll see, would say that Powell's acts weren't guilty, and Texas therefore had no authority to punish him. Likewise, the rights theory would say that Morissette's mind wasn't guilty, and the United States therefore had no authority to punish him. On the conventional theory, the finder of fact would have been obligated to find Powell and Morissette guilty, whereas on the rights theory, the finder of fact would have been obligated to find them not guilty. When someone

[19] The language of Augustine's original sermon was, according to some scholars, "*Ream* linguam *non facit nisi mens rea*," which would translate as: "The only thing that makes a guilty *tongue* is a guilty mind." The passage in which the maxim appears deals with perjury, and specifically with the question: Is someone who swears an oath and who testifies *truthfully*, but who *believes* he's testifying *falsely*, guilty of perjury? Augustine says he is. The full passage reads:

> Take another person, he thinks it's false, and answers to it as if it were true—and it so happens that it is true. For example, to help you understand: "Did it rain in that place?" you ask someone, and he thinks it didn't but it suits his purpose to say, "Yes, it did." But he thinks it didn't. You say to him, "Did it really rain?" "Yes, really," and he swears it did; and in fact it did rain there, but he doesn't know it, and he thinks it didn't; he's a perjurer. What makes the difference is how the word comes forth from the mind. *The only thing that makes a guilty tongue is a guilty mind.*

Saint Augustine, *Sermon 180*, *in* III/5 THE WORKS OF SAINT AUGUSTINE: A TRANSLATION FOR THE 21ST CENTURY—SERMONS 314, 315 (John E. Rotelle, O.S.A. ed., Edmund Hill, O.P. trans. 1992).

commits a crime, but does so without *actus reus* or *mens rea*, as the rights theory construes those expressions, he's immune to state punishment, because the rights reflected in the *actus reus* and *mens rea* requirements disable the state from enacting rules ascribing culpability when doing so would be at odds with those rights.

Actus Reus

Justice Robert Jackson, returning to the Supreme Court from his work as U.S. Chief Prosecutor at Nuremberg, authored the Court's opinion in *Morissette*. In a famous passage, Jackson wrote: "[C]rime . . . [is] a compound concept[] . . . constituted only from a concurrence of an evil-meaning mind with an evil-doing hand."[20] An evil-meaning mind is a guilty mind, or *mens rea*, and an evil-doing hand is a guilty act, or *actus reus*. A crime is thus, according to Jackson, constituted only from a concurrence of *mens rea* and *actus reus*. Without both, no crime is "constituted."

Jackson's words can be read in two different ways. One reading yields the conventional theory, according to which *actus reus* and *mens rea* identify, or refer to, the elements of a statutorily defined crime. If a crime lacks any *actus reus* and any *mens rea*, it would, on the conventional theory, presumably have no elements, and with no elements, no crime would (or could) be constituted in the first place. The other reading yields the rights theory, according to which *actus reus* and *mens rea* stand for something above and beyond the elements of a crime. If an accused commits a statutorily defined crime, but does so without *actus reus* or *mens rea*, the state lacks the authority, on the rights theory, to punish him for committing it. Without both *actus reus* and *mens rea*, no crime can, one might say, be legitimately constituted, because the state would have no authority to punish anyone who commits it.

The task at hand is to explain in more detail, first, what *actus reus* and *mens rea* mean on the conventional theory, and second, what they mean, in contrast, on the rights theory. We begin with the meaning of *actus reus*, on the conventional theory, before turning to the rights theory.

[20] *Morissette*, 342 U.S. at 251. The second ellipsis takes the place of the word "generally." Jackson probably included the qualifier to allow strict liability for what are commonly known as "public welfare" offenses.

The Conventional Theory

The conventional theory's rendering of *actus reus* is the one most lawyers probably have in mind when they use the expression *actus reus*.[21] With one important exception, discussed below, the theory portrays *actus reus* as entirely descriptive. The expression *actus reus*, on the conventional theory, is really nothing more than a way to refer to a criminal statute's "objective" elements, which typically include an act (or failure to act when obligated to act), circumstances attending the act, and the result of the act (when the statute prohibits causing some result).[22]

For example, article 477 of the Texas Penal Code, at issue in *Powell*, provided: "Whoever shall get drunk or be found in a state of intoxication in any public place . . . shall be fined not exceeding one hundred dollars." Under the conventional theory, the *actus reus* of article 477 is the sum of its objective elements. Those elements can be parsed to include some conduct as a result of which the accused "get[s] drunk" in a "place," or as a result of which he is "found" in a "place," where the "place" in which he "get[s] drunk," or in which he's "found," is a "public" place, and if the charge is based on being "found . . . in any public place," he's "in a state of intoxication" at the time he's found. On the conventional theory, *actus reus* is thus reducible to, and has no meaning apart from, the conduct, circumstance, and result elements of a statutorily defined crime.

So understood, *actus reus*, on the conventional theory, doesn't require or demand that anyone to do, or refrain from doing, anything. True, the prosecution is required to prove a crime's objective elements (along with any mental state elements) beyond a reasonable doubt in order to convict. So once a state decides to include an element among a crime's *actus reus*, it obligates itself to prove the existence of those elements beyond a reasonable doubt at trial, but the requirement of proof beyond a reasonable doubt doesn't come

[21] According to Jerome Hall, J.C. Kenny first introduced the expression "*actus reus*," as a free-standing expression, intended to have a meaning all on its own, in 1926 in his *Outlines of Criminal Law*. Jerome Hall, General Principles of Criminal Law 222 (2d ed. 1960). Hall based his claim on personal correspondence with J.W.C. Turner, who wrote: "I can only *guess* that [Kenny] coined it [i.e., the expression '*actus reus*'] for himself." *Id.* at 222 n.24. Insofar as Kenny coined the expression as a useful way to refer to a crime's objective elements, or perhaps just its result elements, *see id.* at 222, it's no wonder "*actus reus*" is often thought to be nothing more than a term of art. *See, e.g.*, Michael S. Moore, *Actus Reus*, *in* 1 Encyclopedia of Crime and Justice 15, 15 (Joshua Dressler ed., 2d ed. 2002) ("*Actus reus* is a term of art in criminal law."). That's all its originator meant it to be.

[22] *See, e.g.*, Vincent Chiao, *Acts and* Actus Reus, *in* The Oxford Handbook of Criminal Law 447, 448 (Markus D. Dubber & Tatjana Hörnle eds., 2014) ("[T]he minimal interpretation [of *actus reus*] treats *actus reus* simply as referring to whatever it is the legislature has decided to criminalize.").

from *actus reus*. It comes from somewhere else. In the United States, it comes from the constitutional requirement of due process.[23] Again, standing alone, *actus reus* doesn't require the state to do, or refrain from doing, anything.

Of course, that's not the whole story. The phrase *actus reus* is often understood to encompass, in addition to a crime's objective elements, what's commonly referred to as the "voluntary act requirement." As its name implies, the voluntary act requirement presents itself as some kind of requirement or demand. So if the conventional theory of *actus reus* encompasses the voluntary act requirement, it would no longer be described as a conventional theory, inasmuch as the conventional theory of *actus reus* is conventional just because it does no more than describe a crime's objective elements, without stating any sort of normative requirement or demand.

Despite its status as a "foundational" principle of criminal law, several outstanding questions continue to surround the voluntary act requirement. Setting aside its obscure historical origin as a legal doctrine, what, for example, does it require? The Model Penal Code tells us that a "person is not guilty of an offense unless his liability is based on conduct that includes a voluntary act," but what does "based on" or "includes" mean here?[24] Moreover, whatever the voluntary act requirement requires, does it require it just because a state has decided to include it in its penal code, or does the Constitution or some higher law require states to include it? For now, assume the voluntary act requirement is put forward, as it would be under the rights theory, as a requirement in the sense that it imposes a limit on a democratic state's authority, and in addition, that the nature of the requirement is such that the state has no authority to ascribe culpability for anything other than *for* a voluntary act.[25] A voluntary act must, on this construal, be the object of liability, and the state has no authority to ascribe culpability for any object other than for a voluntary act.[26]

23 *See In re* Winship, 397 U.S. 358 (1970).

24 Model Penal Code § 2.01(a) (Am. Law Inst. 1985). For a discussion of this Model Penal Code provision, see Douglas Husak, *The Alleged Act Requirement in Criminal Law, in* The Oxford Handbook of Philosophy and Criminal Law 107, 112–14 (John Deigh & David Dolinko eds., 2011).

25 Douglas Husak has argued that the relation between an act and criminal liability, as expressed in the voluntary act requirement, is "best expressed by the 'for' relation. In other words, the act requirement is not satisfied unless criminal liability is imposed *for* an act." Douglas Husak, *Does Criminal Liability Require an Act?, in* The Philosophy of Criminal Law: Selected Essays 17, 26 (2010). Husak nonetheless concludes that this formulation of the act requirement "is almost certainly false—both descriptively and normatively." Husak, *supra* note 24, at 111.

26 Criminal liability is, of course, sometimes based on failing to act in the face of a duty to act. *See, e.g.*, Joshua Dressler, Understanding Criminal Law § 9.07, at 102–05 (8th ed. 2018). Omission liability is usually said to be a "limited" exception to the requirement of a voluntary act, but if you

Next, for the sake of argument, assume a voluntary act is a movement of the actor's body resulting from, as one might say, the actor's "will."[27] A voluntary act is thus a willed bodily movement. Or, what amounts to the same thing, a voluntary act is a bodily movement proximately resulting from a mental state known as a volition, which itself proximately results from the work of something we call the actor's will, or more specifically, what we will later call the actor's "executive will."[28]

For example, suppose Powell was charged with violating article 477 because he got "drunk . . . in [a] public place." Convicting Powell would require the state to prove that Powell's drunkenness, while in a public place, resulted from a voluntary act. If the state proves Powell's drunkenness resulted from a voluntary act, like voluntarily moving his arm to bring the bottle to his lips, the voluntary act requirement is satisfied. The state has conformed to the voluntary act requirement: It has punished Powell for a voluntary act, i.e., for the willed bodily movements in virtue of which he got drunk while in a public place.

If the voluntary act requirement is proposed as a limit on the authority of a democratic state, such that Powell had a right not to be punished for anything other than a voluntary act, the next question is whether the voluntary act requirement so understood states a legitimate limit on the exercise of a democratic state's otherwise legitimate authority over the rules structuring the criminal law.

That brings us back to Chapter 1, and the disagreement between the anarchist and the statist. According to the statist, a democratic state has authority, consisting in the moral power to place its citizens under a moral obligation to conform to the law. Its authority derives from the practical need to reach agreement in the face of disagreement about the requirements of justice, in a way respecting everyone subject to the state's authority as an equal, meaning

count all the administrative regulations imposing duties to act, omission liability looks more expansive than the traditional picture suggests. For the most part, the text ignores omission liability, but that omission shouldn't undermine the main point to be made: that the *actus reus* requirement, on the rights theory, requires as a condition of liability the capacity to choose otherwise than the criminal law demands, where what the criminal law demands is a choice not to do something the criminal law obligates one not to do, or to do something the criminal law obligates one to do.

27 We later distinguish between the "executive will," which produces intentions and volitions, and the "conative will," which contains a shifting collection of occurrent and dispositional motivating reasons.

28 *See* Michael S. Moore, Act and Crime: The Philosophy of Action and its Implications for Criminal Law 113 (1993) ("Acts . . . should be identified with the complex event volitions-causing-movements.").

no one's insight into the requirements of justice is presumed to be superior to anyone else's. No one is an epistemic authority over anyone else. Still, we assume the state's authority is limited, which raises the question: What could possibly ground any proposed limit? We can't ground any such limit on a simple or straightforward appeal to moral truth, for pursuant to the logic of democratic authority, no one's insight into the truth is superior to anyone else's. Yet if we can't appeal to moral truth, then what reason exists not to commit all disputes about justice to the democratic process?

Without going deeper into incredibly difficult, challenging, and contested philosophical terrain, terrain I'm ill-equipped in any event to traverse, I propose to proceed in a lawyerly fashion. I'll try to move forward as a lawyer might if tasked with navigating among a variety of bedrock commitments: to a belief in the existence of moral truth; to the idea that one's fellow citizens are free and equal, with none having epistemic authority over any other; to the need to authoritatively resolve moral disagreements in a democratic fashion for the sake of political peace and order (in light of the first two commitments); and finally, to the belief that democratic authority isn't unlimited authority (despite the first two commitments).

Democratic citizens disagree about what justice truly requires. The need to authoritatively resolve their disagreements, and thus secure political peace in a way in which no one is treated as an epistemic authority or epistemic subordinate vis-à-vis anyone else, supply the reasons for having democratic authority in the first place. Yet if one believes some ground must exist upon which to limit the scope of democratic authority, an appeal to one's beliefs about moral truth, and what justice truly requires, seems, at some point, hard to avoid. It's not immediately obvious where else to turn.

Among a lawyer's stock in trade are standards and burdens of proof. Faced with the above constraints, a lawyer might propose the following: A citizen of a democratic state should believe a proposed limit on democratic authority counts as a legitimate limit only if he believes, having given due regard to the convictions of his fellow citizens,[29] that any state action inconsistent with it

[29] Gerald Gaus distinguishes between an "individual mode" of moral reasoning, which doesn't account for the fact that others disagree with us as to what justice requires when we set out to form beliefs about what justice requires, and a "reconciliation mode," which does. *See* Gerald Gaus, *Self-Organizing Moral Systems: Beyond Social Contract Theory*, 17 Politics, Phil. & Econ. 119, 121–22 (2018). According to Gaus, thinkers associated with the social contract tradition adopted the reconciliation mode. Today, the social contract tradition is often associated with "political liberalism" and "public reason" theories. We won't try to situate the ideas expressed in the text within the literature on "political liberalism" and "public reason." That literature is simply too complex, taking "increasingly esoteric forms" and debating, for example, whether the justification of a "liberal political

would, "now and around here,"[30] and beyond a reasonable doubt, be unjust; moreover, the burden of proof should rest with the proponent of any proposed limit, such that democratically enacted law would enjoy the benefit of a presumption of legitimacy.[31]

This *reasonable doubt test* is intended to give wide berth to democratic politics, without lapsing into dogmatic-sounding assertions about what justice really requires, nor similar-sounding assertions to the effect that we can never have any confidence in our beliefs as to what it requires—all the while acknowledging that the middle ground it seeks might turn to quicksand.[32]

order" needs to be made in terms of "reasons that all persons can reasonably be expected to accept or cannot reasonably reject, if people need to actually accept the political order or whether it is enough that it can be represented as an order they should accept, and so on." Matt Sleat, *Modus Vivendi and Legitimacy: Some Sceptical Thoughts*, *in* THE POLITICAL THEORY OF MODUS VIVENDI 185, 187 (John Horton et al. eds., 2019). For an overview of the literature on "public reason," see Jonathan Quong, *Public Reason*, STAN. ENCYCLOPEDIA PHIL. (2018).

Having said that, the reasonable doubt test advanced in the text tries, as might a theory of public reason, to "distinguish[] what can reasonably be believed and what can reasonably be advanced as the foundation of a society's basic institutions," BRIAN BARRY, 2 JUSTICE AS IMPARTIALITY 188 (1991), but unlike at least some theories of public reason, it doesn't foreswear all appeals to moral truth. For an argument in support of the claim that "normative political theory cannot hover like a blimp over the moral truth without any point of contact," see David Estlund, *The Insularity of the Reasonable: Why Political Liberalism Must Admit the Truth*, 108 ETHICS 252, 253 (1998).

30 BERNARD WILLIAMS, IN THE BEGINNING WAS THE DEED: REALISM AND MORALISM IN POLITICAL ARGUMENT 8 (2005).

31 For other work appealing to a "reasonable doubt" standard, see, for example, GERALD F. GAUS, JUSTIFICATORY LIBERALISM: AN ESSAY ON EPISTEMOLOGY AND POLITICAL THEORY 150 (1996) ("[I]n claiming moral authority over another—claiming to override a person's own judgments and substitute your own—something like the reasonable doubt standard is required."), *id.* at 240 (The sort of claim being advanced by those who claim moral authority over another "are insisting that they have made their case *beyond reasonable doubt*."); Gerald F. Gaus, *On Justifying the Moral Rights of the Moderns: A Case of Old Wine in New Bottles*, 24 SOC. PHIL. & POL'Y 84, 92 (2007) ("[W]hen one person's judgment prevails over another's, there is always the suspicion of 'subjugation.' . . . To 'dispel' this suspicion, we must be able to show that our judgment is valid 'beyond reasonable doubt.'"). Gaus is here relying on JEFFREY REIMAN, JUSTICE AND MODERN MORAL PHILOSOPHY 1 (1990).

Fabienne Peter has recently proposed a theory of the "grounds of political legitimacy," which she describes as a "disjunctive conception," according to which a "political decision is legitimate . . . in virtue of how the decision reflects normative authority, when normative authority can be established, *or*, when normative authority cannot be established, in virtue of how it adjudicates between the conflicting, but valid claims made by citizens." Fabienne Peter, *The Grounds of Political Legitimacy*, J. AM. PHIL. ASS'N (forthcoming 2020) (manuscript at 29–30). Peter's idea resembles the one offered in the text inasmuch as rights against the exercise of democratic authority are legitimate if and when they "reflect normative authority," and the laws of a democratic state are legitimate when, provided they're consistent with any right citizens have against the contrary exercise of state authority, they reflect the result of a democratic process, which is how a democratic state "adjudicates between conflicting, but valid claims made by citizens."

For doubts about the relevance of epistemology and epistemological standards like proof beyond a reasonable doubt to the project of determining when state action is legitimate, see David Enoch, *Political Philosophy and Epistemology*, *in* 3 OXFORD STUDIES IN POLITICAL PHILOSOPHY 132, 159 (David Sobel et al. eds., 2017).

32 *See, e.g.*, JOSEPH RAZ, *Facing Diversity: The Case of Epistemic Abstinence*, *in* ETHICS IN THE PUBLIC DOMAIN: ESSAYS IN THE MORALITY OF LAW AND POLITICS 45, 81 (1994) ("There may be no

One might think the ground it seeks is quicksand, for example, because one might think no meaningful difference really exists in practice between believing a rule is unjust and believing it's unjust beyond reasonable doubt. The sought-after middle ground will in practice, simply and without further ado, collapse into one's beliefs about what justice truly demands. Perhaps, but for what it's worth, that pill would presumably be a hard swallow, at least for those who believe that proof beyond a reasonable doubt—the standard of proof used in criminal prosecutions[33]—is in practice a meaningful standard, not a meaningless pretense. That said, if the sought-after middle ground does collapse, with no middle ground to be found between one's beliefs about what justice truly demands and the belief that one can never know what it truly demands, the upshot would present a choice.

On the one hand, if one harbors no doubt, or is unwilling to harbor any doubt, about one's beliefs about justice, then the legitimacy of any state's laws will depend on how well those laws approximate one's beliefs about justice, which brings us back to the anarchist's theory of legitimacy. It would mean that any citizen who believes a law is, all things considered, unjust will not believe himself morally bound to conform to it. On the other hand, if one's doubts about what justice truly demands go all the way down, then democratic authority (assuming one's doubts don't extend to it as well) would end up being unlimited authority. It would mean that any citizen who believes democratic states have authority will likewise believe himself to be morally bound to conform to any democratically enacted law.

The reasonable doubt test reflects an effort to "avoid the Scylla of supposing that what we reasonably believe is conclusively justified—and therefore can demand as a matter of justice that it be embodied in legislation—and the Charybdis of fleeing from every standing up for our fundamental principles when reasonable people disagree with us, compromising on every issue or always seeking consensus."[34] In the arena of democratic deliberation and politics, we are morally permitted to rely, when proposing what the state should do as a matter of justice, on what we believe to be true, but when we

middle way between actual (including implied) agreement and rational justification."). For a helpful collection of essays on the relationship between truth and democracy, see TRUTH AND DEMOCRACY (Jeremy Elkins & Andrew Norris eds., 2012).

33 *In re* Winship, 397 U.S. 358, 363–64 (1970) ("[A] society that values the good name and freedom of every individual should not condemn a man for commission of a crime when there is reasonable doubt about his guilt.").

34 GAUS, *supra* note 31, at 295.

endeavor to articulate rights limiting democratic authority, we are permitted to rely on what we believe to be true only if we believe it beyond reasonable doubt: claims about rights, among equally free citizens of a democracy, require a good measure of "epistemological restraint."[35]

The reasonable doubt test is like any test: it doesn't apply itself. Someone has to make the hard calls, and the only person who can apply the test to a proposed limit on democratic authority is the person to whom the limit is proposed. "[A]t the apex of one's philosophical system, one's own point of view is what matters, . . . in the epistemic sense that there is no other vantage point from which one can adjudicate."[36] If that's so, all we can do here, and all we'll endeavor to do, is lay our cards on the table and report the verdict we'd reach when applying the test to proposed limits. Those who believe the rights described below pass the test, but are nonetheless too narrow, will believe democratic authority is more limited than proposed. They'll urge more expansive rights limiting a democratic state's authority to define the rules ascribing criminal culpability. Conversely, those who believe the rights described below fail the test, and are too broad, will believe democratic authority is less limited. They'll urge even more narrowly defined rights against democratic authority to ascribe criminal culpability.

Returning to the question at hand: Does the voluntary act requirement, construed as a limit on democratic authority, pass the reasonable doubt test?

Imagine the state of Texas, the jurisdiction in which Powell was prosecuted, considers adding § 102 to its penal code, making it a felony "to firmly intend to commit a crime." The state would be required to prove the requisite intent beyond a reasonable doubt, but proof of the crime wouldn't require proof of any voluntary act taken in furtherance of the illicit intention. Section 102 imposes criminal liability for an act, not in the voluntary act requirement's sense of will bodily movement, but in the sense of a mental act resulting in the formation of a mental state: a firm intent. It wouldn't impose liability for an act qua willed bodily movement, but for an act qua willed mental state. Nonetheless, Section 102 would violate the voluntary act requirement, which requires an act qua willed bodily movement.[37]

35 Barry, *supra* note 29, at 177.

36 Larry Alexander, *Liberalism, Religion and the Unity of Epistemology*, 30 San Diego L. Rev. 763, 796 (1993).

37 Section 102 resembles the Model Penal Code provision on criminal attempts, *see* Model Penal Code § 5.01 (Am. Law Inst. 1985), with at least one notable difference. Section 5.01, unlike § 102, requires the state to prove the defendant acted or failed to act, where his act or omission "constitute[ed] a substantial step in a course of conduct planned to culminate in the commission of a crime." *Id* at § 5.01(1)(c). In other words, it requires the state to prove the defendant performed a

Austin and Dallas are Texas citizens. Austin believes the voluntary act requirement states a legitimate limit on democratic authority, and that § 102 would thus constitute an illegitimate exercise of the state's authority. He doesn't object to criminal liability for attempts, but he does object to defining attempts so as to punish someone for a mental act, rather than for a bodily movement. He believes doing so would amount to punishing someone for a thought crime.[38] On top of that, he imagines § 102 would give the police an incentive to force false confessions, which would mean more innocent people being punished. The voluntary act requirement, as a limit on the authority of the state of Texas, thankfully protects against such abuses.

Dallas disagrees. Austin believes the voluntary act requirement protects against thought crimes, which it does, but Dallas wonders what thoughts § 102 would criminalize. It wouldn't criminalize a passing thought about committing a crime, nor a naughty fantasy popping into the mind unbidden. It would punish someone who forms a distinctive mental state: a firm intention, and firm intentions don't just pop into your head, or arrive there unbidden. The voluntary act requirement disables Texas from criminalizing firm intentions, as well as passing thoughts and fantasies, but Dallas doesn't believe, beyond reasonable doubt, that justice requires the state to be so disabled.

Dallas acknowledges the grave civil-libertarian risks involved in making firm intentions liable to punishment, but believes those risks are, sometimes, worth taking. If the police have strong evidence a terrorist firmly intends to blow up a building, Dallas doesn't believe they should necessarily have to wait for him to do something—perform a willed bodily movement—in furtherance of his terrible intent before making an arrest. Dallas believes Texas should enact § 102, despite the voluntary act requirement, provided anyone convicted for possessing the intent it prohibits could have chosen not to possess it.[39] If the voluntary act requirement disables the state from doing so,

voluntary act or omission. Nonetheless, under the Code, "[c]onduct shall not be held to constitute a substantial step . . . unless it is strongly corroborative of the actor's criminal purpose," *id.* at § 5.01(2), which suggests that attempt liability under the Code, like liability under § 102, is imposed for having formed a "criminal purpose," and not for having taken "a substantial step."

[38] *See, e.g.*, Gabriel S. Mendlow, *Why Is It Wrong to Punish Thought?*, 127 Yale L.J. 2342, 2345 (2018) (stating that "punishment for thought is intrinsically unjust because it's a form of indirect mind control").

[39] *See* Husak, *supra* note 25, at 51 ("When there is overwhelming evidence that a defendant firmly intends to commit a crime, why should punishment be undeserved simply because the act requirement is unsatisfied? I am unaware of a principled answer to this question.").

then Dallas believes the voluntary act requirement constitutes an illegitimate constraint on legitimate democratic authority.

Next, imagine Texas considers adding § 103 to its penal code, which makes it a misdemeanor "to be a member of a designated terrorist organization." Like § 102, § 103 would impose criminal liability for something other than for an act. It would impose, and the state intends for it to impose, liability for possessing a prohibited status: for *being* a member of a terrorist organization. True, one usually has to do something to become a member of a terrorist organization, thereby coming to possess the status of terrorist-organization member, but whatever that something might be, § 103 wouldn't punish it: it would punish *being* a member of a terrorist organization. Section 103 would therefore violate the voluntary act requirement, just like § 102.

Because § 103, like § 102, would violate the voluntary act requirement, that's all Austin needs to know. It too would constitute, he believes, an illegitimate exercise of state authority. Once again, Dallas disagrees. Yes, § 103, like § 102, would violate the voluntary act requirement. Yes, § 103 would mean no longer being able to become a member of a terrorist organization. But Dallas doesn't believe it would be unjust, beyond reasonable doubt, to criminalize being a member of an organization dedicated to spreading terror, provided anyone so charged could have chosen not become or remain a member. Suppose, for example, the forbidden organization is the Ku Klux Klan? If the voluntary act requirement disables a democratic state from enacting § 103, then Dallas doesn't believe it states a legitimate limit on democratic authority.[40]

Austin believes Texas has no authority, pursuant to the voluntary act requirement, to enact §§ 102 and 103. Dallas believes it does. Each appeals to his or her own beliefs when passing judgment, but those beliefs lead them to opposite conclusions. Under the reasonable doubt test, Austin bears the burden of proof. If he truly believes it would be unjust, beyond reasonable doubt, for a democratic state to exercise its authority to enact §§ 102 and 103, then he should also believe the voluntary act requirement states a valid limit on state authority. Before reaching that judgment, however, he should proceed with epistemic modesty and all due deference to the contrary, good faith beliefs of his fellow citizens, especially in light of the non-trivial considerations to which Dallas has pointed in support of her contrary judgment.

[40] *Cf. id.* at 45 ("Punishment for a controlled status is just as legitimate as punishment for a voluntary act.").

If you agree with Austin, and believe that §§ 102 and 103 would, beyond reasonable doubt, constitute an unjust exercise of state authority, such that the voluntary act requirement states a legitimate limit on democratic authority, then you'll regard the enactment of §§ 102 and 103 as *ultra vires*. On the other hand, if you don't believe the enactment of §§ 102 and 103 would be unjust beyond reasonable doubt, or are at least willing to entertain such doubts, as I am, then you'll believe their enactment would, all else being equal, fall within the scope of a democratic state's authority. If so, then read on, where you'll find an alternative proposal, lodged under the heading of *actus reus*, to limit the authority of a democratic state.

The Rights Theory

Actus reus under the rights theory constitutes a limit, expressed in the language of rights, on a democratic state's authority to define conditions of culpability and thus liability to state punishment. The theory pivots on a distinction between knowledge and ignorance. The rights the theory proposes are based on an accused's incapacity, such that the state has no authority to ascribe culpability if the accused was incapacitated in some way, but the incapacity in play depends on the accused's state of mind. When an accused knew he was committing a crime at the time he committed it, one incapacity comes into play; when he didn't, a different one comes into play. Start with the former incapacity, at work when the accused knew he was committing a crime.

Knowledge

When Leroy Powell was arrested, he was drunk and wandering around in public on the 2000 block of Hamilton Street. His drinking and wandering were, we assumed, voluntary acts, insofar as his arms and legs moved as a result of volitions. We also assumed he couldn't have chosen otherwise: He lacked the capacity not to form those volitions. He was, in other words, compelled to drink and appear in public, while drunk, in violation of article 477. Now assume also that Powell, as he drunkenly staggered in public, realized he was committing a crime. That's not an unfair assumption, since Powell had gone through the same routine a hundred times before.[41]

[41] Powell v. Texas, 392 U.S. 514, 555 (1968) (Fortas, J., dissenting).

Powell satisfies the voluntary act requirement, inasmuch as he appeared in public, as one might say, "of his own volition." Fortunately for Powell, the rights theory of *actus reus* doesn't adopt the voluntary act requirement: It proposes a different limit on a democratic state's authority to ascribe culpability. Under the rights theory, if a person realizes φ-ing is a crime, where φ instantiates the elements of a crime, and if he chooses to φ at $t=1$, the state has authority to find him culpable (all else being equal),[42] *unless* he lacked the capacity at that time to have chosen not to φ. In other words, if an accused was *compelled* to choose to φ (i.e., if he lacked the capacity to choose not to φ), the state has no authority to assign guilt to his choice. Because we assumed Powell's choices to drink and appear in public were compelled, those choices weren't guilty, nor therefore were his acts of drinking and appearing, and Texas lacked the authority to punish him for making them, according to the rights theory.[43]

The rights theory replaces the conventional theory's voluntary act requirement with a capacity requirement. We're supposing, for now, that the

[42] The proviso covers three conditions. First, the state has authority to criminalize φ-ing. Second, the state has authority to find the accused culpable consistent with the *mens rea* requirement (discussed below), and third, if the state lacks authority to hold the accused culpable for choosing to φ at $t=1$, it also lacks authority to hold him culpable for choosing to φ based on a prior choice at $t=1\text{-}n$. The third condition is discussed more fully in Chapter 3.

[43] The capacity to choose otherwise is widely thought to describe the type of freedom or control without which an actor isn't morally responsible for the choices he makes. Harry Frankfurt devised a famous story in which an agent (named Jones) makes a choice for which, we're supposed to intuit, he's morally responsible, despite having no capacity to have chosen otherwise. If so, then moral responsibility for our choices doesn't, according to Frankfurt, depend on being able to choose otherwise. *See* HARRY G. FRANKFURT, *Alternate Possibilities and Moral Responsibility*, *in* THE IMPORTANCE OF WHAT WE CARE ABOUT 1, 6–8 (1988) (introducing the famous example of Jones and Black). For a recent collection of essays discussing Frankfurt's thesis, see MORAL RESPONSIBILITY AND ALTERNATIVE POSSIBILITIES: ESSAYS ON THE IMPORTANCE OF ALTERNATIVE POSSIBILITIES (David Widerker & Michael McKenna eds., 2006).

According to one well-known reply to Frankfurt-style cases, Frankfurt was right. Moral responsibility doesn't require an *agent* to be able to choose otherwise. It does, however, require the *mechanism* producing the agent's choice to have been able to respond otherwise, i.e., to be sufficiently responsive to reasons. So even if *Jones* lacked the capacity to choose otherwise, he's still responsible for his choices if the *mechanism* producing those choices could have responded otherwise. *See* JOHN MARTIN FISCHER & MARK RAVIZZA, RESPONSIBILITY AND CONTROL: A THEORY OF MORAL RESPONSIBILITY 38 (1998); Michael McKenna, *Reasons-Responsiveness Theories of Freedom*, *in* THE ROUTLEDGE COMPANION TO FREE WILL 27, 31 (Kevin Timpe et al. eds., 2017) ("Fischer and Ravizza . . . attempt to get around [Frankfurt scenarios] . . . by distinguishing between . . . an *agent*-based and a *mechanism*-based reasons-responsive theory.").

Fair enough, but insofar as we test the capacities of agents and mechanisms in more or less the same way, through the use of counterfactuals, the distinction between agents and mechanisms doesn't seem all that important. *See* Christopher Evan Franklin, *Everyone Thinks That an Ability to Do Otherwise Is Necessary for Free Will and Moral Responsibility*, 172 PHIL. STUD. 2091 (2015); Michael McKenna, *Reasons-Responsiveness, Agents, and Mechanisms*, *in* 1 OXFORD STUDIES IN AGENCY AND RESPONSIBILITY 151, 17–76 (David Shoemaker ed., 2013); Michael S. Moore, *Compatibilism(s) for Neuroscientists*, *in* LAW AND THE PHILOSOPHY OF ACTION 1, 55–59 (Enrique Villanueva ed., 2014).

voluntary act requirement, as a proposed limit on state authority, failed the reasonable doubt test and thus failed to qualify as a legitimate limit on the authority of the state of Texas. Does the rights theory fare any better?

Returning to Austin and Dallas, we might imagine Austin objecting to the capacity requirement, on which the rights theory rests, because he believes it would create insuperable problems of proof. How can a jury tell if someone was powerless to conform? Without some reliable way to sort those equipped with the requisite power from those lacking it, jurors will make mistakes. They'll sometimes wrongfully convict the powerless, and probably more often, wrongfully acquit those who could have conformed, but just didn't. We have reliable ways to test for many things, but modern science has yet to come up with a reliable way to test if someone could or couldn't have chosen to conform to the law.[44] We know Powell didn't conform to article 477, and we've been assuming he couldn't have conformed, but we have no reliable way to test that assumption.

Dallas believes that Austin's worries, though eminently fair, miss the larger point. The problems of proof Austin identifies are important, but the question is whether the rights theory of *actus reus* states a legitimate limit, as a matter of principle, on the state's authority, and the answer depends, pursuant to the reasonable doubt test, on whether one believes, beyond reasonable doubt, that justice immunizes citizens from criminal liability and punishment when *ex hypothesi* they lacked the capacity to conform their conduct to the law.

The rights theory would permit the state to enact §§ 102 and 103, because although they would necessarily violate the voluntary act requirement, they wouldn't necessarily violate the capacity requirement. The rights theory therefore gives more scope to the exercise of democratic authority than does the voluntary act requirement, though not unlimited scope. The rights theory's *actus reus* requirement would intervene only if the state tried to punish a citizen who could not conform to its laws, even if he wanted to conform. Not knowing what a good *argument* in favor of the rights theory's *actus reus* argument would look like, let me just come out and say it: I believe the proposition that justice does not permit a democratic state to punish a citizen who lacked the capacity to conform to the law is a bedrock requirement. I believe it passes the reasonable doubt test. That being so, the rights

44 For more on such concerns, see Stephen J. Morse, *Culpability and Control*, 142 U. Pa. L. Rev. 1587, 1599–602 (1994). Chapter 3 offers a test (the Stephen test) designed to assess an accused's capacity to choose to conform to the law. That test, as we'll see, doesn't eliminate the need for judgment in its application. No test can.

theory's *actus reus* requirement states, to my mind, a legitimate limit on the otherwise legitimate authority of a democratic state to define the conditions of criminal culpability.[45]

When an accused realizes that choosing to φ would mean failing to conform to the law, the *actus reus* requirement, on the rights theory, tells us to investigate his capacity to conform his choices to the law. In contrast, when an accused doesn't realize that choosing to φ would mean failing to conform, the rights theory tells us to investigate a different capacity. We need to excavate this other capacity in more detail, but before doing so, a parting word about terminology.

The rights theory uses the phrase *actus reus* to identify a limit on a democratic state's authority. Those words are usually (but not always) translated as "guilty *act*."[46] Yet inasmuch as the rights theory abandons the voluntary act requirement in favor of the capacity-to-choose-otherwise requirement, the expression *electio nocens* (guilty choice) would more accurately capture the nature of the proposed limit. Nonetheless, in deference to the traditional language, we'll stick with *actus reus*, bearing in mind that the *actus reus* requirement, under the rights theory, constrains the state's authority to ascribe culpability to choices, not actions, though most of the time the two will go hand-in-hand.

Ignorance

When Powell appeared drunk in public, we assumed he realized his drunken appearance was a crime. Now suppose Powell isn't an alcoholic. He's a teetotaler, but when he enters the bar (for a soda) on Hamilton Street, one of the patrons threatens to punch him in the nose unless he agrees to join in a round of drinks. After the first round comes another (also under threat), then another (under threat) and another (under threat), and so on. Thoroughly intoxicated, Powell once again appears in public. This time, unlike last, we'll assume he doesn't realize he's committing a crime. In fact, we'll assume he

[45] *See* HUSAK, *supra* note 25, at 39 n.87 ("Almost no principled opposition has been raised against the claim that persons should not be punished for what they cannot control.").

[46] The phrase "*actus reus*" is sometimes translated as "bad act" or "wrongful act," which might be taken to mean the *actus reus* requirement limits a democratic state's authority to criminalize, such that the state can only criminalize acts, and only those acts that are in some sense "bad" or "wrongful." In contrast, the rights theory construes the *actus reus* requirement as a limit on a democratic state's authority to define culpability, not to criminalize.

lacked the capacity to realize he was committing a crime. The police appear, and he's arrested and charged with violating article 477.[47]

Fortunately for Powell, the *actus reus* requirement under the rights theory isn't limited to compelled choices. It extends to compelled *beliefs* as well. Let φ once again stand for the crime charged. Under the rights theory, if an accused *doesn't* realize φ-ing is criminal, and if he chooses to φ, a democratic state lacks authority to find him culpable (all else being equal),[48] unless he could have realized φ-ing was a crime. If he doesn't, and if he was powerless to have realized otherwise, the state has no authority to assign guilt to his choice. Because we're assuming Powell didn't realize he was committing a crime when he appeared drunk in public, and moreover, lacked the capacity to realize he was, his choice to appear drunk in public wasn't guilty, his act therefore wasn't guilty, and Texas lacked the authority to punish him for making it.

We can now give a full statement of the rights theory's *actus reus* requirement:

> (1) If an accused chooses to φ at t=1, where φ instantiates the elements of a crime, and realizes he's choosing to commit a crime, a democratic state has authority (all else being equal) to attach guilt to his choice, unless he could not have chosen not to φ; or
>
> (2) If an accused chooses to φ at t=1, where φ instantiates the elements of a crime, but doesn't realize he's choosing to commit a crime, a democratic state has no authority (all else being equal) to attach guilt to his choice, unless he could have realized he was choosing to commit a crime.

The first part of the requirement tests an accused's capacity to choose otherwise. The second tests his capacity to believe otherwise. We've supposed the first part passes the test—the reasonable doubt test—needed for it to qualify as a legitimate limit on democratic authority. What about the second part?

47 Texas caselaw provides that "[i]nvoluntary intoxication constitutes an affirmative defense when: the accused has exercised no independent judgment or volition in taking the intoxicant; and as a result of his intoxication he . . . was incapable of conforming his conduct to the requirements of the law he allegedly violated." Mendenhall v. State, 15 S.W.3d 560, 565 (Tex. Ct. App. 2000). Model Penal Code § 2.08(4) likewise provides an affirmative defense when intoxication is "not self-induced" and "if by reason of such intoxication the actor lacks substantial capacity . . . to appreciate . . . its criminality." Model Penal Code § 2.08(4) (Am. Law Inst. 1985).

48 The proviso covers the same three conditions *mutatis mutandis* described in note 42.

An immunity right protecting citizens who lacked the capacity to choose to conform to the law would, we hypothesized above, survive the reasonable doubt test, thus imposing a legitimate limit on democratic authority. As a matter of principle, why should it matter if the source of an accused's incapacity to conform is a defective will or defective reason? Indeed, isn't the capacity to know what the law requires included within the capacity to conform? Doesn't the latter capacity presuppose the former? A citizen who can't know what the law requires can't conform to it.[49] Thus, if someone can't conform to the law, not because his will is incapacitated, but because his reason is incapacitated, I'd submit that justice places him, beyond reasonable doubt, outside the state's authority to ascribe culpability.

At this point, a criminal lawyer will likely object. The second half of the rights theory's *actus reus* requirement immunizes an actor who didn't realize, and couldn't have realized, he was committing a crime at the time he committed it. It provides immunity based on *ignorance of the law* arising from an incapacity. But that means the second half collides with the maxim *ignorantia juris neminem excusat* (ignorance of the law is no excuse), which is a maxim almost universally accepted across the Anglo-American world. How can anyone believe such a near-universally recognized rule of law is unjust? Indeed, how can anyone believe it's not merely unjust, but unjust beyond reasonable doubt?

The *ignorantia* maxim, appearances to the contrary, isn't ironclad. The law already recognizes exceptions to it. Involuntary intoxication is one. When an accused, due to involuntary intoxication, didn't realize he was committing a crime, and was powerless to realize he was, his ignorance would, in many jurisdictions, be an affirmative defense, despite the maxim.[50] Another is insanity. When an accused, due to mental disease or defect, didn't realize he was committing a crime, and was powerless to realize he was, his ignorance would, in many jurisdictions, be an affirmative defense, despite the maxim.[51]

[49] *See, e.g.*, Neil Levy, Hard Luck: How Luck Undermines Free Will and Moral Responsibility 110–11 (2011) ("[T]he epistemic condition [for responsibility] isn't independent of the control condition but built right into it."); Alfred Mele, *Moral Responsibility for Actions: Epistemic and Freedom Conditions*, 13 Phil. Explorations 101, 110 (2010) ("[P]hilosophers who . . . assert[] there are necessary freedom conditions and necessary epistemic conditions for moral responsibility for *A*-ing would do well to articulate a condition of the latter kind that is not also a necessary condition for freely *A*-ing.").

[50] *See, e.g.*, Paul H. Robinson et al., *The American Criminal Code: General Defenses*, 1 J. Legal Analysis 37, 80–84 (2015) (canvassing state law).

[51] *See, e.g.*, Paul H. Robinson & Tyler Scot Williams, Mapping American Criminal Law: Variations Across the 50 States 161–62 (2018) (canvassing state law).

The *ignorantia* maxim is deeply entrenched and nearly universal, but not airtight.

The engine driving these exceptions to the maxim is cognitive incapacity: that the unwitting accused was powerless to realize he was committing a crime. True, these defenses are available only when the incapacity results from involuntary intoxication or a mental disease or defect. But why should cognitive incapacity excuse, despite the maxim, only when it results from involuntary intoxication or mental disease or defect? What purpose do these restrictions serve?

They look like proxies for clean hands. If someone lacked the capacity to realize he was committing a crime because he suffered from a mental disease or defect, or because he was involuntarily intoxicated, chances are his hands are clean: He's not at fault for becoming incapacitated. People aren't usually responsible for having a mental disease or defect or for being involuntary intoxicated, so if one of those conditions undermines his capacity to know the law, chances are he's not culpable for his ignorance.

The rights theory takes these standing exceptions to the *ignorantia* maxim, already reflected in positive law, and modifies them in two ways to craft a limit on democratic authority to ascribe guilt. First, it generalizes. If an accused lacked the capacity to realize he was committing a crime at the time he committed it, he's not culpable, whatever caused his incapacity, as long as he's not at fault for having caused it.[52] Second, it elevates cognitive incapacity from an affirmative defense (arising from the state's decision to exercise its authority to mark the cognitively incapacitated as non-culpable) to an immunity (disabling the state from deciding to exercise its authority to mark the cognitively incapacitated as culpable). It upgrades faultless cognitive incapacity to a limit on state authority, not merely an affirmative defense the state has elected to provide in virtue of its authority.

The rights theory of *mens rea* awaits. Before we proceed, here's a summary describing how the rights theory depicts the *actus reus* requirement. First, if an accused chooses to φ, realizing φ-ing is a crime, the state has authority to assign guilt to his choice to φ (all else being equal), unless he lacked the capacity to choose otherwise. Second, if an accused chooses to φ, without

[52] *See, e.g.*, GARY WATSON, *Excusing Addiction*, *in* AGENCY AND ANSWERABILITY: SELECTED ESSAYS 318, 331 (2004) ("Imagine that someone satisfies the M'Naughton cognitive test, say, but without any showing of disease. It is morally absurd to differentiate between two equally incapacitated individuals solely on the grounds that one of the conditions could be traced to a disease.").

realizing he's committing a crime, the state lacks authority to assign guilt to his choice (all else being equal), unless he had the capacity to believe otherwise.

MENS REA

I distinguished two theories of *actus reus*: the conventional theory and the rights theory. I'll do the same for *mens rea*, starting with the conventional theory.

The Conventional Theory

The conventional theory depicts *actus reus* as an expression used to describe a crime's "objective" elements. It depicts *mens rea* in the same way, only *mens rea* is an expression used to describe a crime's "subjective" or mental state elements.[53] On the conventional theory, *mens rea* is just an expression used to describe a statute's various *mentes reae*.[54] It doesn't impose any disability on a democratic state's authority or confer any immunity on those subject to its authority.

Consider the crime of common law burglary, commonly defined as: "Breaking and entering the dwelling house of another at night with the intent to commit a felony therein." What, according to the conventional theory, does it take to make an accused burglar's mind guilty? It depends on what the statute says it takes, which we'll assume depends on what the state intended it to say.

[53] Negligence is commonly referred to as a "mental state," but that's misleading. An actor is negligent with respect to a result or attendant circumstance element of a statutory offense if he was unaware of that element when a reasonable person, based on facts of which the actor was aware, would have been aware of it. Thus, an actor is negligent if he fails to form a mental state he should have formed, which means negligence is the absence of a mental state, not a mental state itself. Still, it is, as the MPC says, a kind of culpability. *See* MODEL PENAL CODE § 2.02 (AM. LAW INST. 1985).

[54] Francis Sayre first charted *mens rea*'s historical progress from *mens rea* to *mentes reae*. Francis Bowes Sayre, *Mens Rea*, 45 HARV. L. REV. 974, 1026 (1934); Francis Bowes Sayre, *The Present Signification of* Mens Rea *in Criminal Law*, *in* HARVARD LEGAL ESSAYS 399 (Roscoe Pound ed., 1934) [hereinafter Sayre, *The Present Signification of* Mens Rea]. For additional accounts describing the shift from *mens rea* to *mentes rea*, see, for example, Stanislaw Frankowski, Mens Rea *and Punishment in England: In Search of Interdependence of the Two Basic Components of Criminal Liability (A Historical Approach)*, 63 U. DET. L. REV. 393 (1986); Martin Gardner, *The* Mens Rea *Enigma: Observations on the Role of Motive in the Criminal Law Past and Present*, 1993 UTAH L. REV. 635, 641–85; Paul H. Robinson, *A Brief History of Distinctions in Criminal Culpability*, 31 HASTINGS L.J. 816 (1980).

We can probably agree a burglar's mind isn't guilty, under the conventional theory, unless as he breaks and enters another's dwelling house at night, he intends to commit another felony once inside. If that was it, if an intent to commit a felony therein was all it took to make a burglar's mind guilty, then burglary would have only one *mens rea:* (1) "with the intent to commit a felony therein."[55] Or maybe the state intended more, without expressly saying so. Perhaps a burglar's mind isn't guilty unless, in addition to intending to commit another felony, he knew, or at least suspected, that the thing he was breaking and into which he was entering was a (2) "dwelling house" (3) "of another," and that, as we was breaking and entering, he was doing so (4) "at night." If so, that would make a grand total of four *mentes reae*, on the conventional theory, needed to make a burglar's mind guilty. Either way, an accused's mind is guilty, under the conventional theory, if, as he does whatever the crime he's charged with committing tells him not to do, he forms or possesses whatever mental states it tells him not to form or possesses.

The Rights Theory

Every first-year law student learns about another theory of *mens rea*, which they're told is in some vague way, compared to the conventional theory, older and broader.[56] This older theory, associated with the maxim *actus reus non*

[55] Burglary's "intent to commit a felony therein" element is usually described as a "specific-intent" element, and burglary is usually described as a specific-intent crime because it includes a specific-intent element. Specific-intent crimes are distinguished from general-intent crimes, although courts and commentators distinguish the two in different ways, which tends to create confusion. *See* DRESSLER, *supra* note 26, § 10.06, at 132–33. We don't need to dwell on the distinction for present purposes.

[56] *Id.* § 10.02[B], at 114–15 (distinguishing between *mens rea* in a culpability sense and in an elemental sense); GEORGE P. FLETCHER, RETHINKING CRIMINAL LAW § 6.2, at 398–99 (1978) (distinguishing between *mens rea* in a normative sense and a descriptive sense); David O. Brink, *The Nature and Significance of Culpability*, 13 CRIM. L. & PHIL. 347 (2019) (distinguishing between *mens rea* in a broad sense and a narrow sense); Douglas Husak, *"Broad" Culpability and the Retributivist Dream*, 9 OHIO ST. J. CRIM. L. 449 (2012) (same).

A broader theory of *mens rea* arguably explains why the Supreme Court sometimes interprets federal criminal statutes the way it does. If one looks closely at how the Court resolves interpretive questions about the mental states required to convict someone of a federal crime, at least when the statute's plain language is open to interpretation, a principle deeper than the usual roster of interpretive canons may be at work beneath the surface. John Wiley has dubbed this deeper principle the "rule of mandatory culpability." According to this rule, the Court, self-consciously or not, interprets federal criminal statutes, whenever possible, in order to prevent the statute, so far as possible, from being used to convict the "morally blameless," and a person is "morally blameless" if he neither realized, nor should have realized, he was committing a crime when he committed the crime charged.

facit reum nisi mens sit rea, from Saint Augustine, is typically portrayed as a normative requirement of some sort: Justice requires the state to withhold ascriptions of culpability unless the accused satisfies the *mens rea* requirement. An act isn't guilty unless the mind is guilty, and unless the mind is guilty, the person who performed the act isn't guilty. If so, then what, on this older theory, makes a mind guilty?

History's answers include: a "general immorality of motive,"[57] an "evil-meaning mind,"[58] or, perhaps most broadly, "moral blameworthiness."[59] According to William Blackstone, the great eighteenth-century English jurist, the guilty mind was a "vicious will."[60] All these expressions are interesting, but as they stand, they're pretty vague.

The rights theory of *mens rea* refines these expressions in two ways. First, it sharpens them. What emerges is an account according to which a guilty mind is, it turns out, a guilty *will*, a will motivating a choice to commit a crime and expressing insufficient concern for the law. A guilty will might, as Blackstone said, be a vicious will, but an indifferent will is guilty too. Second, it portrays *mens rea* as a normative limit inasmuch as it imposes a limit on a democratic state's authority to assign guilt to an accused's choice to commit a crime. If the state punishes someone who commits a crime, but whose choice to commit it didn't manifest *mens rea*, his punishment isn't only unjust; it's illegitimate.

I formulated the rights theory of *actus reus* one way when the accused realized he was committing a crime, and in another when he didn't. The rights

See John Shepard Wiley, *Not Guilty by Reason of Blamelessness: Culpability in Federal Criminal Interpretation*, 85 Va. L. Rev. 1021, 1023 (1999).

Alan Michaels has identified in the Court's cases what he calls the "principle of constitutional innocence." According to this principle, a state lacks the constitutional authority to punish someone who commits crime φ, when crime φ contains a strict liability element, i.e., an element with respect to which the state need not prove the accused was in any sense culpable, unless the state could, consistent with the Constitution, punish someone for φ-ing with the strict liability element removed from the statute. If a state lacks constitutional authority to make φ-ing a crime, minus its strict liability element, only then does it lack constitutional authority to make φ-ing a crime with the strict liability element included. *See* Alan Michaels, *Constitutional Innocence*, 112 Harv. L. Rev. 828 (1999). Michaels acknowledges that the principle of constitutional innocence doesn't guarantee the "morally blameless" won't be punished. *See id.* at 841. The rights theory of *mens rea* does. The principle of constitutional innocence doubtless explains the Court's existing cases better than does the rights theory, but the rights theory is proposed, not an interpretive theory meant to rationalize an existing body of precedent, but as a normative limit on the authority of a democratic state.

57 Sayre, *The Present Signification of* Mens Rea, *supra* note 54, at 411–12.

58 Morissette v. United States, 342 U.S. 246, 251 (1952).

59 Dressler, *supra* note 26, § 10.02[B], at 114.

60 4 William Blackstone, Commentaries on the Laws of England *21 ("So that to constitute a crime against human law, there must be first, a vicious will . . . .").

theory of *mens rea* follows the same logic. If an accused realized he was committing a crime, his *mens rea* will be expressed, if at all, in his *choice* to commit the crime. If he didn't, his *mens rea* will be expressed, if at all, in the *ignorance* in which he chose to commit it. I'll spell out the knowledge branch first, then turn to the ignorance branch.

Knowledge

Blackstone equated the guilty *mind* with a vicious *will*. The word "will" means different things to different people. We've already encountered, in connection with the voluntary act requirement, what might be called the "executive will," which executes or translates motivational reasons into intentions (and volitions), including the intent to φ, where φ instantiates the elements of a crime. The work of the executive will is thus to make choices. For example, when Morissette picked up the spent casings, picking them up was what he most wanted to do at the moment, and his executive will translated the object of that dominant desire into the object of an intention.[61] It then formed a volition to pick up the spent casings, and *voilá:* Morissette voluntarily did just that, moving from desire to action via the executive will.

The executive will is an important element in the folk psychology of action, but when Blackstone equated *mens rea* with a vicious will, the executive will wasn't the will he had in mind. He wasn't concerned with the will whose job is to transform motivational reasons into intentions. He was talking about a different will, which we'll call the *conative will.*

The choices we make (and intentions we form) result from a contest between competing motivational reasons. Inasmuch as the word "conative" refers to motivation, we can portray the conative will as the field on which competing motivating reasons—intentions, desires, impulses, and so on—join battle. Some of these reasons are occurrent: currently doing battle, exerting causal force in competition with other occurrent desires. Others are dispositional: on the sidelines, waiting to join the fray. If and when they join, they become occurrent, such that they too exert causal force in competition with other occurrent desires. The conative will at $t=1$ is the configuration of

[61] Volitions are a special type of intention, sometimes called a "bare intention," and all bodily movements result from volitions. *See* Moore, *supra* note 28, at 121 ("Volitions . . . are simply . . . bare intentions having as their objects the simplest bits of bodily motions that we know how to do."). When the executive will forms an intention, the intention it forms becomes part of the person's conative will, which can produce further intentions and volitions, and so on.

all the accused's motivational reasons occurrent at $t=1$, in favor of or against choosing to φ.

When Morissette encountered the casings, he wanted to pick them up; he wanted to pick them up to sell them; he wanted to sell them to make money; and so on. At the same time, maybe he didn't want to pick them up. Maybe he didn't want to exert the effort. Maybe he was tired. Maybe he wanted to go home and take a nap. These competing reasons combined in Morissette's conative will, some pushing his executive will to form an intent to pick them up, and others pushing it in the opposite direction. The winner turned out to be the collection of reasons favoring picking them up. Morissette's executive will then obliged: It formed an intention to pick up the casings, along with all the volitions needed to move his body to get the job done.

If φ stands for picking up the casings, and MR for a motivating reason, then ΣMR_{φ} stands for the total motivational force of the reasons contained in Morissette's conative will at $t=1$ in favor of φ-ing. If ~φ stands for some action other than picking up the casings, like going home to nap, then $\Sigma MR_{\sim\varphi}$ stands for the total motivational force of the reasons contained in Morissette's conative will at $t=1$ opposed to φ-ing. Because Morissette chose to φ, we know that the total motivational force of his reasons in favor of picking up the casings at $t=1$ was greater or stronger than the total motivational force of his reasons in favor of doing something else. Because $\Sigma MR_{\varphi} > \Sigma MR_{\sim\varphi}$, at $t=1$, Morissette chose to φ at $t=1$, thereby forming an intent to φ.[62]

When Blackstone equated the guilty mind with a vicious will, the will he had in mind was the conative will. When he described the (conative) will as "vicious," he was characterizing the reasons why the accused chose to φ: the accused's motivation for φ-ing. The balance of a person's motivational reasons for choosing to φ at $t=1$ provides a snapshot of his conative will revealing the quality of his will at the moment of choice.[63] The choice a

[62] All of this might make it seem that we are, as Antony Duff put it, "passive victims" of the "battle of reasons" going on inside of us. In one sense, that's correct. The account given in the text rests on compatibilism and a causal theory of action, and "[c]ompatibilism is at bottom the assertion that our responsibility is compatible with the existence of moral luck in who we are, even though who we are is often not within our control." Michael S. Moore, *The Neuroscience of Volitional Excuse*, *in* PHILOSOPHICAL FOUNDATIONS OF LAW AND NEUROSCIENCE 179, 218 (Dennis Patterson & Michael S. Pardo eds., 2016). In other words, with respect to the proximate causes of our choices, we are passive. In another way, however, it's incorrect, or at least potentially misleading, because the account given in the text is consistent with the fact that we usually experience a sense of agency over our causally determined choices. This sense of agency is discussed in more detail in Chapter 5.

[63] The phrase "quality of will" is most closely associated with Peter Strawson and his effort to develop a compatibilist account of moral responsibility. *See* P.F. Strawson, *Freedom and Resentment*, 48 PROC. BRIT. ACAD. 187 (1962). Strawson didn't say precisely what he meant by the phrase, which has

person makes at $t=1$ thus expresses, or manifests, the quality of his will at that time.[64]

When the state makes it a crime to φ, it takes φ-ing off the table. If throwing car batteries into the trash is a crime, throwing car batteries into the trash is no longer permitted. Everyone is thereafter obligated not to throw car

come to mean slightly different things to different people. *See, e.g.*, NOMY ARPALY, UNPRINCIPLED VIRTUE: AN INQUIRY INTO MORAL AGENCY 15 (2003) ("A person is . . . blameworthy for taking a morally wrong course of action out of lack of good will or out of ill will."); NOMY ARPALY & TIMOTHY SCHROEDER, IN PRAISE OF DESIRE 170 (2014) ("[A] person is blameworthy for a wrong action A to the extent that A manifests ill will (or moral indifference) through being rationalized by it."); MICHAEL MCKENNA, CONVERSATION AND RESPONSIBILITY 18–19 (2012) ("[T]he quality of an agent's will . . . is revealed in her reasons for action, her immediate proximal intention in acting as she did, and the attitudes she has for relevant others, as well as broader motives or plans into which specific reasons and intentions for action are nested."); Holly M. Smith, *Non-Tracing Cases of Culpable Ignorance*, 5 CRIM. L. & PHIL. 115, 129 (2011) ("[T]he moral character of the agent's overall configuration of desires [and aversions] . . . renders the choice blameworthy."); David Shoemaker, *Qualities of Will*, 30 SOC. PHIL. & POL'Y 95 (2013) (distinguishing three different types of "quality of will" theories); Andrew Khoury, Moral Responsibility and Quality of Will 28 (Dec. 2011) (unpublished Ph.D. dissertation, Arizona State University) ("When I speak of an agent's quality of will I am speaking of the motivational structure that issued in the willing."). Some theories of moral responsibility, often described as "quality of will" theories, seem better described as "quality of practical reason" theories, inasmuch as they judge the quality of an actor's practical reasons and judgments, as opposed to his motivational reasons and attitudes. *See, e.g.*, T.M. SCANLON, WHAT WE OWE EACH OTHER (1998); Angela Smith, *Control, Responsibility, and Moral Assessment*, 138 PHIL. STUD. 367 (2008); Angela Smith, *Responsibility for Attitudes: Activity and Passivity in Mental Life*, 115 ETHICS 236 (2005).

Some criminal law theorists look to judgments about the quality of an actor's will in order to explain when and why an actor should be criminally liable for negligence, i.e., for failing to be aware of something, like a fact or a risk of causing some prohibited result, of which he should have been aware, because a "reasonable person" in his situation would have been aware of it. *See, e.g.*, R.A. DUFF, ANSWERING FOR CRIME 296 (2007) (A reasonable person has "proper regard for the values that the criminal law expresses and protects."); MAYO MORAN, RETHINKING THE REASONABLE PERSON: AN EGALITARIAN RECONSTRUCTION OF THE OBJECTIVE STANDARD 13 (2003) (An objective standard of reasonableness should "calibrate[] the standard only for those features of the agent that are not related to his indifference. An objective standard so understood should capture only, but all, culpable indifference."); Kenneth W. Simons, *Punishment and Blame for Culpable Indifference*, 58 INQUIRY 143, 152 (2015) ("[C]ulpable indifference . . . is . . . a lack of proper concern for the right and interests of others."). Peter Westen has argued, more broadly, that an accused is excused under existing doctrines of excuse when and because his choice to commit a crime fails to express a condemnable "attitude." *See* Peter Westen, *An Attitudinal Theory of Excuse*, 25 LAW & PHIL. 289, 358 (2006) ("Criminal convictions are societal judgments that defendants not only engaged in prohibited conduct but were motivated by disparaging attitudes toward what the statutes at hand declare to be the legitimate interests of persons, including the interests of defendants themselves.").

64 Other words can be used to describe this "expression" relation, like "manifest" or "reflect." For more fine-grained analyses of the expression relationship, which may or may not be consistent with simple causal account offered in the text, see, for example, Neil Levy, *Expressing Who We Are: Moral Responsibility and Awareness of Our Reasons for Action*, 52 ANALYTIC PHIL. 243, 248–50 (2011) (arguing that an "act expresses an attitude when the action is caused by the attitude . . . in the right kind of way," and that the "right kind of way" requires awareness of the "facts that make, or at least are believed by the agent to make, the action right or wrong"); Chandra Sripada, *Self-Expression: A Deep Self Theory of Moral Responsibility*, 173 PHIL. STUD. 1203, 1215–19 (2016) (developing what the author calls the "motivational support account" of the expression relationship).

batteries into the trash. If someone nonetheless chooses to φ, knowing φ-ing is a crime, his motivational reasons for choosing to φ, and thereby not conforming to the law, must have been stronger than any competing motivational reasons for choosing not to φ, and thereby conforming to the law. In other words, his will looked like this: $\Sigma MR_{\varphi} > \Sigma MR_{\sim\varphi}$. The state prohibited him (and everyone else) from φ-ing, but its prohibition was insufficient reason for him not to φ. His choice to φ therefore reveals the quality of his will, or his attitude or stance, toward the law. It reveals, *prima facie*, an insufficient concern or regard for the law.

When we say someone's choice to φ reveals an ill or indifferent will, attitude, or stance toward the law, compared to who or what is an accused's quality of will "insufficient"? What's the "law" with respect to which the quality of his will is judged ill or indifferent? We'll say more about what makes an accused's concern or regard for the law "insufficient" later on. For now we can say a little more about the object of his alleged insufficient concern, namely, the "law."

The "law" refers to the law writ large and small. Writ large, it refers to the general good the law serves in resolving disagreements among a democracy's citizens over what the rules making up the criminal law should be. Writ small, it refers to the particular good the criminal prohibition at hand is meant to safeguard. Offenses against the person safeguard bodily integrity. Offenses against property safeguard property interests. Offenses against habitation safeguard the security of the home. Offenses against the administration of justice safeguard fairness in the administration of justice, and so on. An accused's choice to φ thus manifests insufficient concern for the law when it manifests insufficient concern for whatever particular good the law writ small was intended to protect, as well as the general good—authoritatively resolving disagreements—the law writ large secures.

Morissette didn't actually believe he was committing a crime when he took the casings, but suppose he did. He knew the law prohibited taking the casings, but didn't care, or at least didn't care enough. Wouldn't his choice, in light of his knowledge of the law, speak for itself? Wouldn't it show, all by itself, that Morissette lacked sufficient concern for the law? In other words, when someone realizes the criminal law prohibits φ-ing, but chooses to φ nonetheless, doesn't that choice necessarily reflect insufficient concern for the law?

The state sometimes allows a person to commit what would otherwise be a crime if he does so for reasons the state counts as good reasons. For example, if taking the casings was the only way to save his life, or someone else's life, or otherwise avoid some evil greater than the evil involved in taking the casings, the state would probably have permitted Morissette to take them. The criminal law collects these reasons in affirmative defenses, known as justification defenses, like self-defense, defense of others, and necessity (or lesser evils). Crimes committed for reasons the state recognizes as good reasons aren't crimes, all things considered. Morissette, however, had no such reason. He took the casings in order to sell them for profit.

Now imagine a twist on Morissette's story. Imagine Morissette's nemesis—Boris—appears at the Oscoda Air Base, where he finds Morissette hunting deer. In Boris's hands is Morissette's beloved stamp collection, which Boris threatens to burn unless Morissette steals the casings and puts them in Boris's truck, for Boris to sell for profit. What should Morissette do?[65] There's no time to go to the police. His only choice is to commit what he realizes is a crime, or watch his cherished stamps go up in flames. The casings and the stamps are roughly of equal value measured in terms of their fair market value. Torn, Morissette picks up the casings, and puts them in Boris's truck.

When the government prosecutes him for violating § 641, Morissette can't say he acted for reasons the United States would count as reasons making his choice to steal permissible. He didn't, for example, steal to save his life or anyone else's life. So, no self-defense or defense of others. Nor, suppose, did he steal to avoid a lesser evil. The jury, having been properly instructed on the lesser evils defense, found that Morissette didn't choose the lesser evil, and the jury's judgment survived challenge on appeal. So, no necessity defense.[66]

[65] Morissette's predicament is an example of "sacrificial duress," which is discussed in more detail in Chapter 3, *infra* at pp. 133-37. Gary Watson's observations about duress, conceived as what he calls a "prerogative defense," are suggestive when *mens rea* is understood as a limit on state authority:

> [T]he . . . prerogative defense . . . exhibits a principle of legal authority of the first importance: that the criminal law can be legitimate only if it is justifiable to those who are subject to its demands. . . . The recognition [in the defense of duress] of the space of agent-centered prerogatives is . . . the law's acknowledgment of the limits of its own moral jurisdiction. To punish in circumstances of duress (so interpreted) would be to treat the defendant in a way that could not be justified to him as a practical agent; it would be to treat him on grounds that he could reasonably reject.

Watson, *supra* note 52, at 341.

[66] A lawyer defending Morissette would probably argue that he stole the casings under duress (or coercion). As a legal defense, duress has long puzzled criminal law theorists, who typically place affirmative defenses in one of two categories, either justification or excuse. According to several theorists, duress doesn't fit comfortably into either category. Different theorists use different labels to describe the unique theoretical status duress has in law. *See, e.g.*, LARRY ALEXANDER & KIMBERLY KESSLER FERZAN, CRIME AND CULPABILITY: A THEORY OF CRIMINAL LAW 136–41 (2009) (duress as a "personal justification"); ALAN WERTHEIMER, COERCION 168 (1987) (duress as an agent-relative justification or permission); Dan M. Kahan & Martha C. Nussbaum, *Two Conceptions of Emotion in Criminal Law*, 96 COLUM. L. REV. 269, 336 (1996) ("'Duress' captures the interplay of at least some of

Morissette admits he committed a crime. He also admits his reasons for committing it weren't good enough for the United States to permit him to commit it. Still, he doesn't believe he should, under the circumstances, be blamed or punished. It would be one thing if he'd taken the casings, sold them, and used the proceeds for a night on the town, but that's not why he committed the crime. He committed the crime in order to save his beloved stamps.

When someone commits a crime, realizing that's what he's doing, the state is entitled to presume he didn't care as much about the law as he should have. But the presumption is rebuttable.[67] Sometimes sufficient concern and failure to conform can co-exist. Morissette, for example, insists his theft, despite amounting to a § 641 violation, didn't manifest insufficient concern for the law, not in light of Boris's threat. On the contrary, he believes he showed as much concern as the state can legitimately expect of him, or of anyone put to a choice like the one to which Boris's threat put him. Odd as it might sound, he insists he did show sufficient concern for the law, even though, with both eyes open, he committed a crime.

We'll say more about the conditions under which a person who knowingly commits a crime does so without expressing insufficient concern for the law in Chapter 4, but for now, if Morissette's choice to steal the casings didn't express insufficient concern, then on the rights theory his choice to steal the casings lacked *mens rea*: It didn't, all things considered, express or manifest a (conative) will scornful of, or at least indifferent to, the law. Moreover, if an accused's choice to commit a crime, even when he realizes he's committing a crime, lacks *mens rea*, then on the rights theory, a democratic state lacks the authority to punish him for making it, because his mind was guilt-free.

these [complex social] norms and helps to regulate the interaction between the privilege to love one's own and the duty to treat all persons with concern and respect."); Watson, *supra* note 52 at 340 (duress as "prerogative defense").

Another way to capture the distinctive theoretical status of duress is to analogize it to Wittgenstein's famous image of the duck and rabbit. What you see depends on how you look at it. Looked at from the perspective of a law-abiding citizen, duress is a justification. Looked at from the perspective of the state, duress is an excuse. *See, e.g., id.* at 339 ("[T]hose who violate the law [in circumstances of duress] are, in one plain sense, justified in doing so: they act for sufficient reasons. But their conduct is not justifiable from the point of view of the general aims and values of the law.").

67 For the same point made recently in the context of moral excuses, see Paulina Sliwa, *The Power of Excuses*, 47 PHIL. & PUB. AFF. 37, 48 (2019) ("In general, when we witness wrongdoing, we are entitled to infer the lack of a morally adequate present-directed intention. I say 'in general' because this inference is defeasible. This is where excuses come in.").

The rights theory of *mens rea*, like the rights theory of *actus reus*, has two branches. Having canvassed the first branch, which states the *mens rea* requirement when the accused realized he was committing a crime, I turn now to the second, which states the *mens rea* requirement when the accused acted in ignorance.

Ignorance

Suppose Morissette believed, as in fact he said he did, that the casings he took had been abandoned, and because he believed they'd been abandoned, he didn't realize taking them amounted to doing anything criminal. When the FBI comes to arrest him for violating § 641, he wonders how his mind can be guilty when he had no idea he was committing a crime. How can an ignorant mind be a guilty mind? When a citizen of a democratic state chooses to φ, where φ instantiates the elements of a criminal offense, but doesn't even suspect he's doing anything criminal, can his choice manifest a guilty mind?

When someone chooses to commit a crime, and knows he's committing a crime, the quality of his will is expressed in his choice. If, despite choosing to do what he realized was a crime, he cared as much about the law as he should have, then the quality of his will was up to par, and his choice to commit the crime lacked *mens rea*. If not, if he cared less than he should have, then the quality of his will was sub-par, and his choice to commit the crime was made with *mens rea*. When someone chooses to commit a crime but doesn't realize he's committing a crime, his choice once again expresses the quality of his will, but the quality of his will isn't expressed in the choice he makes, at least not directly. Instead, it's expressed in the ignorance in which he makes it.

The quality of a person's will at the moment of choice depends on motivating reasons: on those reasons currently playing a causal role in determining his choice at that moment. The conative will, together with the executive will, work together to produce choices, and thus form intentions and volitions. One thing the conative will doesn't do is form beliefs. That job belongs to a different faculty: theoretical reason.

The beliefs and other cognitive attitudes theoretical reason forms result from the balance of one's epistemic reasons (or evidence) at the moment one forms the belief.[68] Let *p* stand for the proposition that φ-ing is a crime, and

[68] *See* Thomas Kelly, *Evidence*, STAN. ENCYCLOPEDIA PHIL. 5 (2016) ("[I]t is natural to think that 'reason to believe' and 'evidence' are more or less synonymous, being distinguished chiefly by the fact that the former functions grammatically as a count noun while the latter functions as a mass term.").

ER for an epistemic reason: a reason in favor of or against forming the belief that *p*. Thus, ΣER_p represents the total cognitive force of a person's available epistemic reasons at *t*=1 in favor of forming the belief that *p*, and $\Sigma ER_{\sim p}$ represents the total cognitive force of his available epistemic reasons at *t*=1 against forming the belief that *p*. Limiting ourselves for the moment to those cognitive attitudes we call beliefs, if a person doesn't believe *p* at *t*=1, then $\Sigma ER_p < \Sigma ER_{\sim p}$; if he does believe *p* at *t*=1, then $\Sigma ER_p > \Sigma ER_{\sim p}$.

All things considered, we're better off if the beliefs we form reflect the way the world is, not the way we'd like it to be. We generally navigate the world better when we see it as it truly is. So, when our theoretical reason works as it should, it responds only to epistemic reasons, which are, once again, reasons that count in favor of or against some proposition, like φ-ing is a crime, being true or false.

Unfortunately, theoretical reason doesn't always work as it should. The culprit is the will. Sometimes the conative will exceeds its jurisdiction, trespassing on theoretical reason's domain.[69] The desires inhabiting the conative will sometimes interfere with theoretical reason's work, thereby throwing one's cognitive compass off the truth. Sometimes, for example, desire causes theoretical reason to give too much attention, and thus too much weight, to some epistemic reasons, and too little to others. Some facts become more salient, and others less salient. Or, sometimes desire causes some epistemic reasons to be retrieved from memory, allowing them to play a part in forming new beliefs, while causing others to remain buried and causally inert. Beliefs and other cognitive attitudes produced when the conative will misbehaves in ways such as these are products of motivated reasoning. Self-deception and wishful thinking are prime examples.[70]

[69] The conative will can interfere with practical reason as well as theoretical reason. Theoretical reason works to form beliefs (and other cognitive attitudes) about the way the world is. Practical reason works to form beliefs (or judgments) about what one should do, all things considered. The conative will (and the motivational reasons configuring it) can influence practical reason's judgment-forming processes, just as it can influence theoretical reason's belief-forming processes. So, for example, if you judge, all things considered, that you shouldn't have that next slice of cake, or next drink, you might judge in turn that you should, all things considered, resist the motivational reasons (desires) moving you in that direction. Alternatively, those motivational reasons might end up causing you to revise your original judgment as to what you should do, all things considered. In other words, desire might cause you to change your mind, such that you end up believing that having the next slice of cake, or the next drink, is what you should do, all things considered.

[70] Yuval Avnur & Dion Scott-Kakures, *How Irrelevant Influences Bias Belief*, 29 PHIL. PERSPECTIVES, EPISTEMOLOGY 7, 8 (2015) ("The thought that desire or interest can warp inquiry and render us unreliable and sometimes unjustified, has a long and distinguished philosophical pedigree. But it is also familiar in ordinary life."). We ignore for now any conceptual differences between various forms of motivated belief, such as self-deception compared to wishful thinking, as well as differences among

When Morissette spied the casings, suppose it never dawned on him they might be government property. He thought they were abandoned junk. So, when he took them, it never dawned on him he might be committing a crime. At the time he took the casings, the balance of his available epistemic reasons was $\Sigma ER_p < \Sigma ER_{\sim p}$. The causal force of his epistemic reasons for believing the casings had been abandoned defeated the force of his epistemic reasons for believing they were government property, and thus the causal force of his epistemic reasons for believing he wasn't committing a crime when he took the casings defeated that of his epistemic reasons for believing he was. His theoretical reason therefore failed to form the belief that *p*: the belief that he was committing a crime.

Now suppose the casings had been (contrary to fact) gathered together in neat piles, which would have been some evidence they weren't abandoned. Or suppose a sign reading, in all caps, "GOVERNMENT PROPERTY," had been posted near the casings. That would have been more evidence the casings weren't abandoned. Indeed, if Morissette's theoretical reason had registered and responded to these additional facts, let's agree he would've realized the casings weren't abandoned, and so would've realized he'd be committing a crime if he took them. Those additional facts are as plain as plain can be, yet suppose Morissette never notices them. They never gain entry into his theoretical reason, and so he ends up, despite those facts, continuing to believe the casings are abandoned. Or maybe he notices, but those facts never register insofar as they end up playing no causal role in his theoretical reason's belief-forming process. He thus remains oblivious to the fact, when he takes the casings, that he's committing a crime.

Why didn't he notice? Or why did the facts, if he noticed them, nonetheless fail to register? Suppose Morissette ran a fruit stand in the summer, and the

various analyses of self-deception. *See* Kevin Lynch, *Willful Ignorance and Self-Deception*, 173 PHIL. STUD. 505, 513–14 (2016) (sorting theories of self-deception into "unwarranted belief accounts," "implicit knowledge accounts," and "intermediate accounts"). For an influential analysis of self-deception as unwarranted belief based on motivated bias, see ALFRED R. MELE, SELF-DECEPTION UNMASKED (2001).

Cognitive states resulting from self-deception and wishful thinking are usually described as instances of motivated irrationality. They're irrational because they don't result exclusively from epistemic reasons, and they're motivated because they result (at least in part) from motivational reasons. When irrational cognitive states result from motivational reasons, they're sometimes described as resulting from "hot" bias, and when they result from hard-wired heuristics and biases, they're sometimes described as resulting from "cold" biases. For a general discussion of heuristics and biases, see Thomas Gilovich & Dale Griffin, *Introduction—Heuristics and Biases: Then and Now*, *in* HEURISTICS AND BIASES: THE PSYCHOLOGY OF INTUITIVE JUDGMENT 1 (Thomas Gilovich, Dale Griffin, & Daniel Kahneman eds., 2002).

summer hadn't been kind.[71] Rain had been scarce, and the fruit Morissette sold didn't look very good. That was bad for business, and Morissette hadn't made a lot of money. Worse, his only son, age five, had become undernourished, and Morissette's wife had grown increasingly concerned for the boy's well-being. Morissette had become preoccupied with the boy's health, too.

When Morissette spied the casings, neatly piled on the grounds of the Oscoda Air Base, all he could think about was the money he could get for them as scrap, and how the money would put food on the table and help restore his son to full vigor. The desire for his son's well-being blinded him, we might say, to the facts before his eyes. Wanting to help his son, and not wanting to believe the casings were government property, desire kept the unwanted facts from getting through to his theoretical reason. Without those facts to weigh in the balance, Morissette's theoretical reason stood no chance of seeing the truth.

In the hypothetical in which Morissette realized he'd be committing a crime if he took the casings, but took them anyway because Boris threatened his beloved stamp collection, the rights theory of *mens rea* started with the assumption that Morissette's choice to commit the crime revealed a will insufficiently concerned for the law. That assumption was rebuttable, but the presumption was in favor of *mens rea*. In contrast, when an accused commits a crime but doesn't realize he's committing a crime, the rights theory begins from the opposite assumption. It assumes an unwitting choice to commit a crime reveals a will sufficiently concerned for the law. The presumption is against *mens rea*.

When the government prosecutes Morissette for violating § 641, the unwitting Morissette is ready. The government has no authority to punish him for violating § 641, he claims, because he didn't realize he was committing any crime when he took the casings. He thought they'd been abandoned, and property no one wants isn't property you can steal from anyone. He therefore asserts the protection of the presumption against *mens rea*; and without *mens rea*, the government has no authority to punish him.

Not so fast, the government replies. Assuming Morissette didn't realize he was committing a crime, the government nonetheless insists his mind was guilty. According to the government, his ignorance was due to greed, not love for his son and worry about his well-being. He wanted the money

[71] The real Morissette was a "fruit stand operator" during the summer. Morissette v. United States, 342 U.S. 246, 247 (1952).

from the casings to take a vacation. It was avarice, pure and simple, not love for his son, which blinded him to the facts before his eyes. Because his blindness was due to greed, the government insists his choice to take the casings did manifest insufficient concern for the law, not in the choice directly, but in the ignorance in which it was made. If he'd cared as much about the law as he should have, or less about vacationing than he did, he would've realized he was committing a crime. All things considered, therefore, his choice did manifest *mens rea*, and the United States had all the authority it needs to punish him.

Was it love or greed? If it was greed, then the state probably has authority to punish Morissette for violating § 641. If it was love, then it probably doesn't. Where the truth lies will be up to a jury, or some other finder of fact. Discovering the truth won't always be easy, but the ultimate question remains: Did Morissette's ignorance of the law result from insufficient concern for the law? Again, that's not always an easy question to answer, but it's nonetheless the question the rights theory invites us to ask.

The rights theory's *actus reus* requirement, as we saw earlier, conflicts with the *ignorantia* maxim. According to the *actus reus* requirement, and contrary to the maxim, ignorance disables the state from ascribing culpability, provided the accused wasn't only ignorant, but also powerless to have gained knowledge. If so, then whenever the *actus reus* requirement goes toe-to-toe with the *ignorantia* maxim, the maxim should lose. The same goes for the rights theory's *mens rea* requirement. Whenever the *mens rea* requirement conflicts with the maxim, the maxim should lose. The maxim obligates jurors to convict despite an accused's ignorance of the law. The *actus reus* and *mens rea* requirements, pursuant to the rights theory, disables the state's authority to ordain that obligation.

We can now give a full statement of the *mens rea* requirement under the rights theory:

> (1) If an accused chooses to φ at t=1 (where φ instantiates the elements of a crime), and realizes he's choosing to commit a crime, a democratic state has the authority (all else being equal) to attach guilt to his choice,[72]

[72] The proviso covers three conditions. First, the state has authority to criminalize φ-ing. Second, the state has authority to find the accused culpable consistent with the *actus reus* requirement, and third, if the state lacks authority to hold the accused culpable for choosing to φ at t=1, it also lacks authority to hold him culpable for choosing to φ based on a prior choice at t=1-n. The third condition is discussed more fully in Chapter 4.

unless his choice to φ, despite being a choice to commit a crime, nonetheless expressed sufficient concern for the law; or

(2) If a person chooses to φ at $t=1$ (where φ instantiates the elements of a crime), but doesn't realize he's choosing to commit a crime, a democratic state has no authority (all else being equal) to attach guilt to his choice, unless his choice to φ, despite being a choice made in ignorance of the law, nonetheless expressed insufficient concern for the law.

Like the rights theory's *actus reus* requirement, its *mens rea* requirement is tendered as a limit on a democracy's authority to attach culpability to a citizen's choice to commit a crime. In order to enjoy that status, the *mens rea* requirement must pass the reasonable doubt test. We submitted above that the rights theory's *actus reus* requirement passed the test. Does its *mens rea* requirement pass?

In order to answer that question, more needs to be said about the nature of *mens rea*. A choice to φ, I've proposed, manifests a guilty mind when it results, directly or indirectly, from a will whose configuration of motivating reasons reveals insufficient concern for the law. The question is how we can tell if the concern a will expresses for the law is insufficient. We need some benchmark against which we can say of a will that its concern for the law was sufficient or insufficient. We need a test to sort ill wills from healthy ones. Once we have that test, we'll be in a better position to ask if rights theory of *mens rea* passes the reasonable doubt test. We'll call the test for sorting wills the *Jekyll test*, for reasons that should become more perspicuous in a moment.

The Jekyll Test

The Jekyll test is an all-purpose test: It can be used to test the quality of an accused's will whether his choice was witting or unwitting. If his will passes the test, then his choice to commit crime φ would, despite that choice, express sufficient concern for the law, and a citizen who chooses to φ, but whose will nonetheless expresses sufficient concern, lacks *mens rea*, rendering him immune to the ascription of criminal culpability.

We can use Morissette's case to show how the Jekyll test works, beginning with the scenario in which Morissette took the casings knowing they were government property, but took them anyway because Boris threatened to destroy his stamp collection. When Morissette chose to steal the government casings in order to save his beloved stamps from immediate destruction, did his choice express insufficient concern for the law? The Jekyll test is intended to answer, or at least provide a guide to answering, that question. The test has two steps, both of which require some imagination.

Step 1 asks us to imagine injecting Morissette with a serum endowing him with all the care and concern for the law a democratic state can legitimately expect of a *law-abiding* citizen.[73] Everything else about Morissette, and the situation he was in at the moment he took the casings, remains unchanged. The injection changes real Morissette into law-abiding Morissette. Law-abiding Morissette is just like real Morissette, only the latter necessarily cares as much about the law as a law-abiding citizen would have cared. If Morissette cared less than he should have before the injection, he cares as much as he should after. If he was Hyde before the injection, he becomes Jekyll after. On the other hand, if Morissette cared as much as he should have before the injection, then nothing changes. He's the same before the injection as he is after. If he was Jekyll before, he remains Jekyll after.

If the injection of law-abiding concern transforms Morissette, it might do so in one of two ways. First, if Morissette had too little concern for the law before the injection, then the value of $\Sigma MR_{\sim\varphi}$ would be greater afterward. The force of his motivational reasons to conform, and thus not to φ, would increase. Second, if Morissette had too much concern for his own ends before the injection, then the value of ΣMR_{φ} would be less after. The motivational force of his reasons to pursue his own ends, and thus to φ, would decrease. Both mechanisms might be at work at the same time, with $\Sigma MR_{\sim\varphi}$ going up, and ΣMR_{φ} going down.[74] Whatever the mechanism, law-abiding Morissette is the real Morissette's *doppelgänger*, except with sufficient concern for the law, insofar as the real Morissette lacked such concern.[75]

[73] The concern a law-abiding citizen has for the law includes concern for the various goods the obligations the criminal law recognizes or imposes are intended to protect, not least of which are the lives, physical well-being, and property of its citizens, which are protected through the criminal law's core prohibitions. Law-abiding citizens regard their fellow citizens as equals, in the sense that a law-abiding citizen places the same weight on each citizen's interest in life, physical safety, and property without regard to the color of his skin, the faith he professes (or not), who he chooses to be intimate with, and so on. At the same time, however, the Jekyll test assumes a democratic state is obligated, as a matter of justice and beyond reasonable doubt, to recognize that law-abiding citizens have private commitments and attachments, such as their own well-being, to which they're permitted to assign greater weight in their practical deliberations compared to the weight the state, which must be impartial, would assign them, or to the weight other law-abiding citizens, who have different attachments and commitments, would assign them.

[74] *See* Sripada, *supra* note 64, at 1208–11 (describing "a syndrome of dispositional effects" that "cares" have, which includes "motivational, commitmental, evaluative, and affective" effects).

[75] The first step takes the accused (as he really is) and then, as Peter Westen insightfully says, "moralizes" him. *See* Peter Westen, *Individualizing the Reasonable Person in Criminal Law*, 2 CRIM. L. & PHIL. 137, 138 (2008) (arguing that the reasonable person is not an ideal type *individualized*, but

Step 2 asks us to imagine what law-abiding Morissette would have done at the moment real Morissette made off with the casings in order to spare his stamp collection. Once real Morissette has been transformed into law-abiding Morissette, would law-abiding Morissette have taken the casings or would he have left them alone?

If law-abiding Morissette would have taken the casings, then $\Sigma MR_{\varphi} > \Sigma MR_{\sim\varphi}$, despite the transfusion of law-abiding concern. Law-abiding Morissette would've made the same choice as real Morissette, which would mean real Morissette's will wasn't guilty because his choice didn't manifest insufficient concern for the law. Real Morissette had as much concern for the law as law-abiding Morissette would have had, so the injection makes no difference to the choice he would have made.[76] If so, then his reasons

an actual defendant *moralized); id.* at 137 (proposing that a "reasonable person . . . consists of every physical, psychological, and emotional trait an actor possesses, with one exception—the exception being that he possesses proper respect for the values of the people of the state as reflected and incorporated in the statute at hand"); *id.* at 151 ("The proposed test is simple. . . . 'What would a person, who otherwise possessed every trait of the actor but fully respected the interests that the statute at hand seeks to protect, have thought and/or felt on the occasion at issue?'"). Perhaps another way to try to make the point would be to imagine the accused was imbued with "basic decency," where someone with basic decency "cares *enough* about the rights and interest of those affected by his acts and about other important values," and as such his "actions will never warrant . . . retreat from ordinary sociability." Gideon Rosen, *Culpability and Duress: A Case Study*, 88 Proc. Aristotelian Soc'y Supp. 69, 87 (2014).

The criminal law's usual approach to the reasonable person, as academic commentators usually portray it, works from the opposite direction. It starts with the reasonable person (whoever or whatever that is) and then asks how far to "individualize" or "subjectivize" that "idealized, impersonal and disembodied personification of reasonableness." Westen, *supra*, at 148. It then asks if this or that attribute of the accused should be imputed to the reasonable person, but offers no principle according to which one characteristic is in but the next one out. Without some such principle, the "reasonable person in the actor's situation" ends up being an arbitrary construction. *See* Alexander & Ferzan, *supra* note 66, at 81 ("[T]here is no principled and rationally defensible way to define the 'reasonable person in the actor's situation.'"). For a similar critique, see Matt King, *Against Personifying the Reasonable Person*, 11 Crim. L. & Phil. 725, 730 (2017) ("Without knowing something about reasonability itself, we simply have no guidance on what the reasonable person would do. But since the counterfactual test is supposed to be a way of getting at what reasonability involves, it only produces answers when it presumes the very thing it's after.").

[76] Suppose real Morissette didn't steal casings, but tried to kill himself, because he was clinically depressed, meaning he lacked almost all concern, not only for himself, but for anything or anyone. He blows out the pilot light on his stove, turns on the gas, takes some tranquillizers, and falls asleep in front of the stove. The gas leaks into the apartment above Morissette's and kills the occupant. Morissette, however, survives. *Cf.* People v. Feingold, 852 N.E.2d 1163, 1164 (N.Y. 2006). Stipulate that Morissette didn't realize his actions endangered anyone's life but his own. We might suppose that ostensibly law-abiding Morissette, who emerges after real Morissette has been injected with law-abiding concern, is just as depressed as real Morissette. Because real Morissette is clinically depressed, the injection would probably change nothing. If so, then law-abiding Morissette would have acted just as real Morissette did, which means, ironically perhaps, that real Morissette's actions didn't manifest insufficient concern. The moral responsibility of the clinically depressed is discussed in more detail in David Shoemaker, Responsibility from the Margins 126–36 (2015).

for φ-ing, though not good enough to make his choice to take the casings a choice the state would permit, weren't bad enough to make his mind guilty. Taking the casings was still a crime, but Morissette's mind wasn't guilty when he committed it.

On the other hand, if law-abiding Morissette wouldn't have taken the casings, then $\Sigma MR_{\varphi} < \Sigma MR_{\sim\varphi}$, thanks to the transfusion of law-abiding concern. Law-abiding Morissette wouldn't have made the choice real Morissette made, which would mean real Morissette's will was guilty. His choice expressed insufficient concern for the law, because he wouldn't have chosen to φ if his concern had been as robust as it should have been. His upgraded concern for the law, commensurate with the concern a law-abiding citizen would have had, would have defeated whatever countervailing reasons caused real Morissette to choose to steal. Taking the casings was a crime, and Morissette's mind was guilty when he committed it.

So, what would law-abiding Morissette have done? Unfortunately, the Jekyll test doesn't provide easy answers. It only provides the question: What would the accused have done if he'd had as much concern for the law as a law-abiding citizen has? The answer depends on the judgment of law-abiding citizens themselves, called upon to judge the will of a fellow citizen whose law-abidance the state has called into question.

Now go to the scenario in which Morissette believed the casings were abandoned, and so didn't realize he was committing any crime when he took them. Morissette claimed his ignorance was due to an appropriate measure of concern for his son, not an objectionable lack of concern for the law. The government, in contrast, claimed his ignorance was due to greed. Because Morissette didn't realize he was committing a crime, the rights theory tells us to begin with a defeasible presumption against *mens rea*, and then apply the Jekyll test to decide if Morissette loses the benefit of that presumption.

As before, everything about Morissette is held constant at the time he took the casings. He's then injected with a law-abiding citizen's concern for the law. Prior to the injection, where p is the proposition that φ-ing is a crime, the balance of Morissette's epistemic reasons was $\Sigma ER_{p} < \Sigma ER_{\sim p}$, such that his reasons against believing he was committing a crime outweighed his reasons for believing he was, which is why he didn't believe he was committing a crime. Then comes the injection.

If the balance of Morissette's epistemic reasons shifts, so $\Sigma ER_{p} > \Sigma ER_{\sim p}$, then law-abiding Morissette would have realized he was committing a crime. Because nothing else about Morissette has changed, the only explanation for his new-found belief would be his new-found concern for the law. His actual failure to realize he was committing a crime must have been the result of an ill or indifferent will. Morissette would thus lose the benefit of the presumption against *mens rea* with which he started. If so, then his mind was guilty. On the other hand, if the balance of Morissette's epistemic reasons after the injection remains unchanged, so $\Sigma ER_p < \Sigma ER_{\sim p}$, as it was before, then law-abiding Morissette wouldn't have realized he was committing a crime, just as real Morissette didn't. If so, then real Morissette's failure to form the belief that *p* must have some explanation other than insufficient concern for the law.

Maybe his eyesight was bad, so he didn't see the signs saying "Government Property" posted next to the piles of casings. Or maybe he lacked a background belief. Maybe, for example, he didn't realize people usually don't neatly arrange abandoned property they no longer care about. Or maybe he just wasn't bright enough to put two and two together. Whatever the explanation, as long as his ignorance can't be traced to lack of sufficient concern for the law, measured against the concern a law-abiding citizen would have had, then he continues to enjoy the benefit of the presumption against *mens rea*. If so, then his mind wasn't guilty. Again, stating the test is easier than applying it.

With the Jekyll test in hand, we can put the rights theory of *mens rea* to the reasonable doubt test. The theory needs to pass the test in order to earn its proposed status as a legitimate limit on democratic authority. The rights theory tells us that a democratic state lacks the authority to enact rules rendering culpable a citizen who fails to conform to the law, when his failure to conform doesn't manifest, directly or indirectly, insufficient concern for the law. It immunizes from criminal liability any such choice when that choice resulted, directly or indirectly, from a configuration of motivational reasons reflecting sufficient concern, where sufficient concern is measured, pursuant to the Jekyll test, against the standard of a law-abiding citizen.

Suppose we agree that Morissette, when he took the casings, either because Boris threatened his stamp collection, or because, preoccupied with his son's welfare, he didn't realize he was committing a crime, would have made the same choice even if he'd been fortified with sufficient concern for the law: the concern a law-abiding citizen has for the law. If justice permits the United States to punish Morissette under those circumstances, that would mean justice permits a democratic state to punish law-abiding choices. I'll presume to submit the contrary is true. How, as a matter of justice, can a law-abiding choice be a punishable choice? Far from permitting the state to permit itself to punish law-abiding choices, I believe, and beyond reasonable doubt at that, that justice denies the state such permission. If so, then the rights theory of *mens rea*, like the rights theory of *actus reus*, states a legitimate limit on the otherwise legitimate authority of a democratic state to ascribe culpability, such that law-abiding choices are choices beyond the scope of its authority to assign culpability.

Before moving on, I should say a little more about the conative will. The rights theory asks us to judge the quality of the accused's conative will at the moment he chose to commit a crime, where the conative will is understood as the constellation of the accused's motivating reasons at the moment of choice. In order to get a better sense of what it means to judge the quality of an accused's will, we should spend a moment distinguishing the conative will under the rights theory from other accounts of the will with which it might be confused.

Boundaries of the Will

Judging the quality of a person's will involves judging the quality of the person he is, or at least the person he was, at the moment of choice, at least if we equate him—his self—with his will. Inasmuch as the conative will is the configuration of a person's motivating reasons at a particular moment in time, setting the will's boundaries (and thus the self's boundaries) involves identifying which reasons, among all those at work in producing the accused's choice to φ at t=1, to include as part of the conative will (or self), and more importantly, which, if any, to ignore or exclude.[77]

The rights theory presupposes an inclusive theory of the will, according to which the will includes every motivating reason exerting causal influence at the moment the accused chose to φ. It includes, we might put it, all the motivating reasons online at the time. For example, assuming Morissette, when he picked up the casings, realized he was committing a crime, all the motivating reasons causing his choice would be fair game when judging the quality of his will. Likewise, assuming he didn't realize he was committing a crime, all the motivating reasons causing his ignorance would be fair game.

[77] *See, e.g.*, Sripada, *supra* note 64, at 1205 (noting that accounts of moral responsibility based on assessments of the quality of an actor's will might "very well be understood along . . . lines" of accounts that "strike deep self themes"). The philosophical literature uses a variety of terms to refer to the "self": moral personality, practical identity, real self, deep self, and so forth.

The inclusive theory doesn't pick and choose. If a motivational reason was at work, directly or indirectly, when the accused choose to φ, it counts.[78]

Other theories of the self have been proposed. According to one, which might be called the endorsement theory, the self includes all the will's online motivational reasons at t=1, unless the reason is one the accused does, or would on reflection, refuse to endorse; or more broadly, would disown or disavow.[79] In other words, a reason should, on the endorsement theory, be excluded from the will (and the self) if the reason is one the accused does not want to have, or one he wants not to have. Judging the quality is his will is thus a matter of judging the quality of his will so circumscribed, pruned of unendorsed or reflectively rejected motivational reasons.

For example, suppose Morissette, realizing the casings were government property, took them because he wanted money to fund a trip to a sunny beach. As it turns out, however, Morissette wished he didn't care so much, on reflection, about having fun in the sun. Indeed, he hates himself for loving the sun so much, and he's actually alienated from that part of himself. The endorsement theory would banish sun-loving from Morissette's self. As a want he wants not, the endorsement theory would consider it outside of, or external to, who Morissette "really" is. Consequently, if we judge the quality of Morissette's endorsed will at the moment he took the casings, we'd say his choice expressed no disregard for the law, inasmuch as Morissette wouldn't have stolen the casings if his endorsed will had been in charge of his choices.

According to another theory, which might be called the character theory, the self includes all the will's online motivational reasons at t=1, unless the reason is one that doesn't usually or characteristically motivate the accused's choices. A reason counts only if it usually or characteristically motivates the accused's choices. It excludes reasons that aren't part of his character. Judging the quality is his will is thus a matter of judging the quality of his will so circumscribed, pruned of uncharacteristic motivational reasons.

For example, suppose getting to a sunny beach once again motivated Morissette to steal the casings. As it happens, however, taking trips and relaxing on sunny beaches don't characteristically hold much allure for him.

[78] One caveat: The inclusive theory does exclude an online motivational reason if the actor experiences it as external to himself in a sense much deeper than any sense of externality associated with the endorsement and character theories. This deeper sense of externality is discussed in Chapter 5.

[79] *See* HARRY FRANKFURT, *Freedom of the Will and the Concept of a Person*, *in* THE IMPORTANCE OF WHAT WE CARE ABOUT: PHILOSOPHICAL ESSAYS 11, 20 (1988) ("[T]he statement that a person enjoys freedom of the will means . . . that he is free to want what he wants to want.").

He usually prefers clouds and museums. When those who know him best learn he stole casings to steal away to the beach, they're astonished. What, they wonder, got into him? Wanting sun and fun is completely out of character. That's not "really" who he is. Consequently, if we judge the quality of Morissette's characteristic will at the moment he took the casings, we'd say his choice expressed no disregard for the law, inasmuch as Morissette wouldn't have stolen the casings if his characteristic will had been in charge.[80]

The endorsement and character theories describe wills with integrity. According to the endorsement theory, the choices a person makes reflect his will—who he "really" is—only if those choices result from endorsed motivational reasons. An accused's choice to commit a crime reflects the quality of his will, but his will, under the endorsement theory, includes only those motivating reasons the accused would have endorsed, or wanted to have, at the time he made the choice. The endorsed will is thus, we might say, a will with synchronic integrity.

According to the character theory, the choices a person makes reflect his will—who he "really" is—only if those choices result from characteristic motivational reasons. An accused's choice to commit a crime reflects the quality of his will, but his will, under the character theory, includes only those motivating reasons that characteristically or typically motivate the accused's choices: reasons motivating his choices over a range of choices and over time. The characteristic will is thus, we might say, a will with diachronic integrity.

If the endorsement theory is true, then the state can't touch Morissette for theft unless he wanted to want to steal. If the character theory is true, then the state can't touch Morissette for theft unless he's a thief, inasmuch as thieving is something he does characteristically. For my money, neither theory provides a convincing account of the will upon which to rest the

[80] This move would transform a quality of will theory into a character theory. *See, e.g.*, Richard B. Brandt, *A Motivational Theory of Excuses in Criminal Law*, *in* Morality, Utilitarianism, and Rights 235, 235 (1992) ("[P]ersons who have unjustifiably broken valid law should be exempt from punishment unless their behavior is a result of some defect of standing motivation (one might say 'character' instead)." The character theory, as a theory of criminal culpability, is widely believed to be vulnerable on two fronts. One, the criminal law doesn't, as a matter of positive law, stay its hand just because a choice to commit a crime is "out of character," but character theories would presumably be forced to say it should. *See* Michael S. Moore, Placing Blame: A Theory of Criminal Law 578–84 (1997). Second, if in the end the criminal law punishes bad character, as the character theory implies, then punishment shouldn't depend, as it does, on the choice to commit a crime. Bad character should presumably be punished whether or not it's been expressed in a choice to commit a crime. *Id.* at 584–88. The quality of will theory avoids this problem because it grounds culpability in the quality of the actor's will expressed in his choice at the moment of choice.

rights theory of *mens rea*.[81] One finds it hard to believe that justice, beyond reasonable doubt, disables a democratic state from enacting rules ascribing culpability to those who commit crimes expressing insufficient concern for the law, just because those choices are uncharacteristic, or ones the accused wouldn't, on reflection, endorse.

An accused might bear *more* guilt for choosing to φ when he endorses the motivational reasons producing his choice, or when those reasons are for him completely in character. Conversely, he might bear *less* guilt for choosing to φ when he disavows the motivational reasons producing his choice, or when those reasons are for him completely out of character. The rights theory of *mens rea* leaves all that to the democratic process. It assumes that just because Morissette's will lacked integrity, synchronic or diachronic, when he chose to take the casings, doesn't mean the state exceeds its authority when it convicts him of theft, assuming his inclusive will was guilty at the moment he took them. The state doesn't act *ultra vires* just because Morissette wasn't, in one way or another, true to himself when he made off with the casings. A democratic state is nonetheless free find a choice made with *mens rea* more culpable or less culpable, as the case may be, pursuant to the endorsement or character theories of the will.

Time to take stock. The conventional theories of *actus reus* and *mens rea* are useful tools for parsing criminal statutes. They're not very good tools for identifying limits on the authority of a democratic state to establish the rules under which its citizens will be found criminally culpable, and thus eligible for state punishment. If we want *actus reus* and *mens rea* to serve as limits on the state's authority, we need a different theory. The rights theory of *actus reus* and *mens rea* is advanced in the hope of satisfying that need.

The requirements of *actus reus* and *mens rea* can be summarized pursuant to the rights theory as follows:

> If a person realized φ-ing was criminal, and if he chose to φ, his choice presumptively satisfies the *actus reus* requirement, unless he couldn't have chosen not to φ. If a person didn't realize φ-ing was criminal, and if he

[81] *See, e.g.*, Brink, *supra* note 56, at 365 ("[I]t is not clear that we should limit responsibility and blame to culpable states of mind that express an agent's stable character traits or dispositions she endorses, for then we could not hold agents responsible for wrong that were out of character or for familiar forms of weakness of will, in which the agent acts on desires she does not endorse. It seems more reasonable to identify an agent's quality of will with the kind of regard she has for the interests and rights of others.").

> chose to φ, his choice presumptively fails to satisfy the *actus reus* requirement, unless he could have realized φ-ing was criminal.
>
> If a person realized φ-ing was criminal, and if he chose to φ, his choice presumptively satisfies the *mens rea* requirement, unless it expresses sufficient concern for the law. If a person didn't realize φ-ing was criminal, and if he chose to φ, his choice presumptively fails to satisfy the *mens rea* requirement, unless his ignorance expresses insufficient concern for the law.

That lays the foundation, giving a rough understanding of what it might mean to say, as lawyers sometimes do, that criminal liability requires a guilty act and a guilty mind. Criminal law requires a guilty act and a guilty mind because a levy of criminal liability without them exceeds a democratic state's authority, and in particular its authority to impute culpability. The next two chapters add detail to the basics described in this chapter. Chapter 3 examines the *actus reus* and *mens rea* requirements when the accused realized he was committing a crime. Chapter 4 examines them when he didn't.

3
Knowledge

On January 29, 1970, Officers Daly and Larman of the Metropolitan Police Department executed a search warrant for two rooms in the Warren Hotel, located in northwest Washington, D.C.[1] The rooms, according to an informant, were being used to cut heroin. Officer Daly knocked on the door to one of the rooms and announced his purpose. When no one answered, he broke it down. Inside was Raymond Moore, and next to him, lying on the bed, were sixty-seven capsules filled with cut heroin.[2] Another fifty were in his pocket.[3]

Moore was arrested, tried, and convicted on two counts of violating 26 U.S.C. § 4704(a), and two counts of violating 21 U.S.C. § 174, both of which criminalized heroin possession.[4] He was sentenced to two and six years, respectively, on the first two counts, and six years on the other two, the terms to run concurrently. Moore appealed.

He didn't deny having possessed heroin. The state, he admitted, had proven the elements of the crimes charged. The problem, he claimed, was that he wasn't in the habit of possessing heroin for the fun of it. He was an addict, and his habit of possessing heroin was a habit he was powerless to resist. "[H]is conviction was improper," he argued, "because he [had] . . . an overpowering need to use heroin and should not, therefore, be held responsible for being in possession of the drug."[5] In other words, he couldn't help it, and if he couldn't help it, he shouldn't be punished for it. Being powerless to conform to the law should be a defense to a possession charge, Moore argued, under both the common law and the Constitution.

[1] States v. Moore, 486 F.2d 1139, 1141 (D.C. Cir. 1973) (en banc) (opinion of Wilkey, J.).

[2] *Id.*

[3] *Id.* at 1210 (Wright, J., dissenting).

[4] The first statute was known as the Harrison Narcotics Act; the second as the Jones-Miller Act. Neither made simple possession itself a crime, but possession was usually enough to convict under both. By the time Moore's appeal reached the D.C. Circuit, the Comprehensive Drug Abuse Prevention and Control Act of 1970 had replaced both Acts. *See id. at* 1211 & nn.5 & 6.

[5] *Id.* at 1141 (opinion of Wilkey, J.).

Guilty Acts, Guilty Minds. Stephen P. Garvey, Oxford University Press (2020). © Oxford University Press.
DOI: 10.1093/oso/9780190924324.001.0001

In a short *per curiam* opinion, the *en banc* D.C. Court of Appeals affirmed Moore's convictions. The court was badly divided: its multiple opinions, beyond the short *per curiam*, filled over one hundred pages in the *Federal Reporter*. Writing for one group,[6] Judge Wilkey rejected Moore's arguments. As for the common law, recognizing the defense Moore requested would, according to the Wilkey contingent, be ill-advised.[7] Prudence dictated leaving that decision to Congress.[8] As for the Constitution, Judge Wilkey read the relevant Supreme Court precedents more narrowly than did Moore.[9] "There is definitely no Supreme Court holding," he said, to the effect that "it was not criminal to give in to the irresistible compulsions of a 'disease.'"[10]

Judge Wright, writing for another group, disagreed. The "imposition of criminal liability on the non-trafficking addict possessor is," he wrote, "contrary to our historic common law traditions of criminal responsibility."[11] He also read the Court's constitutional precedents more broadly than did Judge Wilkey. They "seem[ed]," he wrote, "to stand for the proposition that an addict cannot constitutionally be subject to criminal process in conduct which is itself inherent in the disease of addiction."[12] Respect for the common law, coupled with the need to read statutes to avoid conflicts with the Constitution, "strongly suggest[ed], if not compell[ed], a construction of the federal narcotics statutes which would avoid inflicting criminal liability upon [a] non-trafficking addict possessor."[13]

The judges in *Moore* were trying to figure out what the law required, circa 1973. The task at hand is to figure out, whatever the law then or now, if the

[6] Judges MacKinnon and Robb joined Judge Wilkey's opinion, while Judges Leventhal and McGowan, writing separately, concurred in affirming all of Moore's convictions. Judges Tam and Robinson, together with Chief Judge Bazelon, joined Judge Wright's dissenting opinion. *See id.* at 1140 (per curiam).

[7] Judge Wilkey saw no principled way to limit the defense Moore sought to crimes of possession, believing its logic would extend to any crime Moore was powerless not to commit, up to and including, for example, robbing a bank for drug money. This conclusion appears, in Judge Wilkey's mind, to have been a *reductio ad absurdum*. *See id.* at 1146 (opinion of Wilkey, J.). The dissent would have limited the defense to possession offenses, but that, so far as Judge Wilkey was concerned, would have been arbitrary and unprincipled. *See id.* Chief Judge Bazelon, in contrast, saw no *reductio*. *See id.* at 1260 (Bazelon, C.J., concurring in part and dissenting in part).

[8] *See id.* at 1148 (opinion of Wilkey, J.). Judge MacKinnon agreed. *See id.* at 1206 (opinion of MacKinnon, J.) ("If a change is to be made in the handling of narcotics it must come from Congress.").

[9] The two precedents were *Powell v. Texas*, 392 U.S. 514 (1968), discussed in Chapter 2, and *Robinson v. California*, 370 U.S. 660 (1962). For an in-depth discussion of *Robinson*, see Erik Luna, *The Story of* Robinson: *From Revolutionary Constitutional Doctrine to Modest Ban on Status Crimes*, *in* Criminal Law Stories 48 (Donna Coker & Robert Weisberg eds., 2013).

[10] 486 F.2d at 1150 (opinion of Wilkey, J.).

[11] *Id.* at 1249 (Wright, J., dissenting).

[12] *Id.* at 1239.

[13] *Id.* at 1250.

United States acted *ultra vires*, beyond its legitimate authority, when it found Moore guilty and punished him for possession. Moore's plea was based on compulsion, and if he truly was compelled, if he truly did lack the capacity to have chosen otherwise, punishing him for possession would, we now know, constitute a trespass on the *actus reus* requirement: If Moore was compelled, his act wasn't guilty.

Moore might have entered a different plea, not about compulsion, but about coercion. He might have claimed, not that his inner demons compelled him to possess, but that they coerced him to do so. A choice to commit a crime, like possessing heroin, is coerced if, under the circumstances, it expressed no lack of sufficient concern for the law, and it would express no such lack of concern if a law-abiding citizen in the accused's situation would have made the same choice. If Moore's choice to possess heroin was truly coerced, then finding him guilty and punishing him for possession would, we now know, constitute a trespass on the *mens rea* requirement: If Moore was coerced, his mind wasn't guilty.

If Moore's choice to possess heroin in the Warren Hotel wasn't guilty, for lack of *actus reus* or *mens rea*, then he should be immune to criminal liability. The authority of the United States to ascribe culpability to his choice would be disabled: It would have no power to enact rules under which a jury would be obligated to find Moore culpable. That assumes the only choice relevant to Moore's liability was his choice to possess heroin in the room of the Warren Hotel, which isn't very realistic. Moore doubtless made a number of other choices, prior to his choice to possess, which one might fairly think should have some bearing on his liability for possession.

For example, focusing only on what happened in the hotel room, would, as Judge Wilkey said, "neglect[] the choice that each addict [including Moore] makes *at the start* as to whether or not he is going to take narcotics and run the risk of becoming addicted to them."[14] The general point behind Wiley's observation is that even if Moore's choice at the hotel was guilt-free, some prior choice or choices resulting in that choice might not have been. If so, then liability for the guilt-free choice in the hotel might, under the right circumstances, be fairly traced back in time to a prior guilty one. Thus, at the end of the day, maybe the United States did have authority to assign guilt to Moore's choice to possess, based on some earlier choice.

[14] *Id.* at 1151 (opinion of Wilkey, J.).

We'll return to that possibility later. Our immediate aim is to add more detail to the *actus reus* and *mens rea* requirements at t=1, the moment in time, or time over which, the crime charged was committed, starting with the *actus reus* requirement, keeping in mind that the analysis is for now limited to defendants who knew they were committing a crime.

Actus Reus

The *actus reus* requirement, according to the rights theory, renders a democratic state helpless to ascribe guilt to someone who chooses to φ, and who realized φ-ing was a crime, if at the time he lacked the capacity to choose otherwise. If Moore was powerless to choose not to possess heroin in the Warren Hotel, then his choice to possess it wasn't guilty. We need now to say more about what must be true of someone before it can be said that he lacked the capacity to choose not to φ at t=1. How can we tell if Moore, as he sat there in the Warren Hotel staring at the heroin, lacked the capacity to leave it alone?

The Capacity to Choose Otherwise

When we choose to do something at t=1, the proximate cause of our choice is the vector sum of the motivational reasons populating our conative will at that moment. Every choice we make results from, and in that sense reflects or expresses, the balance of our motivational reasons at the time we choose. Our conative will is the arena in which competing motivational reasons gather to square off against one another, and the executive will is the mechanism through which the winner gets transformed into choices and intentions.

Once again, ΣMR_{φ} stands for all the motivational reasons at t=1 disposing a person to φ, and $\Sigma MR_{\sim\varphi}$ for all the motivational reasons disposing him not to φ. If the sum of his motivational reasons in favor of φ-ing is greater than the sum of his motivational reasons against φ-ing, such that $\Sigma MR_{\varphi} > \Sigma MR_{\sim\varphi}$, then if the executive will makes any choice, or forms any intent, the choice it makes, or the intent it forms, will be the choice or intent to φ. When someone chooses to φ, $\Sigma MR_{\varphi} > \Sigma MR_{\sim\varphi}$; otherwise, he would've chosen to do something other than φ. But if, at t=1, the balance of someone's motivational reasons favors φ-ing, such that he necessarily chooses to φ, what does it mean to say he could, at t=1, have chosen to do something other than φ?

History offers three answers: libertarianism, hard determinism, and compatibilism.[15] The answer each provides responds in one way or another to an alleged metaphysical truth: Every event in the world necessarily results from past events, combined with the laws of nature. That alleged truth is the thesis of determinism: Everything that happens in the world necessarily results from what happened before, together with the causal laws linking those events together. Determinism leaves nothing to chance. Holding fixed the state of the world at one moment, the laws of nature guarantee what the state of the world will be at the next.

The first answer to our question—what it means to say of someone that he could have chosen otherwise—comes from libertarianism. Libertarianism comes in different forms, many of which are exceptionally subtle, but each in the end represents an attempt to vindicate the thesis that we can indeed choose otherwise, which would mean that determinism, insofar as it denies that we can ever choose otherwise, is false. An agent who's balance of motivational reasons at t=1 is such that $\Sigma MR_{\varphi} > \Sigma MR_{\sim\varphi}$, and who would thus, if determinism were true, necessarily choose to φ, can nonetheless, libertarianism tells us, chose not to φ, despite the fact that the balance of his motivational reasons at t=1 tipped in favor of φ-ing. The question is how that can be. How can an agent choose not to φ when *ex hypothesi* he's most motivated to choose to φ?

One prominent libertarian theory imagines that the conative will is, as we have so far portrayed it, a stage on which different motivational reasons gather to compete, with the victor telling the executive will what to do. Nonetheless, the executive will, with which the agent himself is identified, has a mind of its own, so to speak. Human agents have a contra-causal power, residing in their executive will, to choose not to φ even when the balance of the motivational reasons within their conative will favors φ-ing. All events in the world are necessarily causally determined, as determinism says, with one exception: human choices. Everything is necessarily determined—except the will (and the agent himself insofar as he is identified with his will) and

[15] On free will more generally, and on its relationship to moral responsibility, see, for example, ROBERT KANE, A CONTEMPORARY INTRODUCTION TO FREE WILL (2005); KEVIN TIMPE, FREE WILL: SOURCEHOOD AND ITS ALTERNATIVES (2d ed. 2013); ROUTLEDGE COMPANION TO FREE WILL (Kevin Timpe et al. eds., 2017) [hereinafter ROUTLEDGE COMPANION]; THE OXFORD HANDBOOK ON FREE WILL (Robert Kane ed., 2002); THE OXFORD HANDBOOK ON FREE WILL (2d ed., Robert Kane ed., 2011); Timothy O'Connor, *Free Will*, STAN. ENCYCLOPEDIA PHIL. (2016); Neil Levy & Michael McKenna, *Recent Work on Free Will and Moral Responsibility*, 4 PHIL. COMPASS 96 (2009).

the choices it (he) makes. Libertarianism thus portrays the will's (agent's) freedom (or liberty) and determinism as incompatible. The will prevails.

That's all well and good, assuming the will has the divine metaphysical power libertarianism says it has. A modest libertarian might believe, not that we can always choose otherwise, but only that we sometimes can. If that's so, if we can sometimes choose otherwise, but not always, more will need to be said about the conditions under which we can and those under which we can't. Is our contra-causal power somehow disabled, for example, in the face of intense craving, such as that associated with addiction? A bold libertarian, in contrast, might believe that we can, thanks to the will's *sui generis* power, always choose otherwise. Yet if that's so, then libertarianism presumably can't supply what the *actus reus* requirement needs.[16] The *actus reus* requirement presupposes that at least sometimes we can't choose otherwise, whereas the bold libertarian says we always can. Rather than dive any deeper into the challenging, unfamiliar, and controversial metaphysics on which libertarianism rests, we'll instead simply reserve judgment, set libertarianism aside, and move onto the next theory.

Like libertarianism, hard determinism portrays freedom and determinism as incompatible. Unlike libertarians, who believe the will has contra-causal power and can thus (at least sometimes) defeat determinism, hard determinists don't help themselves to a will with such divine power. On the contrary, they believe the will is hostage to causation, just like everything else. Human choices are events in the world just like any other event, and just as causally determined. If $\Sigma MR_{\varphi} > \Sigma MR_{\sim\varphi}$, then the actor will necessarily choose to φ, and if $\Sigma MR_{\varphi} < \Sigma MR_{\sim\varphi}$, then the actor will necessarily choose not to φ. Nothing can defeat determinism, not even the will, and thus no one has the capacity to choose otherwise.[17] Determinism prevails.

[16] *See* Michael S. Moore, *Compatibilism(s) for Neuroscientists*, *in* Law and the Philosophy of Action 1, 9 (Enrique Villanueva ed., 2014) ("The problem is that attributing contra-causal freedom to human choice as such is too undiscriminating: for if human choices as such is necessarily free, then compelled and ignorant choices are also free, and there are no excuses."). Moore examines several proposals to place "some restrictions on libertarian metaphysics" in order to enable it to "distinguish those who are excused from those who are not," *id.* at 10, but finds none of them persuasive.

[17] Hard determinism is sometimes called "leeway incompatibilism," in contrast to what's often called "source incompatibilism." *See, e.g.*, Kevin Timpe, *Leeway v. Sourcehood Conceptions of Free Will*, *in* Routledge Companion, *supra* note 15, at 213. Hard determinists (leeway incompatibilists) believe the freedom needed for responsibility requires the capacity to choose otherwise, deny anyone has that capacity, and thus conclude no one is ever responsible for his choices. Source incompatibilists, in contrast, believe the freedom needed for responsibility requires us in some sense to be the ultimate source of what causes us to choose as we do, deny anyone is an ultimate source, and thus conclude no one is ever responsible for her choices. Source incompatibilism will be discussed in Chapter 6.

If hard determinism is true, if no one ever has the capacity to choose otherwise, then all choices will necessarily be guilt-free, which would mean no state ever has authority to punish anyone. The *actus reus* requirement would end up eliminating, not just limiting, state authority to ascribe culpability. Any rule attaching culpability to a choice to φ would be *ultra vires*, and the state would have no business being in the business of punishing. That might be music to the ears of anyone dubious about the entire enterprise of state punishment, but not if you come, not to bury state punishment, but to identify limits on the state's authority to impose it. So let's put hard determinism aside too, and turn to the final theory.

Unlike bold libertarianism, which says we can always choose otherwise, and hard determinism, which says we never can, compatibilism says we sometimes can and sometimes can't.[18] Compatibilism affirms that determinism and the capacity to choose otherwise are, as its name implies, compatible: Determinism is true, but that doesn't mean we always lack the capacity to choose otherwise, or at least it doesn't mean we have no way of making sense, in the face of determinism, of propositions asserting that someone had or didn't have the capacity to choose otherwise than he actually did.

When we say an actor could have chosen otherwise than he actually did, we're not, according to the compatibilist, saying he could have chosen otherwise in the libertarian sense. We're not saying he could have chosen otherwise because, as the libertarian says, he as a contra-causal power enabling him to so choose. He can't choose otherwise in that sense, not if determinism is true and the will, like everything else, is at the mercy of causation. Instead, when we say an actor could have chosen otherwise in the actual world, we should be understood to mean he could have chosen otherwise if, contrary to fact, he would have chosen otherwise if θ, where θ stands for some difference between the actual world, in which the actor chose to φ, and some possible or counterfactual world, in which θ is true and the actor chooses not to φ.[19]

[18] For a recent overview of compatibilism, see Michael McKenna & D. Justin Coates, *Compatibilism*, Stan. Encyclopedia Phil. (2016).

[19] Michael S. Moore, *The Neuroscience of Volitional Excuse*, *in* Philosophical Foundations of Law and Neuroscience 179, 209 (Dennis Patterson & Michael S. Pardo eds., 2016) ("[C]apacity statements are disguised counterfactuals *of some form*.") [hereinafter Moore, *Volitional Excuse*]; Michael S. Moore, *Compatibilism(s) for Neuroscientists*, *in* Law and the Philosophy of Action 1, 29 (Enrique Villanueva ed., 2014) ("[T]he seemingly categorical statement that one could have done otherwise is always elliptical for some conditional statement.") [hereinafter Moore, *Compatibilism(s)*]. For recent reviews of the philosophical literature on capacities or abilities to act, see Randolph Clarke, *Abilities to Act*, 10 Phil. Compass 893 (2015), and for abilities generally, see John Maier, *Abilities*, Stan. Encyclopedia Phil. (2014).

In the actual world, if $\Sigma MR_{\varphi} > \Sigma MR_{\sim\varphi}$, the actor will, given the truth of determinism, choose to φ. In order to test someone's capacity to choose not to φ, the compatibilist asks us to imagine a possible world, which is like the actual world in every way except for the change θ introduces, and where θ gives the actor a motivational reason, not present in the actual world, not to φ at *t*=1.

According to compatibilism, if an actor would have chosen not to φ in the possible world (with change θ), then we'd say he could have chosen not to φ in the actual world in which he φ'ed. Thus, his choice to φ in the actual world wasn't compelled. On the other hand, if the actor would have chosen to φ in the possible world (despite change θ), then we'd say he couldn't have chosen not to φ in the actual world in which he φ'ed. Thus, his choice in the actual world was compelled. Or, as it might otherwise be put, he chose under compulsion, or the desires (motivational reasons) causing him to choose to φ were to him irresistible. What, then, is θ?

The usual, though vague, answer is something quite unpleasant. We're asked to imagine if someone would have chosen to φ if θ, where θ is something pretty awful. If he would still have chosen to φ, and thereby suffer θ, then we'd say his choice was compelled; otherwise, we'd say it was free, or at least not compelled. The hard part, of course, is to say what θ is. How bad must θ be? How bad must the consequences of choosing to φ in the imagined world be, such that if the actor would have chosen to φ, and thereby endure θ, we'd be prepared to say he lacked the capacity to choose otherwise, thereby making his real-world choice to φ guilt-free, and placing him, pursuant to the *actus reus* requirement, beyond the state's authority to punish?

One answer takes a page from Kant. "Suppose," Kant said, "that someone says his lust is irresistible when the desired object and opportunity are present. Ask him whether he would not control his passion if, in front of the

We obviously can't put someone into an imagined possible world and watch how he behaves there. The next best thing is to ask how he reacted in the past in different circumstances in the actual world as alike as possible to those in the imagined world, and then make an educated guess as to how he would react in the imagined world. *See, e.g.*, Stephen J. Morse, *Moore on the Mind*, *in* LEGAL, MORAL, AND METAPHYSICAL TRUTHS: THE PHILOSOPHY OF MICHAEL S. MOORE 231, 246 (Kimberly Kessler Ferzan & Stephen J. Morse eds., 2016) ("The metaphysics of counterfactuals will not help with the practical determination that must be made. There will be no easy answers in many cases, but all one can do is attend to the relevant history and compare it to the present facts and circumstances."); Michael Smith, *Responsibility and Self-Control*, *in* RELATING TO RESPONSIBILITY 1, 17 (Peter Cane & John Gardner eds., 2001) ("Regular patterns in actuality are, quite in general, what provide us with such evidence as we have for the similarities and differences that obtain between the actual world and other possible worlds.").

house where he has this opportunity, a gallows were erected on which he would be hanged immediately after gratifying his lust. We do not have to guess very long what his answer would be."[20] For Kant, then, θ was instant death at the end of a rope.

That's one possible value for θ, but it hasn't had many contemporary takers. According to one criminal law theorist not known for being squeamish, Kant's test "give[s] us [a] clear line, but it . . . draw[s] a harsh border. One could imagine a morality this harsh, fitting perhaps for a race of beings made of sterner stuff than are we."[21] According to another, "[A]ll agents with a control problem would manage to resist offending if they were threatened with instant death . . . , [but n]o just legal regime would be so unforgiving."[22] If these theorists are right, Kant's theory of θ sets the bar too high.

But how high is too high? Suppose Kant's proposal for drawing the line between compelled and uncompelled choice was put to the reasonable doubt test. Would it pass? For now, I'll just assume it would, in keeping with those theorists, mentioned immediately above, who believe Kant's test presupposes a "morality . . . . fitting . . . . for a race of beings made of sterner stuff than are we," and no "just" legal regime would be so "unforgiving." If all that's true, it lends at least some support to the idea that Kant's test would pass the reasonable doubt test. If so, the question becomes: Can we come up with another test, which also passes the reasonable doubt test, but that sets a limit short of Kant's immediate-death test, thereby circumscribing even further the scope of a democratic state's authority to ascribe guilt?

[20] Immanuel Kant, Critique of Practical Reason 30 (Lewis White Beck trans., 1985) (1788). Anthony Kenny quotes a Canadian judge who expresses Kantian sympathies when he said: "If you cannot resist an impulse in any other way, we will hang a rope in front of your eyes, and perhaps that will help." Anthony Kenny, Freewill and Responsibility 43 (1978). The quote comes from Justice Riddell, of the Ontario Supreme Court, writing in 1908, in *R. v. Creighton*, (1908) 14 CCC 349, 349 (Can. Ont. Sup. Ct.).

[21] Moore, *Volitional Excuse, supra* note 19, at 215.

[22] Morse, *supra* note 19, at 245. Like-minded sentiments are expressed in John Martin Fischer, *Guidance Control, in* Deep Control: Essays on Free Will and Value 186, 188–92 (2012) (expressing sympathy for the view that someone suffering from agoraphobia is not responsible for, say, not attending his daughter's wedding, if he would leave his home to attend the wedding only if the home was on fire); Alfred R. Mele, Autonomous Agents: From Self-Control to Autonomy 154 (2001) (noting that "many people" are willing to attribute "irresistible desires" even when they can imagine "extreme conditions" in which the actor would have chosen otherwise); Alfred R. Mele, *Akratics and Addicts*, 39 Am. Phil. Q. 153, 163 (2002) ("[A]n agent's desire to A . . . , may properly count as irresistible *even if* he would successfully resist it in some extreme counterfactual scenarios.") (emphasis added).

The Stephen Test

Another proposal turns, not to Kant, but to the eminent Victorian criminal lawyer and judge, Sir James Fitzjames Stephen.[23] Stephen didn't draw the line between compelled and uncompelled choice, as did Kant, with a one-size-fits-all θ, like the gallows. Instead, he proposed that a jury, asked to decide "whether a man could control his actions or not," should be asked: Was "the impulse to commit a crime so violent that the offender would not be prevented from doing the act by knowing that the *greatest punishment permitted by law* for the offence would be instantly inflicted[?]"[24]

Call this the *Stephen test.* According to Stephen, θ should be the instant infliction, not of death, but of the "greatest punishment permitted by law for the offence." Under this test, if an accused would have chosen to φ even if he believed he'd immediately be subject to the greatest punishment the law permitted for φ-ing, then, all else being equal, we should we say he lacked the capacity to choose otherwise. If he passes the test, such that he would've chosen to φ despite θ, we'd say, all else being equal, that he lacked the capacity to choose otherwise, thus making his choice to φ guilt-free. If the state nonetheless imputed culpability to his choice, it would violate the *actus reus* requirement and so exceed the limits of its legitimate authority.

Although Stephen talks about the greatest punishment the law *permits*, we'll amend him to mean, not the greatest punishment the law in fact permits, but instead the greatest punishment it could permit, i.e., the greatest punishment the state could legitimately impose, even if it actually imposes something less. So construed, the Stephen test defines one limit on the state's authority to punish in terms of another. As mentioned in Chapter 1, three limits exist on a democracy's authority to define the conditions under which its citizens can be punished for having committed a crime. According to the third, the state lacks the authority to impose any punishment grossly disproportionate to the crime.

The *actus reus* requirement is part of the second limit, which circumscribes the state's authority to ascribe culpability. The Stephen test (as amended) defines part of the second limit (the *actus reus* requirement applied to

[23] For helpful introductions to Stephen's philosophy, in connection with the criminal law, see generally Marc O. DeGirolami, *James Fitzjames Stephen: The Punishment Jurist*, *in* Foundational Texts in Modern Criminal Law 183 (Markus D. Dubber ed., 2014); Stephen J. Morse, *Thoroughly Modern: Sir James Fitzjames Stephen on Criminal Responsibility*, 5 Ohio St. J. Crim. L. 505 (2008).

[24] 2 Sir James Fitzjames Stephen, A History of the Criminal Law of England 171 (1883) (emphasis added).

defendants who realize they're committing a crime) in terms of the third (the limit on grossly disproportionate punishments). Thus, when an actor realizes φ-ing is a crime, his choice to φ is guilty unless he lacked the capacity to have chosen otherwise, and (pursuant to the Stephen test) he lacked the capacity to have chosen otherwise if, all else being equal, he would've chosen to φ despite believing he'd immediately suffer a punishment just shy of being grossly disproportionate.[25] We'll address the important *ceteris paribus* proviso in a moment, which will in turn require us to modify this statement of the Stephen test, but what we have so far should suffice for now.

The dissenting judges in *Moore* were sympathetic to Moore's predicament. For Moore to stay away from heroin must, they imagined, have been excruciating for him. Although thus inclined to find some way to avoid affirming his punishment for possession, they had a problem. If Moore really was powerless not to possess heroin, as the dissenters believed he might well have been, was he likewise powerless not to rob and steal in order to get the money he'd need to purchase and possess it? As Judge Wilkey, for the less-sympathetic majority, put it:

> If it is the absence of free will [i.e., the capacity to choose otherwise] which excuses the mere possessor-acquirer, the more desperate bank robber for drug money has an even more demonstrable lack of free will and derived from precisely the same factor as [Moore] claims should excuse the mere possessor.[26]

That conclusion, Judge Wilkey thought, was absurd. The dissenters likewise worried about the prospect of letting addicted bank robbers off the hook.[27] All they managed to say in reply, however, was that Congress didn't want

[25] The Stephen test has the virtue of making an accused's capacity not to φ depend on what φ was. An accused's capacity not to φ (and thereby conform to the law) will depend on what φ was, because under the Stephen test, the value of θ (the greatest punishment the state could legitimately impose for φ-ing) will depend on the value of φ (the crime the accused committed). As φ increases (the crime gets more serious), θ increases (the punishment gets more severe). Unfortunately, the test also has the vice of making one relatively indeterminate limit on state authority (*actus reus*) depend on another relatively indeterminate limit (the ban on grossly disproportionate punishments).

[26] United States v. Moore, 486 F.2d 1139, 1146 (D.C. Cir. 1973) (en banc) (opinion of Wilkey, J.).

[27] *Id.* at 1255 (opinion of Wright, J.) ("Perhaps the most troublesome question arising out of recognition of the addiction defense I suggest is whether it should be limited only to those acts—such as mere possession for use—which are inherent in the disease itself."). Chief Judge Bazelon was alone in biting the bullet. *Id.* at 1260 (Bazelon, C.J., concurring in part and dissenting in part) ("I would also permit a jury to consider addiction as a defense to a charge of, for example, armed robbery or trafficking in drugs, to determine whether the defendant was under such duress or compulsion, because of his addiction, that he was unable to conform his conduct to the requirements of the law.").

to excuse addicts for crimes other than possession,[28] nor had the Supreme Court decided to extend an Eighth Amendment ban on punishing addicts beyond the crime of possession.[29] In other words, the dissent offered no principled way to resist Wilkey's *reductio*, as Judge Wilkey was quick to point out.

Moore's capacity to conform to the law, both sides seemed to assume, was all or nothing, no matter what crime he was supposedly powerless not to commit, be it heroin possession, or "bank robberies, street muggings, [or] burglaries."[30] The Stephen test avoids Wilkey's *reductio*, insofar as it couples θ to the punishment a state can legitimately impose, and the punishment a state can legitimately impose depends on the crime.[31] If Moore claimed he was compelled to rob in order to service his addiction, the Stephen test would ask if he would've robbed even if that meant θ, where θ is the greatest punishment the state could legitimately impose for robbery. If he claimed to have been compelled to possess, the test would ask if he would've grabbed the heroin even if that meant the greatest punishment the state could legitimately impose for possession, and so on.

The Stephen test sets a floor. If someone passes the test, then, subject to the proviso below, he was powerless not to φ, and the *actus reus* requirement disables the state's power to declare him culpable. It doesn't set a ceiling. For example, suppose you think the Stephen test, as a matter of justice, is still too unforgiving. Suppose you believe θ should be half the punishment the state is legitimately permitted to impose. If so, then you'd say an accused lacked the capacity not to φ, or his capacity not to φ was diminished, if he would have chosen to φ if faced with $\theta/2$, even if he would have chosen not to φ if faced with θ, as the Stephen test proposes.

If a democratic state wants to create such a defense to liability based on a more forgiving θ, nothing stands in its way. If it wants to call such a defense a lack of capacity defense, or diminished capacity defense, or partial capacity defense, or whatnot, that's fine too. Within the limits of its authority, a democratic state can create any defense it wants, through the usual democratic process. However, if any such proposal is advanced, not simply as a defense

[28] *Id.* at 1256 (opinion of Wright, J.).

[29] *Id.* at 1257.

[30] *Id.* at 1246–47 (opinion of Wilkey, J.).

[31] *See, e.g.*, Moore, *Compatibilism(s)*, *supra* note 19, at 34 ("How badly one has to want not to do something (for acts one did), or to do something (for omissions one didn't do), in order to be excused, should vary with the wrong being excused. As J.L. Austin once put it, it requires a better excuse to excuse stepping on a baby than it does to excuse stepping on a snail."); Moore, *Volitional Excuse*, *supra* note 19, at 184–85 (same).

the state chooses to afford through the exercise of its authority, but as a limit on its authority, then it will need to survive the reasonable doubt test.

We now turn to the proviso mentioned above. The Stephen test is advanced as a tool to sort those who couldn't have chosen not to φ, and who thus couldn't have chosen to conform to the law, from those who could have (but didn't). It purports to give us a test for incapacity, however indeterminate it may be when applied to the facts of a particular case. What the test leaves unexplained is how incapacity happens. It doesn't explain the folk psychology of incapacity, or the folk psychological mechanism underlying incapacity. It doesn't explain what happens in the mind of someone who passes the test and so couldn't have chosen otherwise.

Suppose Moore passed the test (as so far stated): He would've chosen to possess the heroin even if it meant immediately suffering the greatest punishment the United States could legitimately impose for heroin possession. Imagine we then just asked him, "At the time you took possession of the heroin, would you rather have not possessed it than to have to pay that price, or would you rather have possessed and paid?" He sincerely replies, "I'd rather not have possessed. I really, truly wanted to avoid the price a whole lot more than I wanted to possess." Nonetheless, when faced with the heroin, he took possession. If we take what he says at face value, that would mean he wanted not to φ more than he wanted to φ, but ended up choosing to φ. The problem is how to make sense of that. If he really wanted not to φ more than he wanted to φ, he would have chosen not to φ. Right?

Maybe not. If you'll indulge a campy analogy, one speculative possibility is what we'll dub the Hogwarts effect. Hogwarts, of course, is the name of the castle housing the School of Witchcraft and Wizardry, made famous in the Harry Potter books and films. In one of the final scenes of the last film, Hogwarts is under attack from Voldemort and his band of Death Eaters, who use their wands to attack the castle, hurling at it what look like magical cannonballs. But, at least initially, the cannonballs don't connect, never making contact with the target.[32] The school's defenders have used the Protego Maxima charm to erect a barrier around the castle, which the magical volleys of Voldemort and his henchman fail, at least for a while, to penetrate. The volleys don't make it through the barrier and so have no effect.

Sometimes, it appears, a motivating reason, in the form of desire, can erect a barrier around the conative will, like the barrier around Hogwarts.

[32] Harry Potter and the Deathly Hallows: Part 2 (Warner Bros. Pictures 2011).

In the film, the barrier prevented the magical cannonballs from reaching the castle. Something similar may happen to incapacitate the will. The desire to φ, such as the desire to use heroin, might somehow fashion a barrier around the conative will, preventing stronger countervailing motivational reasons (real or counterfactual) from reaching or penetrating it. As a result, those reasons, which would have caused the actor to choose not to φ, fail to compete head-to-head with the accused's reasons in favor of φ-ing. If they had competed, they would have won. But they didn't compete. Instead, the desire to φ shut them out, and so the reasons in favor of φ-ing won. That's the Hogwarts effect.[33]

Once we understand the Hogwarts effect, which forms the folk psychological mechanism underlying incapacitated wills, we need to refine the Stephen test. If someone would've chosen to φ even if threatened with the greatest punishment the law can legitimately mete out, immediately imposed, his choice might be due to the Hogwarts effect, but it might not. We can surely imagine cases in which an accused is threatened with the greatest punishment the law can legitimately dish out, the desire to avoid it competes with the accused's desire to φ, the desire to φ prevails, and the accused chooses to φ. If so, then the accused will choose to φ, not because the imagined countervailing reasons against φ-ing failed to compete with the actor's reasons favoring φ-ing, but rather because those reasons competed, but lost. The desire to φ never produced the Hogwarts effect.

Examples like this require restating the Stephen test as follows: An actor lacks the capacity to choose not to φ if his motivational reasons not to φ are stronger than his motivational reasons to φ, or would be stronger if he believed he'd immediately experience the greatest punishment the state could legitimately impose, but he nonetheless chooses to φ, or would have chosen to φ, because (due to the Hogwarts effect) his reasons not to φ fail to compete, or would fail to compete, with his reasons to φ.

[33] For thoughts along similar lines, see, for example, Moore, *Volitional Excuse, supra* note 19, at 210 ("[T]he alien nature of the tempting desire [e.g., the desire for heroin] *refuses integration* enough to be balanced off against the controlling desire [i.e., the desire not to commit the crime of heroin possession, so that] . . . the tempting desire might cause behavior irrespective of the heightened strength of the controlling desire.") (emphasis added); Michael S. Moore, *Addiction and Responsibility, in* The Palgrave Handbook of Applied Ethics and the Criminal Law 10, 29 (Larry Alexander & Kimberly Kessler Ferzan eds., 2019) ("[C]ravings . . . drive[] out focus on other states . . . and thus *prevent[] them from being . . . integrated* into overall desires.") (emphasis added); Morse, *supra* note 19, at 244–45 ("Generically, the 'ego-alienated' agent's desires [e.g., the desire for heroin] are *sealed off from* the reasons-responsive self.") (emphasis added).

Insanity

A criminal lawyer might, around now, be wondering about insanity. According to the *actus reus* requirement, when an accused realizes he's committing a crime, but chooses to commit it anyway, his act is guilty unless he could've chosen otherwise, unless, in other words, he lacked the capacity to conform to the law, where the Stephen test, as stated immediately above, supplies the test for incapacity. The Stephen test, a criminal lawyer might remark, sounds a lot like a well-known test for insanity, which once enjoyed more popularity than it does now, according to which an accused is insane if, as a result of mental disease or defect, he lacked the capacity (or substantial capacity) to conform to the law. A criminal lawyer might therefore wonder if the *actus reus* requirement is nothing more than insanity in disguise.

As a matter of fact, Stephen offered his test, not as an all-purpose test for incapacity, but as a test for insanity. English law in Stephen's time (and still today) followed the rule or rules derived from *M'Naghten's Case*,[34] according to which (taking more-than-considerable liberties with the actual language in the case) an accused is insane if, as a result of mental disease or defect, he lacked the capacity to realize he was committing a crime.[35] On its face, *M'Naghten* said nothing about being able to conform to the law. Stephen nonetheless believed the law should embrace what would come to be known as the "irresistible impulse" test of insanity, according to which a person is insane if, as a result of mental disease or defect, he lacked the capacity to conform to the law.[36]

[34] M'Naghten's Case, 8 Eng. Rep. 718 (1843).

[35] The language in the text is actually closer to Model Penal Code § 4.01(1) than to the passage from *M'Naghten's Case* most often cited as stating its test for insanity. For present purposes, however, we can safely set aside questions about *M'Naghten*'s original meaning, though we'll touch on some of those questions briefly in Chapter 5. For more on *M'Naghten's Case* and what it stands for, see Stephen P. Garvey, *Insanity*, *in* The Palgrave Handbook of Applied Ethics and the Criminal Law 385 (Larry Alexander & Kimberly Kessler Ferzan eds., 2019).

[36] Based on some of his remarks in *A History of the Criminal Law of England*, it might be thought that Stephen intended his proposed test as a supplement or addition to the rule or rules set forth in *M'Naghten's Case*, but that's probably not how Stephen himself saw it. For example, when the Criminal Code Commission rejected his proposed test, Stephen reacted with indifference: "I have no very strong opinion on the subject," he wrote. "I should be fully satisfied with the insertion in the Code of 'knowledge that an act is wrong' as the best test of responsibility." Stephen had no "strong opinion" because he thought his proposed test and *M'Naghten's Case*, interpreted and understood as he believed it should have been, would produce the same result. As he put it: "It is as true that a man who cannot control himself does not know the nature of his acts as that a man who does not know the nature of his acts is incapable of self-control." 2 Stephen, *supra* note 24, at 171. Unfortunately, Stephen didn't elaborate any further on what he meant.

Insanity also cropped up in *Moore*. Judge Wright, for the dissenters, said: "I believe the development of the common law . . . has reached a new principle: A drug addict who, by reason of his use of drugs, lacks substantial capacity to conform his conduct to the requirements of the law should not be held criminally liable for mere possession."[37] At the time, a person was insane, under D.C. Circuit precedent, if, among other things, he lacked, as a result of mental disease or defect, substantial capacity to conform his conduct to the requirements of the law. The resemblance between Judge Wright's new-found principle and insanity is hard to miss. Judge MacKinnon, for one, didn't miss it. Judge Wright's newly discovered defense was, according to Judge MacKinnon, an insanity defense without a mental disease or defect requirement, which he saw as the "substantial equivalent of insanity without proof of insanity."[38]

One obvious reply to MacKinnon would be to observe that addiction is a mental disease or defect. The latest version of the *Diagnostic and Statistical Manual of Mental Disorders* recognizes, for example, a wide range of "substance-related disorders" as diagnostic categories.[39] That's true, but what makes something a "mental disease or defect" for purposes of the insanity defense is, the courts say, for the law, not the psychiatric profession, to decide, and when pressed, the courts have said addiction, standing alone, is not a mental disease or defect within the meaning of the insanity defense.[40] Unfortunately, they don't say why.[41] Indeed, they say very little about what

[37] United States v. Moore, 486 F.2d 1139, 1209 (D.C. Cir. 1973) (en banc) (Wright, J., dissenting).

[38] *Id.* at 1207 (opinion of MacKinnon, J.).

[39] *See* Am. Psychiatric Ass'n, Diagnostic and Statistical Manual of Mental Disorders 483–589 (5th ed. 2013).

[40] *See, e.g.*, United States v. Lyons, 731 F.2d 243, 245 (5th Cir. 1984) (en banc) ("Today the great weight of legal authority clearly supports the view that evidence of mere narcotics addiction, standing alone and without other physiological or psychological involvement, raises no issue of such a mental defect or disease as can serve as a basis for the insanity defense."). Michigan statutory law defines "mental illness," for the purposes of its insanity test as a "substantial disorder of thought or mood that significantly impairs judgment, behavior, capacity to recognize reality, or ability to cope with the ordinary demands of life." *See* Mich. Comp. Laws §§ 768.21a(1) & 330.1400(g). Insofar as that definition could encompass "virtually any mental condition," Christopher Slobogin, Minding Justice: Laws That Deprive People with Mental Disability of Life and Liberty 252 (2006), it would seem in effect to read the "mental disease or defect" limitation out of the definition of insanity altogether.

[41] What Abraham Goldstein said over fifty years ago, albeit in connection with the *M'Naghten* Rule, and not the irresistible impulse test, appears true today:

> There has been almost no judicial definition of mental disease in cases concerned with the *M'Naghten* rule. The reason commonly advanced is that the more detailed part of the rule—dealing with knowledge—makes it plain that only a limited number of psychoses and the most extreme forms of mental defect can quality. In any event, the words are usually presented, *without explanation*, as part of the charge to the jury.

Abraham S. Goldstein, The Insanity Defense 47–48 (1967) (emphasis added).

makes *any* condition a mental disease or defect and another not. Nor do penal codes.

The mystery only deepens. Setting aside the law's failure to say what makes for a mental disease or defect, one might ask why it insists on a mental disease or defect in the first place. As already mentioned, at the time Moore was decided the law of the D.C. Circuit provided that an accused was insane at the time of the crime if he was powerlessness or unable to conform to the law, provided his powerlessness or inability resulted from a mental disease or defect. What went for D.C. then goes for almost all states today. The only path to insanity is through a mental disease or defect. But if an accused is indeed powerless to conform, why should it matter why he's powerless, as long as he's not at fault for so being? The law doesn't answer that question either.

The law's refusal to define "mental disease or defect," or indeed, to explain why a "mental disease or defect" is needed in the first place, is a sign of something rotten in the state of insanity law. A full diagnosis of the problem will need to wait until Chapter 5, when insanity gets a full-dress treatment. For now, suffice it to say that, yes, the *actus reus* requirement and the irresistible impulse test of insanity are birds of a feather. The *actus reus* requirement is equivalent to the old irresistible impulse test, with two important differences.

First, the mental disease or defect requirement. Whereas the irresistible impulse test provides an excuse only if the accused's incapacity resulted from a mental disease or defect, the *actus reus* requirement protects anyone who's powerless to conform to the law, mental disease or defect or not, provided he was powerless through no fault of his own. Second, normative status. The irresistible impulse test is an affirmative defense, which the state can choose to recognize or not in the exercise of its authority. The *actus reus* requirement, in contrast, is proposed as a limit on state authority, expressed as an immunity right. Thus, if a state chose not to embrace an irresistible impulse test as an affirmative defense, the *actus reus* requirement, reflected in the Stephen test, would render him immune from liability nonetheless.[42]

[42] The U.S. Supreme Court has never held that states are constitutionally required to provide criminal defendants with some form of insanity defense. Five states (Montana, Idaho, Kansas, Utah, and North Dakota) currently have no affirmative defense of insanity. *See* Paul H. Robinson & Tyler Scot Williams, Mapping American Criminal Law: Variations Across the 50 States 160–61 (2018). That may change. The Court has recently agreed to hear a case in which the appellant argues that the Eighth and Fourteenth amendment do not permit a state to abolish the insanity defense. *See* State v. Kahler, 410 P.3d 105 (Kan. 2018), *cert. granted sub nom.* Kahler v. Kansas, 139 S. Ct. 1318 (U.S. 2019). For a persuasive argument to the effect that Due Process requires states to recognize some form of insanity defense, see Stephen J. Morse & Richard J. Bonnie, *Abolition of the Insanity Defense Violates Due Process*, 41 J. Am. Acad. Psychiatry & L. 488 (2013).

Mens Rea

As we saw in Chapter 2, an accused presumptively manifests *mens rea* if he realizes φ-ing is a crime but chooses to φ all the same. We want now to examine two ways in which the presumption of *mens rea* can be defeated, both of which involve choice made under presumption-defeating duress or coercion.

Duress Two Ways

Duress comes in two forms. The first involves *sacrificial* (or external) duress. The second involves *dysphoric* (or internal) duress.[43] Insofar as a defendant chooses to φ under duress in either form, his choice, all things considered, will have manifested no lack of sufficient concern for the law, and his choice will therefore have been made without *mens rea*.

Sacrificial Duress

The criminal law limits the choices we can make, and sometimes requires us to make choices we'd rather not. The criminal law's demands are seldom unduly burdensome, however. Although it usually takes no great sacrifice to conform, sometimes it does. Sometimes the sacrifice it would take to conform is too much for the state legitimately to demand of any law-abiding

[43] The distinction between sacrificial duress and dysphoric duress isn't a doctrinal distinction. Criminal codes don't, for example, have one provision captioned "sacrificial duress" and another captioned "dysphoric duress." The distinction is theoretical, and several commentators have noticed it, though they use different labels to mark its two forms. *See, e.g.*, Larry Alexander & Kimberly Kessler Ferzan, Crime and Culpability: A Theory of Criminal Law 140 (2009) (distinguishing between duress as a "personal justification" (sacrificial) and duress as a "volitional impair[ment]" (dysphoric)); Gary Watson, *Excusing Addiction*, *in* Agency and Answerability: Selected Essays 318, 340 (2004) (distinguishing between duress as a "prerogative defense" (sacrificial) and duress as an "impairment defense" (dysphoric)); Dan M. Kahan & Martha C. Nussbaum, *Two Conceptions of Emotion in Criminal Law*, 96 Colum. L. Rev. 269, 277–78 (1996) (distinguishing between an "evaluative" (sacrificial) and a "mechanistic" (dysphoric) conception of emotion); Dana Kay Nelkin, *Difficulty and Degrees of Moral Praiseworthiness and Blameworthiness*, 50 Noûs 356, 357 (2016) (distinguishing between "degrees of sacrifice" (sacrificial) and "degrees of effort" (dysphoric)). Watson notes:

> Prerogative defenses [like sacrificial duress] . . . raise the issue of whether the defendant's choice was reasonable, rationally defensible. A successful defense must show that it was. The impairment defense [dysphoric duress] grants that this exercise of agency was defective, but argues that it was compatible with the commitments and virtues of the law-abiding citizen. The choice may have been faulty, but that shouldn't be held against him. Therefore, *both defenses require normative judgments at different points*.

Watson, *supra*, at 340 (emphasis added).

citizen, and when that's true, the accused's choice doesn't manifest a guilty mind, having been made under sacrificial duress.

Juan Manuel Contento-Pachon was a cab driver in Bogotá, Colombia in the early 1980s.[44] He swallowed 129 balloons filled with cocaine, and boarded a plane for Los Angeles, with a stop in Panama. When he arrived in Los Angeles, he consented to an x-ray. The cocaine showed up, and he was charged with unlawful possession with intent to distribute a controlled substance, in violation of what was then 18 U.S.C. § 841(a)(1).

At trial he said he'd been coerced. A drug dealer named Jorge threatened to kill his wife and three-year-old unless he smuggled cocaine into the United States. He didn't go to the police in Colombia or Panama for help, because some of them, he believed, were in league with the drug lords.[45] Moreover, Jorge had told him he'd be watched throughout his trip from Columbia to Los Angeles. Contento-Pachon knew the substance in his possession was controlled, and he also knew possession of a controlled substance was a crime. Under the circumstances, did Contento-Pachon violate § 841(a)(1) with a guilty mind?

Isolating that question requires bracketing two others. First, smuggling cocaine is a crime, but given Jorge's threat, was it a crime all thing considered? If the only way for Contento-Pachon to avoid the threat was to commit the crime, then maybe, on balance, the United States wouldn't reckon Contento-Pachon's drug smuggling a crime after all. In the doctrinal language of the criminal law, maybe Contento-Pachon's choice to smuggle the cocaine was, so far as the United States was concerned, permissible inasmuch as it was, under the circumstances, the "lesser evil."[46] If so, then the question of his

[44] *See* United States v. Contento-Pachon, 723 F.2d 691 (9th Cir. 1984). Contento-Pachon wasn't a U.S. citizen, so any moral obligation he had to conform to the law couldn't have been based on his status as a citizen with full rights to participate in the democratic decision-making processes of the United States. For present purposes, we can set that complication aside in order to focus on duress and the circumstances under which it defeats the presumption of *mens rea*. If you like, simply change the facts to make Contento-Pachon a U.S. citizen on vacation in Bogotá. We might also stipulate that all the events take place in a single state with jurisdiction over the crime Contento-Pachon commits and the crime Jorge threatened to commit.

[45] *See id.* at 963.

[46] The Ninth Circuit in *Contento-Pachon* followed what it characterized as the "traditional" rule, according to which, "for the necessity [or lesser evils] defense to apply, the coercion must have its source in the physical forces of nature," not in human agency. *Id.* at 695. Because the coercion Contento-Pachon faced came from Jorge, the Ninth Circuit affirmed the district court's decision denying his request for an instruction to the jury on necessity. *See id.* The Model Penal Code, in contrast to the traditional rule, expands the defense of necessity to encompass threats arising from human agency, as well as from those arising from nature. *See* Model Penal Code § 3.02 (Am. Law Inst. 1985).

mens rea doesn't even get off the ground, and it's not terribly hard to make the case that smuggling cocaine is a lesser evil compared to risking the lives of one's wife and three-year-old child.

Second, Contento-Pachon chose to smuggle cocaine, but given Jorge's threat, could he have chosen otherwise? In other words, wholly apart from any question of *mens rea*, did his choice satisfy the *actus reus* requirement? In order to answer that question, we'd apply the Stephen test, and doing that would require more facts. Suppose the greatest punishment the United States could legitimately impose for smuggling cocaine was fifty years in prison. Contento-Pachon, faced with a choice between fifty years or the lives of his wife and child, chooses his family. If the desire to save his family produced the Hogwarts effect, cordoning off his conative will from countervailing reasons, then his choice to smuggle would have been compelled. But that's a big if. He probably just decided his family was worth any risk of criminal liability, and so chose to take the risk. In any event, for now we'll assume his desire to save his family didn't produce the effect and so wasn't compelled. His choice may have been a hard one, but so far as one can tell, he could have chosen otherwise.

We should in any case be able to bracket those questions if we change the facts and enter a few stipulations. First, designate the crime Jorge orders Contento-Pachon to commit crime φ, and the crime Jorge threatens to commit (unless Contento-Pachon commits crime φ) crime β. Second, assume φ isn't smuggling cocaine into the United States, but serious bodily injury to an innocent stranger named John. Third, assume β is serious bodily injury to Contento-Pachon's wife: Jorge threatens to assault Contento-Pachon's wife unless Contento-Pachon assaults John. Fourth, Contento-Pachon had no other legal options; he had no reasonable opportunity, for example, to get help from the police. Finally, Contento-Pachon, when he assaults John, could have chosen otherwise, thereby satisfying the *actus reus* requirement.

When Contento-Pachon assaults John, he realizes he's committing a crime, which means his choice presumptively satisfies the *mens rea* requirement. He nonetheless pleads not guilty, arguing that his choice to assault John, under the circumstances and all things considered, lacked *mens rea*. In order to evaluate his claim, we apply the Jekyll test, from Chapter 2. When the real Contento-Pachon chooses to φ (assault John), his motivational reasons for doing so (to avoid Jorge assaulting his wife) exceeded his motivational reasons not to φ, such that $\Sigma MR_{\varphi} > \Sigma MR_{\sim\varphi}$. Pursuant to the Jekyll test, we inject the real Contento-Pachon with law-abiding concern, thereby transforming him into law-abiding Contento-Pachon, and see what happens.

If the balance of his motivational reasons shifts, such that $\Sigma MR_{\varphi} < \Sigma MR_{\sim\varphi}$, then law-abiding Contento-Pachon would have chosen not to assault John. Real Contento-Pachon's choice to assault John would therefore have expressed insufficient concern for the law, including the law's interest in the bodily integrity of its citizens, and the presumption of *mens rea* would remain in place. On the other hand, if the balance remains unchanged, such that $\Sigma MR_{\varphi} > \Sigma MR_{\sim\varphi}$, then law-abiding Contento-Pachon would, despite being law-abiding, have chosen to assault John. Real Contento-Pachon's choice to assault John would therefore express no lack of sufficient concern for the law. The presumption of *mens rea* with which we began would be defeated, in which case we'd conclude that the real Contento-Pachon's mind, when he assaulted John, wasn't guilty after all.

From the state's point of view, on the facts of the hypothetical, $\varphi = \beta$. An assault is an assault, and as between its citizens, the state must stand impartial: It must care as much about John and his bodily integrity as it does about Contento-Pachon's wife and her bodily integrity. From the state's impartial point of view, the fact that Contento-Pachon must assault John in order to avoid Jorge's assault on his wife isn't enough for it to permit Contento-Pachon to go unpunished for attacking John. From the state's point of view, in other words, he didn't choose a lesser evil. He chose the same evil.

Nonetheless, from Contento-Pachon's partial point of view, his wife's well-being is more important to him than John's. Contento-Pachon doesn't, I'd contend, lack the concern he should have, as a law-abiding citizen, for the law, including the law of assault intended to protect the bodily integrity of his fellow citizens. Contento-Pachon regards John, as a fellow citizen, with the same concern with which John regards Contento-Pachon, with all the concern one fellow, law-abiding citizen has for, and owes to, any other. Nonetheless, Contento-Pachon legitimately cares more for his wife's welfare than he does for John's, just as he cares more deeply for his own welfare and for the welfare of those with whom he identifies in roles—father, husband, friend—defining who he is: roles which are separate and distinct from his role as citizen.

A democratic state can legitimately ask its citizens to make sacrifices to secure the goods the criminal law exists to protect. If Jorge had blackmailed Contento-Pachon, threatening to expose some deep, dark secret, which would have ruined his reputation, the state could legitimately demand the sacrifice, requiring him to put John's physical well-being above his reputation. Yet, sometimes, the sacrifice it would take to conform to the law is more than the state can legitimately demand, insofar as conformity would demand more concern for the law than the state can legitimately demand of any law-abiding citizen. A citizen who identified completely with the state and the interests its criminal law seeks to protect would conform up to and including the point at which conformity would require choosing, from an impartial point of view, an equal evil, but a law-abiding citizen doesn't, so we aver, cease to be law-abiding just because he doesn't embrace the state's impartial point of view.

Sacrificial duress resembles the affirmative defense of duress found in penal codes across almost all jurisdictions,[47] with two differences. First, any statutory duress defense exists in virtue of the state's exercise of its authority to define the conditions under which an accused isn't culpable. Second, most statutory formulations of duress are, in one way or another, limited in scope. For example, the state might not make the defense available for the crime of murder, or to crimes punishable by death; or might make it available only when the person doing the coercing threatens the bodily integrity of the person being coerced; or it might make it available only when the source of the threat is another person, and not the force of circumstance. All these limitations are fairly common features of positive law.[48]

Sacrificial duress differs from statutory duress, first, because sacrificial duress is meant to serve as a limit on the state's authority to attach guilt to an accused's choice to commit a crime; and second, because it jettisons the restrictions commonly associated with statutory duress. Sacrificial duress can apply when the accused chooses what, in the eyes of the state, in an equal or greater evil, whatever the crime, whatever the threat, and whatever its source. It asks a single question: Did the accused's choice to φ, despite being a choice to commit what he realized was a crime, nonetheless express sufficient concern for the law? The Jekyll test can guide the search for an answer to that question, but the test isn't an algorithm: it doesn't yield determinate answers.[49] For example, if a citizen can legitimately place more weight on an

[47] *See, e.g.*, Paul H. Robinson et al., *The American Criminal Code: General Defenses*, 7 J. LEGAL ANALYSIS 37, 88 (2015) ("At least fifty of the fifty-two [U.S.] jurisdictions recognize some type of [d]uress defense.").

[48] *See id.* (surveying state law and finding that most jurisdictions include these limitations). For an overview of the law of duress, both at common law and under the Model Penal Code, see JOSHUA DRESSLER, UNDERSTANDING CRIMINAL LAW § 23.01[B], at 283–85 (8th ed. 2018) (common law); *id.* § 23.08[A]–[B], at 298–99 (Model Penal Code).

[49] *See, e.g.*, John Lawrence Hill, *A Utilitarian Theory of Duress*, 84 IOWA L. REV. 275, 307 (1999) (emphasizing that a "moralized" test for coercion is "indeterminate.").

interest because the interest is *his*, how far does that principle extend beyond the self? Whose interests can a citizen legitimately treat as an extension of the self? That's not an easy question, nor one we'll make any effort to refine or answer here. One can be uncertain about how the test should to be applied to real cases rich in facts, without harboring doubt about the abstract statement of the test itself.

Sacrificial duress is about choice. It immunizes from criminal liability an actor's choice to φ, when the actor realizes φ-ing is a crime, in order to avoid β, provided the choice, despite being a choice to commit a crime, nonetheless expressed sufficient concern for the law. It depends, in the end, on comparing φ to β, and on the choice between them the accused would have made once infused with sufficient concern. It doesn't require getting inside the accused's mind. It doesn't invite any inquiry into how psychologically difficult the accused would have experienced the choice to conform to the law.[50] A choice made under sacrificial duress will typically be psychologically distressful, but sacrificial duress isn't about any dysphoria, distress, anguish, dread, and so on, which might attend a choice to φ. It's about the nature of the choice itself, not its phenomenology.

The next form of duress, in contrast, is all about the psychological cost it sometimes takes for an accused to conform to the law.

Dysphoric Duress

Unlike Contento-Pachon, no one threatened to do anything to Raymond Moore unless he possessed heroin. The coercion he experienced was internal, not external.[51] It came from within, not from without. Unless he took, and then used the heroin, he'd be forced to endure actual, not just threatened,

[50] Morse, *supra* note 19, at 1617 ("[T]he [legal] criteria [for duress] do not require or imply that the defendant must experience untoward or unpleasant psychological states or that there is anything wrong with the defendant. Most people threatened with dreadful immediate consequences will surely feel fear or 'pressure' to avoid those consequences . . . but such mental or affective states need not be present to claim duress successfully. . . . [N]o matter how much fear or pressure a defendant subjectively experienced, duress will not obtain unless the situation was one in which a person of reasonable firmness would yield.").

[51] Existing state law, as well as the Model Penal Code, typically requires a threat from a third party. *See* Model Penal Code § 2.09 (Am. Law Inst. 1985) (requiring "unlawful" force); Robinson et al., *supra* note 47, at 88 (majority rule in United States requires "unlawful" threat). Some jurisdictions allow the threat to come from nature (duress of circumstances or situational duress), but threats from nature are still external threats. We can imagine cases in which the external-internal distinction gets more complicated. Suppose Ben threatens to put Peter, who suffers from arachnophobia, in a room populated with harmless spiders unless Peter commits crime φ. The dysphoria Peter experiences, and but for which he wouldn't have chosen to φ, makes the threat internal, even though it results from the actions of a third party.

psychological pain or dysphoria. Addicts suffer when they don't use. Can choosing to commit a crime in order to end such distress ever defeat the presumption of *mens rea*?

Moore was a heroin addict, and would, from time to time at least, experience an occurrent desire to use heroin. Assume, however unlikely, that Moore didn't do anything he shouldn't have done to cause himself, nor did he fail to do anything he should have done to prevent himself, from becoming an addict in the first place. Assume as well that he didn't do anything he shouldn't have done to cause, nor fail to do anything he should have done to prevent, his desire for heroin from becoming occurrent and grow in strength. He didn't, for example, head off to the Warren Hotel, while not yet in the grip of desire, in order to buy heroin, only to find himself gripped when he arrived. Instead, he somehow innocently finds himself at t=1 faced with the stark choice to possess or not possess, realizing possession would be a crime.

The balance of Moore's motivational reasons at t=1 is $\Sigma MR_{\varphi} > \Sigma MR_{\sim\varphi}$. That means, as between φ-ing and not φ-ing at t=1, Moore will choose to φ, unless he puts up some resistance: unless he exercises self-control. Absent resistance, his reasons to possess heroin will defeat his reasons not to possess, and with nothing left to stand in their way, his reasons to possess will carry the day. Moore's executive will would then form an intent to possess, along with the volitions needed to move his body so as to come into possession, and he'll choose to φ.

Suppose Moore offers no resistance, and so chooses to φ. Now enter the following stipulations: When Moore chooses to φ, his choice would be a crime, all things considered, i.e., his choice would not be one the United States would permit; he knows heroin possession is a crime; he had the capacity to choose otherwise; and his choice to possess would not qualify as sacrificial duress. In a nutshell: When Moore chooses to possess the heroin, he satisfies the *actus reus* requirement, and nothing in the story so far casts any doubt on the presumption of *mens rea*. If so, then nothing so far disables the state's authority to assign guilt to Moore's choice to possess.

Now suppose Moore does resist. Realizing possession is a crime, Moore judges that, all things considered, he shouldn't possess. At t=1 the balance of his motivational reasons favors possession, but Moore believes he can and should resist the force of his φ-favoring reasons. In other words, he believes he can and should exercise self-control. If Moore wants to resist and exercise self-control more than he wants not to do so ($\Sigma MR_{\text{self-control}} > \Sigma MR_{\sim\text{self-control}}$)

he'll choose to resist and exercise self-control.[52] He'll attempt to diminish the motivational force of his pro-φ reasons, or increase the force of his anti-φ reasons. Or, if that strategy fails, he might just try somehow to block the motivational force of his otherwise dominant pro-φ reasons, preventing them from causing him to reach out and take possession.

The mode of self-control available to Moore at *t*=1 is synchronic.[53] It involves doing something at *t*=1, where the something done is done with the mind. The mental techniques and strategies that someone like Moore might bring to bear—the things he might do with his mind in order to exercise synchronic self-control—take different forms.[54] Count to ten. Frame the choice before you in one way rather than another. Bring to mind the unpleasant costs and consequences you'll endure if you indulge. Focus your mind on something else. Distract yourself. Make this salient and that less so. Bring to mind a prior rule or resolution not to φ,[55] and so on.

[52] At this point, one might wonder how self-control ever gets off the ground. If at *t*=1 $\Sigma MR_{\varphi} > \Sigma MR_{\sim\varphi}$, and if $\Sigma MR_{\sim\varphi}$ already includes motivational reasons to exercise self-control so as not to φ, then won't the actor necessarily choose to φ, inasmuch as his reasons to φ outweigh his reasons not to φ? This is known in the literature as the paradox or puzzle of self-control. *See, e.g.*, Chandra Sekhar Sripada, *Philosophical Questions About the Nature of Willpower*, 5 PHIL. COMPASS 793, 794–96 (2010) [hereinafter Sripada, *Philosophical Questions*]; Chandra Sekhar Sripada, *How Is Willpower Possible? The Puzzle of Synchronic Self-Control and the Divided Mind*, 48 NOÛS 41, 42–55 (2014) [hereinafter Sripada, *Synchronic Self-Control*]. The text presupposes that the solution to this paradox is to assume an actor's reasons for and against φ-ing don't "agglomerate" with, and thus don't compete with, his reasons for and against exercising self-control, such that his reasons to exercise self-control can outweigh his reasons not to exercise it, even while his reasons to φ outweigh his reasons not to φ.

[53] *See, e.g.*, Sripada, *Philosophical Questions, supra* note 52, at 793 ("In [synchronic] self-control, an occurrent desire is prevented from prevailing in action. Synchronic self-control can be contrasted with diachronic control, in which an agent seeks to prevent some non-occurrent future desire from driving action."). Ulysses tying himself to the mast is an example of diachronic self-control.

[54] For helpful discussions of these techniques and strategies of self-management, see, for example, ALFRED R. MELE, IRRATIONALITY: AN ESSAY ON AKRASIA, SELF-DECEPTION AND SELF-CONTROL 26 (1987) [hereinafter MELE, IRRATIONALITY]; ALFRED R. MELE, BACKSLIDING: UNDERSTANDING WEAKNESS OF WILL 91–113 (2012) [hereinafter MELE, BACKSLIDING]; WALTER MISCHEL, THE MARSHMALLOW TEST: MASTERING SELF-CONTROL *passim* (2014); Brendan Dill & Richard Holton, *The Addict in Us All*, *in* ALTERNATIVE MODELS OF ADDICTION 28, 36–43 (Hanna Pickard et al. eds., 2015).

[55] On personal rules or pre-commitment devices, see, for example, GEORGE ANSLIE, BREAKDOWN OF WILL 94 (2001) (describing "personal rules" as "commitments made in your mind, where the stake is nothing but your credibility with yourself."); MELE, BACKSLIDING, *supra* note 54, at 101 ("To use the tactic [of personal rules], one must view what is to be gained by resisting as a series of rewards stretching out over a considerable time."). On resolutions, see, for example, RICHARD HOLTON, WILLING, WANTING, WAITING 9–12 (2009) (describing resolutions as a distinctive form of intention whose function is to resist revision of a prior intention); Richard Holton & Stephen Shute, *Self-Control in the Modern Provocation Defence*, 27 OXFORD J. LEGAL STUD. 49, 54–55 (2007) ("[I]t is plausible that strength of will is the standard *mechanism* by which self-control is achieved: we do the thing that we believe to be right, rather than what we currently want to do, *because of* a prior resolution.").

Such tools and techniques are the tools and techniques of skilled self-control.[56] We deploy them to diminish the motivational force of pro-φ reasons, or increase the force of anti-φ reasons. If all goes well, the motivational force of the pro-φ reasons, once the strongest reasons on the block, will be king no more. Skilled self-control will have dethroned them, the balance of motivational reasons will shift in favor of not φ-ing, and the actor will choose to do something other than φ.

Skilled self-control isn't easy. It usually takes effort, which depletes the motivation needed to carry it on. Of course, not all exercises of self-control involve choice or much effort. Self-control can be mundane. The tempting desire might not be all that tempting, and controlling it might have become a matter of habit.[57] One might not even notice oneself noticing the need to deploy self-control, let alone experience oneself exercising it. In that case, self-control, having become second nature, doesn't really take much, if any, effort at all. Yet when the tempting desire is strong, exercising self-control takes a toll. Exercising one's mind in the service of self-control is like exercising one's body. It doesn't come free of charge. One has to work at it.

Besides skilled self-control, one can also exercise brute self-control.[58] Indeed, when we think about exercising self-control, chances are brute self-control is what first comes to mind. Brute self-control, or what one might have in mind when talking about "willpower," is the mental act of intentionally forming the intent not to form the intent to φ. Not much, if any, skill is involved. Brute self-control is the self-control of first resort, and last. Insofar as one's pro-φ motivational reasons are already dominant, brute self-control is needed to stop or block the intent to φ from forming, at least until skilled self-control can be called upon to shift the motivational balance. If skilled

[56] *See, e.g.*, MELE, IRRATIONALITY, *supra* note 54, at 26 ("In a case of skilled resistance, the agent actively manipulates his motivational condition."); Sripada, *Synchronic Self-Control, supra* note 52, at 43 (describing "[a]ntecedent-focused strategies that alter the appraisal or interpretation of the environmental cues that elicit or sustain the wayward desire").

[57] *See, e.g.*, JEANETTE KENNETT, AGENCY AND RESPONSIBILITY: A COMMON-SENSE MORAL PSYCHOLOGY 139 (2001) (noting that the mental acts involved in synchronic self-control can sometimes "perhaps best be described as cognitive habits with certain triggering conditions").

[58] *See, e.g.*, MELE, IRRATIONALITY, *supra* note 54, at 26 ("To make an effort of brute resistance in support of one's doing *X* is to form or retain an intention to do *X* in order to bring it about that, rather than succumbing to temptation, one *X*-s."); Sripada, *Synchronic Self-Control, supra* note 52, at 43 (describing "response-focused strategies" that "involve either the direct inhibition of motivation or the prevention of action," where the "prevention of action" is a matter of "mentally *blocking* the normal translation of one's motivation to *A* into one's *A*-ing").

self-control fails, brute self-control is all that's left, lest the desire to φ produces an intent to φ. Exercising skilled self-control is hard work; exercising brute self-control is even harder.

When all goes well, exercising synchronic self-control (a mental act or acts) leads to self-control (a shift in the balance of one's motivational reason from φ to -φ). What happens when all doesn't go well, when an actor "*loses*" self-control? What happens when, as we might say, an actor's will is "overwhelmed" or "overcome."

First be clear about what doesn't happen. An actor's "willpower" is sometimes analogized to a muscle. The analogy makes some sense, but like most analogies, it can mislead as well as illuminate. Muscles are physical things, and physical things can physically "give out." Think about trying not to pee. Or about trying to hold on with your fingertips to the edge of a cliff. You'll be able to hold out for a while, thanks to "willpower," but at some point the muscles in your bladder or fingertips will fail you. You pee, or you fall. No matter how much you try not to.[59]

But your will isn't like your bladder. Your bladder is a muscle, and when your bladder gives out, a muscle gives out. That's not what happens when you lose self-control.

Imagine a runner. As he continues to run, the muscles in his legs will eventually give out. At some point, he'll reach the limits of his physical endurance. But something else will probably happen before he gets there. Running over great distances takes effort, and effort depletes the motivation to carry on. As sustained effort and fatigue slowly but surely weaken the motivation to carry on, and as the associated physical pain increases, the motivational force of the reasons in favor of stopping increases, while that of the reasons to keep going decreases. At some point, the force of the reasons to stop will overtake

[59] The analogy between willpower and muscle is frequently associated with the "ego depletion" or "strength" model of self-control. *See, e.g.*, ROY F. BAUMEISTER & JOHN TIERNEY, WILLPOWER (2011). The experiments on which the model is based supports a muscle analogy, but only to an extent. *See,* e.g., MISCHEL, *supra* note 54, at 218 (suggesting that the "reduction in self-control [seen in these experiments] is due not to a loss of resources: it reflects, instead, changes in motivation and attention"); Sripada, *Philosophical Questions, supra* note 52, at 798 ("These self-regulation experiments only demonstrate that willpower has certain properties of a muscle—most importantly the property of exhibiting diminished efficacy immediately following sustained use."). The muscle analogy misleads insofar as it suggests that the will, like a physical muscle, has physical limits, or that the will is a limited resource that can be used up on any particular occasion. Joel Feinberg was probably correct when, some time ago, he observed: "Human endurance puts a severe limit on how long one can stay afloat in an ocean, but there is no comparable limit to our ability to resist temptation." JOEL FEINBERG, *What Is So Special About Mental Illness?*, *in* DOING AND DESERVING: ESSAYS ON THE THEORY OF RESPONSIBILITY 272, 283 (1970).

the force of the reasons to keep going, at which point the runner will choose to stop.[60]

Self-control in the face of strong desire likewise takes effort, and this effort can produce psychic pain, dysphoria, distress, anxiety, and so forth. As this dysphoria persists and grows, it can change the actor's psychology. Perhaps he loses faith in his powers of self-control, coming to believe (falsely) that he can no longer keep his desire to φ in check. Or perhaps he changes his mind about φ, coming to believe that on balance he should choose to φ.[61] Or perhaps he continues to believe he shouldn't choose to φ, but comes to believe on balance that he should stop resisting the desire to φ. Or perhaps his motivation to stop resisting simply becomes greater than his motivation to keep on resisting.[62]

Whatever the underlying nature of the change—whether the beliefs needed to sustain his exercise of self-control change, or whether the balance of motivational reasons needed to sustain his exercise of self-control changes—the end result will be the same: the actor will choose to stop exercising self-control, or at least stop choosing to exercise it. And once the exercise of self-control ceases, the pro-φ forces will carry the day, and the actor will choose to φ. Here's the point: when we say an actor lost self-control, or his will was overwhelmed or overcome, what we usually mean is that, for one reason or another, he decided to abandon his effort to achieve self-control. He chose to give up, or at least chose no longer to endure the dysphoria resulting from not giving up.

[60] *See* Gary Watson, *Disordered Appetites: Addiction, Compulsion, and Dependence*, *in* Agency and Answerability 59, 65 (2004) ("[O]ne who is defeated by appetite is . . . like a collaborationist. . . . "); *id.* at 65 ("Unlike external obstacles (or internal pressures), motivational obstacles work not by defeating one's best efforts but by diverting one from effective behavior."); *id.* at 66 ("The forces that defeat us in motivational compulsion do not do so by opposing our wills but by directing them."); *id.* at 71 ("We are not so much overpowered by brute force as seduced."); Watson, *supra* note 43, at 336 ("Compulsive desire is not a force that moves me independently of my will; it is a 'force' that leads me to make certain choices."); Kevin Zaragoza, *What Happens When Someone Acts Compulsively?*, 131 Phil. Stud. 251, 257 (2006) ("[P]sychological compulsions do not simply 'overwhelm' the will; they 'wear it down' by producing psychological stress.").

[61] *See, e.g.*, Stephen J. Morse, *Culpability and Control*, 142 U. Pa. L. Rev. 1587, 1634 (1994) (observing that dysphoria can impair an "agent's ability to weigh the alternatives rationally" and in that sense to "think straight"); R. Jay Wallace, *Addiction as a Defect of Will*, *in* Normativity & the Will: Selected Essays on Moral Psychology and Practical Reason 165, 183 (2006) ("The focusing of one's attention onto pleasures of consumption that is brought about by [addictive] desires is apt to encourage one to overestimate the value and importance of those pleasures, in reflecting about what one is to do, and this distorting effect can be considered an impairment of the agent's capacities for practical rationality.").

[62] *See, e.g.*, Amelie Oksenberg Rorty, *Where Does the Akratic Break Take Place?*, 58 Australasian J. Phil. 333 (1980); Dill & Holton, *supra* note 54, at 9–10 (identifying "three stages of self-control" and thus three corresponding points at which self-control can "break[] down.").

Not all motivational reasons are created equal: Some are more intent and intransigent than others. This class of reasons might variously be called passions, cravings, addictive desires, recalcitrant desires, or something else along those lines.[63] For now, call them brute desires. The label isn't important. What's important is what distinguishes them from, and makes them more insidious than, other reasons inhabiting and configuring the conative will.

Ordinary, non-brute desires present their objects—the ends they bid us to pursue—under the guise of some good. These plain-vanilla desires motivate us to act so as to achieve their object insofar as they present their object as something not only intelligible, but *prima facie* worth pursuing. They issue an invitation. Go after this. Go after that. Why? Because it's something good, all else being equal. Insofar as run-of-the-mill desires present themselves under the guise of some good, they can be subject to reason's scrutiny. Reason can investigate and interrogate them, and we can rationally entertain the invitation they present and decide whether to accept or reject the offer.

If you judge a desire not worth pursuing, you can decline its offer and resist its call. You can try to diminish its motivational force using reason. For example, you can tell yourself the desire, initial appearances to the contrary notwithstanding, isn't really worth pursuing. Or you can bring to mind the costs involved in pursuing it. You can try to distract yourself and think of something else. In other words, you can try to diminish an ordinary desire's motivational force using skilled self-control, which can be seen as a conversation between reason and rational appetite. Ordinary desires can be reasoned with. We can talk ourselves down from them, reasoning our way loose from their grip. Of course, if reason fails to diminish an ordinary desire's motivational force, you can still use brute self-control, if only as a last resort, in an effort to contain it, thereby preventing an unwanted desire from being translated into a choice to pursue it.

[63] Several collections have recently been published on addiction, all of which contain contributions addressing the responsibility (usually moral, but sometimes legal) of addicts for choices made under the influence of addictive desire. *See* Addiction and Choice: Rethinking the Relationship (Nick Heather & Gabriel Segal eds., 2017); Addiction and Responsibility (Jeffrey Poland & George Graham eds., 2011); Addiction and Self-Control: Perspectives from Philosophy, Psychology, and Neuroscience (Neil Levy ed., 2013); Alternative Models of Addiction (Hanna Pickard et al. eds., 2015).

Efforts to explain addictive behavior based on neuroscientific insights appear to be the inspiration, at least in part, behind this recent attention to addiction. Yet whatever we might learn from neuroscience about addictive behavior, Dill and Holton are persuasive when they observe that the "self-control challenge faced by addicted agents is *not different in kind* from that faced by non-addicted agents—though the two may, of course, differ greatly in degree of difficulty." Dill & Holton, *supra* note 54, at 1 (emphasis added).

Not so with brute desires. Brute desires, besides being especially intense and unremitting, don't invite reason to see things their way. They make no appeal to reason. They just demand. Insofar as a brute desire doesn't present its end as anything worth pursuing, it doesn't motivate. Brute desires, we might say, move us, but they don't motivate us. Because they can't be reasoned with, skilled self-control won't work on brutes.[64] You can't talk yourself down when passion takes hold. Passion, one might say, is blind (or deaf) to reason. You can resist a brute desire, fighting fire with fire through brute self-control, but you can't reason with it. You can only try to contain it and hope its force fades before you give up, and it takes over. When it comes to brute desires, brute self-control isn't a last resort. It's the only one.[65]

Now that we know how self-control gets lost, we can ask: Under what circumstances, if any, does an actor who loses the battle for self-control, and thus chooses to φ, choose without a guilty mind? In order to answer that question, we turn once again to the Jekyll test. Begin with the actor as he is, including the passion he has for his preferred poison. Inject him with all the concern for the law the state can legitimately expect of a law-abiding citizen, and then ask what he would have done had his will been so fortified. He'd presumably have made some effort to resist the pull of his passion, since that's what a law-abiding citizen would've done, insofar as pursuing the passion would mean breaking the law. The question is whether he would, at some point, have abandoned the effort.

Return to Moore and his decision to possess heroin. Once we inject him with law-abiding concern, thereby transforming real Moore into law-abiding Moore, we ask: Would law-abiding Moore have chosen, due to the dysphoria he was suffering, to stop resisting his brute desire for heroin? If yes, then real Moore's choice to give up and his ensuing choice to φ didn't manifest insufficient concern for the law. If no, then it did. Asking that question is easy; answering it isn't.

For one thing, how are we to know what it was like to suffer the dysphoria Moore suffered? How can we feel his pain? We can't, of course. All we can do is imagine as best we can, and reasonable minds applying the Jekyll test to this

[64] *See, e.g.*, WALLACE, *supra* note 61, at 171 ("It is the fact that A-impulses are unresponsive to deliberative reflection . . . that makes them resilient, and resilience in turn is perhaps the philosophically most interesting and salient feature of A-impulses.").

[65] If and when we find ourselves sympathetic to actors who commit crimes in the thrall of desire, we're apt to have in mind those suffering from addictions, manias (like kleptomania or pyromania), and phobias. That makes sense inasmuch as the desires associated with such conditions are, one imagines, brute desires.

or that set of facts will sometimes reach different conclusions. The Jekyll test implements a principle, and principles don't apply themselves. Reasonable citizens called upon to sit in judgment can and will disagree over how the principle embodied in the Jekyll test applies, as when they're asked to apply it to defendants like Moore. But the principle itself, we believe beyond reasonable doubt, reflects a requirement of justice, and as such, it would operate as a legitimate limit on the exercise of otherwise legitimate democratic authority to ascribe culpability to those who, like Moore perhaps, choose to commit a crime under dysphoric duress.

Despite the test's indeterminacy, we can nonetheless confidently observe that the answer it yields will depend on the crime charged. Consider Chester, who was unlucky in the genetic lottery, having been born with two ticking time bombs. One destined him to become afflicted with kleptomania, and the other with pedophilia. One day, through no fault of his own, Chester finds his kleptomaniacal desire triggered at $t=1$, and later, on the same day, again through no fault of his own, his pedophiliac desire triggered at $t=2$. Each desire is as intense as the other, and in his struggle against them, each produces the same measure of dysphoria. On each occasion, he chooses to abandon the struggle, with predictable results. At $t=1$, he steals some trivial object. At $t=2$, he molests a child.

We deploy the Jekyll test in order to decide if Chester's choices manifest *mens rea*. That test entails, at the outset, comparing the dysphoria real Chester would have had to endure in order to resist committing the crime with the nature and seriousness of the crime itself. Understanding what Chester's dysphoria must have been like for him is a tall order, if not a herculean one.[66] We can't, once again, really feel his pain. All that can realistically be done is to try, as best one can, to imagine what it must have been like, relying on all the evidence one can find. With some picture of real Chester's psychic pain in mind, would law-abiding Chester have stolen the trivial object, or molested the child, to end the dysphoria?

Any well-considered verdict would need a more complete description of the facts. Even then, reasonable minds will likely disagree, which is hard to avoid when abstract principle meets messy reality. Still, if we assume Chester's dysphoria, however we go about taking its measure, was the same at $t=1$ and $t=2$, we can at least be confident of the following: Chester's choice

[66] *See* Morse, *supra* note 62, at 1657 ("[J]udging the strength of another's desires and dysphoria, or fear of it, is a herculean endeavor. . . . No established metric exists to determine the magnitude of impulses, desires, or feelings.").

is far less apt to manifest a guilty mind when he steals a trivial object than when he molests a child.[67] One hesitates to believe any amount of dysphoria would cause a law-abiding citizen to give in to relieve the dysphoria, if giving in means sexually harming a child. All else being equal, an accused whose will has been bolstered with law-abiding concern is less apt to give up on the pursuit of self-control the more serious is the crime he would end up committing. As the gravity of φ grows, so too does a law-abiding citizen's resolve to soldier on.

The Jekyll test needs to account for time, too. The desires most likely to defeat self-control tend not to come and go. The afflicted struggle with these desires constantly, causing continual stress and fatigue.[68] When we ask if an accused, fortified with law-abiding concern, would have chosen to abandon the struggle, we need to account for the fact that exercising self-control at $t=1$ depletes the motivational resources—the will to carry on—needed to sustain the struggle at $t=2$.

When we apply the Jekyll test, we assume the accused started out at $t=1$ with a full supply of law-abiding concern, but if he wins the first round, he enters the next round with diminished reserves—with whatever he has leftover from round one, plus any he's managed to build up in the cooldown between $t=1$ and $t=2$. If he loses round two, or any later round, he should be judged, not on what would have happened with a full tank of concern, but on what would have happened with a tank depleted through his prior efforts.

Provocation

Sally is walking down Dauphin Street in Mobile, Alabama. Out of nowhere, Sam comes up from behind and brutally slugs her three times with a large tree branch, causing serious injury. Sam quickly walks away, but doesn't get very far. Sally, overwrought with anger, quickly removes from its holster a concealed Glock 43, which she's licensed to carry. She doesn't believe Sam poses any additional threat. She believes she can walk away without further

[67] *See id.* at 1621–22 ("On the moral view, if the wrong thing desired is small beans, then it may be reasonable to do it, rather than to suffer substantial dysphoria.").

[68] *See, e.g.*, Chandra Sripada, *The Second Hit of Addiction*, *in* 4 Moral Psychology: Free Will and Moral Responsibility 295, 302–03 (Walter Sinnott-Armstrong ed., 2014) (emphasizing the frequency with which addicts must deal with their addictive desires).

harm. She struggles to contain the intense rage, but she succumbs. She takes aim and, intending to kill, pulls the trigger.[69] Sam falls dead.

Sally is charged with murder under Alabama Criminal Code § 13A-6-2(a)(1), defined as causing the death of another "with intent" to cause death. She requests an instruction on manslaughter under § 13A-6-3(1), according to which murder becomes manslaughter if the accused "causes the death due to a sudden heat of passion caused by provocation recognized by law, and before a reasonable time for the passion to cool and for reason to reassert itself."[70]

Sally killed in the "sudden heat of passion," and Sam's attack would probably suffice under Alabama law as "provocation recognized by law," or least the evidence would be enough to get the issue to the jury.[71] Likewise, little time elapsed between Sam's provocation and Sally's lethal act ("before a reasonable time for the passion to cool and for reason to reassert itself"). It all looks good for Sally to avoid a conviction for murder.

Suppose, however, that just weeks before Sally's fatal encounter with Sam, the Alabama legislature voted to abolish the crime of manslaughter under § 13A-6-3(1), and the governor signed the bill into law just days before. When Sally goes to trial, the only charge available to the jury is murder. Manslaughter is no longer an option. If the jury convicts Sally of murder, and Alabama punishes her accordingly, has it acted within the bounds of its authority? Sally says not, insisting she acted without *mens rea*.

[69] Because Sally didn't believe Sam was any threat to her at the moment she pulled the trigger, she can't claim self-defense. *See, e.g.*, ALA. CODE § 13A-3-23 (deadly physical force is justifiable if the "person reasonably believes that another person is [u]sing or about to use unlawful deadly physical force").

[70] The criminal law has long recognized provocation, in some form or another, as a partial defense to a charge of murder. Criminal law theorists have long struggled with why the elements of the provocation defense should have that effect. Why should someone who intentionally causes another's death, but who also satisfies the legal elements of the provocation defense, be convicted of manslaughter, and not murder? The traditional answers divide into what are known as "partial justification theories," and "partial excuse theories," although some commentators offer theories they claim defy these traditional labels, while others attempt to combine partial-justification theories and partial-excuse theories into one. For the traditional theories, compare, for example, Finbarr McAuley, *Anticipating the Past: The Defence of Provocation in Irish Law*, 50 MOD. L. REV. 133 (1987) (partial justification), with Joshua Dressler, *Rethinking the Heat of Passion: A Defense in Search of a Rationale*, 73 J. CRIM. L. & CRIMINOLOGY 421 (1982) (partial excuse). For an account purporting to resist the traditional dichotomy, see Stephen P. Garvey, *Passion's Puzzle*, 90 IOWA L. REV. 1677 (2005), and for an account trying to combine the traditional accounts, see Mitchell N. Berman & Ian Farrell, *Provocation Manslaughter as Partial Justification and Partial Excuse*, 52 WM. & MARY L. REV. 1027 (2011).

[71] *See, e.g.*, Miller v. State, 739 So. 2d 1143, 1145 (Ala. Ct. Crim. App. 1999) (holding that the question of adequate provocation, where the victim "attacked and struck [defendant] with his fist, with or without a weapon," is a question for the jury).

Start with sacrificial duress. Pursuant to the Jekyll test, we need to ask what Sally would have done if she'd been endowed with all the concern for the law the state can legitimately expect, including the good it tries to protect when it makes homicide a crime (here, Sam's life). If we asked Sally why she killed Sam, she might say because she was incredibly angry. If we asked her why she was incredibly angry, she might say because Sam wronged her, and he got what he deserved. If so, then Sally killed Sam because she wanted payback. She wanted to kill Sam in order to punish him for his assault on her.

When Sally killed Sam, her motivational reasons to φ outweighed her motivational reasons not to φ, such that $\Sigma MR_{\varphi} > \Sigma MR_{\sim\varphi}$. Yet, once we inject Sally with sufficient concern, transforming real Sally into law-abiding Sally, the balance would shift, such that $\Sigma MR_{\varphi} < \Sigma MR_{\sim\varphi}$, unless of course we're prepared to say that the desire to kill a fellow citizen, albeit a provocateur, in retaliation for his provocation would outweigh a law-abiding citizen's concern for the life of a fellow citizen, even a provocateur. So long as we're not prepared to go there, then law-abiding Sally wouldn't have chosen to kill Sam, and thus real Sally's choice to kill expressed insufficient concern for the law. Sally's *mens* was *rea*, and Alabama wouldn't have exceeded its authority to convict her of murder.

Now suppose Sally says she killed only because she lost self-control. In other words, she claims not sacrificial duress, but dysphoric duress. Sam's attack enraged her. She realized she shouldn't kill him, and should instead try to resist the urge to unholster the Glock and fire, but the urge was too strong. She could have resisted, but consciously or not, chose not to; or, if she did resist, she ultimately chose to stop, and when she stopped, her desire to kill became her strongest desire, which caused her to form an intent to kill, which caused her to form all the volitions needed to unholster the Glock, point it at Sam, and pull the trigger.

In order to evaluate Sally's claim of dysphoric duress, we apply the Jekyll test, not to Sally's decision to kill (as we did when assessing her claim of sacrificial duress), but to her decision to stop resisting her desire to kill. At the moment real Sally chose to kill, her desire to control her desire to kill was weaker than her desire not to control it, such that $\Sigma MR_{\text{self-control}} < \Sigma MR_{\sim\text{self-control}}$. As a result, she stopped resisting, and her desire to kill, left unchecked, carried the day. We need to ask if the balance of real Sally's reasons to continue resisting her desire to kill would have shifted, such that $\Sigma MR_{\text{self-control}} > \Sigma MR_{\sim\text{self-control}}$, once she'd been transformed into law-abiding Sally.

As long as we're not prepared to say a law-abiding citizen would kill to end dysphoria (however intensely experienced), then law-abiding Sally would've continued to resist, which means she wouldn't have chosen to kill Sam. If so, then real Sally's choice to kill expressed insufficient concern for the law, including the law protecting the life of provocateur Sam. Once again, Sally's *mens* was *rea*, and Alabama wouldn't exceed its authority if it were to convict her of murder. Thus, when Sally kills Sam, she has no claim to have acted under duress, whether dysphoric or sacrificial, and thus no claim to have acted without a guilty mind.

As a partial defense to murder, provocation has in recent years come under heavy fire. Progressive reformers want it abolished, or substantially reformed, believing it provides unjust mitigation for misogynistic men who kill women,[72] and homophobic men who kill gay men.[73] Allowing juries to entertain and perhaps return a manslaughter verdict in these cases is controversial. Sally's case, in contrast, was designed to be uncontroversial. If anyone fits squarely in the heartland of provocation, it's Sally.[74] If the state nonetheless has the authority to convict her of murder, then it has authority to convict any provoked killer for murder. When provoked killers choose to kill, one struggles to see how their mind could, for purposes of the *mens rea* requirement, have been innocent.[75]

[72] *See, e.g.*, Jeremy Horder, Provocation and Responsibility 192–94 (1992). *But see* Joshua Dressler, *Why Keep the Provocation Defense?: Some Reflections on a Difficult Subject*, 86 Minn. L. Rev. 959 (2002); Aya Gruber, *A Provocative Defense*, 103 Calif. L. Rev. 273 (2015).

[73] *See, e.g.*, Robert B. Mison, Comment, *Homophobia and Manslaughter: The Homosexual Advance as Insufficient Provocation*, 80 Calif. L. Rev. 133 (1992). *But see* Joshua Dressler, *When "Heterosexual" Men Kill "Homosexual" Men: Reflections on Provocation Law, Sexual Advances, and the "Reasonable Man" Standard*, 85 J. Crim. L. & Criminology 726 (1995).

[74] The provocation in Sally's case was, after all, one of the categories of provocation—serious assault—recognized as "adequate or reasonable" at common law. *See* Dressler, *supra* note 77, §31.07[B][2][a], at 502 (describing "early common law categories" of adequate provocation). That's not to say the law should accept all the common law's categories of adequate provocation—for example, adequate provocation at common law included observing one's spouse *in flagrante delicto*—but if anything should amount to adequate provocation, serious assault should be in the running.

[75] When someone chooses to kill, after having been provoked and while still in the heat of passion, we can usually fairly assume he could have chosen otherwise, pursuant to the Stephen test, even if we also say that his capacity to conform to the law was "partially impaired," or that he was "partially incapacitated." *See, e.g.*, Joshua Dressler, *Provocation: Explaining and Justifying the Defense in Partial Excuse, Loss of Self-Control Terms*, *in* Criminal Law Conversations 319 (Paul H. Robinson et al. eds., 2009). If so, then provoked killers will usually satisfy the *actus reus* requirement. Nonetheless, the folk psychological processes causing provoked killers to kill can vary from one case to the next, and we can at least imagine cases in which a provoked person fails the Stephen test, in which case the *actus reus* requirement would not be satisfied. We can also imagine cases in which the provoked person's desire to kill might fairly be thought to have undermined his sense of agency, in which case, as we'll see in Chapter 5, he should be found to have been (temporarily) insane at the time of the crime. *See, e.g.*, People v. Harris, 740 N.E.2d 227, 230 (N.Y. 2000) (defendant in provocation case related that, during the killing, "'it was like [he] was looking at a movie [and] didn't have any control' at the time").

Still, having the authority to abolish provocation as a partial defense to murder is one thing. The justice of exercising it to do so is another. The state makes provocation available as a partial defense only if a jury finds the provocation to which the defendant responded was in some sense reasonable, and only if it further finds his loss of self-control was likewise in some sense reasonable. Inasmuch as a provoked killer's culpability is, for those reasons, less than that an otherwise similarly situated but unprovoked killer, one might fairly believe the law should reflect the difference, as a matter of justice, not just in a reduced sentence, but in conviction for a different form of homicide. Nonetheless, those who believe justice requires a provocation defense, in some form or another, will need to persuade their fellow citizens, who believe justice requires no such thing, to change their minds. The justice of the provocation defense is a question whose resolution is properly committed to the democratic process.

The Willing Addict

When we picture addicted Moore in our minds, we're apt to imagine a soul cursed and tortured with addiction who'd do anything to free himself from its grip. For most addicts, that's probably a fair portrait. If he had any "real" choice, we imagine, Moore would choose not to be addicted and not to have reached for that heroin in the Warren Hotel. We imagine he struggles mightily against the forces moving him, and we're at least willing to entertain the thought that he truly was powerless to choose not to possess and use. This is Moore the unwilling addict.

We want now to ponder another Moore, doubtless seldom seen in the real world, but worth contrasting with unwilling Moore all the same. Unlike unwilling Moore, this version of Moore is perfectly contented with who he is, and of course, he's an addict. He's at one, we might say, with his desire to use heroin; in fact, he celebrates it. A life of hedonistic satisfaction is the life for him. Among all his cares and concerns, possessing and using heroin tops the list.[76] This is Moore the willing addict. Does the United States have the authority to punish willing Moore? In order to answer that question we should first ask about its authority to punish unwilling Moore, and in order

[76] Harry Frankfurt introduced the problem of the willing addict in Harry G. Frankfurt, *Freedom of the Will and the Concept of a Person*, 68 J. PHIL. 5, 19 (1971). We can also imagine the willing kleptomaniac, the willing pyromaniac, the willing pedophile, and so on. Here's one apt description of the willing addict:

to answer that question, we need to ask if unwilling Moore's choice to possess heroin satisfies the *actus reus* and *mens rea* requirements.

When unwilling Moore's hand reached out to take the heroin, that's what he most wanted to do at that moment, and his executive will formed the intention to take it, along with the volitions needed to move his hand to reach out for it. Because he chose to possess heroin, knowing it was a crime, his act and mind were presumptively guilty. The question is whether he can rebut that presumption, with respect to both *actus reus* and *mens rea*.

Begin with *actus reus* and the Stephen test. In order to apply the test, we need to ask a series of questions. What, for example, is the greatest punishment a democratic state could legitimately impose for possessing the heroin Moore possessed? Faced with that punishment, would Moore have wanted not to suffer it more than he wanted to possess? If so, would he nonetheless have chosen to possess because (due to the Hogwarts effect) his lesser desire to possess managed to render inert his greater desire not to suffer the law's greatest punishment? If yes, then Moore's choice to possess would've been guilt-free. If not, then it would've been guilty.[77]

Switch to *mens rea* and the Jekyll test. As an unwilling addict, Moore doesn't want to be addicted; he wants not to want to possess the heroin. He therefore struggles against his addictive desire, exercising self-control and trying to reduce the motivational force of his desire to possess, or increase the motivational force of desire not to possess, or if all else fails, to put up brute resistance. The Jekyll test tells us to infuse Moore's will with all the concern for the law the state can legitimately expect of a law-abiding citizen, and then ask what law-abiding Moore would have done. If he would've taken possession, then real Moore's mind wasn't guilty; if not, then it was.

> The willing addict is an adult who cares deeply about hedonic satisfaction of the kind that can be obtained through using narcotics. He didn't get himself addicted in the first place, but he now has narcotic-directed desires and he *genuinely* loves using narcotics; he *truly* would not change a thing.

Chandra Sripada, *Frankfurt's Unwilling and Willing Addicts*, 126 MIND 781, 798 (2017). For "six examples of willing addicts," see Owen Flanagan, *Willing Addicts? Drinkers, Dandies, Druggies, and Other Dionysians, in* ADDICTION AND CHOICE, *supra* note 63, at 68–75.

[77] Whether or not people we describe as "addicts" can choose otherwise continues to be a matter of considerable debate, usually framed in terms of the "disease model" of addiction versus the "choice model." Thankfully, that's a debate we can safely sidestep. It doesn't really matter what criteria we use to describe someone as an "addict." All that matters is whether or not he lacked the capacity to choose otherwise, where we test for that capacity using the Stephen test. *See*, e.g., Sripada, *supra* note 76, at 788 n.9 ("Even if in the actual world, addiction does not involve irresistible desires, the relevant question is whether it is metaphysically possible that there could be a condition, call it *schmaddiction*, in which an agent has irresistible desires to use drugs. I believe it is indeed clearly metaphysically possible.").

The Stephen test and Jekyll test won't always yield a single result on which all reasonable minds will converge. The tests are indeterminate in a variety of ways at a variety of points. For now, for the sake of argument, suppose Moore's choice to possess heroin would satisfy neither the *actus reus* requirement, nor the *mens rea* requirement. Neither his act nor his mind was guilty, and the United States therefore had no authority to ascribe guilt to his choice to possess.

Now return to willing Moore, who's just like unwilling Moore except for the fact that he endorses, rather than repudiates, his desire for heroin. Does the United States have authority to ascribe guilt to his choice?

Begin once again with *actus reus* and the Stephen test. On that score, nothing changes. Even though willing Moore now embraces his addiction, he's still addicted. His desire to possess heroin remains as compulsive as ever, and Moore remains as powerless as ever in the face of it, whether he wants to be addicted or not. The only difference is that willing Moore doesn't care. But that doesn't matter to *actus reus*. When willing Moore chooses to possess, his choice is just as guilt-free as that of unwilling Moore. Willing Moore's *actus*, just like unwilling Moore's *actus*, isn't *reus*.

When we turn to *mens rea* and the Jekyll test, the story changes. Unwilling Moore cared about conforming his conduct to the law, and he at least tried to control his desire to possess. His effort was bound to fail, insofar as he was compelled to possess. Nonetheless, so long as real unwilling Moore put up as much of a fight as would law-abiding unwilling Moore, then real unwilling Moore's choice to possess heroin wouldn't express a lack of sufficient concern for the law, nor would it therefore manifest a guilty mind.

The same doesn't go for willing Moore. On the contrary, willing Moore's love for heroin is second to none, and he makes no effort to stop himself from possessing, not because he believes he lacks the power to choose otherwise,[78] but just because he doesn't want to choose otherwise. When real willing Moore is transformed into law-abiding Moore, all that would change. Once infused with sufficient concern for the law, law-abiding Moore wants to conform and so makes some effort to conform, even though, unbeknownst to him, he's destined to fail. Because real willing Moore made no effort, whereas

[78] We shouldn't, in other words, suppose that willing Moore is defeated Moore. We shouldn't suppose that willing Moore chooses not to put up any resistance only because he's tried in the past and knows he always fails. We should suppose instead that willing Moore believes, albeit falsely, that if he wanted to choose otherwise, he could. He just doesn't want to, and so doesn't make any effort to. *See* Sripada, *supra* note 79, at 792–93 (The unwilling addict "is not a defeated addict who fails to resist *only because* he knows he will fail at resisting.").

law-abiding Moore would have, real Moore's *mens* was *rea*, and his choice to possess would therefore manifest a guilty mind.

Where does that leave us? When unwilling Moore possesses heroin, we assumed the state had no authority to punish him. His act wasn't guilty, nor was his mind. In contrast, when willing Moore possesses heroin, his act isn't guilty, but his mind is. Willing addicts are doubtless hard to find in the real world, but they present an interesting theoretical problem. Does a willing addict's guilt-free act mean the state has no authority to punish him, or does his guilt-laden mind mean it does? What happens to state authority when the mind is guilty but the act isn't?

For an answer we turn to the reasonable doubt test. We should ask if we believe justice, beyond reasonable doubt, would foreclose holding the willing addict criminally culpable for possessing heroin. The willing addict makes no effort whatever to conform to the law, not because he believes he can't, but just because he doesn't want to make any effort. True, if he tried, he'd fail: His choice to possess was compelled. Still, even if he could've conformed, he'd make no effort to do so. Bearing all this in mind, our answer would have to be no: It would not be unjust, beyond reasonable doubt, for the state to ascribe guilt to a willing addict's choice to possess that to which he's happily addicted. The state can, through the democratic process, legitimately decide to ascribe guilt to his choice, just as it can legitimately decide not to do so.[79]

[79] When we think of examples in which it might be plausible to suppose a person lacked the capacity to choose otherwise, we usually bring to mind people who are ostensibly compelled to choose as they do as a result of passion, desire, impulse, or whatnot. But other examples can also be brought to mind, involving choices arising from deep, self-defining cares or commitments, in which choice can be said to be compelled as a "volitional" or "practical" necessity. *See, e.g.*, Harry Frankfurt, *The Importance of What We Care About*, 53 SYNTHESE 257 (1982); Gary Watson, *Volitional Necessities*, *in* CONTOURS OF AGENCY: ESSAYS ON THEMES FROM HARRY FRANKFURT 129 (Sarah Buss & Lee Overton eds., 2002); Bernard Williams, *Moral Incapacity*, 93 PROC. ARISTOTELIAN SOC'Y 59 (1993). The idea appears to be that some cares or concerns, like some desires, produce the Hogwarts effect, such that countervailing motivational reasons, real or counterfactual, are denied entry into the actor's conative will, and so never compete with the motivational reasons grounded in the relevant care or concern.

For example, consider Martin Luther, who said (or is said to have said), standing before Holy Roman Emperor Charles V at the Diet of Worms, "Here I stand; I can do no other. God help me." If we understand him to be saying he could not have chosen to do otherwise, one might reply: "Of course you could have chosen otherwise. You're just saying that in order to emphasize the depth of your conviction, but we don't take you literally." *See, e.g.*, Moore, *Compatibilism(s)*, *supra* note 19, at 57 ("[W]e simply don't believe [Luther]. He literally could have done otherwise. His is merely an emphatic way of emphasizing his deep commitment to what he freely chose to do."). Perhaps, but suspend any disbelief you might have. What if Luther really couldn't have chosen otherwise? What if, in other words, some choices, perhaps Luther's included, are volitionally necessitated or compelled? One wants to say that Luther's compelled choice to do no other, like the willing addict's compelled choice to possess, is one for which he's nonetheless responsible.

TRACING

As noted when Moore was first introduced, we've thus far been assuming he was in no way to blame for the predicament in which he found himself faced with the choice to possess heroin. The time has come to jettison that assumption. First, stipulate that when Moore chose at t=1 to take the heroin his choice was free from guilt, for want of either *actus reus* or *mens rea*. Second, suppose Moore's missing *actus reus* or *mens rea* at t=1 resulted from something he chose to do, or not do, in the past at some undefined point t=1-n. Indeed, chances are, it probably was.

Maybe Moore freely shot up heroin time and again until at some point he was no longer free to refrain, due either to compulsion or coercion (in the form of dysphoric duress). Of course, most addicts don't set out to become addicts. Still, most probably realize, at some point, that that's where the line ends. Anyway, once addicted, maybe Moore freely choose to go to the Warren Hotel even though he realized, or should have realized, that going there would likely cause his forbidden desire to spring to life, at which point he'd be at its mercy. Or maybe, despite realizing he was addicted, he did nothing about it, even when an opportunity to do something was available. No rehabilitation. No AA. No methadone. Nothing. The list of possible choices, made or not made, goes on.

Call any particular prior choice, among the universe of such possible choices, the choice to β, where β is either an act or an omission. Suppose a state wants to enact a rule—a tracing rule—permitting it to ascribe guilt to someone who made an otherwise guilt-free choice to φ at t=1, provided that choice resulted from a prior choice to β at t=1-n.[80] How broad could such a rule legitimately be? For example, could a democratic state legitimately permit itself to punish someone who made a guilt-free choice to φ at t=1 just because he made a prior choice to β to t=1-n, where that prior choice was a

[80] "Tracing" is the word philosophers typically use to refer to arguments to the effect that an actor who *ex hypothesi* lacks responsibility (for some reason) for a choice at t=1 is nonetheless responsible for that choice in virtue of some prior choice at t=1-n. For important discussions, see, for example, JOHN MARTIN FISCHER & MARK RAVIZZA, RESPONSIBILITY AND CONTROL 49–51 (1998); Holly Smith, *Tracing Cases of Culpable Ignorance*, *in* PERSPECTIVES ON IGNORANCE FROM MORAL AND SOCIAL PHILOSOPHY 95 (Rik Peels ed., 2017); Manuel Vargas, *The Trouble with Tracing*, 29 MIDWEST STUD. PHIL. 269 (2005); John Martin Fischer & Neal Tognazzini, *The Truth about Tracing*, 43 NOÛS 531 (2009); Seth Shabo, *More Trouble with Tracing*, 80 ERKENNTNIS 987 (2015). In contrast, criminal law theorists, rather than talk about tracing, tend to use the Latin phrase "*actio libera in causa*," or simply talk about causing the conditions of one's own defense. *See, e.g.*, Susan Dimock, Actio Libera in Causa, 7 CRIM. L. & PHIL. 549 (2013); Paul H. Robinson, *Causing the Conditions of One's Own Defense: A Study in the Limits of Theory in Criminal Law Doctrine*, 71 VA. L. REV. 1 (1985).

but-for and proximate cause of his subsequent guilt-free choice to φ, even if the prior choice itself was otherwise guilt-free? Or would so broad a rule exceed the state's authority?

Presumably, a legitimate limit on a democratic state's authority to trace would, at the least, disable the state from enacting a rule permitting it to trace a guilt-free choice to φ to a prior choice to β unless the prior choice itself satisfied the *actus reus* and *mens rea* requirements. With that presumption in hand, consider the following proposed limit on the state's authority to enact a rule permitting it to trace guilt back in time, where *A* is the accused, φ is a crime the accused chose to commit (without guilt) at *t*=1, and β is some prior choice the accused made at *t*=1-*n*:

> A democratic state has no authority to punish *A* for choosing to φ at *t*=1, where *A* realized φ-ing was a crime, and *A*'s choice to φ was either compelled (no *actus reus*) or coerced (no *mens rea*), *unless A* chose to β at some earlier time *t*=1-*n; A*'s choice to β was a but-for and proximate cause of *A*'s choice to φ; *and*:
>
> (1) β-ing is a crime; *A* realized, or could and should have realized (because law-abiding *A* would have realized), β-ing was a crime; *A* could have chosen not to β; and law-abiding *A* would have chosen not to β; *or*
>
> (2) β-ing is *not* a crime; *A* has no immunity right to β; *A* realized, or could and should have realized (because law-abiding *A* would have realized), β-ing created a state-prohibited risk that *A* might later be compelled or coerced to commit a crime; *A* could have chosen not to β; and law-abiding *A* would have chosen not to β.

This is the *thin ice principle*,[81] tailored here for cases where the accused realized φ-ing was a crime. Later, we'll expand it to cover cases where the accused didn't realize φ-ing was a crime.[82] Formally stated, the principle is

[81] A warmer metaphor, analogous to the thin ice principle, is the fire principle: If you play with fire, don't complain if you get burned.

[82] The first half of the thin ice principle, which will remind criminal lawyers of the much-maligned felony murder rule, reflects what's known as the *versari* doctrine, derived from the maxim *versari in re illicita imputantur omnia quae sequuntur ex delicto*, which Sanford Kadish translates as: "One who traffics in the illicit is responsible for all wrongs that ensue." Sanford H. Kadish, *Reckless Complicity*, 87 J. Crim. L. & Criminology 369, 376 n.19 (1997). Or, as Martin Gardner translates it: "One acting unlawfully is held responsible for all the consequences of his conduct." Martin Gardner, *The* Mens Rea *Enigma: Observations on the Role of Motive in the Criminal Law Past and Present*, 1993 Utah L. Rev. 635, 705. According to Kadish, the *versari* doctrine "plainly responds to a widely shared moral viewpoint." Kadish, *supra*, at 376 n.19.

intricate and unwieldy, but it tries to capture with greater precision a familiar idea: If you skate on thin ice, knowing the ice is thin, don't complain if you fall through. The thin ice principle is broad, but that's as it should be. As a proposed limit on the authority of a democratic state, it's meant to give a wide berth to democratic politics, permitting the state to enact any tracing rule it sees fit, as long as it doesn't go beyond the scope of the thin ice principle. The principle gives the democratic state a wide berth inasmuch as it rests, as it must qua limit on democratic authority, on the conviction that allowing the state to trace beyond its parameters would, beyond reasonable doubt, be unjust.

Imagine the District of Columbia enacted two statutory defenses. Section 101, reflecting the *actus reus* requirement, affords a defense based on compulsion; § 102, reflecting the *mens rea* requirement, affords a defense based on coercion. Washington, D.C. then enacts § 103, which provides: "The defenses afforded by sections 101 and 102 are unavailable if the actor was negligent in placing himself in a situation in which it was probable he would be subject to compulsion or coercion." Section 103 falls within the parameters of the thin ice principle, and as such, constitutes a tracing rule the state can legitimately enact and enforce. So, for example, if Moore, under neither compulsion nor duress, walked by the Warren Hotel, when he could and should have realized doing so would constitute an impermissible risk of awakening his demons, he'd legitimately forfeit any defense he'd otherwise have had, under §§ 101 and 102, to the possession charge.

Some might object that the thin ice principle gives the state authority to permit tracing when doing so would be unjust. They might be right, but the thin ice principle isn't meant to give an account of justice in tracing. It's meant to give an account of legitimacy in tracing. The People are free to adopt a tracing rule narrower than the thin ice principle allows, or indeed, to reject tracing altogether. Or maybe they decide tracing should only be allowed when β is a crime.[83] Or maybe only when the accused realized β-ing, crime or not, was practically certain to result in φ,[84] and so on. The thin ice principle limits a democratic state's authority to trace. It doesn't say how far the state should go, as a matter of justice, within its limits.

[83] *See* Paul H. Robinson & Michael T. Cahill, Criminal Law § 8.0.3, at 293 (2d ed. 2012) ("Where an actor brings about the conditions of his or her defense, but at the time of doing so has no culpability as to the commission of the subsequent offense, it is appropriate to impose liability *only for crimes that address the specific conduct causing the defense conditions.*") (emphasis added).

[84] *See id.* § 8.0.3, at 287–98 (describing the range of existing doctrinal approaches to the problem of culpably causing the conditions of one's own defense).

Consider another objection. Dick is an unwilling kleptomaniac. He enters Macy's and, once inside, his demon takes hold. He desperately wants to steal a wallet. Not because he needs one. He has hundreds. Still, a wallet is what he really, really wants, even if he doesn't understand why. He realizes stealing is a crime, but he steals anyway. When Dick lifts the wallet, he was powerless to have chosen otherwise (no *actus reus*). As it happens, Dick decided, one week earlier, to stop taking the medication he relied on to keep his urge for wallets at bay. Can the state legitimately punish Dick for choosing to steal the wallet, despite the fact that he couldn't have chosen otherwise at the time?

Apply the thin ice principle. Failing to take medication isn't itself a crime, but in Dick's case, it led to one. Assuming Dick realized or should have realized the choice to forego his medication created a risk, which he also knew or should have known the state would prohibit, that he'd later commit a crime under compulsion or coercion, the thin ice principle tells us he's out of luck. The state can legitimately punish him for stealing the wallet, even though he couldn't, at the time, have chosen otherwise. Suppose it does punish him: It gives Dick six months in jail for petit larceny.

Now compare Dick to Harry. Harry is Dick's twin brother, but lucky for Harry, he didn't inherit kleptomania. He suffers from no mental disease or defect rendering him powerless before wallets. Still, he regards himself to be a connoisseur of men's fine accessories. One hour after Dick's theft, Harry walks into Macy's and spies a wallet he fancies for his collection. He knows stealing is a crime, but he doesn't much care. Adding to his collection is more important to him than conforming to the law. When he takes the wallet, his act and mind are as guilty as it gets. The state no doubt has all the authority it needs to punish Harry. Like Dick, Harry gets six months in jail.

Here's the objection. When Harry stole, he could've chosen otherwise. When Dick stole, he couldn't. Harry freely stole a wallet. Dick stole a wallet too, but under compulsion. All he freely did was take a risk, one he realized or should've realized the state forbade, that he might end up compelled to steal if he stopped his medication. Nonetheless, thanks to the thin ice principle, the state can legitimately punish Dick when, albeit under compulsion, he steals a wallet. The objection is that Dick gets the same punishment Harry gets, despite the fact that Harry's choice, unlike Dick's, was as free as free can be. Assuming six months is a proportionate punishment for Harry, Dick's punishment, so the objection goes, must be disproportionate. If the thin ice principle permits the state to impose disproportionate punishment, isn't that a problem?

It might be, if the *actus reus* and *mens rea* requirements were the only limits on a democratic state's authority. But they aren't. A democracy has no authority to punish a citizen absent a guilty act and mind, but as noted in Chapter 1, neither does it have authority to punish someone grossly out of proportion to the crime he committed. If Dick says the state had no authority, under the circumstances, to send him off to jail for six months, he might well be right, but not because his act or mind wasn't guilty. Thanks to tracing, the state can trace his guilt-free choice to steal back to his earlier guilty choice to stop his medicine. But thanks to the ban on grossly disproportionate punishments, the state may have no authority to impose on Dick six months in jail for choosing not to take his medicine, even though at the time he realized or should have realized he was taking a prohibited risk that he would or might, at some later time, be compelled into the commission of a crime.

Tracing can easily trap addicts like Moore. Even if Moore was innocent at the moment he possessed, chances are he made prior choices, not themselves compelled or coerced, without which he wouldn't have been compelled to possess while sitting in a room at the Warren Hotel on January 20, 1970. If the United States had enacted a tracing rule pursuant to which it permitted itself to trace Moore's compelled choice to some earlier free choice, if Moore's earlier choice fell within the scope of that rule, and if that rule itself fell within the scope of the thin ice principle, then Moore rolled the dice. He skated on thin ice, fell through, and the United States can legitimately ascribe guilt to his choice to possess heroin, despite that choice having been compelled.[85]

The discussion has thus far tried to add detail to the *actus rea* and *mens rea* requirements when the accused realized he was committing a crime. We turn next to the *actus reus* and *mens rea* requirements when the accused was ignorant: when he didn't realize he was committing a crime at the time he committed it.

[85] *See* Stephen J. Morse, *Hooked on Hype: Addiction and Responsibility*, 19 LAW & PHIL. 3, 26 (2000) ("[M]ost addicts are responsible for becoming addicted."); Stephen J. Morse, *Addiction, Choice and Criminal Law*, *in* ADDICTION AND CHOICE, *supra* note 63, at 441 ("The . . . seemingly most decisive reason [for the criminal law's 'unforgiving' response toward addicts] is the potential for diachronous responsibility."). Even when a state can legitimately trace an addict's culpability back to a prior act or omission, that doesn't mean it should, as a matter of justice, refuse to give addicts any break. *See, e.g.*, WATSON, *supra* note 43, at 350 (suggesting that systematic mitigation for addicts at sentencing "would allow us to record the defendant's complicity in her own plight and, at the same time, to do at least some justice to the special difficulties under which she labors.").

4
Ignorance

On February 2, 1955, two police officers stopped Virginia Lambert, a "poor black woman,"[1] on a street in Los Angeles. They suspected she was carrying drugs. Lambert was taken to the Wilshire Police Station, strip-searched and interrogated for two hours.[2] No drugs were found.

That, for Lambert, was the good news. The bad news was L.A. Municipal Code § 52.39(a), which made it "unlawful for any convicted person to be or remain in the City of Los Angeles for a period of more than five days, without . . . registering with the Chief of Police,"[3] along with § 52.38(a), which defined a "convicted person" as "[a]ny person who, subsequent to January 1, 1921, has been or hereafter is convicted of an offense punishable as a felony in the state of California."[4] Lambert, the police discovered, had pled guilty

[1] Warren Christopher, Chances of a Lifetime: A Memoir 23 (2001). Lambert was represented by Samuel C. McMorris, who would later represent Lawrence Robinson in *Robinson v. California*, 370 U.S. 660 (1962). Lambert was apparently McMorris's legal secretary at the time of her arrest. *See L.A. Officials Unhappy over Court's Ruling*, L.A. Times, Dec. 17, 1957, at 6 ("Samuel C. McMorris . . . said Mrs. Lambert was his legal secretary at the time she was arrested for failing to register as an ex-convict . . . ."). In fact, McMorris was apparently with Lambert at the time of her arrest. *See* Appellant's Opening Brief at 5, Lambert v. California, 335 U.S. 225 (1957) (No. 47) ("[A]ppellant, while in the company of her attorney-employer, was accosted on a street corner by two police officers.").

McMorris's brief in *Lambert* "consisted of a scattergun array of assertions, some of which hit their mark, but most of which were clearly wide of the target." Peter W. Low & Benjamin Charles Wood, Lambert *Revisited*, 100 Va. L. Rev. 1603, 1608 (2014). Because "neither Lambert's lawyers nor the attorneys for the City of Los Angeles had fully addressed the issues," Christopher, *supra*, at 24, the Supreme Court set the case for re-argument the following Term, and in a move apparently never before or since made, appointed another lawyer, future Secretary of State Warren Christopher, to submit an *amicus* brief and argue on Lambert's behalf. McMorris was later disbarred for "willful failure to communicate with several of his clients and to perform the services for which he was retained during the period from November 1969 to September 1978." *See* McMorris v. State Bar of Cal., 672 P.2d 431, 432 (Cal. 1983).

[2] The Supreme Court sometimes deploys the "void for vagueness" doctrine to scrutinize laws especially prone to being enforced in an "arbitrary and discriminatory" manner, *see, e.g.*, Papachristou v. City of Jacksonville, 405 U.S. 156 (1972), and the circumstances surrounding Lambert's arrest suggested the L.A. registration ordinance was in fact being enforced in such a manner. The ordinance in *Lambert* wasn't vague, however. If you were a felon, you had to register. Nothing terribly vague about that. Still, inasmuch as the Court's underlying concern in *Lambert* was the fact that the ordinance readily lent itself to arbitrary and discriminatory enforcement, it makes sense to describe *Lambert* as a "quasi-vagueness decision." *See* Low & Wood, *supra* note 1, at 1662.

[3] Brief of Amicus Curiae for Appellant app. at 3, Lambert v. California, 355 U.S. 225 (1957) (No. 47).

[4] Lambert v. California, 355 U.S. 225, 226 (1957).

Guilty Acts, Guilty Minds. Stephen P. Garvey, Oxford University Press (2020). © Oxford University Press.
DOI: 10.1093/oso/9780190924324.001.0001

four years earlier to forgery (a felony in California), but never registered with the Chief of Police, as § 52.39(a) required. Having found no drugs, the police charged Lambert with having violated § 52.39(a) instead.

According to the trial judge, § 52.39(a) required the state to prove Lambert realized she'd been convicted of a felony. Lambert had spent time in jail on the forgery conviction,[5] but didn't think that made her felon, because (in the United States at least) felons typically go to prison while misdemeanants typically go to jail. Consequently, she claimed not to have realized she was a felon, and the trial judge allowed her to explain all that to the jury. On the other hand, § 52.39(a) didn't, according to the trial judge, require the state to prove that Lambert realized that, as a felon, she was required to register, let alone that failing to register was a crime. So, when Lambert tried to explain that she wasn't aware of the registration requirement, the judge sustained the state's objection.[6]

The jury found Lambert "guilty as charged," apparently convinced, despite her testimony to the contrary, that she did know forgery was a felony; moreover, her professed ignorance of the registration requirement was, as a matter of law, neither here nor there. The judge placed Lambert on probation, and ordered her to pay $250.[7]

On appeal to the U.S. Supreme Court, Lambert had no choice. If California law didn't recognize her ignorance of the registration requirement as a defense,[8] she'd have to insist that her ignorance of the requirement, no matter what California law said, meant her conviction for violating § 52.39(a) was

[5] Lambert's sentence for forgery had been suspended, and she was placed on probation for five years in 1951. Her probation was "modified" in 1952, as a result of which she spent six months in jail, after which her probation ended. *See* Appellant's Opening Brief, *supra* note 1, at 4.

[6] In a supplemental brief to the Supreme Court, the Los Angeles City Attorney included a letter from Harold R. Muntz, then-Chief Probation Officer of the Los Angeles County Probation Office. Muntz wrote that his Office's "records [on Lambert] further show the following notation dated October 30, 1951: 'Advised to register.' In accordance with our practice that [notation] indicates that Mrs. Lambert was advised by the Deputy Probation Officer to register with the Los Angeles Police Department in accordance with the City's Registration Ordinance." Supplemental Brief of Appellee app. at 2, Lambert v. California, 355 U.S. 225 (1957) (No. 47). Nonetheless, for purposes of her appeal before the Supreme Court, Justice Douglas wrote: "We must assume that appellant had no actual knowledge of the requirement that she register under this ordinance, as she offered proof of this defense, which was refused." 355 U.S. at 227.

[7] A violation of the registration ordinance was punishable by six months imprisonment, a $500 fine, or both. Each day a felon went unregistered counted as a separate violation. *See* Brief of Amicus Curiae for Appellant, *supra* note 3, at 9 n.**

[8] A criminal lawyer would characterize this defense as a "failure of proof" defense. If § 52.39 had been read to require the state to prove Lambert knew she was duty-bound to register, and if the state had failed to prove beyond a reasonable doubt that Lambert realized she was required to register, then the state would have failed to carry its burden to prove all the elements of the crime charged: Its proof against her would have failed.

unconstitutional. The Supreme Court agreed. "[W]e now hold," wrote Justice Douglas, in a five-page opinion for a five-member majority, "that the registration provisions of the [Los Angeles] Code as sought to be applied here violate the Due Process requirement of the Fourteenth Amendment."[9] Unfortunately, Justice Douglas's opinion didn't explain very clearly how or why that was so.

Justice Frankfurter wrote for three of the four dissenters. His tone was dismissive:

> If the generalization that underlies, and alone can justify, this decision were to be given its relevant scope, a whole volume of the United States Reports would be required to document in detail the legislation in this country that would fall or be impaired. I abstain from entering upon consideration of such legislation, and adjudications upon it, because I feel confident that the present decision will turn out to be an isolated deviation from the strong current of precedents—a derelict on the waters of the law. Accordingly, I content myself with dissenting.[10]

The "generalization" to which Justice Frankfurter referred (and to which he objected) was apparently something like: A citizen can, consistent with Due Process, be punished only if he is blameworthy, and no one who commits a crime is blameworthy unless he realized, or at least should have realized, he was acting or failing to act contrary to the criminal law. If this, or something close to it, was the generalization Justice Frankfurter saw behind *Lambert*'s holding, it would run headlong into the well-entrenched maxim *ignorantia juris neminem excusat*: ignorance of law doesn't excuse.[11] The safe bet, that this entrenched maxim would eventually prevail, and that *Lambert* would indeed be a derelict, was with Justice Frankfurter.

Still, at the time, some commentators thought otherwise, speculating that *Lambert* might well signal the *ignorantia* maxim's eventual demise. Soon after the decision, one writer opined: The Supreme Court in *Lambert* "clearly told us that it detests the immoral use or misuse of the criminal sanction in the case of a morally blameless defendant,"[12] and that "[a]bsolute criminal

[9] 355 U.S. at 227.

[10] *Id.* at 232 (Frankfurter, J., dissenting).

[11] The maxim entered American law from English common law, which inherited it from Roman law. *See, e.g.*, Edwin R. Keedy, *Ignorance and Mistake in the Criminal Law*, 22 Harv. L. Rev. 75, 75–81 (1908) (surveying the maxim's origins).

[12] Gerhard O.W. Mueller, *On Common Law Mens Rea*, 42 Minn. L. Rev. 1043, 1104 (1958).

liability is beginning to end in America."[13] Others offered more modest assessments. Perhaps ignorance is a constitutional defense, but only if the crime charged was an omission, making it a crime not to do something, like register, rather than do something, like steal or kill. That reading would limit *Lambert*'s scope, but what principle would explain why ignorance excused omissions, but not acts? One could doubtless come up with some such principle, but we'll put that possibility aside for now.

Lambert's meaning remains a matter of debate,[14] but whatever its legacy, it hasn't, so far, been the thin edge of a wedge leading to the *ignorantia* maxim's demise. *Lambert* isn't exactly a dead letter. Courts still rely on it from time to time to invalidate criminal statutes and reverse convictions,[15] but Justice Frankfurter's prediction was more or less on the money. "Derelict" might be a little strong, but probably not by much. Ignorance of the law didn't excuse before *Lambert* was decided, and by and large, it doesn't excuse today, sixty years later.

At any rate, set aside the Constitution, Due Process, and *Lambert*'s tea leaves. Our concern isn't with § 52.39(a)'s constitutionality, but rather with the state of California's authority to punish Virginia Lambert for failing to do what § 52.39(a) required her to do, assuming she had no idea the law required her to do what she failed to do. We want to know if, and under what circumstances, the requirements of a guilty act and mind limit the state's authority to punish someone who unwittingly commits a crime. In other words, when, if ever, do the requirements of *actus reus* and *mens rea* trump the *ignorantia* maxim? Before getting to that, we first need to look more closely at the *ignorantia* maxim itself, and what can be said on its behalf.[16]

[13] *Id.*

[14] *See, e.g.*, Low & Wood, *supra* note 1, at 1605 (*Lambert* as a "variant on the vagueness doctrine"); Alan C. Michaels, *Constitutional Innocence*, 112 Harv. L. Rev. 828, 862 (1999) (*Lambert* as a "right-to-travel" case).

[15] *See, e.g.*, Conley v. United States, 79 A.3d 270, 288–89 (D.C. 2013) (holding unconstitutional, under *Lambert*, a District of Columbia statute making it a felony offense for a person to be present in a motor vehicle if the person knows the vehicle contains a firearm).

[16] The best philosophical examination of the *ignorantia* maxim to date is Douglas Husak, Ignorance of Law: A Philosophical Inquiry (2016) (arguing that justice requires an affirmative defense precluding the conviction of anyone charged with a crime who wasn't at least reckless with respect to the fact that he was doing something morally wrong independent of the law).

The *ignorantia* maxim permits criminal liability when a citizen unwittingly violates a criminal prohibition even if his ignorance of law was reasonable. This contrasts with the law of qualified immunity, which (roughly) permits civil liability when a public official unwittingly violates a citizen's statutory or constitutional rights only when his ignorance of the law was unreasonable. *See* Harlow v. Fitzgerald, 457 U.S. 800, 818 (1982) (holding that "government officials performing discretionary functions generally are shielded from liability for civil damages insofar as their conduct does not

Ignorantia Juris

If the *Lambert* Court had simply applied the *ignorantia* maxim, disregarding whatever metes and bounds Due Process might impose on it, the case would have been easy. Lambert would have lost, hands down. The maxim is a powerful force, in law and in the legal mind. Having been dutifully passed down from generation to generation, the maxim has become a mantra.

When all is said and done, *ignorantia juris neminem excusat* is a rule of law that provides (as a first approximation): The absence of a mental state (ignorance) with respect to a specific object (the law) will have a prescribed legal effect (no defense to criminal liability). That sounds simple, but there's more to the maxim than meets the eye. First, we need a more complete account of the maxim's scope. Does ignorance of the law never excuse? Second, when ignorance, even reasonable ignorance, fails to excuse, we deserve to know why. What can be said in the maxim's defense? Finally, we need a more precise account of the maxim's two key concepts. What does it mean to say that someone is "ignorant" of the "law"?

The Maxim's Scope

The maxim presents itself as an ironclad rule, but like most rules, its armor has chips. Most of the time ignorance doesn't excuse, but sometimes it does. Not often, but sometimes. The state has sometimes, in the exercise of its authority, decided to make an exception to the rule.

Section 32(a) of the Securities Exchange Act of 1934 establishes penalties for violations of the securities laws. Among those violations is conduct known as "insider trading." At the same time, § 32(a) provides that "no person shall be subject to imprisonment . . . if he proves that he had no knowledge" of the law he violated.[17] Section 32(a) thus protects the ignorant from prison, though not from conviction. A more obscure provision protects the

violate clearly established statutory or constitutional rights of which a reasonable person would have known"); Barbara E. Armacost, *Qualified Immunity: Ignorance Excused*, 51 Vand. L. Rev. 581, 584 (1998) ("[E]ven if an official's conduct actually violated the Constitution, she is immune from liability if a reasonable official could have believed that her actions were lawful. In other words, ignorance of law—at least reasonable ignorance—is excused."); Kit Kinports, *The Supreme Court's Quiet Expansion of Qualified Immunity*, 100 Minn. L. Rev. Headnotes 62, 65–68 (2016) (describing how the standard for qualified immunity set forth in *Harlow* has been subtly expanded in subsequent cases).

[17] Securities Exchange Act of 1934, § 32(a), 15 U.S.C. § 78ff(a).

ignorant from criminal liability altogether. Section 1902 of Title 18 makes it a crime for a federal official with confidential information, which "might... affect the market value of any product of the soil," to disclose that information "to any person not entitled" to it "under the [relevant agency's] ... rules," but "no one shall be deemed guilty" unless he had "actual knowledge" of the rule prohibiting the disclosure.[18]

Nothing stops a democratic state from abrogating the *ignorantia* maxim and enacting an ignorance of law defense, applicable not just to a particular crime, but across the board. German law, for example, includes a provision making ignorance of law a defense when the accused's ignorance, whatever the crime, was "unavoidable."[19] Similarly, according to New Jersey Penal Code § 2C:2-4(c)(3): "A belief that conduct does not constitute an offense is a defense to a prosecution for that offense ... when ... [t]he actor *otherwise diligently pursues* all means available to ascertain the meaning and application of the offense to his conduct and honestly and in good faith concludes his conduct is not an offense in circumstances in which a law-abiding and prudent person would also so conclude."[20] Among the states, however, New Jersey stands alone, with most states continuing to cleave to the maxim.

Even when a state doesn't abrogate the maxim with a generic affirmative defense (and most don't), courts sometimes interpret an offense to make knowledge of the law an element of the offense itself, which the state must then prove beyond a reasonable doubt. For example, 26 U.S.C. § 7201 makes it a felony to "*willfully* attempt[] in any manner to evade or defeat any tax."[21] According to the Supreme Court, when Congress spoke of "willful" evasion, it meant to require the government to prove the "law imposed a duty on the defendant, that the *defendant knew of this duty*, and that he voluntarily and intentionally violated that duty."[22] Similarly, 18 U.S.C. § 1512(b)(2)(A) makes it a crime, punishable by up to 20 years, to "*knowingly* ... *corruptly persuade[]* another person ... with intent to ... cause ... any person

18 18 U.S.C. § 1902.

19 According to § 17 of the German Penal Code: "If at the time of the offense the offender lacks awareness that he is acting unlawfully, he shall be deemed to have acted without guilt if the mistake was unavoidable. If the mistake was avoidable, the sentence may be mitigated." THE GERMAN CRIMINAL CODE: A MODERN ENGLISH TRANSLATION 41 (Michael Bohlander trans., 2008). Much, of course, depends on what makes a mistake "unavoidable." According to one commentator, "unavoidability" is "not a mere psychological criterion, but requires of D that he exerts all his individual intellectual abilities and if need be consult with reliable specialists, such as lawyers, as to whether or not his intended action is lawful." MICHAEL BOHLANDER, PRINCIPLES OF GERMAN LAW 120 (2009).

20 N.J. REV. STAT. § 2C:2-4(c)(3) (emphasis added).

21 26 U.S.C. § 7201 (emphasis added).

22 Cheek v. United States, 498 U.S. 192, 202 (1991) (emphasis added).

to withhold testimony . . . from an official proceeding," thereby obstructing justice. Construing this ungainly locution, the Supreme Court said that "[o]nly persons *conscious of wrongdoing* can be said to 'knowingly . . . corruptly persuade[].' "[23]

Adding mental states to an offense, when none plainly appears on the face of a statute, is another way courts sometimes protect the ignorant, albeit indirectly. For example, 26 U.S.C. § 5861(d) makes it "unlawful . . . to . . . possess a firearm which is not registered to him in the National Firearms Registration and Transfer Record." That statutory language contains no mental state whatsoever.[24] Harold Staples possessed an unregistered AR-15. Ordinarily, an AR-15 can't fire automatically, but Staple's AR-15, having been modified, could. That made Staple's AR-15 a "firearm" within the meaning of § 5861(d), which meant he was obliged to register it. Taking § 5861(d) at face value, Staples was guilty: He was in possession of an unregistered firearm. End of story.

Staples was convicted, but didn't give up. Despite § 5861(d)'s plain language suggesting otherwise, he argued that Congress didn't intend to punish him for violating it unless the government proved he realized, as he claimed he didn't, that his AR-15 could fire automatically. Staples was, in other words, asking the Supreme Court to read § 5861(d) to require the government to prove he had a mental state that, based on the statute's plain language, the government wasn't required to prove. The Court agreed with Staples.[25]

The logic behind the Court's opinion, as others have noticed,[26] went something like the following. First, begin with the sensible assumption that Congress wouldn't, all else being equal, want its criminal statutes to be used to punish anyone who was "morally innocent." Punishing the morally innocent doesn't seem like something Congress (or anyone) would want to do. Next, equate "moral innocence" with reasonable ignorance of the law. If

[23] Arthur Andersen LLP v. United States, 544 U.S. 696, 706 (2005) (emphasis added).

[24] Acts unlawful under § 5861(d) are punishable by up to ten years in prison, pursuant to 28 U.S.C. § 5871.

[25] Staples v. United States, 511 U.S. 600 (1994).

[26] *Staples* is one in a line of Supreme Court cases in which the Court has construed federal criminal statutes with the aim of protecting the "morally innocent" or "morally blameless." *See, e.g.*, Aziz Z. Huq & Genevieve Lakier, *Apparent Fault*, 131 Harv. L. Rev. 1525, 1564 (2018) ("In a wide array of cases . . . the Court has construed diverse federal criminal laws to avoid imposing liability on 'innocent' or 'apparently innocent' conduct—that is, on the conduct of reasonable law-abiding persons."); John Shepard Wiley, Jr., *Not Guilty by Reason of Blamelessness: Culpability in Federal Criminal Interpretation*, 85 Va. L. Rev. 1021, 1023 & 1029 (1999) ("When reading [federal criminal] statutes, the Justices today suppose that Congress does not want blameless people to be convicted of serious federal crimes," and people are blameless "if they break laws about which they [neither] knew [nor] should have known."); *id.* at 1023 (The Court's "method [of statutory interpretation] amends the medieval slogan that ignorance of the law is no excuse.").

someone didn't know he was committing a crime, and if his ignorance was reasonable, then he's "morally innocent." Third, find a way, if possible, to read § 5861(d) such that it can't be used to punish anyone who's morally innocent.

Now comes the controversial part, on which the majority and the dissent split ways. According to the majority, and contrary to the dissent, a person who didn't realize the weapon in his possession could fire automatically would have no reason to believe he was committing a crime (and would thus be morally innocent), while a person who did realize it could fire automatically would have reason to believe he was or might be committing a crime (and would thus not be morally innocent). The dissent rejected that premise, but if you accept it, the conclusion follows: In order to convict someone for violating § 5861(d), Congress intended the government to prove he realized the weapon in his possession could fire automatically. The syllogism in support of that conclusion goes like this: Congress wouldn't and didn't intend to punish the morally innocent; someone who didn't realize the weapon in his possession could fire automatically would be morally innocent (insofar as a reasonable person who didn't realize the weapon in his possession could fire automatically wouldn't have realized he was or might be committing a crime); therefore, Congress wouldn't and didn't intend to punish anyone for violating § 5861(d) unless the government proved he realized the weapon in his possession could fire automatically.

The *ignorantia* maxim is a rule of law, and like any other rule of law, the state is free to make exceptions to it.[27] Indeed, in the United States the state lacks the authority, as a matter of constitutional law, to give the *ignorantia* maxim its full scope. These exceptions are grounded formally in the Constitution's guarantee of Due Process, and substantively in some principle to the effect that the state loses its authority to blame the ignorant when the state itself bears the lion's share of the blame for their ignorance.

The first limit, from *Lambert*, involves notice. *Lambert*'s outer limits are obscure, but it does have a solid, if relatively tiny, core. Suppose the Los Angeles City Council passed an ordinance making it a crime for felons to fail to register, but published the ordinance in "print too fine to read," or in Rotokas, a language known only to about 4,000 native speakers in Papua

27 Although not often portrayed as such, insanity, in one of its more influential formulations, is another exception to the *ignorantia* maxim. Under what's usually described as a cognitive test for insanity, an accused is, generally speaking, insane if, as a result of mental disease or defect, he lacked the capacity to know he was committing a crime; or in other words, if, as a result of mental disease or defect, he was ignorant of the criminality of his conduct. *See infra* notes 52–56 and accompanying text.

New Guinea. A law "written in print too fine to read or in a language foreign to the community" would, Justice Douglas observed in *Lambert*, violate Due Process.[28] Whatever else Due Process requires, failing to publish a law at all, publishing it in print too fine to read, or publishing it in Rotokas, would fall short. States can't pretend to rule by law if they don't even try to make the law known, let alone if they try to hide it.

The second limit, from a line of cases going back to 1959,[29] involves estoppel. Suppose Lambert, after entering her plea on the forgery charge and having been told to report to the Probation Office, asked the Chief Probation Officer for Los Angeles County, "Is there anything I need to do now? Do I need to register or something?" Suppose he told her in reply, and in no uncertain terms, "No. You're not required to do anything. If you were thinking about § 52.39(a), don't worry. That doesn't apply to you." As it turned out, the Chief was wrong. New to the job, he misunderstood the ordinance. If Lambert's reliance on the Chief's erroneous assurances was reasonable, and if Lambert was later prosecuted for violating § 52.39(a), the Due Process Clause, assuming the chief was a "government official,"[30] would probably afford a defense. One state agent can't, consistent with Due Process, prosecute a citizen for doing something after another state agent has assured him he was permitted to do whatever he did (or not obligated to do whatever he failed to do). Reasonable reliance on the first official's statement of the law, albeit erroneous, would estop the second official from bringing a prosecution.

Defending the Maxim

The various exceptions to the *ignorantia* maxim, reflected in positive law, constitutional or otherwise, are interesting, but the maxim remains the rule. A rule so deeply entrenched in the legal landscape must enjoy especially

[28] Lambert v. California, 355 U.S. 225, 230 (1957). For the Model Penal Code's statutory version of the defense, see Model Penal Code § 2.04(3)(a) (Am. Law Inst. 1985). The Code's notice defense is probably narrower than *Lambert*'s constitutional defense. *See* Model Penal Code and Commentaries § 2.04 cmt. 3, at 276 (Am. Law Inst. 1985) (*Lambert* "indicates the possible appropriateness of the defense in some extraordinary situations" that § 2.04(3)(a) would not reach.).

[29] *See* Raley v. Ohio, 360 U.S. 423 (1959). For the Model Penal Code's statutory version of the defense, see Model Penal Code § 2.04(3)(b) (Am. Law Inst. 1985). The Code's estoppel defense, like its notice defense, is probably narrower than the constitutional defense. *See* Gabriel J. Chin et al., *The Mistake of Law Defense and an Unconstitutional Provisions of the Model Penal Code*, 93 N.C. L. Rev. 139, 143–44 (2014).

[30] *See* Chin et al., *supra* note 29, at 171–72 ("Taking the Supreme Court's cases as a binding baseline, . . . the constitutional defense . . . cannot be limited to particular officers.").

strong reasons of principle to back it up. As it turns out, those reasons are surprisingly frail.

For starters, ignorance of the law is said not to excuse because those subject to the law are presumed, conclusively, to know the law, whether they really do or not, just in virtue of being subject to the law. However often repeated, this supposed defense is no defense at all. On the contrary, it presupposes that ignorance *does* excuse: Ignorance would excuse, if anyone was ignorant, but happily no one is, not in the law's eyes anyway, thanks to the law's conclusive (but unrealistic) presumption that everyone knows the law.

Back in the day when the criminal law reached murder and mayhem, but not much more, a conclusive presumption of knowledge made some sense. It makes much less sense today, when the criminal law's reach has expanded, and when, for example, violating one of the administrative state's countless regulations can be a crime, even if prosecutors don't routinely use their discretion to indict folks who violate, knowingly or otherwise, the mass of rules contained in the Code of Federal Regulations or state regulatory codes. Appealing to a conclusive presumption to defend the maxim does little more than change the question from why ignorance is no excuse to why knowledge is conclusively presumed.

Another false start proclaims, not that everyone is presumed to know the law, but that everyone has a duty to know it. Anyone who unwittingly commits a crime is guilty of breaching this supposed duty. This defense might convince the choir, but not the rest of the congregation. Imagine the state enacts a statute imposing on its citizens a duty to know whether φ-ing is a crime. Frank chooses to φ, but doesn't realize φ-ing is a crime. He therefore breaches his duty not to φ as well as his duty to know φ-ing is a crime, which means he can't (on this line of thought) rely on his ignorance to excuse his choice to φ. Frank protests: He didn't know he had a duty to know the law. In response, one might postulate yet another duty: a duty to know the duty to know that φ-ing is a crime, which Frank also breached. Frank protests again: He didn't know about this postulated meta-duty either, and so on.[31] Defending the maxim on the back of imagined add-on duties does little more than kick the can, deferring the day of reckoning.

[31] Douglas N. Husak, *Ignorance of Law and Duties of Citizenship*, 14 Legal Stud. 105, 107 (1994) (arguing that several arguments offered in defense of the *ignorantia juris* maxim that invoke an "alleged" duty to know the law are "unsound").

These makeweight defenses aside, the *ignorantia* maxim's standard defense trades on worries about what would happen if ignorance, even reasonable ignorance, defeated liability.[32] Oliver Wendell Holmes, for example, thought the no-excuse maxim was a good idea: It encouraged people to learn the law, and if that meant sometimes punishing the reasonably ignorant, then so be it.[33] Making omelets means cracking eggs. Some defenders of the maxim go further, imagining, almost apocalyptically, that the rule of law itself will perish if ignorance allowed criminals to escape liability. As Jerome Hall put it: "To permit an individual to plead successfully that he had a different opinion or interpretation of the law would contradict the . . . postulates of a legal order."[34] If ignorance excused, the law would (for all practical purposes) end up being whatever the defendant believed it to be, which wouldn't be good for good order.

The maxim's supposed benefits may indeed turn out to be greater than its imagined costs. Much depends, of course, on what counts as a cost and a benefit and on whether the no-ignorance maxim actually delivers the promised benefits and produces the imagined costs. Maybe the cost-benefit calculus favors retaining the maxim in some cases (e.g., when the crime is *malum in se* and the actor realized, or should have realized, he was doing something morally wrong, and therefore likely legally wrong), but not in others (e.g., when the crime is *malum prohibitum* and the actor didn't realize, and had no reason to realize, he was doing something morally wrong, and therefore likely legally wrong).[35] The maxim's fate, on

[32] *See* HUSAK, *supra* note 16, at 76–81.

[33] O.W. HOLMES, JR., THE COMMON LAW 48–49 (1881). For a challenge to Holmes's calculus, concluding that "if the goal were truly to maximize private knowledge of the law, a negligence standard would be unambiguously superior to a strict liability standard," see Dan M. Kahan, *Ignorance of the Law Is an Excuse—But Only for the Virtuous*, 96 MICH. L. REV. 127, 133 (1997).

[34] JEROME HALL, GENERAL PRINCIPLES OF CRIMINAL LAW 383 (2d ed. 1960). The standing reply to Hall's worry, credited to George Fletcher, is to say that Hall confused ignorance as a justification with ignorance as an excuse. *See* GEORGE P. FLETCHER, RETHINKING CRIMINAL LAW § 9.3.4, at 734 (1978). If ignorance only excuses, then offenders don't get to say what the law is. All they get is the chance to be excused for having been unaware of what the law is. One might say in response that allowing an excuse based on ignorance would (in any case in which the excuse is found to exist) establish the "law of the case," and the "law of the case *is* the law for that actor." Samuel W. Buell, *Novel Criminal Fraud*, 81 N.Y.U. L. REV. 1971, 2030 n.177 (2006). True, but that wouldn't mean someone excused in virtue of having been ignorant was permitted to commit the crime charged. He's still just excused, whatever the "law of the case" is. Finally, we should note, for the record, that Hall wasn't, strictly speaking, offering a consequentialist or instrumental defense of the *ignorantia* maxim. As Fletcher observes, Hall's "argument [in defense of the maxim was] a supposed claim of conceptual necessity." *See* FLETCHER, *supra*, at 735.

[35] One potential benefit of an ignorance defense would be to offset, to some degree, the putative costs arising from over-criminalization, inasmuch as fewer people will go to prison with the defense

this defense of it, would depend on its consequences and how they shake out.[36]

We offered our verdict on the maxim, and its relationship to the *actus reus* and *mens rea* requirements, in Chapter 2. The maxim, despite its long history and the law's habitual, almost reflexive, deference toward it, conflicts with the *actus reus* and *mens rea* requirements. Whatever might be said in the maxim's defense, I propose it would be unjust, beyond reasonable doubt, for a democratic state to ascribe culpability to someone who, through no fault of his own, didn't realize he was committing a crime, unless he had the capacity to so realize (thus establishing *actus reus*), and unless his ignorance (even if he did have the requisite capacity) was itself the product of insufficient concern for the law (thus establishing *mens rea*). Unless those provisos are met, the state has no authority to adhere to *ignorantia juris neminem excusat* and ascribe guilt to ignorant choices.[37]

If so, then the next task is to describe in more detail the *actus reus* and *mens rea* requirements as limits on a democratic state's authority to ascribe culpability to an accused when the accused is charged with having chosen to φ, but claims he didn't realize he was, at the time, committing a crime. A step preliminary to that task is to explain, with more precision, what it means to say of someone that he was "ignorant" of the "law."

"Ignorance" of "Law" Defined

When someone who's "ignorant of the law" chooses to φ, his act and mind are presumptively guilt-free. The state has no authority to impute guilt to

than without it. For more on this point, see, for example, Paul J. Larkin, Jr., *A Mistake of Law Defense as a Remedy for Overcriminalization*, CRIM. JUST. (Spring 2013), at 10.

36 Following Sanford Kadish, most criminal law theorists, it appears, believe the criminal law's excuses must be grounded in something other than the calculus of consequences. *See, e.g.*, JOSHUA DRESSLER, UNDERSTANDING CRIMINAL LAW § 17.03[A], at 201 (8th ed. 2018) ("[E]xcuses in the criminal law are far more plausibly defended in non-utilitarian terms.") (citing Sanford H. Kadish, *Excusing Crime*, 75 CALIF. L. REV. 257, 264 (1987)). If so, it would be odd to suppose that ignorance of law, as an excuse, should, alone among excuses, stand or fall depending on the consequences of recognizing it or failing to do so.

37 Unless perhaps the consequence would be, as Hall might have imagined, a catastrophic end to the "legal order" itself, in which case the demise of the *ignorantia* maxim would presumably undermine the reason for having a state with authority in the first place, which is to establish order and secure peace in the face of disagreement among equal citizens over what the law should be. But it's hard to believe the *ignorantia* maxim is necessary for legal order, Hall possibly to the contrary notwithstanding.

his choice unless he could have realized he was committing a crime, and if so, only if his ignorance was the result of insufficient concern for the law. Conversely, when someone who's not "ignorant of the law" chooses to φ, his act and his mind are presumptively guilty. The state has authority to punish him for φ-ing, unless he couldn't have chosen otherwise, or if his choice to φ expressed sufficient concern for the law.

Which way the presumption runs depends on the accused's state of mind. Was he "ignorant of the law" or not? Answer that threshold question one way, and the accused's act and mind are presumed innocent; answer it the other way, and his act and mind are presumed guilty. Because so much turns on the answer, we should get as clear as we can on the question. When we say someone was "ignorant of the law" what, first, does "ignorance" mean, and what, second, does "law" mean?

"Ignorance"

Begin with "ignorance." Ignorance is the absence of a cognitive mental state, i.e., a mental state as to the truth of some proposition *p*. Cognitive mental states are cognitive attitudes, and for present purposes, cognitive attitudes vary along two main dimensions: confidence and consciousness.[38]

First, confidence. If someone says he *knows* that *p*, he implies a cognitive attitude toward the truth of *p* held with considerable confidence. A person who *knows* that *p* is confident *p* is true (even if he's wrong). In contrast, if someone says he *believes* that *p*, he implies a cognitive attitude toward the truth of *p* held with comparatively less confidence. He *believes p* is true, but he doesn't *know* it's true. Finally, if someone says he *suspects* that *p*, he implies a cognitive attitude toward the truth of *p* held with even less confidence; indeed, maybe not much confidence at all. He *suspects p* is or might be true, but lacks the confidence needed to say he *believes* it's true, let alone to say he *knows* it's true.[39] The lines between knowledge, belief, and suspicion lack

[38] For a discussion of the various ways in which one cognitive attitude varies from another, see Eric Schwitzgebel, *Belief*, STAN. ENCYCLOPEDIA PHIL. § 2, at 23–35 (2015) ("Types, Degrees, and Relatives of Belief").

[39] A criminal lawyer schooled in the "culpability kinds" described in Model Penal Code § 2.02 might wonder how "suspicion" would translate, if at all, into the Code's terminology. The best translation would be "recklessness," i.e., an actor who suspects that *p* is one who (in the Code's language) is "reckless" with respect to *p*. The translation isn't perfect because the Code's definition of "recklessness," especially as it applies to "attendant circumstance" elements, raises a raft of interpretive problems not worth trying to sort out here. For a thorough analysis of the Code's definition of "recklessness" and a survey of these problems, see David M. Treiman, *Recklessness and the Model Penal Code*, 9 AM. J. CRIM. L. 281 (1981). For an especially careful analysis of the Code's definition of "recklessness" as it applies to attendant circumstances, see Larry Alexander, *Lesser Evils: A Closer Look*

mathematical precision. When does suspicion fade into belief? When does belief shade into knowledge? The borders between these cognitive attitudes are shadowy, but that's only to be expected. The criminal law speaks in the workaday language of folk psychology, not mathematics.

Second, consciousness. If an actor is currently considering or entertaining his cognitive attitude toward *p*, we'll say he's *occurrently* aware or conscious of his cognitive attitude (whatever it may be) toward *p*. His attitude toward proposition *p* is, one might put it, present before his mind's eye. For example, if he believes he's committing a crime, he's occurrently aware of his belief if he's thinking to himself: "I believe I'm committing a crime." If an actor isn't currently considering or entertaining his cognitive attitude toward *p*, but could summon it to mind with little or no effort (thereby making it occurrent), we'll say he was *dispositionally* aware or conscious of his attitude toward *p*.[40] For example, if an actor, as he commits a crime, were to ask himself if he believes he's committing a crime, and if an honest answer were an immediate "yes, of course," then he would be dispositionally aware or conscious of his attitude toward *p*. The attitude is there. All it takes to make it occurrent is for him to direct attention to it.

We should mention one other possibility. A dispositional cognitive attitude toward *p* is one an actor could easily bring to mind. All it takes is for him to advert to it, in response to a simple prompt. But suppose an actor wouldn't summon his attitude toward *p* to the forefront of his mind without some appreciable effort. Maybe he wouldn't become occurrently aware of it unless, for example, he underwent psychoanalysis or something similarly arduous. In that case, the actor's attitude toward *p* is neither occurrent nor dispositional, but rather, as we'll say, *unconscious*. An actor's unconscious cognitive attitudes can influence the occurrent and dispositional cognitive attitudes he forms, as well as the choices he makes and the actions he performs, but

at the Paradigmatic Justification, 24 LAW & PHIL. 611, 624–26 (2005) (arguing that the "concept of a recklessly held belief is incoherent").

40 A "dispositional" attitude might also be described as "latent" or "personally available." For more on dispositional belief, see, for example, HUSAK, *supra* note 16, at 193–201 (providing a detailed and nuanced discussion of "dispositional" belief and highlighting the difficulties involved in formulating a precise account); NEIL LEVY, CONSCIOUSNESS & MORAL RESPONSIBILITY 32–33 (2014) ("Information is personally available . . . when the agent is able to effortlessly and easily retrieve it for use in reasoning *and* it is online," that is, "playing a role in guiding his behavior"); Schwitzgebel, *supra* note 38, § at 25 ("A subject dispositionally believes *P* if a representation with the content *P* is stored in her memory or 'belief box' . . . . When that representation is retrieved from memory for active deployment in reasoning or planning, the subject occurrently believes that *P*.")

an unconscious attitude exercises its influence behind the curtain of awareness. As it might be put, an unconscious cognitive attitude toward *p* can be "online"—it can causally influence the formation of other cognitive attitudes, and so choices and actions—despite being "off-stage," i.e., off the stage of consciousness, either occurrent or dispositional.

What measure of confidence and consciousness must an accused's cognitive attitude toward the law obtain, for present purposes, in order to ascribe to him "knowledge" of the law, such that the absence of that attitude makes him "ignorant" of the law?

Starting with the question of confidence, how much confidence would it take in the truth of the proposition that φ-ing is a crime before a law-abiding citizen would choose not to φ? Presumably not much. A law-abiding citizen would, we believe, err on the side of caution. If he suspected φ-ing was a crime, he'd refrain from φ-ing, and choose to do something else. If φ-ing was something he nonetheless wanted to do, he might look into the law more carefully, not to find a loophole, but to confirm or disconfirm his suspicion. It would be odd for a law-abiding citizen to say he suspected φ-ing was a crime, but then to go ahead and φ anyway. If so, then suspicion that φ-ing is a crime is all the confidence a law-abiding citizen should need in order to defeat any claim that he was "ignorant of the law." Moreover, if suspicion suffices to defeat ignorance, then so too *a fortiori* do belief and knowledge.

One additional observation should be entered at this point in order to dispel a potential confusion. Suppose we agree that someone was ignorant of the law, but we also agree that his ignorance was "willful," adjourning for a moment what it means to describe someone as "willfully ignorant." Do we mean to suggest that someone who's ignorant of the law, when his ignorance was "willful," is presumptively immune to criminal liability? The short answer is no, the willfully ignorant would not, on the analysis of "ignorance" offered above, be presumptively immune.

In order to see why not, we need to get clear on what it means to describe someone as "willfully ignorant." Courts and commentators disagree on the details,[41] but a rough-and-ready rendering is as follows: A person is "willfully ignorant" of some fact *p* if he suspected that *p*, could easily have done

[41] *See, e.g.*, Alexander F. Sarch, *Willful Ignorance, Culpability, and the Criminal Law*, 88 St. John's L. Rev. 1023 1039–1043 (2014) (describing disagreement among the federal circuit courts of appeals on the elements of "willful ignorance"). For a recent and detailed examination of the willful ignorance doctrine, see Alexander Sarch, Criminally Ignorant: Why the Law Pretends We Know What We Don't (2019).

something to gather additional evidence to confirm or disconfirm his suspicion that *p*, but for no good reason chose not to make the effort.[42] Under these conditions, the law ascribes to him "willful ignorance" of the fact that *p*, and in turn treats "willful ignorance" of the fact that *p* as legally equivalent to "knowledge" of the fact that *p*. If so, then a person isn't willfully ignorant of the fact that *p* unless he starts out suspecting that *p*. Anyone who's willfully ignorant of the fact that he's committing a crime must therefore start out suspecting he's committing a crime: Suspicion is a necessary condition for establishing willful ignorance. On the analysis offered above, however, a person who suspects that φ-ing is a crime is *not* ignorant of the law. On the contrary, the fact that a person suspected that φ-ing was a crime suffices to establish that he wasn't ignorant of the law.

Turning from confidence to consciousness, the choice is between occurrent awareness and dispositional awareness.[43] As between the two, occurrent awareness sets the bar too low. We find it hard to believe a law-abiding citizen would regard himself as ignorant of the law unless, while in the midst of committing a crime, the thought "I'm committing a crime" was then and there coursing through his consciousness. A law-abiding citizen wouldn't let himself off the hook so easily. Suppose a law-abiding citizen were to ask himself *sua sponte*: "Do you suspect, if you choose to φ, that you'd be committing a crime?" And suppose his honest answer is: "Yes, I suspect it is." Under those circumstances, a law-abiding citizen would do something other than φ. Or, if he chose to φ, he wouldn't plead ignorance to avoid the consequences. If so, then as between occurrent awareness and dispositional awareness, dispositional awareness should suffice to defeat any claim of "ignorance" of the law.

We can summarize as follows. For present purposes, when we hereafter say that an accused was "ignorant" of the fact that he was committing a crime—was ignorant of the law—we mean that, at the time he chose to φ, he didn't (dispositionally) suspect that φ-ing was a crime. Conversely, when we hereafter say that an accused "knew" or "believed" or "realized" he was

[42] *See* Douglas N. Husak & Craig A. Callender, *Willful Ignorance, Knowledge, and the "Equal Culpability" Thesis: A Study of the Deeper Significance of the Principle of Legality*, 1994 Wis. L. Rev. 29, 41 ("[A] defendant is willfully ignorant of an incriminating proposition p when he is suspicious that p is true, has good reasons to think p true, fails to pursue reliable, quick and ordinary measures that would enable him to learn the truth of p, and, finally, has a conscious desire to remain ignorant of p in order to avoid blame or liability in the event that he is detected.").

[43] If someone unconsciously believes he's committing a crime, it seems safe to assume he shouldn't be said to "know" or "believe" or "realize" he's committing a crime.

committing a crime we mean that, at the time he chose to φ, he at least (dispositionally) suspected that φ-ing was a crime.

"Law"

The state presumptively lacks the authority to ascribe guilt to someone who commits a crime but who was "ignorant" of the "law." Having explained what it means to say someone is "ignorant," we now need to say more about the "law." When an accused is ignorant of the "law," thus rendering him presumptively immune to the ascription of guilt, what's the "law" about which he must be ignorant in order to gain this presumptive immunity?

For help with that question, we turn to Sillasse Bryan. Bryan bought handguns from people who'd purchased them legally from dealers in Ohio. After filing off the serial numbers, Bryan sold the guns on the streets of Brooklyn. He was charged with violating 18 U.S.C. § 922(a)(1)(A), which made it unlawful to "engage in the business of . . . dealing in firearms" without a license, and § 924(a)(1), which made a "willful" violation of § 922(a)(1)(A) a crime. By the time the case reached the Supreme Court, everyone agreed the statue's use of the word "willful" meant the government had to prove that Bryan knew his conduct failed to conform to the "law." The question was what law, specifically, the government had to prove he knew.[44]

The Court was divided. The majority thought it was enough for the government to prove Bryan realized he was committing some crime, thereby violating some criminal law, when he sold the guns. On the majority reading, Bryan "willfully" violated § 922(a)(1)(A) if he knew, while performing the "conduct" defined in the crime with which he'd been charged, that he was doing something "unlawful."[45] Assuming Bryan engaged in the conduct prohibited under § 922(a)(1)(A), and assuming he realized, while engaged in that conduct, that he was doing something unlawful, it didn't matter exactly which crime Bryan thought he was committing.

The dissent thought the Government needed to prove more. It needn't prove the defendant could cite the law chapter and verse. The Government shouldn't be forced to prove Bryan knew, as he sold the guns, that he was committing a crime because he was violating *18 U.S.C. § 922(a)(1)(A)*. But

[44] Bryan v. United States, 524 U.S. 184 (1998).

[45] *Id.* at 1926 ("[K]nowledge that the conduct is unlawful is all that is required" to prove a willful § 922(a)(1)(A) violation). The U.S. Court of Appeals for the District of Columbia has recently stated that, under *Bryan*, the "conduct that [a defendant] must know was unlawful is the *actus reus* of the crime with which he is charged." United States v. Burden, 934 F.3d 675, 693 (D.C. Cir. 2019).

it should, according to the dissent, be obliged to prove he realized he was committing a crime because, as he was dealing in firearms without a licence, he realized *dealing in firearms without a license* was a crime. According to the dissent, it wasn't enough for the Government just to prove Bryan realized, as he was engaged in the conduct prohibited under § 922(a)(1)(A), that he realized he was doing something unlawful. His knowledge of the law had to be more specific than that: he had to know dealing in firearms without a license was unlawful.

The question in *Bryan* was what meaning to assign to the word "willful" in § 924(a)(1). Our question is what meaning to assign to the word "law" in the expression "ignorance of law." The questions are different, but the answers end up being roughly the same.[46] For our purposes, consider how a law-abiding citizen would conduct himself. Presumably, a law-abiding citizen who believed that he was engaged in conduct amounting to a crime wouldn't choose to engaged in that conduct, no matter what specific crime he may have thought his conduct added up to. For a law-abiding citizen, a crime is a crime is a crime: a categorical prohibition, not a price. Unlike Holmes's "bad man,"[47] a law-abiding citizen doesn't do a cost-benefit analysis, and then decide to conform to the criminal law or not. If he suspects the conduct in which he's engaged is a crime, he toes the line. If someone suspects he's crossing the line into crime, he's not ignorant of the law, no matter what particular crime he happens to think he's walking into.

The conclusion to which we arrive is as follows, taking p to stand for the proposition "φ-ing is a (any) crime," where φ instantiates the elements of a crime. When someone chooses to φ, but is ignorant of the fact that p, his choice to φ presumptively fails to satisfy the *actus reus* and *mens rea* requirements. He can nonetheless lose the benefit of that presumption if (1) he had the capacity to believe that p (thus defeating the presumption

[46] The *Bryan* majority interpreted the word "willful" in § 924(a)(1) to require the government to prove Bryan knew, while engaged in the conduct defined in § 922(a)(1)(A), that he was doing something "unlawful," whereas we've interpreted the word "law," in the expression "ignorance of law," to mean an accused didn't (dispositionally) suspect, while engaged in the conduct prohibited under the statute charged, that his conduct was "criminal." Suppose an accused believed that his conduct violated a legal obligation for which the remedy was a "civil penalty," but didn't realize it in fact violated a legal obligation for which the consequence was punishment. In other words, he believed his conduct was unlawful, but not criminal, when it was in fact criminal. Does he have "knowledge of the law" for present purposes? The answer would presumably depend on whether a law-abiding citizen would treat a legal obligation the violation of which incurred a "civil penalty," but not punishment, as a prohibition (in which case we'd say he had knowledge of the law) or a price (in which case we'd say he didn't).

[47] Oliver Wendell Holmes, Jr., *The Path of the Law*, 10 HARV. L. REV. 457, 459 (1897).

against *actus reus*), and (2) he would have believed that *p* if he'd had sufficient concern for the law (thus defeating the presumption against *mens rea*). If he satisfies those two conditions, and thus loses the presumption's benefit, his choice to φ goes from being innocent to being guilty, despite his ignorance, and the state can legitimately ascribe guilt to his choice to φ.

We can now examine in more detail the two conditions an accused's choice to φ, when made in ignorance of the law, must satisfy in order to shift from innocence to guilt, beginning with *actus reus.*

Actus Reus

The *actus reus* requirement is about power or capacity. When someone realizes he's committing a crime but chooses to commit it anyway, the *actus reus* requirement guarantees he had the power to choose otherwise. Likewise, when someone *doesn't* realize he's committing a crime, the *actus reus* requirement guarantees he had the power to believe otherwise. The *actus reus* requirement forms a shield, immunizing those powerless to choose not to commit a crime, or powerless to realize they were committing a crime in the first place.

When we looked, in Chapter 3, for a suitable way to test an accused's capacity to choose otherwise, we settled on the Stephen test,[48] which was designed to test the power of an accused's will. We now need an analogous test for an accused's capacity to believe otherwise, which is designed to test the power of his theoretical reason. How can we tell if an accused's (theoretical) reason is capable of responding to compelling epistemic reasons to believe φ-ing is a crime? The Stephen test, designed for the will, won't work for reason, but we can jigger it a bit to get a test that can: the *Lex test.*[49]

[48] *See* Chapter 3, *supra* at pp. 124–29.

[49] The Stephen test measures an actor's capacity to have chosen otherwise, and presupposes a compatibilist account of the relevant capacity. Compatibilism is a thesis about the relationship between freedom and determinism with respect to the choices we make (and thus the intentions and volitions we form), and the compatibilist theory relied on in Chapter 3 says that we "freely" form intentions (make choices), that our choices aren't "compelled," or that we have "control" over our choices, despite the truth of determinism, as long as our conative will, as the folk-psychological mechanism by and through which we form intentions, has the capacity, or sufficient capacity, to respond to motivational reasons.

The Lex test measures an actor's capacity to have believed otherwise, and presupposes a doxastic compatibilist account of the relevant capacity. Doxastic compatibilism is a thesis about the relationship between freedom and determinism with respect to the beliefs we form, and the doxastic compatibilist theory relied on here says that we "freely" form beliefs, that our beliefs aren't

The Lex Test

The Stephen test, designed as a stress test for the will, involves among other things asking what an accused would have chosen if faced with a punishment just this side of gross disproportionality. In order to retool the test for theoretical reason, we can ask what an accused would have believed if faced with the law's sharpest and clearest pronouncement telling him φ-ing is a crime.

Imagine the Bureau of Infallible Declaratory Judgments (Criminal Division). The Bureau speaks for the state, issues on-the-spot legal judgments, and has one agent: Lex. Santa knows when someone's been naughty. Lex knows when they *will* be. Whenever someone is about to commit a crime, but before they do, Lex sends a text: "This is the state speaking. If you choose to do that, you'll be committing a crime."[50] Lex, as the voice of the state, knows a crime when he's about to see one. Real-life state actors, including courts, say at various times and in various settings what the law is, but they can get it wrong. Lex, in contrast, is infallible.

Lex gives us what we need: a stress test for theoretical reason. The Lex test works much like the Stephen test does. Applying the Lex test requires holding everything about the accused and his situation constant. Before receiving Lex's text, the accused doesn't suspect that *p*, i.e., that φ-ing is a crime.

"compelled," or that we have "control" over our beliefs, despite the truth of determinism, as long as our theoretical reason, as the folk-psychological mechanism by and through which we form beliefs, has the capacity, or sufficient capacity, to respond to epistemic reasons.

The literature on doxastic compatibilism, though not as vast as the literature on compatibilism with respect to choices and actions, is still formidable. For more on doxastic compatibilism, see, for example, Conor McHugh, *Attitudinal Control*, 194 SYNTHESE 2745 (2017); Sharon Ryan, *Doxastic Compatibilism and the Ethics of Belief*, 114 PHIL. STUD. 47 (2003); Matthias Steup, *Doxastic Freedom*, 161 SYNTHESE 375 (2008). For an overview of the literature on our moral responsibility for the beliefs we form, see generally Andrew Chignell, *The Ethics of Belief*, STAN. ENCYCLOPEDIA PHIL. § 3.4 (2018).

Having compatibilist "freedom" or "control" over our beliefs doesn't mean we can "will to believe." Our conative will, together with our executive will, forms intentions. Our theoretical reason forms beliefs. Each has its own proper and limited domain. That's not to say, however, that the desires populating the (conative) will don't sometimes indirectly influence how one's theoretical reason goes about forming beliefs. Sometimes they do, and when they do, the resulting beliefs are said to arise from self-deception or some other form of motivated cognition. *See infra* notes 57–58 and accompanying text. Moreover, though we normally experience a sense of agency (and an associated sense of control) when our will forms intentions, we normally experience no such sense of agency (nor associated sense of control) when our theoretical reason forms beliefs. *See* Chapter 5, *infra* at pp. 228–30 (discussing sense of agency).

50 Compare the instruction Judge Weinstein gave, in a case in which a defendant claimed to have been insane under the federal test for insanity, which, among other things, required the state to prove he was "unable to appreciate the . . . wrongfulness of his act," pursuant to 18 U.S.C. § 17(a). According to Judge Weinstein, the jurors should ask themselves the following counterfactual: "*If [the defendant] were told that the act was illegal*, would he have been able to understand . . . that he would be breaking the law"? U.S. v. Polizzi, 545 F. Supp. 2d 270, 277 (E.D.N.Y. 2008) (emphasis added).

He then receives Lex's text telling him it is. We then ask: Does he now believe that *p*? If yes, then his theoretical reason wasn't incapacitated: He had the capacity to believe otherwise, and his choice to φ, despite having been made in ignorance, nonetheless satisfies the *actus reus* requirement. If no, if he still doesn't believe that *p*, despite Lex's text, then all bets are off. His reason was incapacitated: He couldn't have believed otherwise, he was compelled to believe as he did, and his choice to φ, which started out innocent, remains innocent.

When someone fails the Stephen test he chooses to φ even though he actually wanted, or counterfactually would have wanted, not to φ more than he wanted to φ. He so chooses because (due to the Hogwarts effect) the actual or counterfactual desire to φ failed, or would have failed, to compete with, or be balanced against, the stronger actual or counterfactual desire not to φ. The desire to φ sets up a metaphorical barrier around the conative will, denying entry to any stronger countervailing desire, actual or counterfactual. With the competing desire shut out, the desire to φ did or would have prevailed, causing the executive will to translate it into intentions and volitions and from there into action.

Something similar may happen when someone fails the Lex test. The Lex test presents the accused with a compelling counterfactual reason to believe *p*. If he nonetheless continues to believe not-*p*, maybe that's because something prevents the counterfactual reason he has to believe *p*, along with any other reasons he has to believe *p*, from competing with, or being balanced against, his reasons to believe not-*p*. The belief that not-*p* is thus a compulsive belief, inasmuch as it stands immune to countervailing evidence. We have a name for beliefs like this: delusions.[51] The Lex test, when all is said and done, immunizes from criminal liability someone who delusionally believes he's not committing a crime.

Suppose Lambert didn't realize she was committing a crime when she failed to register. Her ignorance would presumptively place her beyond the state's reach (for want of *actus reus*). Now suppose Lex had sent Lambert a text, after she plead guilty to forgery, which read: "Having been convicted of a felony, you must register with the Chief of Police. If you don't, you'll be guilty of another crime." Would Lambert have realized her failure to register was a crime? Nothing we know about her from the public record suggests

[51] For more on the nature of delusions, see Chapter 5, *infra* at pp. 233–39.

otherwise. No one claimed she was delusional, in which case she would satisfy the *actus reus* requirement.

Insanity

When we introduced the Stephen test as a test for an accused's capacity to choose otherwise, we noticed its resemblance to the so-called volitional test for insanity, commonly known as the "irresistible impulse" test. Under this test an accused is insane if, at the time of the crime, he lacked the capacity, due to "mental disease or defect," to conform to the law. The Stephen test mirrors the irresistible impulse test, minus the "mental disease or defect" requirement. Moreover, whereas the irresistible impulse test is an affirmative defense, available (when it is) as a result of state authority, the Stephen test operationalizes a limit on state authority.

What goes for Stephen goes for Lex. A criminal lawyer will notice the Lex test mirrors another brand of insanity, usually referred to as a "cognitive" test, a generic statement of which might go like this: "A person is not responsible for criminal conduct if, at the time of such conduct, as a result of mental disease or defect, he lacked the capacity to know he was committing a crime." Statutory variations on this generic statement abound. For example, should the test speak in terms of "lack of capacity" or "lack of substantial capacity"? Should "know" be replaced with something else, like "appreciate"? Should "wrong" be substituted for "crime"? We'll take up some of these questions in Chapter 5, when we deal with insanity head-on, but for now they can safely be set aside.

The Lex test differs from the cognitive test for insanity in the same two ways the Stephen test differs from the volitional test. First, the mental disease or defect requirement. The Lex test, unlike the cognitive test, imposes no such requirement. It doesn't matter why, under the Lex test, an accused lacked the capacity to realize he was committing a crime, provided he wasn't at fault for being so incapacitated. Someone who passes the Lex test will typically be someone we'd generally believe to be suffering from a mental disease or defect, and he'd usually be able to find a diagnosis somewhere in DSM-V. But no mental-disease-or-defect requirement is baked into the test itself.

Second, normative status. Cognitive insanity tests are available in positive law (when they are) because the state has exercised its authority to make them available. They're there because the state wants them there. In contrast, the *actus reus* requirement, reflected in the Lex test, is a limit on state authority: It exists as a legitimate limit on state authority to ascribe culpability, whether the state has chosen to recognize it in positive law or not. If an accused would have been found insane under a cognitive insanity test, but positive law doesn't recognize it as an affirmative defense, the Lex test would fill the void, precluding liability all the same.

Not many people will fail the Lex test, but we can invent some who might. One example comes from Herbert Wechsler, Chief Reporter of, and intellectual force behind, the Model Penal Code. Wechsler drafted a lengthy model jury charge on insanity. The charge describes a fictitous person, we'll call him Peter, who delusionally imagined he was an "Oriental monarch, with absolute dominion over those about him, including the privilege to deal with or terminate their lives as he [saw] fit."[52] Suppose Peter killed Paul, delusionally believing he had the "privilege to . . . terminate" Paul's life. Believing he had "absolute dominion," Peter presumably didn't think killing Paul was a crime. Now, if Peter got a text from Lex telling him killing Paul would indeed be a crime, would Peter believe it?

Peter's imagined delusion is probably rare, if not one of a kind. He doesn't, for example, suffer from delusions of persecution, familiar in cases involving insanity pleas. On the contrary, far from being a target of persecution, Peter sees himself as an "absolute monarch," which we assume would mean he also believes he's a law unto himself, or at least not subject to anyone else's law. He delusionally believes he's outside and above the law governing everyone else.

Imagine the text he gets from Lex includes the following language: "Just to be clear: Whatever you might think, you're *not* above the law. You're subject to it, just like everyone else. If you kill Paul, you'll be guilty of murder, and murder is a crime." Would that change Peter's mind? One imagines not. Inasmuch as Peter delusionally believes he's a monarch, with the privilege to terminate life on a whim, countervailing evidence, no matter how compelling to a rational mind, won't compel Peter's mind. The nature of a delusion is to seal itself off from evidence contradicting it. Anti-psychotic medicine might help dislodge a delusion, but countervailing evidence won't.

Consider another case described in Wechsler model charge. This time Peter delusionally believes he's heard the voice of God commanding him to kill Paul. If Peter also believes God would never tell him to do anything against the law, chances are he believes too that no crime is afoot as he

[52] Model Penal Code and Commentaries § 4.01 app. C at 214 (Am. Law. Inst. 1985).

prepares to kill Paul. Now he gets Lex's text: "Sorry to disappoint you, but if you kill Paul, then whatever God told you, you'll be guilty of murder, and murder is a crime." Unlike Peter's delusion in the prior example, nothing about Peter's delusion this time around implies he wouldn't understand the message.[53] If so, if Peter would have realized, after getting Lex's text, that killing Paul is a crime, he'd face a hard choice, assuming he was thinking rationally: either disobey God or commit a crime. That's not an easy choice, but if Peter goes with God and kills Paul, he wouldn't be immune to criminal liability on the ground that he was powerless to know the criminality of his conduct.[54]

An ignorant choice isn't a guilty choice, unless the accused had the power to realize he was committing a crime (and even then only if his ignorance itself manifested insufficient concern for the law). Most folks who unwittingly commit crimes have that power, thereby satisfying the *actus reus* requirement, despite being unwitting. Wechsler's imaginary defendant who delusionally believed himself to be a monarch with absolute dominion over others is, if anything, a rare exception, not the rule. Still, even if most unwitting defendants will pass the Lex test, thereby satisfying the *actus reus* requirement, that still leaves the *mens rea* requirement. Even if nearly all unwitting actors could have believed otherwise, we also need to ask if their

[53] We could, of course, complicate the story and make it even harder to apply the Lex test to the facts. For example, suppose Peter delusionally believes God told him not to trust any messages he gets from Lex. Or suppose Peter delusionally believes God told him that Lex is Satan.

[54] Peter's delusion is an example of what legal doctrine refers to as a "deific-decree." *See, e.g.*, Lundgren v. Mitchell, 440 F.3d 754, 784–87 (6th Cir. 2006) (Merritt, J., dissenting) (discussing the history of the deific-decree doctrine). The facts of such cases have inspired a rule according to which an accused is insane, under a cognitive test, as long as he didn't believe his conduct was morally wrong, even if he believed it was legally wrong. The argument begins from the premise, based on intuition, that a person who kills pursuant to a deific decree should be acquitted on grounds of insanity. If a cognitive insanity test defines the wrong about which the accused must be ignorant as a "legal" wrong, and if in most deific-decree cases the accused does realize he's committing a crime (a legal wrong), then in most deific-decree cases, the verdict would be that the accused was sane. In contrast, if a cognitive insanity test defines the wrong about which the accused must be ignorant as the fact that he's committing a "moral" wrong, then in most deific-decree cases, the verdict would be that the accused was insane, at least if you assume the accused believed God doesn't command people to commit moral wrongs. Thus, defining the wrong about which the accused must be ignorant as a moral wrong, rather than a legal wrong, reaches what's assumed to be the right result, an acquittal on grounds of insanity.

For more on deific-decree cases, including the famous case of James Hadfield, see Chapter 5, *infra* at p. 235; Stephen P. Garvey, *Insanity*, *in* THE PALGRAVE HANDBOOK OF APPLIED ETHICS AND CRIMINAL LAW 385, 389 (Larry Alexander & Kimberly Kessler Ferzan eds., 2019); Linda Ross Mayer, *Unreasonable Revelations: God Told Me to Kill*, 39 PACE L. REV. 745, 748 (2019) (concluding that "assessing someone's claim of 'revelation' as insane or not is not within the jurisdiction of the law, and therefore, a claim of deific command, absent some other evidence of insanity, cannot be a grounds for exculpation either as an excuse or justification, though the circumstances may be grounds for mercy or mitigation").

ignorance reflected a guilty mind, for if it didn't, they'd remain immune to any state effort to ascribe guilt to their choice.

Mens Rea

When someone chooses to commit a crime but doesn't realize he's committing a crime, his choice is presumptively innocent, for want of both *actus reus* and *mens rea*. The presumption of innocence yields, for *actus reus*, if the defendant passes the Lex test. It yields, for *mens rea*, if he passes the Jekyll test. When applied to knowing defendants, the Jekyll test allows us to detect ill and indifferent wills expressed directly, in the choice not to conform. When applied to ignorant defendants, it allows us to detect ill or indifferent wills expressed indirectly, in the ignorance from which the choice was made.

The Jekyll Test

When an accused chooses to φ at $t=1$, where φ-ing is a crime, but doesn't realize φ-ing is a crime, he's ignorant of the fact that *p*, where *p* stands for the proposition "φ-ing is a crime." If an accused is ignorant of the fact that *p* at $t=1$, then the causal force of his available epistemic reasons against believing that *p* outweighed the causal force of his available epistemic reasons in favor of believing that *p*, such that $\Sigma ER_p < \Sigma ER_{\sim p}$. That, for our purposes, means his theoretical reason failed even to suspect that *p*. In order to tell if his ignorance was born of a guilty mind, we deploy the Jekyll test, which enables us to discover if the fact that $\Sigma ER_p < \Sigma ER_{\sim p}$ was the result of an ill or indifferent will.

When all goes well, theoretical reason forms cognitive attitudes (at a given moment) based on our available epistemic reasons (our available evidence). Unfortunately, sometimes all doesn't go well. Motivational reasons, which properly belong to the conative will, sometimes interfere, knocking theoretical reason off task. Theoretical reason should, when it works as it should, track only the truth, but motivational reasons can sometimes cause theoretical reason to attend to some evidence more than other evidence; to retrieve some evidence stored in memory, but not other evidence; to cast some evidence in a more favorable light than other evidence; and so on. Whatever the causal pathway by which the conative will's motivational reasons lead theoretical reason astray, motives can, and sometimes do, end up influencing the beliefs theoretical reason forms.

The will influences reason indirectly. We can't (directly) will ourselves to believe anything.[55] Our executive will doesn't form beliefs. It forms intentions and volitions. Nonetheless, our conative will, and the motivational reasons it contains, can influence the balance of epistemic reasons to which theoretical reason responds, causing us to form beliefs we otherwise wouldn't have formed, or to fail to form beliefs we otherwise would have formed. That might not be true of Mr. Spock, of course. His theoretical reason is air-tight. His theoretical reason responds only to the desire for truth. Alas, we're not Vulcans. Being mere mortals, our motives sometimes influence our beliefs, causing us to see the world as we do because that's how we want to see it.

All this is just an abstract way to describe an all-too-familiar phenomenon. Psychologists call it motivated cognition or reasoning.[56] Philosophers tend to speak of self-deception, wishful thinking, and the like.[57] Whatever the idiom, the basic idea is the same: What we want can influence what we believe. Again, the influence is indirect: The will can't and doesn't tell theoretical reason what beliefs to form. Instead, the will works its mischief offstage, massaging and manipulating the evidence to which theoretical reason responds, altering its overall epistemic force in one direction or another, and thus changing the beliefs we form.

The Jekyll test is designed to detect cases in which an accused's ignorance resulted from the indirect influence of an ill or indifferent will. It tests for guilty ignorance, and thus for *mens rea*. As we've seen, the test has two steps. First, inject the accused with a law-abiding citizen's care and concern for the law, holding everything else about him and his situation constant, thereby transforming him into a law-abiding clone of his actual self (if he wasn't law-abiding already). Second, ask: Is he still ignorant of the fact that *p*, or does he now at least suspect that *p*?

[55] For just one argument against "direct doxastic voluntarism," see Andrei A. Buckareff, *Deciding to Believe* Redux, *in* THE ETHICS OF BELIEF 33 (Jonathan Matheson & Rico Vitz eds., 2014). Having said that, some philosophers have tried to identify limited circumstances in which it may make sense to say we can "will to believe."

[56] *See, e.g.*, Ziva Kunda, *The Case for Motivated Reasoning*, 108 PSYCHOL. BULL. 480 (1990).

[57] Philosophers disagree about what it means to say someone is self-deceived or in a state of self-deception. For an introduction to the literature, see Ian Deweese-Boyd, *Self-Deception*, STAN. ENCYCLOPEDIA PHIL. (2016). We can thankfully bracket these disagreements. All that matters for now is the fact that conative states (desires, motives, motivational reasons, and so forth) can causally influence the formation of cognitive states. For the analysis of self-deception relied on here, see ALFRED R. MELE, SELF-DECEPTION UNMASKED 50–51 (2001); ALFRED R. MELE, IRRATIONALITY: AN ESSAY ON AKRASIA, SELF-DECEPTION, AND SELF-CONTROL 127 (1987).

If the balance of the accused's epistemic reasons remains unchanged—if he remains ignorant of the fact that *p*—then his ignorance must not have been the result of an ill or indifferent will: It must have been due to something else. Maybe he just didn't have enough evidence in *p*'s favor available to him at *t*=1. That's one possibility. Or maybe he just lacked the cognitive wherewithal to form the belief that *p*, based on the available evidence. The evidence available to the accused might have caused someone with more mental horsepower (with access to the same evidence) to form the belief that *p*, but it wasn't enough for the accused, who would have required more evidence in order to form that belief.[58] That's possible too. But whatever the explanation, if an injection of sufficient concern wouldn't shift the balance, resulting in the accused realizing he's committing a crime, then whatever the cause or causes of his ignorance, it couldn't have been due to an ill or indifferent will.

On the other hand, if the balance does shift, such that the accused would have realized φ-ing was a crime, then his ignorance must have been due to indifference, because the only thing the Jekyll test changes is the quality of the accused's will, bringing it up to the standard of the law-abiding citizen. So, if the accused, once brought up to par, would have realized φ-ing was a crime, then his ignorance must have resulted from insufficient concern, where that lack of sufficient concern is reflected, not directly in the choice itself, but indirectly in the ignorance from which the choice was made.

Return to Virginia Lambert. Assume she was unaware of the registration requirement and so didn't realize she was committing a crime when she failed to register with the Chief of Police. That would mean the balance of her epistemic reasons (throughout the entire time she failed to register) must have been $\Sigma ER_p < \Sigma ER_{\sim p}$. Moreover, because she didn't realize her failure to register was a crime, she's entitled, at the start, to the protection of the no-*mens rea* presumption.

[58] The Jekyll test requires holding everything about the accused constant, including "intelligence," whatever that amounts to. The only thing it changes is the accused's quality of will. This contrasts with how the Model Penal Code instructs us to test for negligence. According to the Code, the "intelligence . . . of the actor would *not* be held material in judging negligence." Model Penal Code and Commentaries § 2.02 cmt. 4, at 242 (Am. Law Inst. 1985) (emphasis added). On this point, we agree with those who believe the Code is mistaken. *See* Michael S. Moore & Heidi M. Hurd, *Punishing the Awkward, the Stupid, the Weak, and the Selfish: The Culpability of Negligence*, 5 Crim. L. & Phil. 147, 170 (2011) ("Being generically stupid is not a plausible vice, however undesirable such a characteristic might be."); Peter Westen, *Individualizing the Reasonable Person in Criminal Law*, 2 Crim. L. & Phil. 137, 149 (2008) (rejecting the "MPC commentary's confident pronouncement that, for purposes of culpability for negligence, an actor's 'intelligence' is always irrelevant").

Now add some made-up facts. Immediately after pleading guilty to forgery and being placed on probation, imagine Lambert heads to the Probation Office, where the probation officer tells her, first thing: "You need to register with the Chief of Police. His office is just across the street, in the Police Department. You have one day. If you don't register, it's another crime." "No problem," replies Lambert, "I'll take care of it."

The rest of the meeting with the probation officer lasts about an hour. When it's over, Lambert packs up her things and starts walking to the Police Department to register, but along the way, starts to think. "He probably meant felons had to register, but I'm not a felon. Felons get sent to prison, and I only got probation. Besides, if I really had to register, my lawyer would have told me so. The judge would have, too." By the time Lambert gets to the other side of the street, she's convinced herself the constable had blundered. The law might require dangerous felons to register, but not her. Thus, when she reaches the Police Department door, she doesn't even suspect, as she turns around and heads home, that in one day's time she'll be committing a crime, nor does she realize she's committing a crime when that day arrives.

In order to tell, under these fictional facts, if Lambert's mind was guilty, throughout the period she failed to register when she was required to have registered, we apply the Jekyll test. First, introduce into Lambert's will a dose of law-abiding concern, transforming real Lambert into law-abiding Lambert. Second, ask if law-abiding Lambert would have realized failing to register was a crime. On this meager rendition of the facts, what result?

The state would probably say something like the following: Lambert's ignorance was nothing but a rationalization, which a dose of law-abidance would obviously have prevented. No law-abiding citizen would have been so quick to convince herself that the probation officer didn't know what he was talking about. Lambert didn't register because she didn't want to. Simple as that. So, the balance of Lambert's epistemic reasons, once reinforced with law-abiding concern, would have shifted, from $\Sigma ER_p < \Sigma ER_{\sim p}$ to $\Sigma ER_p > \Sigma ER_{\sim p}$, and her epistemic reasons favoring *p* would have prevailed. She would've realized she was required to register, her actual ignorance thus resulted from insufficient concern, and she should therefore lose the benefit of the no-*mens rea* presumption.

Of course, the defense will make the opposite case:

> Go ahead. Inject my client with all the law-abiding concern you want. It won't change a thing. She was ignorant of the law before, and will be after.

> Was she rationalizing? Of course not. She was just trying to figure out, honestly in light of what she'd been told, if she really was required to register, or if the probation officer got it wrong. She concluded he got it wrong. Simple as that. We concede, of course, that she was the one who got it wrong. She knows that now, but she didn't know it then. Her ignorance was perfectly innocent. Insufficient concern for the law? Absolutely not.

If the defense story is true, then Lambert's ignorance wasn't due to an ill or indifferent will, but to something else. The balance of her epistemic reasons, pre-injection and post-, would have remained tipped in favor of not-*p*, her ignorance was innocent, and the no-*mens rea* presumption would remain intact.

Deciding who to believe is what finders of fact are for, and having available a well-stocked set of facts typically makes it easier for them to decide. The Jekyll test presents the question: Did the accused's ignorance reflect insufficient concern for the law? It also offers a heuristic to help answer it, asking us to imagine what the accused would have believed if he'd had sufficient concern for the law, holding everything else about him constant. But that's all the guidance the test gives. Reasonable citizens, called upon to apply it to a set of rich and messy facts, will sometimes, in good faith, reach different verdicts. That's as inevitable as it is unavoidable.

Assume, when Lambert's will is put to the test, the jury discovers indifference at the root of her ignorance. When it returns a "guilty" verdict, Lambert protests: "Look, I'm a law-abiding citizen! If I knew I needed to register, I would have. Yes, I admit I would've taken the probation officer a little more seriously if I'd taken the law a little more seriously. But I usually do. Really. I have character witnesses. They'll back me up." Lambert puts on witness after witness to attest to her good and law-abiding character. Lambert is, we can stipulate, characteristically law-abiding: her ignorance on this occasion resulted from indifference, but her indifference was truly out of character.

Alas, Lambert's mind would still be guilty. The Jekyll test gauges the quality of an actor's will, not her character. We could, of course, amend the test to make it a test of character, but we should resist the temptation. The quality of an accused's will, for purposes of the *mens rea* requirement, should be understood to reflect who he was at the time he chose to φ, not who he characteristically is. If he wasn't law-abiding at the moment, that's enough to ascribe *mens rea* to his unwitting choice. A democratic state can always decide, in the exercise of its legitimate authority, to assign criminal liability only if an accused's ignorance manifests an ill or indifferent character, and not just an ill or indifferent will, but that should be a question resolved through the ordinary course of democratic politics.

Putting Jekyll to Work

The easiest way to build a case against the *ignorantia* maxim is to dwell on defendants who stand at risk of punishment for unwittingly committing regulatory offenses, like the poor unsuspecting soul who could find himself in jail because he took his beagle for a walk in a national park on a leash longer than six feet.[59] These defendants aren't indifferent to the law. They just had no clue the law outlawed what they did, or didn't, do. But some charges against unwitting defendants are more serious, like manslaughter or murder, and some defendants wilier. The Jekyll test should help orient our thoughts about hard cases, as well as easy ones. We next put Jekyll to work on a sampling of hard cases.

Forgetting

Miles Harrison, a forty-nine-year-old businessman, followed his usual routine on the morning of July 8, 2008. He dressed Chase, his twenty-one-month-old son, in a T-shirt and shorts, put sunscreen on him, and strapped him into the child seat in the back of the family GMC Yukon. Being Virginia in July, the temperature would reach 90 degrees. Harrison stopped at a dry cleaner, leaving Chase briefly in the car, then made or received 13 calls on his cell phone.[60] Harrison was supposed to drop Chase off at the KinderCare day care center, but amid all the calls, he forgot. He arrived at work, got out of the car, and another busy day was off. He didn't look in the backseat, where Chase, nine hours later, would be found dead, his core body temperature at 108 degrees.

[59] *See* 36 C.F.R. § 2.15 (prohibiting "[f]ailing to . . . restrain on a leash which shall not exceed six feet in length" a pet within a "park area"); 36 C.F.R. § 1.3 (providing that any "person convicted of violating [36 C.F.R. § 2.15] . . . shall be punished by a fine as provided by law, or by imprisonment not exceeding 6 months, or both, and shall be adjudged to pay all costs of the proceedings").

[60] Tom Jackman, *On Stand, Man Tells of Son's Death in Car*, WASH. POST, Dec. 17, 2008 (Harrison "had taken Chase to day care several times in the previous week, had left him in the car while dropping off laundry and had made or received 13 phone calls while driving."). On none of the prior occasions had Harrison forgotten to make the drop off at KinderCare. Harrison and his wife had adopted Chase, originally named Dmitri Yakovlev, from Russia. *See* Ellen Barry, *Russian Furor Over U.S. Adoptions Follows American's Acquittal in Boy's Death*, N.Y. TIMES, Jan. 3, 2009.

When Harrison left Chase in the backseat, he unleashed a risk. That risk, unless stopped, was almost certain to leave Chase dead, which it did. Assume Harrison was oblivious. He never suspected he was committing a crime, not even dispositionally, as he went about his day at work.[61] Harrison is charged, as in fact he was, with involuntary manslaughter, also known as negligent homicide: Harrison "negligently" caused his son's death, because a "reasonable person" in Harrison's situation would have realized his acts and omissions created an unjustifiable risk to his son's life, that risk materialized, and Chase died as a result.

Was Harrison "negligent"? That was the question on which Harrison's liability for negligent homicide turned.[62] Our question is related, but different. Assuming Harrison didn't realize he was failing to do something the criminal law obliged him to do (i.e., to remove his infant son from a seat in a car in which the temperature had reached 90 degrees), did his ignorance of the fact that he was committing a crime (i.e., failing to do something the criminal law obliged him to do) manifest a guilty mind?[63]

Apply the Jekyll test. Imbue Harrison with law-abiding concern for the law, including the law of homicide, which protects human life, including the life of Chase. Hold everything else about Harrison constant, including the stress of the day and his powers of memory.[64] Would law-abiding Harrison have realized Chase was still in the car? Or, would law-abiding Harrison have remembered, at some point during the day, and before it was too late, that Chase was still in the Yukon's child seat? If he would have remembered, he'd also no doubt have realized that leaving him there would get him in trouble with the law, and that would mean real Harrison's ignorance of the law,

[61] In some cases involving forgetting or distraction, the accused is in fact dispositionally aware of the risk he's creating, even if he's not occurrently aware. *See* Douglas Husak, *Negligence, Belief, Blame and Criminal Liability: The Special Case of Forgetting*, 5 Crim. L. & Phil. 199 (2011); Doug Husak, *Distraction and Negligence*, *in* Principles and Values in Criminal Law and Criminal Justice: Essays in Honour of Andrew Ashworth 81 (Lucia Zedner & Julian V. Roberts eds., 2012). But Harrison might not in fact have been dispositionally aware. For example, when Harrison's attorney asked him, "If anyone had asked you on that day, where did you think [Chase] was?," Harrison said he would have replied, "Day care." Jackman, *supra* note 60. Taken at face value, Harrison's reply suggests he lacked not only occurrent awareness of the risk, but dispositional awareness as well.

[62] Harrison waived a jury trial, putting his fate in the hands of Fairfax County Circuit Judge R. Terrence Ney, who found Harrison not guilty. Gene Weingarten, *Fatal Distraction: Forgetting a Child in the Backseat of a Car Is a Horrifying Mistake. Is It a Crime?*, Wash. Post. Mag., Mar. 8, 2009.

[63] You might at this point be thinking that Harrison should he have done something to remind himself that Chase was in the backseat, like set an alarm on his iPhone. Perhaps, but that thought raises the question of tracing, to which we will turn below.

[64] *See, e.g.*, Samuel Murray et al., *Responsibility for Forgetting*, 176 Phil. Stud. 1177, 1195 (2019) (reporting results of a study according to which participant responses to various vignettes suggested that "stress partially excuses forgetting when the agent is not at fault for the stress").

which followed from his ignorance of fact that Chase was still in the car, was at bottom due to indifference.

That might have happened, but law-abidance, we should bear in mind, isn't omniscience. Law-abidance means sufficient concern for the law and the interests it protects, including life. Sometimes a dose of law-abidance will make the difference between ignorance and awareness. But not always. Sometimes, a distraction, or series of distractions, will be just as distracting post-dose as they were in reality. Sometimes forgetting is just forgetting. Whatever small cue would've brought memory back online, moving the mind from ignorance to awareness, just doesn't happen, and no amount of good will would have made it happen. Sometimes bad things happen to good-willed people.

Harrison was distraught when he learned of his son's death. An emergency room nurse, present at the scene when the police first brought him in, reported that Harrison "was virtually catatonic . . . his eyes shut, rocking back and forth."[65] When offered sedation, he refused. According to the nurse, he said "he didn't deserve any respite from pain."[66] By all accounts, Harrison was a loving father who would never have done anything to harm his son. "I've never seen a father cherish a child like Miles did Chase," said one witness.[67] All of which attests to the quality of Harrison's character, not necessarily the quality of his will on the day in question. But his character isn't irrelevant. As a loving father, Harrison probably had as much concern for his son on that July morning as he characteristically had, and that concern was probably well beyond the concern a law-abiding citizen has for his fellow citizens. If so, then Harrison's ignorance on that day resulted in a tragedy, but it didn't result from indifference.

Every year, between fifteen and twenty-five children die as Chase did.[68] Reactions to these cases run pillar to post. Some see a crime; others, a tragedy. Some prosecutors bring charges; others think the crime is punishment enough.[69] This disagreement is no surprise, and the Jekyll test won't magically bring consensus, stating as it does a standard or principle whose

[65] Weingarten, *supra* note 62.

[66] *Id.*

[67] Jackman, *supra* note 60.

[68] *See, e.g.*, Weingarten, *supra* note 62; Skip Hollandsworth, *This Can Happen to Anyone*, Tex. Monthly, Aug. 23, 2018. Before the 1990s, child deaths from hyperthermia were relatively rare. Thereafter, safety experts said to put children in the back in car seats, which is when parents started to forget they were there. *See* Hollandsworth, *supra*.

[69] Allen G. Breed, *Sentences Vary When Kids Die in Hot Cars*, Wash. Post, July 28, 2007.

application rests on judgment. It guides, but it doesn't dictate. Even with Jekyll as chaperone, disagreement will linger. One person will wonder how a truly loving parent could forget a baby; another will think "there but for the grace of God go I." Judging the quality of another's will, at a moment in time, or over an interval of time, isn't easy, but that's what Jekyll requires.[70]

Lookin' for a Loophole

Cleora King was being held in a county jail in Minnesota, having been sentenced to ten days for prostitution.[71] King was searched, and phentermine (a stimulant used to promote weight loss) was found, "concealed in a small foil package in her undergarments."[72] Possession of a "controlled substance" was a crime in Minnesota, and phentermine was among the substances Minnesota law controlled.[73] However, at the time King possessed phentermine, it wasn't listed as a controlled substance in any statute. Instead, it was controlled because the State Board of Pharmacy, to which the legislature had delegated authority to designate controlled substances, had filed with the secretary of state a regulation designating it as such, even though the regulation itself hadn't been published.[74]

King moved to dismiss the charge, claiming "she was without notice that the possession of phentermine was a crime." On appeal, the Minnesota Supreme Court disagreed. Citing Blackstone's *Commentaries*, the Court observed: "It is a deeply rooted concept of our jurisprudence that ignorance of the law is no excuse."[75] The regulation controlling phentermine

[70] Another case, well-known known among criminal law theorists and likewise involving a charge of negligent homicide, is *State v. Williams*, 484 P.2d 1167 (Wash. Ct. App. 1971). Walter (aged twenty-four) and Bernice (aged twenty) Williams, both Native Americans with little formal education, were convicted because the judge believed they should have realized their fourteen-month-old son Joseph's life was in danger from an infected tooth. According to the Washington Court of Appeals, the "evidence showed that the defendants did not understand the significance of the baby's symptoms," *id.* at 1174, but the court nonetheless upheld their convictions. Under the Jekyll test, a respectable case can be made the other way: The Williamses were ignorant of the law, and their ignorance was itself innocent, manifesting no lack of sufficient concern for the law or their son's welfare. For an excellent discussion of the case, see Westen, *supra* note 58, at 152–55.

[71] State v. King, 257 N.W.2d 693, 698 n.4 (Minn. 1977).

[72] *Id.*

[73] *See id.* at 695.

[74] *See id.* at 698 n.1 (Otis, J., dissenting). The facts were actually more complicated. Even if the Minnesota State Board of Pharmacy hadn't designated phentermine a controlled substance under Minnesota law, it would have been controlled anyway, because Minnesota law automatically controlled any substance federal law controlled, and phentermine had been controlled under federal law for two years prior to King's arrest. *See id.* at 696.

[75] *Id.* at 697.

was available in the office of the secretary of state, and that, according to the Court, was notice enough.

Now imagine hypothetical King. Before possessing any phentermine, hypothetical King suspects phentermine possession is a crime, but isn't sure. Before going out to make a purchase, she decides to look into it, to confirm her suspicion or put it to rest. She discovers, to her pleasant surprise, that phentermine isn't on Minnesota's statutory list of controlled substances. Her suspicion vanishes, and she now harbors no doubt: phentermine possession, she believes, is not a crime. Thus, at the moment she comes into possession of some phentermine, she mistakenly thinks she's free and clear.

One more thing. Although hypothetical King doesn't even suspect she'd be committing a crime if she possessed phentermine, she also believes the legislature made a mistake. She believes the legislature would have made phentermine possession a crime had it squarely confronted the question. Its failure to criminalize phentermine possession, she believes, must have been on oversight. In other words, hypothetical King believes she's discovered a legal loophole: a gap in the law the legislature would fill if only it realized it was there.[76] Of course, the loophole she thinks she's discovered doesn't exist. Phentermine possession is a crime. Hypothetical King nonetheless jumps through the loophole she thinks she's found and possesses phentermine.

Under these imagined circumstances, does hypothetical King's choice to possess phentermine manifest a guilty mind? At the outset, we're assuming she didn't even suspect she was committing a crime, which entitles her to the no-*mens rea* presumption. The question is whether she loses the benefit of that presumption, which she would if her ignorance was itself the product of a guilty mind. Applying the Jekyll test, the first thing to do is to imbue hypothetical King with law-abiding concern, transforming her into law-abiding King. Let's assume that Law-abiding King, like hypothetical King, wouldn't even suspect phentermine possession is a crime. Like hypothetical King, law-abiding King believes she's found a loophole, and that belief wasn't itself a result of insufficient concern for the law. Hypothetical King decided to exploit that imagined loophole. What would law-abiding King have done?

On the one hand, insofar as law-abiding King doesn't suspect phentermine possession is a crime, hypothetical King's ignorance can't be traced to indifference. On the other hand, it would be odd to describe

76 If hypothetical King didn't think the legislature would have filled the gap she thought she'd discovered, then what she thought she found would have been a hole, but not a loophole.

as law-abiding someone who stands ready to slip through every loophole he thinks he's come across, even if he otherwise diligently toes the line. A law-abiding citizen, unlike W.C. Fields, doesn't go "lookin' for loopholes,"[77] and if he happens to find one, doesn't go through it. If that's right, then law-abiding King, having found what she thought was a loophole, would have steered clear. The "bad man" immortalized in Holmes's *The Path of the Law* might jump through loopholes,[78] but law-abiding citizens forbear. Because hypothetical King, like Holmes's bad man, chose to exploit the loophole she mistakenly thought she'd discovered, a fair case, though not an open-and-shut one, can be made against the no-*mens rea* presumption, and in favor of finding hypothetical King to have acted with a guilty mind.[79]

Imaginary Crimes

The story we've told about King so far is one in which King doesn't believe (or even suspect) possessing phentermine is a crime because she thinks she's found a loophole, which unfortunately for her didn't really exist. She believed she was acting lawfully, when in fact she wasn't.

Now flip the facts. Suppose Minnesota decides to decriminalize possession of all controlled substances, such that possession of any substance, whether previously declared to be "controlled" or not, is no longer a criminal offense. The citizens of the Land of 10,000 Lakes are therefore free to possess as much phentermine as their hearts desire. Nonetheless, suppose hypothetical King, for some reason, never got the memo. Maybe she just moved to Minnesota from Alabama, where possession of a controlled substance is still a crime, and phentermine, along with much else, is on the controlled list. When King receives delivery of phentermine capsules from an online distributor, she believes she's committing a crime under Minnesota law, when in fact she isn't.

[77] Quote Investigator, *I'm Looking for Loopholes*, at <https://quoteinvestigator.com/2016/05/08/loopholes/>.

[78] Holmes, *supra* note 47, at 993 ("If you want to know the law and nothing else, you must look at it as a bad man, who cares only for the material consequences which such knowledge enables him to predict, not as a good one, which finds his reasons for conduct, whether inside the law or outside it, in the vaguer sanctions of conscience.").

[79] For a similar reaction to folks who exploit imagined loopholes, see Peter Westen, *Two Rules of Legality in Criminal Law*, 26 LAW & PHIL. 229, 260 (2007) (An actor's mistake of law isn't "reasonable" when "(i) he realized all along that conscientious members of the political community who knew everything he knew would say that he deserved to be punished for what he did, and (ii) their conscientious views turn out to be *correct* as a matter of law.").

After receiving the phentermine in the mail, King experiences an epiphany. Believing she's committed a crime, she wants to atone. So she confesses her "crime" to the local police. But she can't be charged with the crime of possessing a controlled substance. No such crime exists in Minnesota. Nor can she be charged with attempted possession of a controlled substance. If possession of a controlled substance is no crime in Minnesota, then neither is attempted possession. Things would probably be different under Minnesota law if Minnesota criminalized possession of controlled substances, but didn't include phentermine on the controlled list. If King had then possessed phentermine, erroneously believing phentermine was listed, when it wasn't, she might be liable for attempted possession inasmuch as she would have committed a crime had the law defining "controlled substance" been as she imagined it to be.[80]

Still, didn't King's choice to commit what she thought was a crime express indifference to, or even contempt for, the law, even though the law she believed she was violating, and thereby expressing indifference to, or contempt for, existed only in her head? Suppose Minnesota had enacted a statute, known as the contempt law, making it a crime to "act in a way that one believes to be criminal."[81] Anyone who believed she was committing a crime would in fact, thanks to the contempt law, be committing a crime. Assuming King knows all about the contempt law, she has a guilty mind when she comes into possession of phentermine, not toward an imaginary crime, but toward a real crime, embodied in the contempt law. Can Minnesota legitimately punish her for violating the contempt law, and thereby expressing indifference to, or contempt for, the law making it a meta-crime to act in a way one believes is a crime?

The *mens rea* requirement is one constraint on the state's authority, limiting its power to define culpability, and we're assuming King satisfies that requirement when she violates the contempt law. But as we saw in Chapter 1,

[80] *See* MINN. STAT. § 609.17(2) ("An act may be an attempt notwithstanding the circumstances under which it was performed or the means employed to commit the crime intended or the act itself were such that the commission of the crime was not possible, unless such impossibility would have been clearly evidence to a person of normal understanding."). Cases involving "impossibility" arise when the accused mistakenly believes facts exist and those facts, if they really did exist, would satisfy the attendant circumstance elements of a statutorily defined crime. A structurally analogous case arises when facts exist that satisfy the elements of a statutorily defined defense, but the accused doesn't realize those facts exist. These latter cases involve what's known as "unknowing justification." In both cases, the accused thinks he's committing a completed crime, but isn't, though he would be if the facts had been as he supposed they were.

[81] R.A. DUFF, CRIMINAL ATTEMPTS 157 (1996).

the state's authority to define crimes—like the contempt law—is also limited. We didn't say much about what those limits might be, beyond observing that citizens in democratic states likely have rights defining freedoms traditionally associated with liberal democratic states, and that those rights immunize from penal liability conduct falling within their parameters. The question now is whether there exists, among those rights, a right not to be punished for doing nothing more than acting in a way one believes is a crime, and thereby expressing indifference to, or contempt for, the law, as reflected in the contempt law.

A democratic state is empowered to alter the normative status of those subject to its authority, levying moral obligations where none existed before, and tailoring existing moral obligations so they're owed to the state. Democracies enjoy this power in order to resolve disagreements over what the rules of collective co-existence should be, including disagreements over what interests should, as a matter of justice, be protected through the deployment of the criminal law.[82] But the imagined contempt statute presses the envelope. The interest it protects is the law itself (and thus the state itself) from what, so far as the state is concerned, are nothing more than bare expressions of indifference to, or contempt for, the power in which its democratic authority consists, untethered to any exercise of its authority to resolve disagreements over the particular ends or interests the criminal law should be used to safeguard.[83]

Yet suppose citizens disagree over the contempt statute itself. Some believe the state should exercise its authority to protect its authority, while others disagree. If we adhere to the reasonable doubt test, one would need to ask: Do I believe it would be unjust, beyond reasonable doubt, for a democratic state to punish a citizen who makes a choice manifesting indifference to, or contempt for, the state's authority as such, insofar as he commits a crime, under the contempt law, whenever he believes he's committed a crime, whether the crime he believes he's committed is otherwise a crime or not.

The contempt statute, to our mind, would fail the reasonable doubt test. On the one hand, the contempt statute would resolve the disagreement we've imagined to exist over enacting such a statute (though the disagreement is

[82] *See* Chapter 1, *supra* at pp. 62–64.

[83] *See* Duff, *supra* note 81, at 159 (Someone who's culpable for the crime of "contempt of law" "displays a willingness to flout a second-order value: a willingness, on this occasion, to break (what he believes to be) the law. . . . However, he does not . . . display a willingness to injure any first-order, substantive interest which the law actually protects.").

only imagined, since no democratic state of which I'm aware has enacted anything like the contempt statute). On the other hand, the only purpose the contempt statute serves, beyond resolving that disagreement, is to protect from insult the power in which the state's authority itself consists. But expressing contempt for the state's authority, without in any other way running afoul of an otherwise legitimate criminal prohibition, looks like a freedom whose exercise should, as a matter of justice, be immune to state censure and punishment. Punishing expressions of contempt for its authority, without more, looks like the kind of thing an authoritarian state would do. Democratic citizens are bound to conform to democratically enacted law, but only if that law doesn't exceed a democratic state's authority. The contempt law, I would aver, exceeds that authority, which commits me to the proposition that it would be unjust, beyond reasonable doubt, for a democratic state to punish a citizen for choosing to commit a crime whose only point is to protect the state's authority itself from expressions of disrespect through the commission of what would otherwise be, in the eyes of the state, no crime at all.[84]

Stand Your Ground

A drunken Charles Keitt, twenty-three years old, parked his car in an alley located behind nineteen-year-old Bennie Peterson's home, in the District of Columbia.[85] Keitt tried to steal the windshield wipers from Peterson's wrecked car. By the time Peterson emerged from his house and confronted him, Keitt was back in his car. Things got verbally tense. Peterson went back in the house, emerging with a pistol. He stopped to load it, and again confronted Keitt, telling him not to move or he'd shoot. Keitt moved, but Peterson didn't shoot, not yet. Keitt retrieved a lug wrench from the trunk of his car. Wrench raised, he approached Peterson, who warned him not to take another step. Keitt didn't listen. Peterson shot, from a distance of about ten feet, hitting Keitt square in the face.[86]

Charged with murder, Peterson claimed self-defense, but the jury convicted. On appeal, Peterson claimed (among other things) that the

[84] George Fletcher has argued that cases of pure legal impossibility, or "legally imaginary attempts," involve actors who have "displayed hostility toward the legal order," GEORGE P. FLETCHER, BASIC CONCEPTS OF CRIMINAL LAW § 10.3, at 181 (1998), and that "[t]here is no reason why criminal codes should not include a catchall provision covering any intent to violate the law." George P. Fletcher, *Constructing a Theory of Impossible Attempts*, 5 CRIM. JUST ETHICS 53, 59 (1986). The idea here is that such a reason does exist: Namely, a democratic state would lack the authority to enact into law a catchall provision of the sort Fletcher imagines.

[85] United States v. Peterson, 483 F.2d 1222, 1225 n.15 (D.C. Cir. 1973).

[86] *Id.* at 1225–26.

trial judge misinstructed the jury on the elements of self-defense, mistakenly telling its members Peterson was required to retreat, if he could, before using deadly force. The Court of Appeals for the District of Columbia sided with the judge. Some jurisdictions don't require retreat, but the District of Columbia did, and the "undisputed fact [was] that at no time did Peterson endeavor to retreat from Keitt's approach with the lug wrench."[87]

Stipulate the following. First, when Peterson killed Keitt, he intended to kill him.[88] Second, he realized intentionally killing another human being was a crime, at least if the other human being isn't threatening to kill you. Third, he wasn't responsible for creating the situation giving rise to his need to use deadly force. In other words, Keitt was the aggressor, not Peterson.[89] Fourth, he realized he safely could have retreated, thereby avoiding the need to shoot. But he chose not to retreat, not because he believed he couldn't, but because he believed the law didn't require it. Fifth, he didn't pull the trigger until he thought he had to: He believed it was necessary to use deadly force at the moment he used it in order to avoid being killed, albeit only because he didn't believe the law required him to retreat. Finally, believing the law entitled him to stand his ground, and believing deadly force was necessary, he didn't realize he was committing a crime when he pulled the trigger.

Under existing law, Peterson would go to prison. According to the *ignorantia* maxim, ignorance of the law is no excuse. That goes not only for the law defining crimes, but also for the law defining defenses, like self-defense.[90] Nonetheless, if Peterson, at the moment he pulled the trigger, didn't even suspect he was committing a crime, then his mind was presumptively innocent,

[87] *Id.* at 1234. Does justice require a person to retreat before using deadly force? Not surprisingly, theorists disagree. For a defense of the no-retreat rule, see, for example, Heidi Hurd, *Stand Your Ground*, *in* The Ethics of Self-Defense 254 (Christian Coons & Michael Weber eds., 2016). For doubts about Hurd's argument, see Kimberly Kessler Ferzan, *Stand Your Ground*, *in* Palgrave Companion to Applied Ethics and the Criminal Law 731 (Larry Alexander & Kimberly Kessler Ferzan eds., 2019).

[88] Peterson didn't testify at trial, but the government introduced a statement he made to the police after his arrest in which he said, "I did not mean to shoot him . . . I just wanted to scare him." 483 F.2d at 1226. That statement, if true, would support a failure of proof defense: When he shot, Peterson lacked the intent to kill.

[89] In the actual case, the trial court instructed the jury on the "aggressor rule," under which Peterson would be denied the defense if the jury determined that he, not Keitt, was the aggressor, provided he didn't renounce his aggression. The evidence presented to the jury was insufficient, Peterson claimed, to support such a finding. The Court of Appeals disagreed. *See id.* at 1234 ("We think the evidence plainly presented an issue of fact as to whether Peterson's conduct was an invitation to and provocation of the encounter which ended in the fatal shot."). For an insightful discussion of aggressors and provocateurs, including the distinction between them, and when and why they should lose their moral right to self-defense, see Kimberly Kessler Ferzan, *Provocateurs*, 7 Crim. L. & Phil. 597 (2013).

[90] *See, e.g.*, Model Penal Code § 3.09(1) (Am. Law Inst. 1985).

for want of *mens rea*, unless his ignorance itself was guilty, which bring us once again to the Jekyll test.

We're assuming Keitt was the aggressor. He went after Peterson, not the other way around. The law of self-defense in the District of Columbia nonetheless demanded that Peterson retreat, so long as doing so wouldn't jeopardize his own safety. In most states, however, the law of self-defense wouldn't have forced Peterson to retreat. Not being the aggressor, he didn't do anything wrong. Keitt was the aggressor, and most states permit innocent victims of another's lethal aggression to stand their ground.[91] Peterson mistakenly believed the law in D.C. was like the law in most other states. With all that in mind, but without more, would law-abiding Peterson, not knowing D.C. law required him to retreat, have stood his ground or stood down?

Or take a harder case. Suppose Keitt attacked Peterson inside Peterson's home.[92] Even in jurisdictions, like D.C., where retreat is required, a person is permitted to stand his ground in his own home.[93] That's known as the "castle doctrine." But suppose the District of Columbia had decided to get rid of the castle doctrine. Life is sacred, and a person should be permitted to kill in self-defense only if he can't retreat, inside his castle or out. That, we might suppose, was the logic behind the District of Columbia's imagined decision abolishing the castle doctrine. If Peterson, now inside his castle, kills Keitt without retreating, erroneously thinking D.C. law permitted him to stand his ground, at least in his castle, does his ignorance manifest, under those circumstances, a guilty mind?

91 *See* DRESSLER, *supra* note 36, at § 18.02[C][2], at 217 ("A majority of jurisdictions today apply a 'no-retreat' rule: a non-aggressor is permitted to use deadly force to repel an unlawful deadly attack, even if he is aware of a place to which he can retreat in complete safety."). George Fletcher once described a theory of self-defense according to which the "significant feature is not the conflict of interests, but the unilateral violation of the defender's autonomy. If a person's autonomy is compromised by the intrusion, then the defender has the right to expel the intruder and restore the integrity of his domain." FLETCHER, *supra* note 34, § 10.5.3, at 860. German law, he claimed, reflected this theory: "The basic maxim underlying the German conception of the defense is: *Das Recht braucht dem Unrecht nicht zu weichen* (Right need never yield to Wrong). If a defender is obligated to retreat, he is obligated to give way to the forces of *Unrecht* or the Wrong. The issue is not balancing the value of autonomy against the value of the aggressor's life, but whether the defender enjoys autonomy to begin with." FLETCHER, *supra* note 34, § 10.5.4, at 865.

92 In the actual case, Peterson claimed he was, for purposes of self-defense, within his home (or "castle") at the time he shot, because he was standing in his yard, i.e., the "curtilage" of his home. *See* 483 F.2d at 1236–37. Thus, claimed Peterson, he wasn't required to retreat, even if he otherwise would have been. The Court never reached this claim, apparently because it believed the jury found Peterson was the aggressor, and aggressors are always required to retreat, even in their castles.

93 *See* DRESSLER, *supra* note 36, at § 18.02[C][3], at 218 (noting the castle doctrine is a "universally recognized exception" to the duty to retreat).

The main point is that questions like these can't be avoided. The requirement of a guilty mind applies to all defendants and all crimes. It applies to easy cases, like those involving defendants who didn't realize they were committing a crime because the crime charged was tucked away in some corner of the Code of Federal Regulations. Yet it also applies to hard cases, like those involving defendants who commit serious crimes believing the law nonetheless grants them permission to do so. The requirement of a guilty mind protects those charged with walking a dog in a national park on too-long a leash. It also protects those charged with murder.

Tracing

At the end of Chapter 3, we met Dick, a kleptomaniac who stole a wallet from Macy's. He realized he was committing a crime, but couldn't help himself. At the moment he took the wallet, his choice wasn't guilty, for want of *actus reus*, and the state had no authority to say otherwise. That wasn't the end of the story, however. We formulated a tracing rule, dubbed the thin ice principle, according to which the state could legitimately trace Dick's guilt-free choice to φ at *t*=1 back to some prior guilty choice, which placed him back on the hook for φ-ing.[94]

The thin ice principle offered in Chapter 3 limited itself to cases in which the accused realized or should have realized his prior choice (labeled β) was itself a crime, or created a state-prohibited risk that he'd later be compelled (no *actus reus*) or coerced (no *mens rea*), at some later time, to φ. We now need to expand the thin ice principle to accommodate cases in which the accused's choice to φ was lacking *actus reus* or *mens rea* due to ignorance. Modified for the ignorant defendant, the thin ice principle provides:

> A democratic state has no authority to punish *A* for choosing to φ at *t*=1, where *A* didn't realize φ-ing was a crime, and *A* either could not have realized φ-ing was a crime (no *actus reus*), or law-abiding *A* would not have realized φ-ing was a crime (no *mens rea*), *unless A* chose to β at some earlier time *t*=1-*n; A*'s choice to β was a but-for and proximate cause of *A*'s choice to φ, *and:*

[94] *See* Chapter 3, *supra* at pp. 153–58.

(1) β-ing is a crime; *A* realized, or could and should have realized (because law-abiding *A* would have realized), β-ing was a crime; *A* could have chosen not to β; and law-abiding *A* would have chosen not to β; *or*

(2) β-ing is *not* a crime; *A* has no immunity right to β; *A* realized, or could and should have realized (because law-abiding *A* would have realized), β-ing created a state-prohibited risk that *A* might later unwittingly, and without *actus reus* or *mens rea*, commit a crime; *A* could have chosen not to β; and law-abiding *A* would have chosen not to β.

This version of the thin ice principle, tailored for those who are innocently ignorant of the law at $t=1$, is a challenge to digest, as was the version, tailored for the compelled or coerced, proposed in Chapter 3. Still, with a little effort, the basic idea should come through.

We can take the principle for a test ride with Bruce.[95] Suppose New York enacts a tracing rule co-extensive with the thin ice principle, which sets the outer limit on its authority to trace. Bruce is an investment banker on Wall Street. The market had a bad day, and so did Bruce, so he heads to Shorty's, on Pearl Street, for a drink. He has a martini. Then another. Then another. After becoming intoxicated, but not falling-down drunk, he decides to drive home. He turns on the ignition, leaves the parking lot, and heads out, driving erratically. He's pulled over on the FDR and arrested.

Bruce is charged with violating § 1192.3 of New York's Vehicle and Traffic Law: "No person shall operate a motor vehicle while in an intoxicated condition."[96] The crime is simple. Roughly, it has two objective elements: operating a motor vehicle, and doing so while in an intoxicated condition. If Bruce says he was so intoxicated he didn't realize he was operating a motor vehicle, or indeed, if he says he was so intoxicated he didn't realize he was intoxicated, it won't do him any good. Section 1192.3 doesn't require the state to prove any mental state with respect to its objective elements.[97]

[95] When philosophers discuss tracing and moral responsibility, the discussion often features hypotheticals involving drunk drivers. *See, e.g.*, JOHN MARTIN FISCHER, *The Triumph of Tracing*, *in* DEEP CONTROL: ESSAYS ON FREE WILL AND VALUE 206, 207 (2012) (describing Dan, a drunk driver who runs over a pedestrian, as "of course" responsible for the pedestrian's death); Matthew T. Flummer, *In Defense of Tracing*, 41 J. PHIL. RES. 439, 439–40 (2016) (showcasing a hypothetical involving two drunk drivers); Seth Shabo, *More Trouble with Tracing*, 80 ERKENNTNIS 987, 987 (2015) ("In the classic example, someone is morally blameworthy for her impaired decision to drive because it was a foreseeable consequence of her unimpaired decision to drink.").

[96] N.Y. VEH. & TRAF. LAW § 1192.3.

[97] When a criminal offense includes a mental state, as § 1192.3 does not, a defendant is permitted, under New York law, as under the Model Penal Code, to introduce evidence of an intoxicant's effects to negate intent with respect to result and attendant circumstance elements, but not recklessness. *See*

Guilty or not under existing law, our question is whether New York has the authority to punish Bruce for violating § 1192.3. Answering that question turns out to be more involved than one might think. We'll eventually get to the thin ice principle, but we need to take a couple other steps first, making a number of assumptions along the way.

Step 1. Did Bruce realize he was committing a crime as he was operating his motor vehicle in an intoxicated condition? It depends on how intoxicated he was, and what effect the multiple martinis had on his mind as he was operating his motor vehicle while intoxicated. How an intoxicant changes the mind depends on the intoxicant and the mind.

Assume Bruce's multiple martinis messed up his theoretical reason, the equipment though which he forms beliefs about the world, including beliefs about whether he's driving a car, whether he's intoxicated, and whether driving a car while intoxicated is a crime. His mind-on-martinis made it harder for him to get a clear cognitive picture of the world, compared to his mind-not-on-martinis. The martinis, not to put too fine a point on it, made him temporarily dumb. Of course, despite his martini-induced dumbness, he might still have suspected he was committing a crime as he was driving. If so, New York can send him off to jail with a clear conscience.

Step 2. Now assume the martinis really messed with Bruce's theoretical reason, such that he didn't even suspect he was committing a crime. If so, his ignorance would make him presumptively immune to state punishment. That presumption would, of course, give way if he wasn't powerless to realize he was committing a crime (thus satisfying the *actus reus* requirement); and if his ignorance itself was the result of insufficient concern for the law and its ends, including the lives and limbs of others who might get in his way on his drunken drive home (thus satisfying the *mens rea* requirement).

In order to test for *actus reus*, we turn to the Lex test. If Lex had opened the car door, sat down next to Bruce and told him in no uncertain terms he'd be committing a crime if he drove the car out of the parking lot, would Bruce have gotten the message? Again, it would depend on how much the martinis had managed to undo his capacity for theoretical reasoning, but let's assume

N.Y. Penal Law § 15.05(3); Model Penal Code § 2.08 (Am. Law Inst.). Other states use different rules to regulate the admissibility of evidence related to an intoxicant's effect on the accused's mental state. *See* Mitchell Keiter, *Just Say No Excuse: The Rise and Fall of the Intoxication Defense*, 87 J. Crim. L. & Criminology 482 app. (1997) (summarizing various approaches regulating the admission of intoxication evidence among the states as of 1997). The distinction between crimes requiring specific intent (admissible) and those requiring general intent (inadmissible) is still used in some states, as it is in the United Kingdom. *See* Dir. Pub. Pros. v. Majewski, [1977] A.C. 443.

they hadn't degraded Bruce's mind to the point where, faced with Lex's unequivocal declaration, he would have failed to register the fact that φ-ing was a crime. If so, then Bruce satisfies the *actus reus* requirement, and his presumptive immunity is halfway to defeat.

In order to test for *mens rea*, we turn to the Jekyll test. Would Bruce have realized that he was committing a crime at t=1 if he cared as much as a law-abiding citizen would have cared about the law and the welfare of his fellow citizens? You might think so. After all, isn't drunk driving the height of indifference? Yes and no. First, bear in mind what, for now, we're testing. We're testing the quality of Bruce's will during the time he was violating § 1192.3, not before. The state of his will while getting drunk is, for now, neither here nor there.

Second, we're assuming the martinis corrupted the quality of Bruce's mind (his theoretical reason), not the quality of his will.[98] We're assuming he didn't realize he was committing a crime, based on all the evidence available to him at t=1, because, and only because, the martinis mucked up the gears of his theoretical reason. The martinis transformed not-so-dumb Bruce into dumb Bruce. So unless good will makes you smarter, injecting Bruce with law-abiding concern wouldn't change a thing, assuming Bruce otherwise had sufficient concern for the law. He still wouldn't have realized he was committing a crime. If so, then Bruce's presumptive immunity remains only half-way beat, which means it isn't beat, and Bruce remains immune, for want of *mens rea*.

Step 3. We come at last to the thin ice principle. Assuming Bruce's choice to φ fails the *mens rea* requirement, such that he remains immune to criminal liability, is Bruce nonetheless liable for φ-ing, thanks to the thin ice principle? Can his (assumed) guilt-free choice to φ at t=1 be traced to a prior choice to β, where that choice meets the conditions set out in the thin ice principle?

The obvious place to look for a suitable β is Bruce's choice to have those multiple martinis, thereby impairing his powers of theoretical reason. New York law doesn't make it a crime to consume martinis, nor does it make it a crime to get drunk.[99] It makes it a crime to drive while drunk. That being

[98] One should hasten to add that Bruce's multiple martinis may well have degraded, not the quality of his mind, but the quality of his will, rendering him temporarily indifferent, rather than temporarily stupid. If Bruce's ignorance was due, not to martini-induced stupidity, but to martini-induced indifference, then he'd lose the benefit of the presumption against liability, inasmuch as he retained the capacity to realize he was committing a crime, and inasmuch as his ignorance itself was the result of self-induced indifference. *See* Douglas Husak, *Intoxication and Culpability*, 6 Crim. L. & Phil. 363 (2012).

[99] German law does make it a crime to get drunk, provided you end up committing an "unlawful act" while in a "drunken state." *See* Strafgesetzbuch [StGB] [Penal Code] § 323a.

so, the hard question under the thin ice principle would be: At some point after putting the first martini to his lips and before operating his motor vehicle while intoxicated, did Bruce realize he was thereby creating a state-prohibited risk that he might unwittingly commit a crime (driving while intoxicated); or, if he didn't so realize, could he have so realized, and if so, would he have so realized if he'd had the concern of a law-abiding citizen?

Any attempt at an answer depends on more facts. For example, suppose Bruce, just one week before *t*=1, had gone to Shorty's, ordered the same number of martinis, gotten into the same car, driven the same route home, and ended up under arrest for DWI. With those memories still fresh in mind, and having no plan to have someone drive him home, Bruce would probably have realized, at some point between his first drink and his decision to turn on the ignition, that he was thereby taking a risk, which the state wouldn't permit, that he might later and unwittingly commit a crime, including violating § 1192.3. If so, then despite having no authority to punish Bruce for violating § 1192.3 while he was violating it, New York could legitimately punish him for its violation, pursuant to the thin ice principle, based on the choices he made at Shorty's to indulge his taste for martinis.

In contrast, suppose just before bringing the first martini to his lips, Bruce solicited a solemn promise from Betty, whom he had every reason to trust, that under no circumstances would she let him get into his car and drive home. Betty assured him she wouldn't. Cross her heart and hope to die. But Betty let him down. When Bruce was on his third martini, and slipping into oblivion, Betty slipped out, leaving Bruce behind. Intoxicated, Bruce got into his car and headed home. At no point beforehand did he suspect he was committing a crime, nor at any point beforehand did he suspect he was taking any prohibited risk that he'd later end up unwittingly committing a crime. On those facts, the thin ice principle would seem less likely to come to New York's aid, and if it doesn't, then New York lacked authority to punish Bruce for violating § 1192.3. Once Bruce has been invested with the concern of a law-abiding citizen, would he have realized in light of the assurances he'd solicited from Betty that he was creating a prohibited risk that he'd later end up unwittingly committing a crime? That looks to be the main question.

The next chapter takes up another problem. The *actus reus* and *mens rea* requirements presuppose that the person whose choice is being tested against the demands of those requirements experiences the choice being tested as *his* choice. Chapter 5 asks what would happen to the state's authority to ascribe guilt if the person charged with the crime *doesn't* experience the choice being judged as his choice.

5
Agency

Around 4:00 on January 20, 1843, a man was walking down Parliament Street, crowded with people,[1] heading to Downing Street. Another man approached him from behind, withdrew a pistol, put it to his back, and pulled the trigger. A nearby Bobbie saw what happened, rushed over, and seized the assailant, who was reaching for another pistol. The assailant was Daniel M'Naghten,[2] a wood-turner from Glasgow.[3] The victim was Edmund Drummond, private secretary to Queen Victoria's Prime Minister, Robert Peel. M'Naghten wanted to kill Peel, not Drummond, but mistook the latter for the former. Drummond died five days later. The case against M'Naghten has become a defining moment in the law of insanity.[4]

M'Naghten was delusional. He attacked Drummond because he believed members of the Tory party were out to get him, relentlessly persecuting him. In reality, of course, the Tories weren't after him, but M'Naghten wasn't in reality. He was in a world of his own, at least when it came to the Tories. Earlier, M'Naghten had told the Glasgow police commissioner "he was the object of some persecution, and . . . that he thought it proceeded from the priests at the Catholic chapel on Clyde Street, who were assisted by a parcel of Jesuits."[5] Two days later, he told the commissioner the "Tories had joined the Catholics,"[6] and thereafter it was the Tories who, as some witnesses later put

[1] *See* Arlie Loughnan, *M'Naghten's Case (1843)*, *in* Landmark Cases in Criminal Law 125, 130 (Philip Handler et al. eds., 2017).

[2] M'Naghten's name is spelled in different ways in different sources. *See, e.g.*, Richard Moran, Knowing Right from Wrong: The Insanity Defense of Daniel McNaughtan xi–xii (1981); Bernard L. Diamond, *On the Spelling of Daniel M'Naghten's Name*, 25 Ohio St. L.J. 84 (1964). We'll use the spelling from the case bearing his name. M'Naghten's Case, 8 Eng. Rep. 718 (1843). For historical accounts of the case, see, for example, Moran, *supra*; Richard D. Schneider, The Lunatic and the Lords (2009); Daniel McNaughton: His Trial and the Aftermath (Donald J. West & Alexander Walk eds., 1977).

[3] Schneider, *supra* note 2, at 143.

[4] Most U.S. jurisdictions today continue to define insanity in ways traceable the original formulation of the M'Naghten Rules. *See* Paul Robinson et al., *The American Criminal Code: General Defenses*, 7 J. Leg. Analysis § 2.2.1, at 77 (2015) (stating that the "majority view" of the insanity defense provides that "[a]n actor is not responsible for criminal conduct if at the time of such conduct as a result of mental disease or defect he did not know his conduct was wrong").

[5] Schneider, *supra* note 2, at 208 (citing transcript).

[6] *Id.*

Guilty Acts, Guilty Minds. Stephen P. Garvey, Oxford University Press (2020). © Oxford University Press.
DOI: 10.1093/oso/9780190924324.001.0001

it, "haunted" him.[7] Today, M'Naghten would likely be diagnosed with paranoid schizophrenia or paranoid psychosis.[8]

"The delusions were of such intensity," M'Naghten's father testified at trial, "that the Tories were with him day and night spying on him . . . they were there every time he turned around . . . they laughed at him and shot their fists in his face."[9] M'Naghten sought help from the police, from Sir James Campbell, the Lord Provost of Glasgow,[10] and from Alexander Johnston, M.P. for Glasgow,[11] all to no avail. According to Johnston, M'Naghten "complained about being attacked in the newspapers, and said the persons of whom he complained followed him night and day . . . . [H]e thought his persecutors would be satisfied with nothing less than his life."[12] M'Naghten, so far as one can tell, apparently believed killing the Tory prime minister was the only way out, a last desperate attempt to end the torment.

M'Naghten was tried for murder.[13] When the defense rested, the presiding judge, Chief Justice Tindal, asked the Solicitor General, William Follett: "[A]re you prepared, on the part of the Crown, with any evidence to combat [the defense] testimony . . . , because we think if you have not, we must be under the necessity of stopping the case. Is there any medical evidence on the other side?"[14] Follett threw in the towel. "No, my Lord,"[15] he replied. Justice Tindal then all but directed an acquittal by reason of insanity.[16] M'Naghten was sent to Bethlem Hospital, also known as Bedlam,[17] and thereafter to Broadmoor Asylum, where he died in 1865.[18]

M'Naghten's case would eventually produce a test for insanity bearing his name. We'll get to that in a minute, but assume M'Naghten had actually been

[7] *Id.* at 204 (Jane Drummond Patterson, in whose house M'Naghten had lodged two years before the trial, testified that M'Naghten, after three or four months, mentioned being "haunted by devils."); *id.* at 207–08 (testimony of Rev. Alexander Turner that M'Naghten "talked about being haunted" by a number of persons).

[8] *See id.* at 253.

[9] *Id.* at 254.

[10] *See id.* at 207.

[11] *See id.* at 205.

[12] *Id.* at 205–06.

[13] *See id.* at 225. M'Naghten had savings of £750 (probably somewhere between $67,000 to $97,000 today) and was able to hire the Victorian equivalent of a defense dream team. *See id.* at 55.

[14] *Id.* at 222. Justice Tindal would later speak for the Law Lords in announcing what became known as the *M'Naghten* Rule(s). The reason for the equivocation between the *M'Naghten* Rule (singular) and the *M'Naghten* Rules (plural) is explained *infra* note 26.

[15] *Id.*

[16] *Id.* at 223–24.

[17] *See id.* at 225.

[18] *See id.* at 265–66.

tried under what would become known as the *M'Naghten* test. It's anyone's guess as to what the verdict would have been, but according to some, the test, honestly applied, should have produced a verdict of guilty.[19] If so, M'Naghten would have become, not a patient in Bethlem, but an inmate at Newgate. He wouldn't have been there long: A conviction for murder in 1843, in Victorian England, meant a quick trip to the gallows unless the Home Secretary intervened with the royal prerogative of mercy.

If M'Naghten had been convicted, did the Crown have the authority to ascribe guilt to his choice? If, when he shot Drummond, M'Naghten acted without *actus reus* or *mens rea*, then the Crown would have had no authority to convict, let alone hang him. So: When M'Naghten pointed his pistol at Drummond and pulled the trigger, were his act and mind guilty?

The question looks simple, but it's actually not. The problem, as we'll see, is with the question itself. M'Naghten, it assumes, was the one who shot Drummond, and with that assumption in hand all we need to do is ask if M'Naghten's choice to pull the trigger satisfies the *actus reus* and *mens rea* requirements. Here's the problem: Suppose M'Naghten didn't experience himself as the one who pulled the trigger. True, the finger of M'Naghten pulled the trigger. But suppose M'Naghten didn't experience himself as the agent who moved his finger? What if he thought someone else was in control?

If that sounds paradoxical, it should. We'll attempt to dispel the paradox in due course, but not before taking, as a necessary prelude, an extended detour into the law of insanity as an affirmative defense to criminal liability. We'll look first at the traditional tests for insanity, then move to the irrationality theory, the most prominent proposal to displace the traditional tests. As we'll see, none does an unimpeachable job explaining exactly what it means for a person's choice to be insane.[20] Our trip begins in 1843, with the law of *M'Naghten's Case*. It ends with the mind of Daniel M'Naghten, and a different theory of insanity, which resolves the paradox, and moreover, elevates insanity from an affirmative defense to a limit on state authority.

[19] *See, e.g.*, Michael S. Moore, *The Quest for a Responsible Responsibility Test: Norwegian Insanity Law After Breivik*, 9 Crim. L. & Phil. 645, 662 (2015).

[20] For a more detailed analysis of the traditional theories and the irrationality theory, see Stephen P. Garvey, *Insanity*, *in* The Palgrave Handbook of Applied Ethics and the Criminal Law 385 (Larry Alexander & Kimberly Kessler Ferzan eds., 2019).

Tradition

Courts usually announce new rules of law when deciding appeals. Usually, that is. The most famous test for insanity, the *M'Naghten* Rule,[21] didn't come to the world in the usual way. The Queen at the time, Queen Victoria, had been an assassin's target three years before M'Naghten tried to kill her prime minister. Her assailant, Edward Oxford,[22] had been acquitted on grounds of insanity, and the Queen was none too happy when M'Naghten got the same treatment.[23] She told the House of Lords to ask the judges of the Queen's Bench to explain, once and for all, what made a person insane in the eyes of English law. Their pronouncement became the *M'Naghten* Rule. Fall within the rule, and you go to a hospital; fall outside, and you go to prison (or the gallows).

Criminal lawyers today tend to talk about *the M'Naghten* Rule or test, but that's misleading. In reality, we have not one *M'Naghten* test, but two. The old *M'Naghten* is the one the Queen's Bench judges announced in 1843. The new *M'Naghten* is a modern-day descendant of the old, and can be found, in one form or another, in many state penal codes,[24] as well as the federal criminal code.[25] The two belong to the same family, or at least they share the same family tree, but the words of the old *M'Naghten* differ from the words of the new in more ways than one.

Five questions were put to the judges in *M'Naghten's Case*. Their answers to three of the five have, regrettably, faded into history.[26] What's passed into the modern canon is the single answer they gave to questions two and three,

[21] Daniel M'Naghten's Case, 8 Eng. Rep. 718 (1843).

[22] For an account of Oxford's life after the attempt, see Jenny Sinclair, A Walking Shadow: The Remarkable Double Life of Edward Oxford (2012).

[23] Queen Victoria would be attacked on eight separate occasions between 1840 and 1882. *See* Paul Thomas Murphy, Shooting Victoria: Madness, Mayhem, and the Rebirth of the British Monarchy 1 (2012) (providing a narrative history of the attacks).

[24] For surveys of insanity law in U.S. jurisdictions, see Paul H. Robinson & Tyler Scot Williams, Mapping American Criminal Law: Variations Across the 50 States 163–65 (2018); Robinson et al., *supra* note 4.

[25] *See* 18 U.S.C. § 17(a) ("It is an affirmative defense to a prosecution under any Federal statute that, at the time of the commission of the acts constituting the offense, the defendant, as a result of a severe mental disease or defect, was unable to appreciate the nature and quality or the wrongfulness of his acts.").

[26] Commentators who attend to the judges' answers to all the questions naturally tend to speak about the *M'Naghten* Rules (plural), while those who focus only on the answer to the second and third questions, dealing with the "proper questions to be submitted to the jury, when a person alleged to be afflicted with insane delusion . . . is charged with the commission of a crime," *M'Naghten's Case*, 8 Eng. Rep. at 720, tend to speak of the *M'Naghten* Rule (singular). For a more detailed examination of the judges' answers, see Garvey, *supra* note 20, at 386–88.

which asked how a jury should be instructed when a defendant pleads insanity. The judges answered:

> [T]o establish a defence on the ground of insanity, it must be clearly proved that, at the time of the committing of the act, the party accused was labouring under such a defect of reason, from disease of the mind, as not to know the nature and quality of the act he was doing; or, if he did know it, that he did not know he was doing what was wrong.[27]

So says the old *M'Naghten*. The test is easier to quote than understand. Entire books have been devoted to deciphering it,[28] but its meaning remains elusive. Indeed, maybe it doesn't even state an all-purpose test for insanity, good for any case in which insanity is alleged. The judges may, for example, have intended to limit their answers to cases involving defendants who, like Daniel M'Naghten, were suffering from what were known circa 1843 as "partial delusions."[29] We won't add to the existing commentary on (and confusion over) *M'Naghten*'s original meaning. Instead, we'll set the old *M'Naghten* aside, and move onto the new.

[27] *M'Naghten's Case*, 8 Eng. Rep. at 722. In one important, though nowadays neglected passage, the judges expressly say in response to the fourth question that someone "labour[ing] under . . . partial delusion only, and . . . not in other respects insane, . . . must be considered in the same situation as to responsibility as if the facts with respect to which the delusion exists were real." *Id.* at 723. According to at least two influential treatises, this language doesn't add anything to the language cited in the text. *See* 1 Wayne R. LaFave, Criminal Law § 7.2(b)(5), at 509 (6th ed. 2017) ("[I]t is undoubtedly fair to conclude that this particular part of *M'Naghten* does not set up a unique formula differing from the right-wrong test."); A.P. Simester et al., Simester and Sullivan's Criminal Law: Theory and Doctrine § 19.1(ii)(f), at 723 (5th ed. 2013) ("This express provision for partial delusions does not appear to add anything to the substance of the Rules.").

Other courts and commentators, however, appear to have construed it as a separate test. *See, e.g.*, Parsons v. State, 2 So. 854, 865 (Ala. 1887) ("The rule in *McNaghten's Case* . . . is that the defense of insane delusion can be allowed to prevail in a criminal case only when the imaginary state of facts would, if real, justify or excuse the act."); Davis v. State, 28 S.W.2d 993, 996 (Tenn. 1930) ("Under [*McNaughten's Case*] . . . a homicide committed under an insane delusion is excusable, if the notion embodied in the delusion and believed to be a fact, if a fact indeed, would have excused the defendant."); Walter Sinnott-Armstrong & Ken Levy, *Insanity Defenses*, *in* The Oxford Handbook of Philosophy of Criminal Law 299, 301–02 (John Deigh & David Dolinko eds., 2011) ("[T]he judges in *M'Naghten*'s case proposed a counterfactual test[,]" according to which an accused was insane if his acts would have been justified if his delusions had been true.).

Whatever the relationship between the answer to questions two and three, and the answer to question four, the test for insanity contained in the answer to the fourth question mirrors the delusion theory discussed below. *See infra* notes 81–92 and accompanying text.

[28] For an in-depth analysis of the old *M'Naghten*, see Herbert Fingarette, The Meaning of Criminal Insanity 234–42 (1972). Fingarette's theory of insanity is commonly characterized as an irrationality theory. *See infra* note 60. If that characterization is accurate, and because Fingarette "read[s] the *M'Naghten* test as saying much the same thing" as the theory he proposed, *id.* at 197, then perhaps the old *M'Naghten* should be understood as an irrationality test.

[29] *Id.* at 721–22.

The new *M'Naghten* comes in different shapes and sizes, with different jurisdictions formulating the test in slightly different ways. We'll work with the following generic statement: A person is not responsible for criminal conduct if at the time of such conduct, as a result of mental disease or defect, he lacks the capacity to know the criminality of his conduct.[30] The new *M'Naghten* differs from the old in a few ways, only one of which needs emphasis for present purposes.[31]

The difference centers on capacity. The old *M'Naghten* made no explicit mention of capacity, asking only if the accused was laboring under a defect of reason, from disease of the mind, so as not to know the nature and quality of what he was doing, or if he did know it, he did not know he was doing what was wrong. Not a word about capacity. The new *M'Naghten*, in contrast, puts capacity front and center.[32] An actor isn't insane unless, as a result of mental disease or defect, he not only didn't realize he was committing a crime, but was powerless to so realize.[33]

30 This generic statement of the new *M'Naghten* tracks the corresponding language of Model Penal Code § 4.01(1). *See* Model Penal Code § 4.01(1) (Am. Law Inst. 1985).

31 Here are the other differences: (1) The generic statement sidesteps the protracted debate over the meaning of the word "wrong" contained in the old *M'Naghten*. *See* Sinnott-Armstrong & Levy, *supra* note 27, at 302–06 (describing all imaginable meanings of the word "wrong"). It simply assumes "wrong" means "criminally wrong," which is how it's been construed in the land where *M'Naghten* was born. *See* R. v. Windle, [1952] Q.B. 826, 844 (Eng.) ("The test must be whether an act is contrary to law."); Andrew Ashworth & Jeremy Horder, Principles of Criminal Law § 5.2(b), at 143 (7th ed. 2013); James Manwaring, *Windle Revisited*, 12 Crim. L. Rev. 987, 987 (2018) (stating that "*Windle* interpreted insanity's wrongness limb to require ignorance of legal wrong," but arguing that its "reasoning for this interpretation was seriously flawed"). (2) The generic statement omits the reference to the accused's failure to "know the nature and quality of the act he was doing." This language is commonly omitted because, it's thought, it adds nothing to "he did not know he was doing what was wrong," which in the end does all the work needed to defeat liability. *See, e.g.*, Clark v. Arizona, 548 U.S. 735, 753 (2006) ("In practical terms, if a defendant did not know what he was doing when he acted, he could not have known that he was performing the wrongful act charged as a crime."). (3) The generic statement omits the reference to "defect of reason." This language is commonly omitted because, it's probably thought, it adds nothing to the disease-of-the-mind element. *See* Fingarette, *supra* note 28, at 178. Fingarette, for one, thought otherwise, calling it a "profound mistake" to omit the defect-of-reason element from the formulation the test. Fingarette, *supra*, at 198.

32 The Law Commission of England and Wales has recently proposed a new defense, called "not criminally responsible by reason of a recognized medical condition," which likewise centers on capacity. According to the Commission, the "essence of a lack of capacity defence is that, at the time of the alleged offense, the accused could not have done otherwise." The Commission goes on to explain that this basic incapacity defense encompasses "three relevant capacities," which include the capacity "to understand that you are doing something wrong" and the capacity "to control your body." Law Commission, Criminal Liability: Insanity and Automatism. A Discussion Paper—Summary for Non-Specialists 16–18 (July 23, 2013). Thanks to Antony Duff for this reference.

33 *See* Sinnott-Armstrong & Levy, *supra* note 27, at 311 ("[T]he M'Naghten rule hinged on actual knowledge rather than ability to know."). The Supreme Court has slipped easily from the original non-capacity language of the old *M'Naghten* to the capacity language of the new *M'Naghten*, without noting the difference. *See Clark*, 548 U.S. at 747 (describing the "second part" of the original language

Before continuing, return for a moment to Daniel M'Naghten and confront his responsibility head on. Ignore the law and its various tests for insanity. Instead, consult your intuitions. Whatever the law says, should M'Naghten have been found criminally responsible and sent to the gallows, or should be have been found not responsible and sent to Bethlem?

If you agree with many thoughtful commentators, then you'd say Bethlem.[34] If anyone's insane, M'Naghten was. If so, then M'Naghten provides a litmus test for insanity tests. M'Naghten is to insanity what Linda Brown—the plaintiff in *Brown v. Board of Education*—is to equal protection. A theory of insanity telling us M'Naghten was sane is (for that reason) a bad theory of insanity, just as any theory of equal protection telling us Brown wasn't denied it is (for that reason) a bad theory of equal protection.[35] If a test for insanity pronounces Daniel M'Naghten insane, it passes the test (which makes it a plausible test for insanity); if not, it fails (which makes it implausible). Call this the *M'Naghten litmus test*, not to be confused with the M'Naghten test itself, old or new.

Perhaps the biggest criticism of the new *M'Naghten* focused not on what the test said, but on what it didn't say. Suppose, the critics imagined, someone realized what he was doing, and that what he was doing was a crime, but as a result of mental disease or defect, just couldn't help himself. He was, as one might colloquially put it, *driven* to commit the crime, or as the law sometimes puts it, he experienced an "*irresistible impulse*" to commit it.[36]

from *M'Naghten*, i.e., the language stating that the accused "did not know he was doing what was wrong," as a test for "lack of moral capacity").

[34] *See* MORAN, *supra* note 2, at 4 (describing this as the "conventional wisdom" and citing the work of Fingarette, Biggs, Goldstein, and Rollin); Moore, *supra* note 19, at 662 ("Daniel M'Naghten himself . . . would be considered in popular understanding as quite crazy."). The Queen, of course, didn't think so. Nor did the public at the time. If M'Naghten could plan, as he could and did, then he wasn't insane. Then again, neither the Queen nor the public heard first-hand the evidence presented at trial. If they had, maybe they would've thought differently. Moran challenges the conventional wisdom, or at least sets out "to demonstrate that [M'Naghten's] mental condition and alleged delusions of persecution were, at the very minimum, rooted in the political reality of his day." MORAN, *supra*, at 5. *See also* Richard Moran, *McNaughtan, [McNaghten] Daniel* (1802/3–1865), OXFORD DICTIONARY OF NATIONAL BIOGRAPHY (online ed. January 2008) (M'Naghten was a "former actor and medical student [who] was familiar with the symptoms of insanity, and . . . may have been feigning . . . .").

[35] Nathaniel Persily, *The Meaning of Equal Protection: Then, Now, and Tomorrow*, GPSOLO, Nov.-Dec. 2014, at 13 ("As momentous as [*Brown*] was for starting the constitutional ball rolling forward toward full equal citizenship for all Americans regardless of their race, *Brown* is now also a litmus test for what the Constitution, and especially the Equal Protection Claus, actually *mean*."). The M'Naghten litmus test might not be as reliable as the *Brown* litmus test, at least not if you believe more people are likely to intuit M'Naghten was sane than they are Brown wasn't denied equal protection.

[36] A standard citation is to Parsons v. State, 2 So. 854, 866 (Ala. 1887).

If you think such a person should be regarded as insane in the law's eyes, a point of considerable controversy,[37] the new *M'Naghten* would need to be amended.[38] The fix would be easy: add another prong (sometimes referred to, a little misleadingly, as the "irresistible impulse" prong), to wit: A person is not responsible for criminal conduct if at the time of such conduct, as a result of mental disease or defect, he lacks the capacity to conform his conduct to the requirements of law.

The new *M'Naghten*, together with the irresistible impulse addition, comprise what we'll call the "traditional test" for insanity. The traditional test has an elegant and simple structure. It takes two conditions, compelled ignorance and compelled choice, and bars criminal liability when either of those conditions is satisfied, provided those conditions resulted from a "mental disease or defect." Insanity equals compelled choice or compelled ignorance resulting from mental disease or defect.

We've seen that an accused's *actus* wasn't *reus*—his choice to commit the crime wasn't guilty—if he realized he was committing a crime, but lacked the capacity to choose otherwise (compelled choice); or, if he didn't realize he was committing a crime, he lacked the capacity to believe otherwise (compelled ignorance). We've also seen that the *actus reus* requirement is

[37] Stephen Morse is the most prominent and thoughtful critic of volitional or control tests for insanity. *See, e.g.*, Stephen J. Morse, *Against Control Tests for Criminal Responsibility*, *in* Criminal Law Conversations 449 (Paul H. Robinson et al. eds., 2009). Richard Bonnie likewise "favor[s] narrowing the defense by eliminating its so-called volitional prong or control test." Richard J. Bonnie, *The Moral Basis of the Insanity Defense*, A.B.A. J., Feb. 1983, at 196. Michael Corrado is probably the foremost defender of an approach to insanity based entirely on volitional impairment. *See, e.g.*, Michael Corrado, *The Case for a Purely Volitional Insanity Defense*, 42 Tex. Tech. L. Rev. 481 (2009). For a recent criticism of Corrado's position in favor of Morse's, see Paul Litton, *The Mistaken Quest for a Control Test: For a Rationality Standard of Sanity*, *in* The Insanity Defense: Multidisciplinary Views on Its History, Trends, and Controversies 185 (Mark D. White ed., 2017).

Any plausible case in which one might be inclined to believe an actor couldn't have done otherwise than commit the crime charged will, Morse argues, typically be one in which the actor would be insane under the irrationality theory he defends. He says, for example:

> Suppose . . . that an agent's desire is so powerful and insistent that it compromises the agent's ability to think straight, to bring reason to bear on the reasons not to act. Some people in the throes of intense desires may be virtually unable to think of anything except satisfying the desire. Indeed, some addicts, for example, describe seeking and using in almost *automaton-like terms*. Their minds are blank, and seeking and using "*just happens*." This is a textbook example of irrationality.

Morse, *supra*, at 457 (emphasis added). For present purposes, notice the italicized phrases. The phenomenon those phrases describe looks, as we'll see, like the phenomenon we'll later characterize as "lost agency."

[38] We should note for the record that some defenders of the *old M'Naghten* Rule believed that the rule, properly understood and applied, could reach and exonerate those who acted on irresistible impulse. *See, e.g.*, 2 James Fitzjames Stephen, History of the Criminal Law of England 167–71 (1883); Jerome Hall, General Principles of Criminal Law 520–22 (1960).

equivalent to the traditional test for insanity, with two differences.[39] First, the traditional test is an affirmative defense the state adopts (or not) in the exercise of its authority, whereas the *actus reus* requirement is a limit on the state's authority to ascribe culpability. Second, the traditional test is limited to incapacities resulting from a "mental disease or defect," whereas the *actus reus* requirement insists only on the accused not being at fault for his incapacity, whatever its proximate cause.

For purposes of the *actus reus* requirement, we used the Stephen test to assess an accused's capacity to choose otherwise (and thus conform his conduct to the requirements of law),[40] and the Lex test to assess his capacity to believe otherwise (and thus realize his conduct didn't conform to the law).[41] The Stephen test and the Lex test rely on counterfactuals. Stephen tells us an accused lacked the capacity to conform to the law if he chose to φ even though his motivational reasons not to φ were greater than his reasons to φ, or would have been greater if he believed the greatest punishment the state could legitimately impose for φ-ing would immediately befall him. Meanwhile, Lex tells us an accused lacked the capacity to realize he was committing a crime if he would have continued to believe φ-ing was not a crime even after receiving Lex's text telling him it was.

Although the traditional test is silent on how to test for the incapacities it associates with insanity, the Stephen test and the Lex test can fill the void. The traditional test for insanity is, rightly or wrongly, typically understood to require "total" incapacity, which suggests that the possible world in which the accused's capacities are tested should be especially unforgiving.[42] Rare indeed should be the case in which the requisite capacity is found lacking. The Stephen test and the Lex test, both designed to be rarely satisfied, fit the bill.

With those tests in hand, the first problem for the traditional test comes into sight. Daniel M'Naghten was, as we've said, probably suffering from paranoid schizophrenia or paranoid psychosis. He was in pretty bad shape, believing the Tories were out to get him, haunting him day and night, and so forth. If we apply the traditional test, using the Stephen test and the Lex test to fix the relevant counterfactuals, then maybe, under the circumstances,

[39] *See* Chapter 3, *supra* at 129–32; Chapter 4, *supra* at 178–81.
[40] *See* Chapter 3, *supra* at 124–29.
[41] *See* Chapter 4, *supra* at 177–78.
[42] *See* Model Penal Code and Commentaries § 4.01 cmt. 3, at 171 (Am. Law Inst. 1985) (implying that the "M'Naghten and 'irresistible impulse' criteria," understood to require "lack of capacity" to know the law, or to control oneself so as to conform to the law, "call[ed] for *complete* impairment of ability to know or to control") (emphasis added).

M'Naghten was insane. Maybe, under the circumstances, he either couldn't have realized he was committing a crime, or if he did, couldn't have done otherwise. Maybe, in other words, he fails the Stephen test, or the Lex test, or both.

But probably not. He probably passes both. If Lex, now embodying the Crown, had appeared and told M'Naghten he would, if he killed the person walking along Parliament Street, offend the king's peace and commit a crime, would M'Naghten have "known" he'd be committing a crime? One might insist not, but a fair case can be made, not only that he could have realized he was committing a crime, but that he did. According to one knowledgeable observer, M'Naghten "made no *mistakes* about what he was doing—he knew he was shooting, and he knew that he was killing—*nor* was he ignorant of the legal and moral prohibitions against killing."[43] True, he believed "if he did not strike first, he himself would be hurt or worse," but "such beliefs, even if true, would not give rise to any valid duress defense (there being no threats of immediate harm), nor can such preemptive strikes against non-imminent harm be justified as self-defense."[44] If so, then M'Naghten would appear to have been sane under the traditional test's first prong.

Likewise, if we allow, pursuant to the Stephen test, that the gallows was, at least at the time, the greatest punishment the state could legitimately dish out for murder, would M'Naghten have done an about-face if he believed death would be his immediate fate for choosing to kill the person on Parliament Street? Again, according to our knowledgeable observer, "there is no very persuasive case for saying that M'Naghten was *compelled* to do what he did."[45] If the gallows had materialized, a fair case can be made that a desire to avoid its thirteen steps would have competed and prevailed against the desire to stop the Tory persecution. If so, then M'Naghten was sane under the second prong, too.

If we nonetheless agree, when we listen to our intuitions, that M'Naghten *was* insane, then the traditional test fails the M'Naghten litmus test: It would send M'Naghten to the gallows when he should be sent to Bethlem. Indeed, the traditional test, faithfully applied, probably does a pretty poor job overall sorting defendants who most people would intuit to be sane from those who most people would intuit to be insane.[46] Worse, its tendency is for false

[43] Moore, *supra* note 19, at 662.

[44] *Id.*

[45] *Id.*

[46] With respect to the decisions juries actually make, the rule they're told to apply may in the run of cases make little to no difference. Jurors, so far as one can tell, tend in general to return the same

negatives. It probably sends to prison more folks who should go to a mental hospital than it sends to mental hospitals folks who should go to prison.

A natural response to this worry is to loosen the language, moving away from total incapacity to something less than total. The Model Penal Code showed the way, declaring in § 4.01:

> A person is not responsible for criminal conduct if at the time of such conduct as a result of mental disease or defect he lacks *substantial* capacity either to *appreciate* the criminality of his conduct or to conform his conduct to the requirements of law.[47]

Section 4.01 preserves the traditional test's basic structure. Its innovation was (more) vagueness, ushered in through the italicized words. First, it replaces "know" with "appreciate," on the theory that insanity may not preclude "knowledge," but does preclude "appreciation," where appreciation is meant to convey some deeper, but ill-defined, mode of understanding.[48] Second, recognizing that capacities come in degrees,[49] the Code spurned the traditional test's total-incapacity requirement, watering it down with a substantial-incapacity requirement.[50] Section 4.01 is thus the traditional test, only more open-ended, thus enabling juries to acquit when the traditional test, honestly applied, might lead to conviction.[51]

verdict whatever the test. *See, e.g.*, Rebecca K. Helm et al., *Unpacking Insanity Defence Standards: An Experimental Study of Rationality and Control Tests in Criminal Law*, 8 European J. Psychol. Applied in Legal Context 63, 68 (2016) ("This study confirms existing research suggesting that jurors use their own conceptions of insanity rather than legal standards when making insanity determinations."); James R.P. Ogloff, *A Comparison of Insanity Defense Standards on Juror Decision Making*, 15 Law & Hum. Behav. 509, 526 (1991) ("[F]or whatever reason, the particular insanity defense standards employed do not seem to strongly influence a juror's decision making.").

[47] Model Penal Code § 4.01(a) (Am. Law Inst. 1985) (emphasis added).

[48] *See* Model Penal Code and Commentaries, *supra* note 42, § 4.01 cmt. 3, at 169 ("The use of 'appreciate' rather than 'know' conveys a broader sense of understanding than simple cognition.").

[49] Michael S. Moore, *The Neuroscience of Volitional Excuse*, *in* Law and Neuroscience 179, 214 (Dennis Patterson & Michael S. Pardo eds., 2016).

[50] *See* Model Penal Code and Commentaries, *supra* note 42, § 4.01 cmt. 3, at 172 (Substantial capacity means "a capacity of some appreciable magnitude when measured by the standard of humanity in general, as opposed to the reduction of capacity to the vagrant and trivial dimensions characteristic of the most severe afflictions of the mind.").

[51] The story of *M'Naghten*'s evolution ends, of course, with John Hinckley's attempt on the life of then-President Ronald Reagan, apparently in an effort to win the affections of actress Jody Foster. Prior to Hinckley's attempt, the Model Penal Code's test was on the rise; afterward, in a reaction echoing Queen Victoria's to M'Naghten's acquittal, many jurisdictions retreated to the some version of the new M'Naghten. Congress's retreat is recorded in the definition of insanity under federal law, 18 U.S.C. § 17.

Does § 4.01 pass the M'Naghten litmus test? Hard to say. Some might think so; others might think not. That's the beauty of vagueness. Compared to the traditional test, it gives juries discretion, inviting reliance on judgment and intuition. That makes it harder to say what verdict § 4.01 would return when applied to M'Naghten. Of course, the Code, being softer than the traditional test, naturally offers M'Naghten a better chance, all else being equal, to persuade a jury to send him to Bedlam instead of the gallows.

Even if the Code, unlike the traditional test, passes the M'Naghten litmus test, it faces another problem, which the traditional test also faces. The Code, like the traditional test, has two elements: a mental-disease-or-defect element and a liability-precluding element. Both tests presuppose the mental-disease-or-defect element must cause the liability-precluding element: No one is insane unless the liability-precluding element results from the mental-disease-or-defect element.[52]

The mental-disease-or-defect requirement is puzzling.[53] Set aside the glaring fact that the criminal law seldom, if ever, defines "mental disease or defect." That's bad enough. Worse is its failure to explain why it insists on the mental-disease-or-defect requirement in the first place, leaving one to wonder what work the requirement is meant to do. We mentioned this problem earlier, promising a full-dress treatment later on. Time to redeem the promise.

Maybe the mental-disease-or-defect requirement is a proxy for something else. Perhaps it serves as a guarantee that anyone pleading insanity qua incapacity isn't to blame for being incapacitated. It guarantees, in other words, that the accused doesn't have dirty hands. You're not to blame for being incapacitated if your incapacity arises from a mental disease or defect. Mental disease just happens. No one sets out to make himself suffer from a mental disease. That's sensible, but this proxy theory makes the mental-disease-or-defect requirement out to be nothing more than a clean-hands rule.[54]

[52] You might say that anyone who lacks the capacity to know he's committing crime, or who can't conform to the law if he does know it, must necessarily be suffering from something fairly called a mental disease or defect. Perhaps that's right. It's hard to know without some account of what counts as a "mental disease or defect." Even so, the traditional test tells us a mental disease or defect must cause an incapacity. If mental disease or defect is just another way to identify the relevant incapacity, then it can't cause that incapacity.

[53] *See, e.g.*, Gary Watson, *Excusing Addiction*, *in* Agency and Answerability: Selected Essays 318, 331 (2004) ("[T]he disease-requirement is not really cogent.").

[54] In addition to incapacity resulting from mental disease or defect, incapacity resulting from involuntary intoxication is another widely recognized defense. *See, e.g.*, Model Penal Code § 2.08(4) (Am. Law Inst. 1985). The involuntary-intoxication defense also suggests that the mental-disease-or-defect requirement is really nothing more than a clean-hands proxy. Incapacity resulting from

Here's one problem with the proxy theory. If the mental-disease requirement is merely a proxy for clean hands, it suffers, like any proxy, from over- and under-inclusion. First, under-inclusion. Suppose Sally is faultlessly incapacitated: Her incapacity was the result of mental disease or defect. When Sally kills Jane, she's not guilty, because she's insane. Contrast Sally with John, who's also faultlessly incapacitated, but John's incapacity is due to something other than a mental disease or defect. When he kills Jane, he's out of luck. No insanity defense for him. Nor, let's suppose, can he avail himself of any other defense. That doesn't seem fair. As long as you're not at fault for being incapacitated, it shouldn't otherwise matter why you're incapacitated.

Second, over-inclusion. Go back to Sally, who's once again incapacitated, due to mental disease or defect, at the time she kills Jane. This time, however, Sally had decided, a week before, to stop taking her medicine. Without the medicine, the symptoms from which she suffers will return, and she'll be incapacitated once more. All this she knows, but decides to stop taking her medicine anyway. If Sally, now incapacitated, kills Jane, she'll still be entitled to plead insanity, at least under existing law in most places.[55] That doesn't seem fair either. Because Sally's at fault for being incapacitated, one wonders why she should be allowed to plead insanity.

The traditional test gives us the following simple recipe for insanity. Step one: Start with a standard liability-precluding condition (compelled ignorance or compelled choice). Step two: Add a mental-disease-or-defect condition (leave undefined). Step three: Require the element in step one to result from the element in step two. *Voilá*, insanity.

Maybe one lesson from the traditional test's shortcomings is to rethink step one. Rather than a traditional excusing condition, like compulsion or ignorance, maybe one should start instead with the mental disease or defect condition, and in particular, with the idea that mental disease or defect in itself is somehow the key to insanity, rather than just an ill-fitting proxy for clean hands. Mental disease or defect isn't simply a gateway to insanity: It's the whole ball of wax.

mental disease or defect is one way a person can be blamelessly incapacitated. Involuntary intoxication is another.

[55] One possible exception to this generalization, the only one of which I'm aware, is Washington law, which provides that "[n]o condition of mind induced by the voluntary act of a person charged with a crime shall constitute insanity." WASH. REV. CODE § 10.77.030(3).

History gives one famous example of this approach. It comes from the Court of Appeals for the District of Columbia in 1954, in *United States v. Durham*.[56] It began with promise, but didn't end well. The *Durham* court's members, and especially *Durham*'s author, Judge David Bazelon, were dissatisfied with the traditional test. For Bazelon, the test left the jury without a complete portrait of the accused's state of mind at the time of the crime, and without a complete portrait, how could the jury fairly say whether he was insane? *Durham* thus threw out the traditional test, and replaced it with a single-sentence alternative: "[A]n accused is not criminally responsible if his unlawful act was the product of mental disease or mental defect."[57]

This rule, known as *Durham* Rule or product test, is as notable for what it doesn't say as for what it does. Unlike the traditional test, it makes no mention whatsoever of incapacity. Indeed, it makes no effort to identify anything amounting to a liability-precluding condition, like the compelled ignorance or choice associated with the traditional test.

On the contrary, what precludes liability under *Durham* is the simple fact that the actor suffered from a mental disease or defect, provided it caused his unlawful act. Besides wanting a test allowing the jury to hear more about the accused's state of mind than the traditional tests allowed, why Judge Bazelon opted for the particular language he did is hard to know. Whatever the motivation, the *Durham* Rule itself presupposed that mental disease or defect, or at least *some* mental diseases or defects, sufficed to preclude criminal responsibility all by themselves, no incapacity required, as long as the accused wouldn't have committed the crime but for the mental disease or defect.

The *Durham* court may have been onto something. Alas, the court didn't see what it was, and the rot soon set in. Its source was the court's failure to define "mental disease or defect." At trial, the prosecution would present its experts, who would solemnly testify that the accused suffered from no mental disease or defect. The defense would then present its experts, who with equal solemnity would testify that he did, and moreover, his crime was a product

[56] 214 F.2d 862 (D.C. Cir. 1954).

[57] *Id.* at 874–75. The *Durham* Rule never said why a person who wouldn't have committed a crime but for the fact that he was suffering from something called a mental disease or defect shouldn't be criminally liable. Some take the Rule to rest on what's been called a "causal theory" of excuse, which isn't really a theory of excuse at all. A theory of excuse is supposed to separate those who are responsible for their choices from those who aren't, but the causal theory entails that no one is responsible for any choice: All choices are excused. For some, this conclusion represents a *reductio* of the causal theory; for others, it represents enlightenment, spelling as it does the end of the criminal law as a blaming institution. For if no one is responsible for anything, then no one should be blamed for anything. This argument is discussed in greater detail in Chapter 6.

of it. Who was to say who was right? The experts were, after all, the experts, at least when it came to saying what was and wasn't a mental disease or defect. The battle of the experts left the jury caught in the crossfire. Far from bringing its normative judgment to bear on the question of insanity, the jury was reduced to arbitrating credibility.

When the court finally got around to defining "mental disease or defect," it changed course. Rather than identifying what it was about some mental diseases and defects, such that suffering from them was in itself somehow inconsistent with criminal responsibility, the court returned to familiar territory. A "mental disease or defect," the court said almost a decade after *Durham*, included "any abnormal condition of the mind which substantially effects mental or emotional processes and substantially impair behavior controls."

Ring any bells? It should. Under the traditional test, a mental disease or defect had to cause a liability-precluding condition, which included a lack of capacity to conform to the requirements of law. Under the upgraded *Durham* Rule, now with a definition of "mental disease or defect," a mental disease or defect had to cause "substantially impaired behavior controls," which in turn caused the crime charged, otherwise it wasn't a "mental disease or defect" at all, at least not so far as the law of insanity was concerned. When push came to shove, the D.C. Circuit thus did an about face and returned to tradition,[58] with something like volitional incapacity—"substantially impaired behavioral controls"—coming to the fore.[59] The gravitational pull of the old ways proved hard to escape.

[58] The court's ongoing efforts to patch up the *Durham* Rule in response to problems arising from its application eventually led the court to abandon it altogether, in favor of the then-recently promulgated Model Penal Code rule. *See* United States v. Brawner, 471 F.2d 969 (D.C. Cir. 1972). The product rule survives in New Hampshire, where it first took root, and in the Virgin Islands. *See* State v. Pike, 49 N.H. 399, 438 (1869); Petric v. People, 61 V.I. 401, 408 (2014).

[59] When *Durham* was finally laid to rest in *Brawner*, Judge Bazelon made another effort to formulate a way to sort the sane from the insane. Here's what he settled on: "[A] defendant is not responsible if at the time of his unlawful conduct his mental or emotional processes or behavior controls were impaired to such an extent that he cannot justly be held responsible for his act." *Brawner*, 471 F.2d at 1032 (Bazelon, C.J., concurring in part and dissenting in part).

Bazelon thus went one step (or more) beyond the Model Penal Code on the vagueness path. He dispensed with anything like a rule or test for insanity; instead, his formulation got all of the facts in front of the jury but gave no guidance. It presented the jury with the ultimate question: Can the defendant justly be held responsible for his act? That was also more or less the majority recommendation of the Royal Commission on Capital Punishment. *See* Royal Commission on Capital Punishment, Report, 1949-1953, para. 333(iii), at 116 (1953) ("[A] preferable amendment of the law would be to abrogate the [*M'Naghten*] Rule and to leave the jury to determine whether at the time of the act the accused was suffering from disease of the mind (or mental deficiency) to such a degree that he ought not to be held responsible."). Getting the ultimate question to the jury, without any

Irrationality

The D.C. Circuit eventually abandoned the *Durham* Rule altogether, replacing it with the Model Penal Code's version of the traditional test (which Congress eventually replaced with its own version of *M'Naghten*). Indeed, the traditional test, in one form or another, now prevails across the law of the land (except in New Hampshire and the Virgin Islands).

Still, the traditional test's victory in positive law doesn't mean everyone's happy about it. At bottom, the discontented believe that the traditional test misunderstands insanity because it sees nothing special about the insane. That, so say the discontented, must be wrong. The traditional test takes the oldest excuses in the book—ignorance and compulsion—and finds insanity when those excuses happen to result from a mental disease or defect, mysteriously left undefined. That can't be right. Insanity can't just be a traditional excuse outfitted with an obscure mental disease or defect requirement. It must, tradition's detractors believe, be something else. But what?

Enter the irrationality test. The test's champions agree that, at the heart of insanity, lies irrationality, but their accounts differ in detail and nuance, making it hard to tell exactly what the reported versions of the theory stand for. In fact, as we'll see in a moment, it might be better to talk about irrationality theories (plural), with different theories bearing a family resemblance to one another but differing in important ways.[60] As always, the devil is in the details.

more by way of guidance from the law, was also probably the hoped-for effect of the New Hampshire doctrine, which is usually, though perhaps mistakenly, taken to be equivalent to the *Durham* Rule. *See* John Reid, *Understanding the New Hampshire Doctrine of Criminal Insanity*, 69 Yale L.J. 367, 396 (1960) (claiming that the "ends sought by New Hampshire [were] . . . to discard legal presumptions and give the jury the full fact-finding duty.").

[60] Michael Moore and Stephen Morse are today's most prominent irrationality revisionists. They don't agree on everything, however. First, Moore defends irrationality-as-unintelligibility, while Morse defends (or at least sometimes seems to defend) irrationality-as-delusion. Second, Moore believes insanity is a status defense that defeats liability for any and all crimes the accused commits, while Morse believes it's an excuse that defeats liability for some crimes the accused commits, but not necessarily all. Third, Moore would make room for a separate "volitional" excuse based on lack of capacity to control one's choices or conform one's choices to the requirements of law. *See* Michael S. Moore, *The Neuroscience of Volitional Excuse*, in Philosophical Foundations of Law and Neuroscience 179 (Dennis Patterson & Michael S. Pardo eds., 2016) (offering an analysis of "volitional excuse"). Morse sees no need for any such volitional excuse; or if a need exists, he believes the costs associated with it would exceed its benefits; ergo, the law shouldn't adopt it.

For earlier discussions commonly included in the irrationality camp, see Fingarette, *supra* note 28; Herbert Fingarette, *Insanity and Responsibility*, 15 Inquiry 6 (1972); Joel Feinberg, *What Is So Special About Mental Illness?*, *in* Doing and Deserving: Essays in the Theory of Responsibility 272 (1970); Herbert Morris, *Criminal Insanity*, 17 Inquiry 345 (1974) (reviewing Herbert Fingarette, The Meaning of Criminal Insanity (1972)). Robert Schopp is also

What supposedly unites all irrationality theories is the proposition that insanity is (in some sense) irrationality. Everyone who's insane is necessarily irrational, though not everyone who's irrational is necessarily insane. We might therefore formulate the irrationality theorist's test for insanity thusly: An actor is insane if he's (in some sense) irrational.

If that's all the theory tells us, it doesn't tell us as much as we need.[61] M'Naghten was irrational in some sense, but then again, he knew how to put two and two together. He knew how to plan an attack on the prime minister. He knew how to work a gun. That looks instrumentally rational at least. Moreover, we're all more or less irrational, more or less of the time.[62] Weakness of will, for example, is an all-too-human species of practical irrationality, and self-deception is an all-too-human species of epistemic irrationality. What we need to know, with some measure of precision, is when irrationality veers into insanity. Without an answer—if all we say is that insanity equals irrationality—then insanity becomes like pornography: You know it when you see it.

We can try to make irrationality more precise. For starters, we can distinguish two different irrationality theories: the unintelligibility theory and the delusion theory.[63] Both theories relate insanity to psychosis. The

commonly included. *See* ROBERT F. SCHOPP, AUTOMATISM, INSANITY, AND THE PSYCHOLOGY OF CRIMINAL RESPONSIBILITY: A PHILOSOPHICAL INQUIRY 215 (1991). Lumping all these theorists in the same camp makes sense, insofar as they all stand in opposition to the traditional test and in so doing make some appeal to the idea of irrationality, but it also risks obscuring important differences among them. For example, some passages in Feinberg's important essay on insanity actually echo the lost agency theory:

> "[S]enseless" desires, because they do not cohere, are likely to seem alien, not fully expressive of their owner's essential character. When a person acts to satisfy them, it is *as if he were acting on somebody else's desires*. And, indeed, the alien desires may have a distinct kind of unifying character all their own, as if a new person were grafted onto the old one.

Feinberg, *supra*, at 288 (emphasis added). Indeed, in a footnote to this passage, Feinberg writes: "Hence the point of the ancient metaphor of 'possession.'" *Id.* at 288 n.4.

61 *See* FINGARETTE, *supra* note 28, at 179 ("[T]he word 'irrational' is used in a number of very different senses."); Sinnott-Armstrong & Levy, *supra* note 27, at 317 ("[T]he term 'rational' is vague and controversial."); Walter Sinnott-Armstrong, *Insanity and Irrationality*, 1 PUB. AFF. Q. 1, 14 (1987).

62 Morse emphasizes that rationality is a "continuum concept." *See, e.g.*, Stephen J. Morse, *Diminished Rationality, Diminished Responsibility*, 1 OHIO ST. J. CRIM. L. 289 (2003). Consistent with that emphasis, he argues in favor of a partial defense of irrationality, when the accused is irrational, but not so irrational as to warrant a complete defense. *See id.* That's all well and good, but what's needed, if possible, is a more precise delineation between not sufficiently irrational and sufficiently irrational to warrant a partial defense, as well as the line between not sufficiently irrational and sufficiently irrational to warrant a full defense.

63 Prior to Thomas Erskine's defense of James Hadfield in 1800, existing English authority, such as it was, appears to have limited legal insanity to what was then called "total" insanity, or what's here called irrationality-as-unintelligibility. Erskine argued that "total" insanity was sufficient for legal insanity, but not necessary. He argued that what was then called "partial" insanity should also suffice. As Erskine said in *Hadfield*, in some cases "reason is not driven from her seat [i.e., total insanity],

unintelligibility theory says insanity consists in being psychotic, where being psychotic is a "degree-vague assessment of severity in a variety of mental abilities" indicating "*severe* abnormalities of behavior."[64] The delusion theory says insanity consists in psychotic choices, where a psychotic choice is a choice based on delusion.

Unintelligibility

Irrationality is a matter of degree. The insane are just that much more irrational than the rest of us, insofar as the "irrationality associated with insanity is a deep[], . . . radical kind of irrationality."[65] But "deep" and "radical" how? The unintelligibility theory portrays insanity's irrationality as deep and radical in two ways.[66] First, insanity's irrationality is deep insofar as it's a property, not of acts, but of actors. It attaches not just to what a person does. It goes deeper, attaching to the person himself. Second, insanity's irrationality is radical insofar as the insane are unintelligible to us, so unintelligible it no longer makes sense to regard the insane as moral agents.[67]

When a person ceases to be a moral agent, it makes no sense to get angry at him for anything he does, crimes included. Resentment and indignation are misplaced, just as they are when an animal causes harm, inasmuch as animals aren't moral agents. Non-agent persons are, an unintelligibility theorist might say, "beyond good and evil,"[68] or perhaps "not operating within the realm of reason at all."[69] Or, perhaps, "stranger to us than birds in our

but . . . [instead] distraction sits down upon it along with her, holds her, trembling, upon it, and frightens her from propriety [i.e., partial insanity]." *The Trial of James Hadfield*, 27 How. St. Tr. 1281, 1313 (1800).

[64] Moore, *supra* note 34, at 656.

[65] Fingarette, *supra* note 28, at 179.

[66] Moore's latest and most extended discussion of his theory of insanity can be found in Moore, *supra* note 34. Earlier statements can be found in Michael S. Moore, Law and Psychiatry: Rethinking the Relationship 217–45 (1984); Michael S. Moore, *Mental Illness and Responsibility*, 39 Bull. Menninger Clinic 308 (1975) (reprinted as Chapter 14 in Michael S. Moore, Placing Blame: A Theory of Criminal Law 595–609 (1997)).

[67] What does it take to make someone a "moral agent"? Moore identifies nine criteria, *see* Moore, *supra* note 34, at 673–77, with emphasis on the capacity for "practical rationality." *See id.* at 677 ("In particular, very crazy human beings are most importantly deficient in . . . practical rationality.").

[68] *Id.* at 678.

[69] *See* R.A. Duff, Answering for Crime: Responsibility and Liability in the Criminal Law 289 (2007). Duff suggests that "if a person is so disordered that he is not operating within the realm of reason at all, he should be described as a-rational or a-reasonable rather than irrational or unreasonable." *Id.*

gardens."[70] We should treat them, as sentient creatures, with compassion, and if they're dangerous, we might want to confine them. But blaming them makes no sense. Blame presupposes moral agency, and calling someone "insane" is just another way of saying he's not a moral agent.

The unintelligible are often afflicted with schizophrenia. Schizophrenia is commonly associated with hallucinations and delusions, but also manifests in "word salad," "thought-blocking," and neologisms, as well as agitated and repetitive movements; or, at the opposite extreme, catatonia.[71] Or think about the more florid inmates of the Bridgewater Asylum for the Criminally Insane, depicted in Frederick Wiseman's 1967 documentary *Titicut Follies*. Other words for the unintelligible come to mind: raving, rambling, bizarre, deranged, delirious, incoherent, and so on. Or: "totally deteriorated, drooling."[72] You get the idea. Most of us would doubtless have a hard time regarding such beings as fellow travelers. We are, as the unintelligibility theory says, apt to look upon them as beings so disintegrated or disordered as to be non-agents.

Insanity's history is replete with analogies. For the unintelligibility theory, the insane are likened to wild beasts or brutes.[73] The analogy is usually traced to Judge Robert Tracy in his charge to the jury in the 1724 trial of Edward Arnold, but its antecedents go back almost 500 years earlier, to 1256.[74] Early English law distinguished between the "totally insane" and "partially insane,"[75] and the wild-beast analogy was meant to illuminate what it was to

[70] Moore, *supra* note 34, at 678 (quoting Manfred Bleuler, described as the "'father' of schizophrenia").

[71] *See* Am. Psychiatric Ass'n, Diagnostic and Statistical Manual of Mental Disorders 99 (5th ed. 2013); Nat'l Inst. Mental Health, Schizophrenia, at 4 (NIH Pub. No. 15-3517).

[72] Gregory Zilboorg, Mind, Medicine and Man 273 (1943).

[73] *See* Moore, *supra* note 34, at 678–79.

[74] *See* Anthony Michael Platt & Bernard L. Diamond, *The Origins and Development of the "Wild Beast" Concept of Mental Illness and Its Relation to Theories of Criminal Responsibility*, 1 J. Hist. Behav. Sci. 355, 361 (1965) (tracing the history of the "wild-beast" analogy back from Tracy to Hale to Coke and finally to Bracton). According to Platt and Diamond:

> The "wild beast" concept emerged finally in the seventeenth century as a result of a mistranslation of "*brutis*" . . . Bracton's use of "*brutis*" was in fact shorthand for "*brutis animalibus*," which may literally be translated as "brute" or "dumb animals." This expression and idea was used particularly by the canonists to distinguish man from animals. Bracton correctly observed that "animals which lack reason" do not possess the will or intent to do harm; consequently, they are not to be considered legally accountable. It was quite legitimate for Bracton to include the insane in this conceptual framework because they too, like dumb animals, were considered lacking in will and understanding.

Id. at 360–61. The wild-beast analogy might actually fit the lost agency theory as well as, if not better than, the unintelligibility theory, at least if animals (or some animals) lack a sense of agency.

[75] *See, e.g.*, Joel Peter Eigen, *Delusion in the Courtroom: The Role of Partial Insanity in Early Forensic Testimony*, 35 Med. Hist. 25, 27 (1991) ("Legal tracts written by Sir Matthew Hale and Lord Coke, together with judicial instructions dating to the late eighteenth century, reveal that juries were

be totally insane. As Judge Tracy said: A person isn't insane unless "*totally* deprived of his understanding and memory, and doth not know what he is doing, no more . . . than a brute, or a wild beast."[76] The unintelligibility theory, which embraces the wild-beast analogy,[77] thus limits insanity to what in days gone by was called total insanity, but total insanity is a procrustean theory of insanity.

Don't misunderstand. If someone qualifies as insane under the unintelligibility theory, then insane he is. No doubt about that. The unintelligibly insane fail even to pass the threshold into moral agency. That's not the theory's problem. Its problem is under-inclusion. The unintelligibility theory, being under-inclusive, will too often certify the sanity of those who are, intuitively at least, certifiably insane.

Take M'Naghten. M'Naghten was mentally disordered, but not so disordered we can't make any sense of him. We might not understand why he thought the Tories were out to get him, but if killing the prime minster was the only way to stop it, then killing the prime minister was an intelligible thing to do. Nor was M'Naghten so disordered he couldn't figure out how to make the attempt. He could, and did, come up with a plan and put it into action. He wasn't "*totally* deprived" of reason. If a theory of insanity is plausible only if it passes the M'Naghten litmus test—thereby certifying M'Naghten to be insane—then the unintelligibility theory is implausible, inasmuch as it would certify M'Naghten to be sane. That's strike one.[78]

traditionally instructed that only a total want of memory and understanding—a *total* insanity—would satisfy the law's criterion for exemption from culpability.").

[76] *Trial of Edward Arnold*, *supra* note 63, at 765.

[77] Moore, *supra* note 34, at 678–79.

[78] Moore maintains that (the real) M'Naghten *would* qualify as insane under the unintelligibility test. *See* Moore, *supra* note 34, at 662. That's hard to fathom, given what we know about M'Naghten. This disagreement—was M'Naghten unintelligible or not—highlights another point Moore makes; namely, that the "line separating persons from non-persons," the intelligible from the unintelligible, is more gray zone than bright line. Still, portraying M'Naghten as having passed some threshold into unintelligibility, as having entered a zone wherein he's "stranger to us than birds in our gardens," doesn't seem like an accurate description of the historical M'Naghten. History's descriptions of M'Naghten, and the unintelligibility theory's description of the insane, don't mesh very well. Here's an account of how M'Naghten behaved while in prison awaiting trial:

> What would become increasingly interesting about M'Naghten was the fact that his demeanor throughout his time in prison was always precisely the same. He always appeared calm and composed. He had a hearty appetite and ate well. He appeared very attentive to conversations between other people in the jail: other prisoners, attorneys, police guards, and is said to have frequently laughed at any jocular observations that were made.

SCHNEIDER, *supra* note 2, at 29–30. On its face, that doesn't sound like someone who's stranger to us than birds in our gardens. Morse makes much that same observation more generally about people suffering from psychotic disorders. *See* Stephen J. Morse, *Moore on the Mind*, *in* LEGAL, MORAL, AND

Now change the facts. Suppose, for argument's sake, that M'Naghten was indeed as disordered as the unintelligibility theory requires, akin to a wild beast. If so, he shouldn't be held criminally liable for killing Drummond. But if he'd truly been as disordered as the unintelligibility theory requires, he probably wouldn't have committed the crime in the first place. Crimes don't necessarily require cunning, but they usually require coherence. The non-agents of the unintelligibility theory are, one imagines, so disordered it would be miraculous for them to pull themselves together enough to pull off a crime.[79] Maybe some can, but probably not many. The unintelligibility theory is thus a test for insanity that will seldom be used or needed. That's strike two.

The unintelligibility theorist might nonetheless insist that M'Naghten *was* irrational enough to count as insane. That seems unlikely, but suppose we go along. Now assume M'Naghten decides not to kill the prime minister, but instead to steal a bowler, not because he was irresistibly driven to it, but just because he wants to look dapper and doesn't feel like paying. He knows full well he's stealing and stealing is a crime, and his theft has nothing to do with his delusions. He doesn't, for example, believe stealing the bowler will strike a blow against the Tory establishment.

On the unintelligibility theory, insanity attaches to people, not choices or acts; or better, because it attaches to people, it attaches to all of their choices and acts. Thus, if M'Naghten was insane under the unintelligibility theory, he's not guilty of theft. Indeed, if he was insane under the unintelligibility theory, he's not guilty of anything. Not being a moral agent, he could literally do no wrong, inasmuch as he could bear no responsibility for any wrong he did.

But, once again, M'Naghten's delusions had nothing to do with hats. They had to do with Tory persecution, which stealing the bowler would do nothing to stop. Under those circumstances, it wouldn't seem out of line for

Metaphysical Truths: The Philosophy of Michael Moore 233, 240 (Kimberly Kessler Ferzan & Stephen J. Morse eds., 2016) ("People with psychotic disorders . . . are not 'stranger to us that the birds in our gardens,' nor are they 'beyond good and evil' . . . . Each is recognizably one of us.").

[79] Fingarette, *supra* note 28, at 206 ("[T]here as those whose mental powers have generally so deteriorated for one reason or another that the individual has become permanently incapable of the most elementary self-care or interpersonal intercourse."); Morse, *supra* note 78, at 241 ("[T]hose people who are omni-disabled are usually too disorganized to engage in criminal conduct other than simple assaultive or disorderly conduct, for which no sensible defendant raises an insanity defense."). As Thomas Erskine said in his defense of Hadfield, cases in which "reason is not merely disturbed, but wholly driven from her seat . . . are not only extremely rare, but never can become the subjects of judicial difficulty." *Trial of James Hadfield*, *supra* note 63, at 1313.

the state to condemn him for pinching the bowler,[80] and if it wouldn't be out of line, then insanity can't be based on status, as the unintelligibility theory says. If so, then insanity can't be like infancy, which is the stock example of a status defense. Children, being globally non-responsible, might be able to do no wrong, but the same doesn't go for the insane, unless of course insanity is limited to those who really and truly are unintelligible to us, in which case we're back to the procrustean problem.

All of which leaves the unintelligibility theory in a bind. If it says M'Naghten was sane, it fails the M'Naghten litmus test, because it deems M'Naghten sane when the received wisdom regards him as insane. If it insists M'Naghten was insane, then M'Naghten gets a pass for any crime he commits, because insanity is a status defense. Neither horn has much appeal. Strike three.

Delusion

Now tack to the other irrationality theory: the delusion theory.[81] For starters, stipulate that delusions are irrational beliefs. They're irrational inasmuch as they don't respond to evidence contradicting them, no matter how compelling the countervailing evidence may be. M'Naghten, for example, believed the Tories were out to get him. Time and again he was told that was not the case, to no avail. Nothing, we're to imagine, would have convinced him otherwise.

[80] FINGARETTE, *supra* note 28, at 208 ("[T]here seems no good moral reason why, in general, a person who is persistently irrational about food should not nevertheless be held responsible in connection with his business dealings."); Morse, *supra* note 78, at 241 ("[P]eople with severe mental disorders . . . may be competent or morally responsible for some conduct."); Anthony Kenny, *Can Responsibility Be Diminished?*, *in* LIABILITY AND RESPONSIBILITY 1, 24–25 (R.G. Frey & Christopher Morris eds., 1991) ("Treating madness as a status rather than a factor . . . gives a certified mental patient a license which is not given to others: He knows there are certain things he may do without being held criminally responsible, while all others not of the same status will be held responsible."). Morse and Kenny also argue that treating insanity as a status defense or exemption is, in one way or another, to some extent or another, potentially stigmatizing. *See* Morse, *supra*, at 243 (expressing concern that treating insanity as a status excuse "would contribute, albeit marginally, to common misunderstandings and fear of mental disorder that continue to stigmatize and exclude people with such disorders"); Kenny, *supra*, at 25 ("Treating madness as a status . . . attaches stigma to insanity by assuming, without any need of proof, that insanity predisposes to criminal action.").

[81] The test for insanity contained in the *M'Naghten* judges' answer to question four, *see supra* note 27, states the same test as the irrationality-as-delusion theory, namely, that an accused suffering from delusions is insane if, assuming his delusions had been real or true, he wouldn't have been guilty under existing law of the crime charged.

Delusions come in different shapes and sizes. Some are self-contained. If you suffer from what's known as Capgras delusion, you delusionally believe your spouse is an imposter, but the delusion usually just sits there. You don't, for example, decide to confront the imposter, go out looking for your real spouse, or turn to the police for help.[82] Other delusions don't just sit there. Delusionally believing the Tories were out to get him, M'Naghten decided to take action. His only option, he reasoned, was to assassinate Peel. M'Naghten's delusion was irrational, but once it became fixed in his mind, the decision to kill Peel looks not only intelligible, but rational. M'Naghten did the cost-benefit analysis. Better to kill than (eventually) be killed. Still, at the root of his rational decision to go after Peel was the irrational delusion that Peel and his lot were coming after him.

The delusion theory differs from the unintelligibility theory in two ways. First, on the delusion theory, irrationality is understood, not as a property of persons, but as a property of choices or acts. Second, a choice or act is irrational insofar as it rests on one type of irrational belief; namely, a delusion, and it rests on a delusion inasmuch as a delusion forms part of the practical syllogism leading to choice. M'Naghten's choice to make an attempt on Peel's life was insane because the practical reasoning leading him there was irrational, and the practical reasoning leading him there was irrational because it was based on an irrational belief: the delusion that the Tories were out to get him.[83] According to the delusion theory, M'Naghten's choice to kill Peel was insane just because it rested on a delusion of persecution.[84]

A traditionalist, who endorses the traditional test, is apt to be unpersuaded. M'Naghten's decision, he'll gladly concede, rested on a delusion. He tried to kill Peel only because he irrationally believed the Tories were ruining his life. But, the traditionalist will ask: So what? If we assume M'Naghten, despite his delusions, could have realized he was committing a crime, and if so, could have conformed to the law, what difference does his delusion make? In other words, the traditionalist wants to know why a delusion-inspired choice

[82] Every rule has an exception: Christopher Frith and Eve Johnstone describe "one extreme case [in which] a [Capgras] patient who believed that his step-father had been replaced by a robot and subsequently decapitated him to look for batteries and controls in his head."). *See* Christopher Frith & Eve Johnstone, Schizophrenia: A Very Short Introduction 140 (2003).

[83] Morse, *supra* note 78, at 240 ("We excuse [a person as insane] when substantive irrationality [i.e., delusion] impairs the agent's practical reasoning in the context in question.").

[84] Thomas Erskine advanced this version of the delusion theory in his defense of James Hadfield. *See* Garvey, *supra* note 20, at 399–400 (discussing Erskine's defense of Hadfield).

should preclude liability, if and when the choice was neither compelled nor made in compelled ignorance.[85]

The delusion theorist might at this point reply that he's been misunderstood. Not all choices based on delusions are insane. Some are; some aren't. Properly understood and refined, the delusion theory tells us that a choice based on a delusion is an insane choice, but only if, had the actor's delusions been true, the choice wouldn't have been a crime.[86] For example, if M'Naghten's delusions about the Tory spies had all been true, his decision to steal a bowler, say, would still be a crime. His delusions about the Tories, if they'd been true, would do nothing to shield him from liability for the crime of larceny. On the other hand, eliminating Peel was, M'Naghten delusionally believed, the only way he could end his torment. If killing Peel really was the only way M'Naghten could find peace, would he be guilty of murder? That, according to the delusion theory, is the critical question.

Unfortunately, when we try to answer that question we encounter another problem. At the start, we can safely take self-defense off the table. Assuming

[85] *See*, e.g., Moore, *supra* note 34, at 671 ("[U]sually . . . paranoid schizophrenics do not make any mistakes about what they are doing or that morality or the criminal law prohibit the doing of it.").

[86] Morse rejects the unintelligibility theory. Does he embrace the delusion theory? It's hard to tell. On the one hand, he writes: "Some agents . . . act for such irrational reasons that it would be unjust to blame and punish them *whether or not* they would be justified if the facts and circumstances were as they delusionally believed." Stephen J. Morse & Morris B. Hoffman, *The Uneasy Entente Between Legal Insanity and Mens Rea: Beyond* Clark v. Arizona, 97 J. CRIM. L. & CRIMINOLOGY 1071, 1129 (2007) (emphasis added). The "whether or not" suggests Morse doesn't embrace the delusion theory. On the other hand, he later writes: A delusional actor "must be convicted," unless his "moral compass has been independently compromised by mental disorder," i.e., when, "[e]ven if all the facts and circumstances he believes them to be were true, he would still be guilty of a crime." Morse, *supra* note 78, at 243. Should the last clause be read to imply that a delusional actor must *not* be convicted if, assuming all the facts and circumstances as he believes them to be were true, he would *not* be guilty of a crime? If so, that suggests Morse does embrace the delusion theory.

The delusion theory is similar to Christopher Slobogin's "integrationist" alternative to insanity. Insanity, according to this alternative, would be abolished as an affirmative defense. Instead, existing criminal law doctrines would be applied to the facts as the defendant believed them to be, whether those beliefs were delusional or not. The defendant's fate would turn on the result. *See* Christopher Slobogin, *An End to Insanity: Recasting the Role of Mental Disability in Criminal Cases*, 86 VA. L. REV. 1199, 1199–1208 (2000) [hereinafter Slobogin, *An End to Insanity*]. Alas, the criminal law isn't as "subjective" as Slobogin imagines, and "subjectifying" it to the extent he needs for his alternative to work would require a significant departure from existing doctrine. *See, e.g.*, Morse & Hoffman, *supra*, at 1128 (stating that Slobogin is "incorrect about the extent of subjectivization current law accepts"). Slobogin later notes that if the law isn't sufficiently "subjective," then a "'special defense' for offenders with mental illness would still be needed, albeit one that focuses on whether, at the time of the crime, they lacked subjectified *mens rea* or believed they were confronted by circumstances that would be justifying or coercive if true." Christopher Slobogin, *A Defense of the Integrationist Test as a Replacement for the Special Defense of Insanity*, 42 TEX. TECH. L. REV. 523, 532–33 (2009). At any rate, Slobogin expressly remarks that his integrationist alternative is "virtually identical" to the "Partial Delusion defense announced in M'Naghten" in response to question four. *See* Christopher Slobogin, *The Integrationist Alternative to the Insanity Defense: Reflections on the Exculpatory Scope of Mental Illness in the Wake of the Andrea Yates Trial*, 30 AM. J. CRIM. L. 315, 335 (2003).

self-defense requires an imminent threat, M'Naghten wouldn't prevail on a self-defense claim because he attacked Drummond (thinking he was Peel), not the other way round. True, M'Naghten thought the Tories were out to get him, but M'Naghten didn't think he faced an imminent attack on his life when he killed Drummond.[87] What about a necessity, or lesser evils, defense? M'Naghten faced a choice: kill Peel or let the Tories (eventually) kill him (or at least continue their torment). If those were in fact the two evils he faced, was killing Peel the lesser evil under the law of necessity circa 1843?

Doubtful, if only because necessity at common law didn't extend to murder,[88] nor does it extend to murder under English law today.[89] Much the same would go for common-law duress, which likewise wasn't available for murder. M'Naghten might have had better luck in a different time or place. The Model Penal Code, for example, contemplates necessity and duress, under the right circumstances, as defenses to homicide, though most jurisdictions don't follow the Code on necessity or duress. If a jury, instructed on the law of necessity and duress under the Code, were asked if M'Naghten, assuming his delusions were true, chose the lesser evil, or killed under duress, who knows what it would decide.[90]

The delusion theory rests its verdict—sane or insane—on the law applied to the accused's delusional world, thus requiring fact-finders to step into a delusional world and apply the law to the facts they find there. That's not easy to do. Trying to do it for M'Naghten was hard enough, but now try to do it for James Hadfield. Hadfield, a former English soldier who'd been struck in the head with a sabre during the Battle of Tourcoing in 1794, believed death was his divine fate, because his death would bring forth the second coming of Christ. He also believed his death had to be at someone's hand other than

87 *See* Slobogin, *An End to Insanity*, *supra* note 86, at 1203 ("Whether M'Naghten would have been acquitted under the . . . [integrationist] proposal would depend on whether he believed the harassment would soon lead to his death or serious bodily harm and whether he thought there was any other way to prevent that occurrence.").

88 According to one contemporary treatise on English law, "[u]nder current law, *Dudley [and Stephens]* is regarded as authority that necessity is unavailable for murder. But, on the facts, *Dudley* need not have decided any specific rule for murder." Simester et al., *supra* note 27, § 21.3(ii)(e), at 805. *Dudley and Stephens* is the famous English cannibalism case, but it wasn't decided until 1884, over forty years after *M'Naghten*.

89 *See id.*

90 M'Naghten, one might argue, couldn't claim lesser evils or duress, even in a Model Penal Code jurisdiction, insofar as he had options to protect himself from the Tories other than killing the prime minister. Why, for instance, didn't he go to the police and tell them what the Tories where up to? Well, he did, and was told nothing could be done. Within his delusional world, maybe M'Naghten believed the state had abandoned him. An analogy might be to a battered spouse who, after repeated but failed efforts to get help from the authorities, comes to believe the state has abdicated, and so decides to take matters into her own hands.

his own, else the second coming wouldn't come. So Hadfield decided he had to kill the king, which would cause the king's successor to execute him for treason, and thus would Christ come again. Was Hadfield, under the delusion theory, sane or not?

According to the delusion theory, it depends: Is it a crime to kill the king if killing the king is necessary to bring Christ back into the world? Once again, necessity probably wasn't at the time a defense to murder, completed or attempted, let alone when the target is the king. Then again, it is Christ we're talking about.[91] Is it permissible to sacrifice the king (in order to sacrifice oneself) in order to bring about the second coming? That probably depends on whether you believe in Christ in the first place, but set that complication aside. The real problem is the question itself. The delusion theory forces the question, but the question itself borders on the bizarre.[92] All else being equal, a test that turns on the fantastical is a test better avoided.

All the tests discussed above have one thing in common. The traditional test (and its Model Penal Code descendant) ask if the *accused* had the power, more or less, to know he was committing a crime, or whether he had the power, more or less, to choose otherwise. The *Durham* Rule asks if mental illness caused the *accused* to commit the crime. The irrationality tests ask if the *accused* was so irrational he was no longer an agent at all, or if his crime wouldn't have been a crime had his delusions been real. For all their

[91] James Fitzjames Stephen (a judge at the time) had this to say about the verdict in *Hadfield's Case*: "My own opinion . . . is that if a special Divine order were given to a man to commit murder, I should certainly hang him for it unless I got a special Divine order not to hang him. What the effect of getting such an order would be is a question difficult for anyone to answer till he gets it." 2 STEPHEN, *supra* note 38, at 160 n.1.

[92] Moreover, as Glanville Williams observed long ago, the test assumes the "lunatic [can] be reasonable in his unreason, sane in his insanity." GLANVILLE WILLIAMS, CRIMINAL LAW: THE GENERAL PART § 161, at 504 (2d ed. 1961). Williams wasn't the first to make this point. Earlier critics made the same point. *See, e.g.*, Parsons v. State, 2 So. 854, 866 (1886) ("If [a delusional accused] dare fail to reason, on the supposed facts embodied in the delusion, as perfectly as a sane man could do on a like state of realities, he receives no mercy at the hands of the law."); State v. Jones, 50 N.H. 369, 388 (1871) (The test "is, in effect, saying to the jury, the prisoner was mad when he committed the crime, but he did not use sufficient reason in his madness."); ISAAC RAY, TREATISE ON THE MEDICAL JURISPRUDENCE OF INSANITY § 34, at 47 (3d ed. 1860) ("This is virtually saying to a man, 'You are allowed to be insane; the disease is a visitation of Providence, and you cannot help it; but have a care how you manifest your insanity; there must be method in your madness.'"); HENRY MAUDSLEY, RESPONSIBILITY IN MENTAL DISEASE 97 (1874) ("Here is an unhesitating assumption that a man, having an insane delusion, has the power to think and act in regard to it *reasonably*; that, at the time of the offense, he ought to have and to exercise the knowledge and self-control which a sane man would have and exercise, were the facts with respect to which the delusion exists real; that he is, in fact, bound to be reasonable in his unreason, sane in his sanity."); 1 FRANCIS WHARTON & MORETON STILLÉ, MEDICAL JURISPRUDENCE § 520, at 548–49 (5th ed. 1905) ("This rule is based on the theory that an insane man must act with reason and moderation; he must measure his acts strictly by a rational standard; but insane men do not do this; and for the reason that they are insane.").

differences, all these tests assume the act and mind behind the crime were those of the *accused*. What, though, if they weren't? That brings us to insanity as lost agency.

Lost Agency

When all goes well, and you move your hand, you experience your hand moving, and you experience yourself moving it. Your hand is moving, and you're the one moving it. In other words, when you move your hand, you experience a sense of *ownership* (it's *my* hand) and a sense of *agency* (it's *me* moving it).[93] The author or agent of your hand's movement is you. Indeed, our experiences of ownership and agency are mundane. We take them for granted. So much so that they fade into the phenomenal background, such that we hardly ever notice them. Simple, right?

Not always. Enter Dr. Strangelove. The character in Stanley Kubrick's 1964 film of the same name was an odd duck, but perhaps the oddest thing about him was that hand. It seemed to have a mind and will of its own. The good doctor's affliction has a name: alien hand syndrome. Those, like the doctor, who suffer from it experience and believe the hand that's moving is theirs. What they don't experience or believe is that they're the ones moving it. They experience a sense of ownership without a sense of agency.[94] Their hand is moving, but they're not moving it. Someone, or something, external or alien to them, to their sense of agency, is in control. Many "refer to their alien hands as 'imps' or 'devils.'"[95]

[93] Research on the sense of agency is a relatively recent development. *See* Tim Bayne & Elisabeth Pacherie, *Narrators and Comparators: The Architecture of Agentive Self-Awareness*, 159 SYNTHESE 475, 475 (2007) ("Until recently, neither philosophers nor psychologists had much interest in awareness of one's own agency. This is no longer the case, and there is now a burgeoning literature on the mechanisms underlying 'the sense of agency.'"); Patrick Haggard, *Sense of Agency in the Human Brain*, 18 NATURE REVIEWS: NEUROSCIENCE 197, 197 (2017) ("[S]ense of agency has received surprisingly little attention in cognitive neuroscience until recent times."). For recent collections on the phenomenon, see, for example, AGENCY AND SELF-AWARENESS: ISSUES IN PHILOSOPHY AND PSYCHOLOGY (Johannes Roessler & Naomi Eilan eds., 2003); DECOMPOSING THE WILL (Andy Clark, Julian Kiverstein & Tillmann Vierkant eds., 2013); NEUROPSYCHOLOGY OF THE SENSE OF AGENCY: FROM CONSCIOUSNESS TO ACTION (Michela Balconi ed., 2010); SENSE OF AGENCY: EXAMINING AWARENESS OF THE ACTING SELF (Nicole David, James W. Moore & Sukhvinder Obhi eds., 2015); THE SENSE OF AGENCY (Patrick Haggard & Baruch Eitam eds., 2015).

[94] Researchers sometimes distinguish *anarchic* hand syndrome from *alien* hand syndrome, where the former involves a loss of a sense of agency without a loss of a sense of ownership and the latter involves a loss of a sense of agency and ownership. *See, e.g.*, Clelia Marchetti Sergio Della Sala, *Disentangling the Alien Hand and Anarchic Hand*, 3 COGNITIVE NEUROPSYCHIATRY 191 (1998).

[95] SAM KEAN, THE TALE OF DUELING NEUROSURGEONS 257 (2014).

Most of us are lucky. We don't suffer from alien hand syndrome. But most of us have driven a car, and driving a car, or any other over-learned behavior, can provide a glimpse of what it's like to lose one's sense of agency, though the experience falls far short of alien hand syndrome.[96] We sometimes go on auto-pilot. We drive, but have no sense of driving, in which case we might colloquially speak of "highway hypnosis." Psychologists might use the language of automaticity.[97] Some musicians and athletes might describe it as "flow," or being "in the zone."[98] A virtuoso might say, in order to try to explain the experience, that the "music just took over." Of course, zoning out is a far cry from alien hands. For one thing, the flow stops if something interrupts it, and once interrupted, the actor regains the sense of agency. He zones back in. Focus won't restore the sense of agency to an alien hand, however.

The theory of insanity described below portrays insanity as alien hand syndrome writ large. What makes an act insane is the fact that the person whose act it is has no sense of agency at the time he performs it. He experiences the action as the action of his body, but fails to experience himself as its author. He doesn't experience himself as being "in control" of what he's doing, because he doesn't experience himself as doing it.

Imagine Dr. Strangelove's hand suddenly hits you: You'd be upset, but presumably you wouldn't (once you calm down) blame *him*. *He* didn't hit you. His hand did. Likewise, on the theory described below, if insane Jane kills John, Jane's not guilty. *Jane* didn't kill John. Her *body* did. Ascriptions of guilt presuppose a sense of agency; the insane are insane because they lack a sense of agency; therefore, if Jane was insane, it makes no sense to ascribe guilt to her choice to kill John.

[96] *See* Tim Bayne & Neil Levy, *The Feeling of Doing: Deconstructing the Phenomenology of Agency*, *in* Disorders of Volition 49, 56 (Natalie Sebanz & Wolfgang Prinz eds., 2006) ("Although it seems to be true that experiences of authorship are recessive or dampened in the context of automatic actions (or, at least, action we experience as automatic), we doubt that the phenomenology of agency is entirely lacking from such experiences.").

[97] John A. Bargh & Tanya L. Chartrand, *The Unbearable Automaticity of Being*, 54 Am. Psychologist 462, 468 (1999). Some psychologists might describe this phenomenon as shifting from what they call System 2 (the automatic system) back to System 1 (the deliberative system), where the shift itself is under the command of System 2. Something happens to interrupt the flow, at which point System 2 relinquishes control back to System 1. On System 1 and System 2 generally, see Daniel Kahneman, Thinking, Fast and Slow 19–30 (2011).

[98] *See, e.g.*, László Harmat et al., Flow Experience: Empirical Research and Applications (2016); Matti Vuorre & Janet Metcalfe, *The Relation Between the Sense of Agency and the Experience of Flow*, 43 Consciousness & Cognition 133 (2016).

This is the lost sense of agency theory of insanity—or lost agency theory, for short.[99] Of course, like most things having to do with the mind, one's sense of agency can doubtless be diminished or reduced, as opposed to being lost altogether.[100] For ease of exposition, however, we introduce the theory on the assumption that the sense of agency, retained or lost, is all-or-nothing.[101]

[99] For what looks like an earlier and inchoate—and regrettably overlooked—presentation of the lost agency theory, see JOHN DEIGH, *Moral Agency and Criminal Insanity*, *in* EMOTIONS, VALUES, AND THE LAW 196, 207–10 (2008):

> One must also show [in order for mental illness to excuse] something further about the illness, that it so impaired the offender's agency, say, as to render it idle. The illness could do so, for instance, by rendering the offender passive with respect to the internal forces that bring about his commission of the offense. The offense, in this case, would be like action done under the influence of hypnosis or some powerful psychoactive drug, for typically when an action is done under either of those influences, the actor is passive with respect to the external forces that induce him to act. Hence, the action does not issue from the actor's exercise of his agency. He is not its author.

Deigh's essay was originally written in 2000, but not published until 2008. Deigh draws on the work of Harry Frankfurt. Roughly, Frankfurt maintained that a person is responsible for choosing to φ when his first-order desires, which cause him to φ, mesh with what Frankfurt calls his higher-order volitions (such that the person wants to do what he wants to do), and isn't responsible when they don't. If they don't mesh, he observes, we might say you qua your higher-order volitions are alienated from you qua your first-order desires. Needless to say, the sense of alienation involved in alien hand syndrome and lost agency is of a far different and more profound sort than the sense Frankfurt had in mind.

The lost agency theory also dovetails with the "ownership" condition described in John Martin Fischer's reasons-responsiveness theory of moral responsibility. Fischer says a person is morally responsible for an action "insofar as he has guidance control of it, where guidance control consists in the action's issuing from the agent's own, moderately reasons-responsive mechanism;" ownership of the mechanism is "defined in terms of taking responsibility" for it; and "taking responsibility" requires among other things that the person "must see himself as the source of his behavior . . . That is, the individual must see himself as an agent." JOHN MARTIN FISCHER & MARK RAVIZZA, RESPONSIBILITY AND CONTROL: A THEORY OF MORAL RESPONSIBILITY 230–31, 210 (1998). It stands to reason that someone who lacks a sense of agency will not "see himself as the source of his behavior."

[100] The sense of agency is probably a matter of more or less, and when lost or diminished, it's lost or diminished intermittently. *See* Matthis Synofzik et al., *The Experience of Agency: An Interplay Between Prediction and Postdiction*, 4 FRONTIERS IN PSYCHOLOGY 1, 6 (2013) ("Agency attribution in patients with delusions of influence [control] . . . fails only episodically and only in certain contexts.").

[101] Psychologists use various methods for measuring the sense of agency. Self-reports are one measure, and a phenomenon known as "intentional binding" is often used as an implicit measure. *See, e.g.*, James W. Moore & Sukhvinder S. Obhi, *Intentional Binding and the Sense of Agency: A Review*, 21 CONSCIOUSNESS & COGNITION 546 (2012). Psychologists have also offered different theories describing the psychological processes believed to produce the sense of agency, with what's called the "comparator model" apparently being the dominant (but not uncontested) theory. *See, e.g.*, Glenn Carruthers, *The Case for the Comparator Model as an Explanation of the Sense of Agency and Its Breakdowns*, 21 CONSCIOUSNESS & COGNITION 30 (2012). For more or less accessible introductions to this very large and specialized literature, see, for example, ANIL ANANTHASWAMY, THE MAN WHO WASN'T THERE: TALES FROM THE EDGE OF THE SELF 112–15 (2015); James W. Moore, *What Is the Sense of Agency and Why Does it Matter?*, 7 FRONTIERS IN PSYCHOL. 1, 3–4 (Aug. 2016); Markus Schlosser, *Agency*, STAN. ENCYCLOPEDIA PHIL. 29–30 (2015).

The Demon Within

Metaphors are a risky business. They can illuminate, but they can also mislead. Having put that disclaimer on the table, here's a metaphor for the lost sense of agency: We'll name it the *alien-self metaphor*.

Before an actor loses his sense of agency, the only self around is the actor himself. That's the *real self*. When the sense of agency is lost, another self can emerge. That's the *alien self*. Now we have two selves, so to speak, in the same body. The actor has become disintegrated. Before the split, the real self was in charge, at the helm, calling the shots, in the driver's seat, and so forth.

Once the sense of agency is lost, the real self loses command, and the alien self takes over. The real self becomes a passive bystander to the actions of a body he continues to experience as his own, but no longer experiences himself as the author of what his body does. His actions are thus at once both his and not his. Intentions and volitions are being formed, with bodily movements resulting. Yet the real self doesn't experience himself as the author of any of it.

The alien-self metaphor has buried antecedents in the history of insanity. Once upon a time, the insane were, as we've seen, thought to be like wild beasts or children. Once upon a time, even further back, they were thought to be something else: possessed.[102] An insane person was thought to be a demoniac, whose mind and body a demon had overtaken: someone with a demon within.[103] The lost agency theory gives new meaning to this old idea. "The devil made me do it" is a lame excuse,[104] but when it comes to insanity, it contains a kernel of truth. In fact, possession may have been behind the old wild-beast analogy, inasmuch as "animals and the insane were both considered embodiments of evil spirits."[105]

[102] *See, e.g.*, ROY PORTER, MADNESS: A BRIEF HISTORY 10–33 (2002) (chapter titled "Gods and Demons"); ROY PORTER, MIND-FORG'D MANACLES: A HISTORY OF MADNESS IN ENGLAND FROM THE RESTORATION TO THE REGENCY 63 (1987) ("One mark of possession by the Devil was insanity."); DANIEL N. ROBINSON, WILD BEASTS & IDLE HUMOURS: THE INSANITY DEFENSE FROM ANTIQUITY TO THE PRESENT 74–112 (1996) (chapter titled "Possession and Witchcraft"); ANDREW SCULL, MADNESS IN CIVILIZATION 67–69 (2015) (section titled "Demonic Possession and Spiritual Healing"). For a recent historical account of possession and exorcism in sixteenth- and seventeen-century Europe, see BRIAN P. LEVACK, THE DEVIL WITHIN: POSSESSION & EXORCISM IN THE CHRISTIAN WEST (2013).

[103] *See, e.g.*, LEVACK, *supra* note 102, at 60 ("[M]ost theologians in the scholastic tradition . . . argue[d] that . . . the Devil seized control of the demoniac's mental faculties, [and] he could thereby gain control of the will.").

[104] *See* Moore, *supra* note 60, at 201.

[105] Platt & Diamond, *supra* note 74, at 363 ("Catholic dogma distinguished human beings from animals, assigning to Man the possibility of an immortal soul. At the same time, animals were considered appropriate objects of punishment and excommunication. One means of reconciling these

The insane themselves sometimes use the language of possession to make sense of their lost sense of agency. Consider two well-known cases. First, Andrea Yates, who drowned her children to save their souls. According to one account: "Mrs. Yates believed that *Satan was within her* and tormented her and her children. She thought after she drowned her children, she would be arrested and executed. She indicated that Satan would be executed along with her."[106]

Next, Andrew Goldstein, who in January 1999 "picked up [Kendra Webdale], and threw her onto the tracks in front of . . . [a New York City subway] train just as it entered the station." In a statement to the police, Goldstein said:

> As I was standing on the platform there was a woman standing waiting for the train. She was facing the incoming train and I was standing behind her. I got the urge to push, kick or punch. I pushed the woman who had blonde hair. I don't recall what she looked like. But I know she was a white female. When I pushed her she fell onto the track and was struck by the train . . .
>
> I feel like an aura, or a sensation like you're losing control of your motor systems. And then, you lose control of your senses and everything. *And then you feel like something's entering you. Like you're being inhabited.* I don't know. But—and then, and then it's like an overwhelming urge to strike out or push or punch.[107]

When the alien self takes charge, the real self is still on-board, but helpless. The alien self responds to reasons as it goes about its business. It can plan and premeditate, and indeed, its plans can be quite intricate. The alien self in Daniel M'Naghten had a plan to kill Peel, just as the alien self in James Hadfield had one to kill the king. It can look out for the police. It can lock doors, flee from danger, and so forth. It can also be impulsive, acting with what appears to be utter disregard for the consequences. The alien self has a mind and will of its own, responding to reasons to which the real self would

views, endowing animals with intelligence and souls without contradicting Christian dogma, was to assume that they were incarnations of evil spirits.").

106 Phillip J. Resnick, *The Andrea Yates Case: Insanity on Trial*, 55 CLEV. ST. L. REV. 147, 149 (2007) (emphasis added).

107 CHARLES PATRICK EWING, INSANITY: MURDER, MADNESS, AND THE LAW 116 (2008) (emphasis added).

never respond, and failing to respond to reasons to which the real self would regularly respond.

Lost agency isn't the traditional irresistible impulse test in disguise, though it's easy to get the two confused. Someone claiming to be insane under the irresistible impulse test might say, "I couldn't control myself." Someone claiming to be insane under the lost agency theory might say the same thing. The similarity is superficial, however. Under the traditional test, the question is whether the actor could have chosen otherwise than he did. Under the lost agency theory, in contrast, the question is whether the actor at the time of choice experienced himself as the one doing the choosing. "I couldn't control myself," is a plea of a different order from "I wasn't in control." The former pleads compulsion; the latter, lost agency.

The real self can react to its lost sense of agency in different ways, and different actors can describe the experience of lost agency in different language. Faced with the "vague and strange experience"[108] of having one's body move without the sense of its movement having been "done by me,"[109] one possibility is bewilderment. The real self knows his body did something, but having failed to experience himself as its author, might have no idea why his body did what it did. Or he might report having acted for one reason or another but with no experience of those reasons as being his reasons. He might describe himself as an onlooker or detached observer. Asked why he did what he did, he might reply: "It wasn't me." "I don't know what happened." "It just happened." "I don't know why I did it." Or he might be reduced to paradox: "I did it, but I didn't do it," as in "I (my body) did it, but I (as agent) didn't."

Or, he might go a step further, into delusion.[110] Faced with the experience of his body moving but without the experience of being the author of its movement, he might entertain the thought of having been—must have been—under the control or influence of some alien or external force. Moreover, having entertained the thought of someone or something external to his real self being in charge of what he does, he might come to believe it. Indeed, he might believe it no matter what the evidence to the contrary. He

[108] Synofzik et al., *supra* note 100, at 5.

[109] Matthis Synofzik et al., *Beyond the Comparator Model: A Multifactorial Two-Step Account of Agency*, 17 Consciousness & Cognition 219, 228 (2008).

[110] *See, e.g.*, Philip Gerrans, *Passivity Experience in Schizophrenia*, *in* Disturbed Consciousness: New Essays on Psychopathology and Theories of Consciousness 325, 338 (Rocco J. Gennaro ed., 2015) ("[P]assivity experience [i.e., loss of a sense of agency] is rarely reported as such but more often reported in the form of a delusion of alien control.").

might, in other words, form and maintain what are known as delusions of alien control or influence.[111]

According to a twenty-nine-year-old shorthand typist diagnosed with schizophrenia:

> When I reach my hand for the comb it is my hand and arm which move, and my fingers pick up the pen, but I don't control them. . . . I am just a puppet who is manipulated by cosmic strings. When the strings are pulled my body moves and I can't prevent it.[112]

In the mind of someone so afflicted, the metaphor of alien control will no longer be just a metaphor. It will have become reality. Someone or something external to the real self has taken over: a demon, a device, God, and so forth.

The sense of agency can be lost over the mind as well as the body.[113] One might experience a thought in one's head but have no experience of having put it there. Instead, it must have been inserted into one's mind. This experience might in turn give rise to its own particular brand of delusion,

[111] For helpful overviews of the large literature on delusions, see, for example, Lisa Bortolotti, *Delusion*, STAN. ENCYCLOPEDIA PHIL. (2016) [hereinafter Bortolotti, *Delusion*]; Lisa Bortolotti & Kengo Miyazono, *Recent Work on the Nature and Development of Delusions*, 10 PHIL. COMPASS 636 (2015); Max Coltheart et al., *Delusional Belief*, 62 ANN. REV. PSYCHOL. 271 (2011); Louis Sass & Greg Byrom, *Phenomenological and Neurocognitive Perspectives on Delusions*, 14 WORLD PSYCHIATRY 164 (2015). For book-length treatments, see, for example, LISA BORTOLOTTI, DELUSIONS AND OTHER IRRATIONAL BELIEFS (2010); PHILIP GERRANS, THE MEASURE OF MADNESS: PHILOSOPHY OF MIND, COGNITIVE NEUROSCIENCE, AND DELUSIONAL THOUGHT (2014); JENNIFER RADDEN, ON DELUSION (2011); LAWRIE REZNEK, DELUSIONS AND THE MADNESS OF THE MASSES (2010).

The literature on delusions tends to organize around four questions. First: Are delusions beliefs or something else? For defenses of the traditional doxastic account against critics, see, for example, Lisa Bortolotti, *In Defence of Modest Doxasticism About Delusions*, 5 NEUROETHICS 39 (2011); Tim Bayne & Elisabeth Pacherie, *In Defence of the Doxastic Conception of Delusions*, 20 MIND & LANGUAGE 163 (2005). Second: Is the formation and maintenance of a delusion best explained along the lines of what's known as the two-factor model or what's known as the prediction-error model? *Compare, e.g.*, Coltheart et al., *supra*, at 282–93 (discussing the two-factor model applied to monothematic delusions), *with* Philip Robert Corlett & Paul Charles Fletcher, *Delusions and Prediction Error: Clarifying the Roles of Behavioural and Brain Responses*, 20 COGNITIVE NEUROPSYCHIATRY 95 (2015) (defending prediction-error model); Philip R. Corlett et al., *Toward a Neurobiology of Delusions*, 92 PROGRESS IN NEUROBIOLOGY 345 (2010) (same). Third: Can the two models be reconciled? *See, e.g.*, Kengo Miyazono et al., *Prediction-Error and Two-Factor Theories of Delusion Formation: Competitors or Allies?*, *in* ABERRANT BELIEFS AND REASONING 34 (Niall Galbraith ed., 2015). Fourth: Can the two-factor-model account for polythematic, as well as monothematic, delusions? *See, e.g.*, Max Coltheart, *On the Distinction Between Monothematic and Polythematic Delusions*, 28 MIND & LANGUAGE 103, 110–11 (2013) (suggesting possible ways in which the two-factor theory can explain polythematic delusions).

[112] ANDREW C.P. SIMS, SYMPTOMS IN THE MIND: AN INTRODUCTION TO DESCRIPTIVE PSYCHOPATHOLOGY 153 (2d ed. 1995).

[113] *See, e.g.*, Joëlle Proust, *Is There a Sense of Agency for Thought?*, *in* MENTAL ACTIONS 253 (Lucy O'Brien & Matthew Soteriou eds., 2009).

commonly known as "thought insertion."[114] Someone or something, the actor comes to believe, is putting thoughts in his head. According to another twenty-nine-year-old, also diagnosed with schizophrenia:

> I look out the window and think the garden looks nice and the grass cool, but the thoughts of Eamonn Andrews come into my mind. There are no other thoughts, only his. . . . He treats my mind like a screen and flashes his thoughts into it like you flash a picture.[115]

One might likewise experience a voice in one's head but have no experience of being its author. The actor loses his sense of agency over his own "inner speech," attributing it to some external source or entity. This phenomenon too has a name: "auditory verbal hallucination."[116] Thought insertion and auditory verbal hallucinations can each be grounded in a lost sense of agency, not over the movements of one's body, but over the movements of one's mind.

One form of auditory verbal hallucination, so-called command hallucinations, has attracted special attention from the law, at least when

[114] The literature on thought insertion focuses on two questions. First: Does thought insertion involve a lost sense of agency or a lost sense of ownership? *Compare* G. Lynn Stephens & George Graham, When Self-Consciousness Breaks: Alien Voices and Inserted Thoughts (2000) (agency); Shaun Gallagher, *Relations Between Agency and Ownership in the Case of Schizophrenic Thought Insertion and Delusions of Control*, 6 Rev. Phil. Psychol. 865 (2015) (same); Patrizia Pedrini, *Rescuing the "Loss-of-Agency" Account of Thought Insertion*, 22 Phil., Psychiatry & Psychol. 221 (2016) (same), *with* Lisa Bortolotti & Matthew Broome, *A Role for Ownership and Authorship in the Analysis of Thought Insertion*, 8 Phenomenology & Cognitive Sci. 205 (2009) (ownership); Michelle Maiese, *Thought Insertion as a Disownership Symptom*, 14 Phenomenology & Cognitive Sci. 911 (2015) (same); Jean-Remy Martin & Elisabeth Pacherie, *Out of Nowhere: Thought Insertion, Ownership and Context Integration*, 22 Consciousness & Cognition 111 (2013) (same). Second: Does the same mechanism that explains lost agency over action explain lost agency over thoughts? *Compare, e.g.*, Philip Gerrans, *The Feeling of Thinking: Sense of Agency in Delusions of Thought Insertion*, 2 Psychol. Consciousness: Theory, Res., & Prac. 291 (2015) (yes), *with* Agustin Vincente, *The Comparator Account on Thought Insertion, Alien Voices and Inner Speech: Some Open Questions*, 13 Phenomenology & Cognitive Sci. 335 (2014) (raising questions).

[115] Sims, *supra* note 112, at 152.

[116] For a sampling of the literature on auditory verbal hallucinations, see Stephens & Graham, *supra* note 114; Raymond Cho & Wayne Wu, *Mechanisms of Auditory Verbal Hallucination in Schizophrenia*, 4 Frontiers in Psychiatry 1 (2013); Remko van Lutterveld et al., *The Neurophysiology of Auditory Hallucinations—A Historical and Contemporary Review*, 2 Frontiers in Psychiatry 1 (2011); Lauren Swiney & Paulo Sousa, *A New Comparator Account of Auditory Verbal Hallucinations: How Motor Prediction Can Plausibly Contribute to the Sense of Agency for Inner Speech*, 8 Frontiers in Hum. Neurosci. 72 (2014); Rachel Upthegrove et al., *Understanding Auditory Verbal Hallucinations*, 133 Acta Psychiatrica Scandinavica 352 (2016); Sam Wilkinson & Ben Alderson-Day, *Voices and Thoughts in Psychosis*, 7 Rev. Phil. & Psych. 529, 531 (2016) ("[T]he orthodox view of AVHs [is that] they are to be understood as a result of disrupted monitoring of inner speech.").

God is doing the commanding. According to the "deific-decree" doctrine, if God tells you to kill, you're insane.[117] If an actor heard the voice of God commanding him to commit the crime, that's some evidence the real self wasn't in charge. Hearing God's command might mean the actor has come to see himself as an instrument of God's hand, and seeing oneself as an instrument is one way of trying to make sense of lost agency. Yet, insofar as the doctrine extends only to those who hear God's voice, it sweeps too narrowly. It shouldn't matter who's doing the commanding. Wholly apart from any First Amendment worries,[118] what matters is the experience of being commanded, which is evidence of what really matters: to wit, the experience of not being the agent in charge.

Of course, not all delusions involve alien control and inserted thoughts. Delusions run the gamut. Some are monothematic, involving "a single delusional belief or a small set of delusional beliefs all related to a single theme."[119] Others, of the variety typically seen in schizophrenia, are polythematic, involving "delusional beliefs about a variety of topics unrelated to each other," some of which can be quite bizarre.[120] John Nash, for example, believed he'd become the Emperor of Antarctica, not to mention being the left foot of God on Earth.[121] Some are self-contained, leaving other beliefs untouched. Others metastasize, infecting the whole mind, with other beliefs forming around them, some of which are themselves delusions (secondary delusions), while

[117] For an overview of the doctrine's history, see Lundgren v. Mitchell, 440 F.3d 754, 784–88 (6th Cir. 2006) (Merritt, J., dissenting).

[118] Wilson v. Gaetz, 608 F.3d 347, 354 (7th Cir. 2010) (Posner, J.) ("[T]o distinguish between 'deific' and all other delusions and confine the insanity defense to the former would present serious questions under the First Amendment."). For critiques of the deific decree doctrine, see, for example, Grant H. Morris & Ansar Haroun, *"God Told Me to Kill": Religion or Delusion?*, 38 San Diego L. Rev. 973, 978 (2000) ("[T]he insanity defense should not be available to those who kill at God's commands.").

[119] Max Coltheart et al., *supra* note 111, at 280 (Monothematic delusions include the Capgras delusion, Cotard delusion, Fregoli delusion, mirrored-self misidentification, somatoparaphrenia, delusion of alien control, and delusion of thought insertion).

[120] How might one explain the bizarre content of some delusions? According to one account:

> Bizarre delusions . . . represent inappropriate use of metaphor in an attempt to establish some inter-subjective meaning, albeit futile. During the formative delusional mood, the world becomes ineffable. Prodromal patients use relative terms (similes) to describe their experiences: "It is *as if* people are actors, walking down the street wearing masks." As these experiences persist, the relative terms subside (people *are* wearing masks, they *are* in disguise); the simile becomes a metaphor as the delusion develops and the metaphor becomes a top-down prior around which perception and cognition are organized.

Philip R. Corlett, *Answering Some Phenomenal Challenges to the Prediction Error Model of Delusions*, 14 World Psychiatry 181, 182 (2015).

[121] *See* Donald Capps, *John Nash's Delusional Decade: A Case of Paranoid Schizophrenia*, 52 Pastoral Psychol. 193, 200–01 (2004). The Nash character was also depicted as having visual hallucinations, but these are very rare. The real Nash's hallucinations were only auditory.

others seem like rational responses to the irrationality of the primary delusion. Delusions form a motley crew.

Delusions of alien control and thought insertion tend to arise when, having lost a sense of agency, the actor locates the source of his bodily movements in the agency of someone or something else. Other delusions are different. Consider delusions of reference (or megalomania),[122] for example, which "involve beliefs that unrelated or commonplace phenomena in the world (events, objects, or other people) refer directly to oneself and carry a special personal significance."[123] The John Nash character in Ron Howard's *A Beautiful Mind* suffered from delusions of reference, searching papers, magazines and whatnot looking for secret messages and codes only he could decipher. Such delusions don't involve attributing agency to an external source, but as it turns out, they too, like delusions of alien control, can also arise from the experience of lost agency.

The basic idea is simple. A lost sense of agency arises when the internal mechanism through which we gain a sense of agency fails to work as it should. Delusions of alien control arise when the actor tries to make sense of that experience, and some further defect prevents the actor from rejecting the hypothesis that some alien force is in control of his thoughts and actions.[124] Another response, when one's internal mechanism for self-monitoring fails, is to rely on external cues in an effort to compensate.[125] These external cues

[122] On delusions of reference generally, see Mike Startup et al., *Delusions of Reference: A New Theoretical Model*, 14 Cognitive Neuropsychiatry 110 (2009); Mike Startup & Sue Startup, *On Two Kinds of Delusions of Reference*, 137 Psychiatry Res. 87 (2005).

[123] Coltheart et al., *supra* note 111, at 277.

[124] This explanation presupposes a so-called bottom-up account, according to which a delusion arises from an abnormal experience. So-called top-down accounts put the causal relation in the opposite direction, with abnormal experience arising from the delusion. One challenge top-down theories face, of course, is the need to explain where the delusion comes from in the first place. Bottom-up accounts claim that the abnormal experience, which gives rise to the delusion, is itself a result of some defect in how the brain works. *See* Bortolotti, *Delusion, supra* note 111, § 3.2, at 19–21.

[125] Ananthaswamy, *supra* note 101, at 117 (noting that schizophrenic patients "have to rely more heavily on their judgments about the external environment to augment their sense of agency[,]" because their internal mechanism for self-monitoring is defective); Joëlle Proust, The Philosophy of Metacognition: Mental Agency and Self-Awareness 258 (2013) ("Many [schizophrenic] patients . . . present an inflated, rather than deflated sense of agency . . . . [T]hey seem to rely more heavily on observed consequences to attribute to themselves authorship of actions for consequences that either are independently salient ('I caused the Iraq War'), or that are congruent with their present motivations. They end up over-attributing to themselves actions they did not perform."); Shitij Kapur, *Psychosis as a State of Aberrant Salience: A Framework for Linking Biology, Phenomenology, and Pharmacology in Schizophrenia*, 160 Am. J. Psychiatry 13, 15 (2003) ("It is proposed that in psychosis . . . [a] neurochemical aberration usurps the normal process of contextually driven salience and leads to *aberrant assignment of salience to external objects and internal representations*."); Synofzik et al., *supra* note 100, at 6 ("[A]s a consequence of giving up the usually most robust and reliable internal action information source, i.e., internal predictions, the sense of agency in psychotic patients is at constant risk of being misled by *ad-hoc* events, invading beliefs, and confusing

then take on out-sized significance and meaning, becoming aberrantly salient. In order to make sense of it all, the actor assigns them special and personal importance. Delusions of reference result: Mundane objects "speak" to the actor, for example.

Delusions of reference commonly go hand-in-hand with delusions of persecution.[126] As with delusions of reference, the link between lost agency and persecutory delusions isn't obvious or direct. Still, a link there might well be.[127] When an actor loses a sense of agency over his thoughts and inner speech, let alone his body, anxiety is a natural response. He might come to believe the thoughts he experiences, and the words he hears in his head, aren't just external: They might be part of a malevolent conspiracy.[128] Compared to seeing oneself as someone's or something's puppet, it might be easier to see

emotions and evaluations."); Matthis Synofzik et al., *Misattributions of Agency in Schizophrenia Are Based on Imprecise Predictions About the Sensory Consequences of One's Actions*, 133 Brain 262, 270 (2010) ("[S]chizophrenic patients might over-attribute external events to their own agency whenever stronger weighted external agency cues are in fact not veridical and misleading."); Martin Voss et al., *Altered Awareness of Action in Schizophrenia: A Specific Deficit in Predicting Action Consequences*, 133 Brain 3104, 3110 (2010).

[126] Daniel Freeman & Philippa Garety, Paranoia: The Psychology of Persecutory Delusions 122 (2004) ("Internal sensations of significance and reference may lead to delusions of reference that are understood within a persecutory belief system."); Coltheart et al., *supra* note 111, at 277 ("Delusions of persecution and reference commonly co-occur (often along with hallucinations)."); Startup et al., *supra* note 122, at 112 ("[I]t appears that the traditional association between referential delusions and persecutory delusions applies primarily to referential delusions of observation, [not communication].").

[127] Freeman & Garety, *supra* note 126, at 117 (developing a model of persecutory delusion in which "[i]nternal anomalous experiences are important," including "thoughts being experienced as voices; actions being experienced as unintended; more subtle cognitive alternations such as perceptual anomalies; depersonalization; or a sense of significance or reference."); Daniel Freeman & Philippa Garety, *Advances in Understanding and Treating Persecutory Delusions: A Review*, 49 Soc. Psychiatry & Psychiatric Epidemiology 1179, 1179 (2014) (noting that "anomalous internal experiences and reasoning biases" are among the "causal factors" for persecutory delusions); Daniel Freeman, *Suspicious Minds: The Psychology of Persecutory Delusions*, 27 Clinical Psychol. Rev. 425, 425 (2007) ("There is also evidence that anomalous internal experiences may be important in leafing to odd thought content and that a jumping to conclusions reasoning bias is present in individuals with persecutory delusions."); Daniel Freeman, *Persecutory Delusions: A Cognitive Perspective on Understanding and Treatment*, 3 Lancet Psychiatry 685, 687 (2016) ("[P]aranoia thrives when an individual is in a subjectively anomalous internal state: odd internal sensations and perceptions provoke fearful explanations."); Robyn Langdon et al., *The Cognitive Neuropsychological Understanding of Persecutory Delusions*, *in* Persecutory Delusions: Assessment, Theory, and Treatment 221, 229 (Daniel Freeman et al., 2008) ("[N]europsychological impairments . . . might precipitate a train of thought leading (more or less directly) to a persecutory delusion.").

[128] *See, e.g.*, Paul C. Fletcher & Chris D. Frith, *Perceiving Is Believing: A Baysian Approach to Explaining the Positive Symptoms of Schizophrenia*, 10 Nature Reviews Neuroscience 48, 56 (2009) ("Ultimately, someone with schizophrenia will need to develop a set of beliefs that must account for a great deal of strange and sometimes contradictory data. Very commonly they come to believe that they are being persecuted: delusions of persecution are one of the most striking and common of the positive symptoms of schizophrenia.").

oneself as the object of persecution.[129] Persecutory delusions typically draw content from the actor's preexisting stock of beliefs.[130] M'Naghten, for example, may have believed the Tories were after him because, according one author, he "hat[ed] . . . the Tories and the policies they represented."[131]

We started with the experience of lost agency and the delusions of alien control and thought insertion to which that experience can give rise. Those delusions aren't uncommon to find in those who are exemplars of insanity. But, as we've seen, other delusions, also not uncommon, such as delusions of reference and persecution, can likewise arise from lost agency, or so it seems. If so, then insanity doesn't always or necessarily come with a demon within. Lost agency can manifest in delusions other than in delusions of alien control. What matters in the end, however, is the lost sense of agency—of not being in control, of being a passive onlooker—not the content of the particular delusions, if any, it generates.

Of course, not all delusions spring from lost agency. Some delusions find root in other abnormal experiences. Someone with Capgras delusion, for example, can recognize a familiar face, but doesn't experience the affective reactions which usually accompany it. That absent affect, together with some further defect in way the actor tests hypotheses, produces a delusion: The person with the familiar face (one's mother, for example) must really be a robot or an imposter.[132] Likewise, a lost sense of agency doesn't always give rise to delusion. Still, when someone commits a crime in the grip of delusion, red flags should go up. With delusion comes the possibility, and maybe probability, of lost agency.[133]

[129] FREEMAN & GARETY, *supra* note 126, at 120 ("Believing that something is wrong with them (for instance, that they are becoming mad) may be a more distressing belief (and less plausible and compelling) than that they are being persecuted.").

[130] *Id.* at 119 ("In the search for meaning, pre-existing beliefs about the self, others, and the world will be drawn upon.").

[131] MORAN, *supra* note 2, at 45.

[132] *See, e.g.*, Neralie Wise, *The Capgras Delusion: An Integrated Approach*, 15 PHENOMENOLOGY & COGNITIVE SCI. 183 (2016) (offering an account of the Capgras delusion drawing on phenomenological and analytic traditions). The Cotard delusion is the belief that you're dead, or that parts of your body are rotting. "[T]he experiential states underlying the Capgras and Cotard delusions are different: whereas the Capgras delusion appears to involve a fairly focal impairment in face processing, the Cotard delusion seems to involve a global alteration in affective experience. Rather than experiencing only familiar faces as alien, the Cotard patient experiences *everything* as strange, devoid of meaning and lifeless." Tim Bayne, *Delusions*, *in* THE OXFORD COMPANIONS TO CONSCIOUSNESS 218, 220 (Tim Bayne et al. eds., 2009).

[133] John Hinckley's attempted assassination of then-President Ronald Regan, together with his subsequent acquittal on grounds of insanity under the Model Penal Code test, was a pivotal moment in the history of the insanity defense in the United States. How would Hinckley have fared under the lost agency theory?

Schizophrenia is probably first among equals when it comes to the mental disorders most commonly associated with insanity. On the lost agency theory, that makes sense. "Schizophrenia is the classic disorder of sense of agency,"[134] and the "delusion of alien control is particularly associated with schizophrenia."[135] Indeed, lost agency appears capable of underwriting a number of delusions characteristic of schizophrenia.[136] On the other hand, not everyone we might intuitively regard as insane will be diagnosed as schizophrenic, since "aberrant experiences of agency are strikingly common in a range of different disorders,"[137] nor should we assume anyone diagnosed as schizophrenic is necessarily insane.

What, for example, about disorders whose stock-in-trade is intense, unremitting, and unwanted desire, like manias, philias, addictions, and phobias? When an actor commits a crime in the grip of a desire associated with these disorders, does an alien self or the real self commit the crime?

If we attend to how maniacs, phobics and so forth sometimes describe their experiences, it might be tempting to believe that, for example, the

Without having heard all of the evidence, offering a prediction is probably ill-advised. Having said that, Hinckley might have been thought to have suffered from erotomania (also known as De Clerambault syndrome): He delusionally believed Jodie Foster was in love with him, which somehow prompted his assassination attempt. But that wasn't so. Hinckley realized Foster was *not* in love with him, and that's what apparently prompted the attempt. *See* BONNIE ET AL., *supra* at 42 (testimony of Park Dietz). Hinckley may nonetheless have been delusional. The experts disagreed. The defense psychiatrists testified Hinckley was psychotic, suffering in particular from delusions of reference; the government's psychiatrists testified Hinckley was non-psychotic. *See, e.g.*, RICHARD J. BONNIE ET AL., A CASE STUDY IN THE INSANITY DEFENSE: THE TRIAL OF JOHN W. HINCKLEY, JR. 31 (3d ed. 2008) ("Perhaps the most significant divergence of clinical opinion about Hinckley's mental disorder at the time of the offense pertained to whether Hinckley had 'delusions' and 'ideas of reference.'"). If the government's witnesses were right, then one red flag indicating lost agency would have been missing in Hinckley's case. That's about as much as one can say.

[134] Moore, *supra* note 101, at 4.

[135] Coltheart et al., *supra* note 111, at 288; *id.* at 278 ("[C]ontrol delusions . . . are considered to be more specifically characteristic of schizophrenia.").

[136] FRITH & JOHNSTONE, *supra* note 82, at 141–41 ("Many of the delusions reported by patients with schizophrenia seem to result from a combination of an abnormal experience with a willingness to develop extremely unlikely explanations for that experience.").

[137] Moore, *supra* note 101, at 6. For example, a diminished sense of agency has also been associated with obsessive-compulsive disorder, although it manifests in ways different from the ways it manifests in schizophrenia. *See id.* at 5 ("In Obsessive Compulsive Disorder . . . it has been shown that patients have deficits in sensorimotor prediction resulting in a reduction in sensory suppression. This finding echoes those from patients with schizophrenia."); Antje Gentsch et al., *Dysfunctional Forward Model Mechanisms and Aberrant Sense of Agency in Obsessive-Compulsive Disorder*, 71 BIOLOGICAL PSYCHIATRY 652, 658 (2012) ("In schizophrenia, the noisy sensory input seems to be integrated into a cognitive system of biased beliefs about passivity and outside influence, whereas in OCD, it may inform a system searching for conscious control and motivate behavioral strategies for regaining control over external events."); Lea Oren et al., *Intentional Binding and Obsessive Compulsive Tendencies: A Dissociation Between Indirect and Direct Measures of the Sense of Agency*, 20 J. OBSESSIVE-COMPULSIVE & RELATED DISORDERS 59, 64 (2019) ("It is becoming clear that for OC individuals, the experience of agency is impaired.").

pyromaniac didn't really choose to set the fire, because his desire to set it somehow bypassed his will, causing his body to move all by itself.[138] What, though, could it possible mean to say that desires move the body without the help of the will?

When the doctor taps your patellar ligament, your knee goes up without your will doing any work, but desires don't move the body in the way reflexes do. Desires cause intentions; intentions cause volitions; and volitions cause the body to move. That's how desires move bodies. Desires don't move bodies all by themselves. They require the will to form intentions and volitions in their service, since volitions are in the end what make the body move, at least when its motion isn't due to mechanical reflex. If so, then the idea of desires bypassing the will is incoherent, or at best metaphorical.

Still, we can't completely eliminate the possibility that there's more than just metaphor to the metaphor of the bypassed will. Maybe the metaphor is sometimes reality.[139] A maniac, phobic, or kindred spirit likewise suffering from a disorder of desire, might not experience the desire causing his body to move as *his* desire, nor the intention arising from that desire as *his* intention, nor the volition arising from that intention as *his* volition. If so, then the alienation the actor experiences from the pertinent desire might not be just the alienation associated with a desire one wishes he didn't have. It might instead be the more profound alienation associated with lost agency. If so, then talk of bypassed wills may in some cases be another way of saying the actor's sense of agency was lost.[140]

[138] Moore, *supra* note 60, at 195–97 (discussing the idea of desires "bypassing" the will).

[139] *See, e.g.*, Bayne & Levy, *supra* note 96, at 52 ("It is sometimes suggested that one of the pathological features of the phenomenology of addiction and obsessive-compulsive spectrum disorders is that the individuals concerned experience their actions as caused by their desires and urges rather than as having their source in *them*. We suspect that as one begins to experience one's movements as caused by one's mental states, one no longer experiences them as one's own actions.").

[140] When Joel Feinberg talks about the desires associated with kleptomania, he describes them as "senseless," because "they do not cohere, as likely to seem alien, not fully expressive of their owner's essential character. When a person acts to satisfy them, it is *as if he were acting on somebody else's desires*." Feinberg, *supra* note 60, at 288 (emphasis added). When Stephen Morse discusses people afflicted with some form of volitional disorder, he notes how they sometimes describe their actions using language associated with lost agency, e.g., they act like "automatons." *See supra* note 37.

Now is as good a time as any to mention psychopathy. Students of the criminal law, as well as ethicists, have spent considerable effort wondering if psychopaths can be morally responsible for the crimes they commit. We couldn't possibly do justice here to the enormous literature on the subject. *See, e.g.*, Being Amoral: Psychopathy and Moral Incapacity (Thomas Schramme ed., 2014); Handbook on Psychopathy and Law (Kent A. Kiehl & Walter P. Sinnott-Armstrong eds., 2013); Responsibility and Psychopathy: Interfacing Law, Psychiatry, and Philosophy (Luca Malatesti & John McMillan eds., 2010). For now, suffice it to say that psychopathy, so far as one can tell, doesn't involve any lost sense of agency.

Defects of Consciousness

The traditional insanity test invites us to see insanity as a defect of reason (cognition) or will (volition). The lost agency theory puts insanity in a new light, seeing it as neither a defect of reason nor will. Instead, it's seen as a defect of consciousness: a lost sense of agency. So understood, insanity doesn't stand alone. It belongs in the company of other defects of consciousness.

Consider three such defects popular in the criminal law: hypnosis, somnambulism (sleepwalking), and multiple personality disorder (now known as dissociative identity disorder).[141] These phenomena are the criminal law's exotica: interesting to ponder but rarely seen in the real world. Moreover, criminal lawyers usually put them, or at least hypnosis and sleepwalking, in one doctrinal category (no voluntary act), and insanity in another (affirmative defense). The lost agency theory suggests that's a mistake. We should see them instead as members of the same family, whatever the doctrinal category to which they're assigned.

Hypnosis

In Robert Wiene's 1920 film *The Cabinet of Dr. Caligari*, a character named Cesare, under the hypnotic control of Dr. Caligari, commits a string of murders.[142] In the 1959 novel *The Manchurian Candidate*,[143] post-hypnotic suggestion leads Raymond Shaw to attempt an assassination. That's all film and fiction,[144] not the real world. In the real world, hypnosis is, at least today, more about stage entertainment and smoking cessation. Indeed, one searches in vain for real crimes committed under hypnosis.[145] Maybe that's because

[141] Epileptic fugue, associated with *petit mal* seizures, is another example. For a fascinating discussion of such cases in nineteenth-century England, see JOEL PETER EIGEN, UNCONSCIOUS CRIME: MENTAL ABSENCE AND CRIMINAL RESPONSIBILITY IN VICTORIAN LONDON (2003).

[142] THE CABINET OF DR. CALIGARI (Decla-Bioscopt 1920); Bernard Williams, *The Actus Reus of Dr. Caligari*, 142 U. PA. L. REV. 1661, 1670 (1994) (describing the film's plot).

[143] RICHARD CONDON, THE MANCHURIAN CANDIDATE (1959).

[144] On hypnosis in film generally, see STEFAN ANDRIOPOULOS, POSSESSED: HYPNOTIC CRIMES, CORPORATE FICTION, AND THE INVENTION OF CINEMA (2008); Deirdre Barrett, *Hypnosis in Film and Television*, 49 AM. J. CLIN. HYPNOSIS 13 (2006).

[145] *See* Michael Heap, *Hypnosis in the Courts*, *in* THE OXFORD HANDBOOK OF HYPNOSIS 745–66 (Michael R. Nash & Amanda J. Barnier eds., 2008); Graham F. Wagstaff, *Hypnosis and the Law: Examining the Stereotypes*, 35 CRIM. J. & BEHAV. 1277 (2008). Newspapers, including *The New York Times*, reported in 1895 that Thomas McDonald, acquitted of murder, claimed at trial to have been under the hypnotic control of Anderson Gray. *See, e.g., The Hypnotist Made Principal: His Subject Found Guiltless of Murder by a Kansas Court While He Bears Penalty for the Crime*, N.Y. TIMES, Apr. 7, 1895. Just a few days later, however, the *Times* ran another story, reporting that the "defense of hypnotism was not raised at trial; that no evidence concerning hypnotism was given, and that the word 'hypnotism' was mentioned but once, in a remark of McDonald's counsel, after Gray, the first man tried, had been convicted." *Hypnotism Not a Factor: Gray Made McDonald a Murderer Merely by*

hypnosis can push a person only so far: No one will do under hypnosis something he wouldn't otherwise have done.[146] Still, the prospect of hypnotic crime has become, for whatever reason, part of the legal imagination.

The experts disagree about what really happens when someone enters a hypnotic trance.[147] According to one school of thought, what happens isn't much. Hypnotized subjects just get more relaxed and willing to follow orders. They play-act. If so—if nothing special happens when someone is hypnotized—then hypnotic crime is no different from other crime, and neither are the culprits who commit them. The other school makes hypnosis more interesting, inasmuch as a hypnotic state is a dissociated state in which the hypnotist takes control of the subject's mind and actions.[148] The subject becomes "mesmerized."[149] If so, then hypnotic crimes aren't just like other crimes, and hypnotized villains aren't really villains. They're innocent pawns, and their manipulators bear all the guilt.

Return to the metaphor of the alien self. If we take the dissociation account as true, the family resemblance between hypnotism and insanity becomes easy to see. The insane and the hypnotized both experience a lost sense of agency. Indeed, what hypnotists call the "classic suggestion effect" is just a lost sense of agency.[150] With the sense of agency lost, the self divides. The real self becomes disassociated from the alien self, and the alien self takes

Argument, N.Y. TIMES, Apr. 15, 1895. In any event, McDonald was acquitted, apparently on grounds of self-defense. *See Hypnotism Not a Factor, supra*. Gray was convicted and hung. *See* State v. Gray, 39 P. 1050, 1054 (Kan. 1895) (affirming conviction).

[146] *See, e.g.*, MODEL PENAL CODE AND COMMENTARIES, *supra* note 42, § 2.01 cmt. 2, at 221 ("The widely held view that the hypnotized subject will not follow suggestions repugnant to him was deemed insufficient to warrant treating his conduct while hypnotized as voluntary; his dependency and helplessness are too pronounced.").

[147] *Compare* Erik Z. Woody & Pamela Sadler, *Dissociation Theories of Hypnosis*, *in* THE OXFORD HANDBOOK OF HYPNOSIS: THEORY, RESEARCH, AND PRACTICE 81 (Michael R. Nash & Amanda J. Barnier eds., 2008) (discussing state theories), *with* Steven Jay Lynn et al., *Social Cognitive Theories of Hypnosis*, in *id.* at 111 (discussing non-state theories).

[148] Vince Polito et al., *Sense of Agency Across Contexts: Insights from Schizophrenia and Hypnosis*, 2 PSYCHOLOGY OF CONSCIOUSNESS: THEORY, RES., & PRAC. 301, 309–10 (2015) ("[T]he 'dissociated control' and 'dissociated experience' theories of hypnotic responding are conceptually very similar to the comparator accounts of passivity experiences in schizophrenia.").

[149] So named after Franz Anton Mesmer. *See* ALAN GAULD, A HISTORY OF HYPNOTISM 1 (1992).

[150] David A. Oakley & Peter W. Halligan, *Hypnotic Suggestion: Opportunities for Cognitive Neuroscience*, 14 NATURE REVIEWS: NEUROSCIENCE 565, 568 (2013) ("[A]n effect is considered a 'classical suggestion-effect' only if it is experienced as involuntary; as 'happening all by itself.'"); Vince Polito et al., *Measuring Agency Change Across the Domain of Hypnosis*, 1 PSYCHOLOGY OF CONSCIOUSNESS: THEORY, RES., & PRAC. 3, 3 (2014) ("[E]xperiencing . . . action in hypnosis as occurring without effort or conscious volition . . . has been considered an essential element of hypnotic responding.").

control.[151] The real self of hypnosis, like the real self of insanity, becomes a passive observer to what his mind and body do under the alien self's control. In fact, those under hypnosis sometimes attribute what they do to alien control, just like the insane sometimes do.[152]

Still, the phenomenology of hypnosis differs from insanity in at least three ways. First, the lost sense of agency in hypnosis results from hypnotic induction, whereas the lost sense of agency in insanity is constitutive of some mental disease or defect, some defect in the brain. Second, the alien (hypnotized) self of hypnosis is under the hypnotist's control. The hypnotist is the puppeteer; the alien self is the puppet. In contrast, the alien self of insanity controls the real self but is itself under no one's control. Nonetheless, insane or hypnotized, the real self remains a helpless bystander.[153] Third, when the hypnotized actor is told to snap out of it, the lost sense of agency ends, the alien self disappears, and the self reintegrates. For the insane, reintegration doesn't come with a snap of the fingers.

Hypnotic crimes are, once again, the stuff of film and fiction. Still, if such a crime were to occur, most students of the criminal law, at least inasmuch as the dissociation theory accurately depicts the hypnotic subject's state of mind, would agree: Criminal liability would be inapposite. But they'd disagree, doctrinally speaking, about why. According to some, the actor hasn't acted: He hasn't voluntarily moved his body, and so fails to satisfy the voluntary act requirement. Others find that implausible: How can it be that the accused hasn't acted when his body performed whatever complex action it took to commit the crime? Volitions must have formed, which means the resulting movements were voluntary. If so, the reason for letting the hypnotic criminal

[151] *See* Woody & Sadler, *Dissociation Theories of Hypnosis, supra* note 147, at 89 ("[A]cross [the] diverse matrix of hypnotic behavior there is an essential denominator: in hypnosis all these behaviors are accompanied by the subjective experience that the self is not the origin of the response."); *id.* at 92 (suggesting that the dissociation arising from hypnosis involves a "breakdown" in the same mechanism that produces a loss of the sense of agency in "psychotic disorders, such as schizophrenia"); *id.* at 94 ("[D]issociation theories [of hypnosis] hypothesize that for highly hypnotizable people, hypnosis transiently brings about a disruption of [the] mechanism . . . for discriminating the internal versus external origins of events.").

[152] *See* Michael H. Connors, *Hypnosis and Belief: A Review of Hypnotic Delusions*, 36 Consciousness & Cognition 27, 38 (2015); Rochelle E. Cox et al., *An Hypnotic Analogue of Alien Control: Modeling the Delusion and Testing Its Impact on Behavior and Self Monitoring*, 1 Psychol. of Consciousness: Theory, Res., & Prac. 407, 425 (2014).

[153] Hypnotic actions combine lost agency and manipulation, i.e., the hypnotist induces a lost sense of agency and then manipulates the actions of the alien self. Hypnosis and manipulation are discussed in a different context in Chapter 6.

go free can't be that he didn't act. It must be something else, for which an affirmative defense should be provided.[154]

Both sides have a point. Indeed, they might be talking past one another. Those in the no-act camp, who think the hypnotized don't act, are looking at the real self, and rightly observe that the real self didn't act. The real self was just a bystander, albeit a bystander to the movement of his own body.[155] In contrast, those in the act camp, who think that the hypnotized do act, are looking at the alien self, and rightly observe that the alien self did act, albeit at the hypnotist's behest.

At stake in this dispute, from a legal point of view, is mainly the burden of proof. If the no-act camp wins, the state should bear the burden. If the act camp wins, the defense should bear it. Yet rather than make the burden question turn on who you look at—real self or alien self—the question should be answered directly. Are the usual reasons for assigning the burden to one side or the other better served if the state must prove the accused was in command, or if the defense must prove he wasn't? Rather than ask if the accused "really" acted, better just to cut to the chase.

Sleepwalking

Unlike hypnotic crimes, which exist only in film and fiction, people actually do commit crimes while asleep.[156] Mrs. Cogdon laid out her nineteen-year-old daughter Pat's pajamas, placing a hot-water bottle in her bed and a glass

[154] *See, e.g.*, JOSHUA DRESSLER, UNDERSTANDING CRIMINAL LAW § 9.02[C][3][a], at 89 (8th ed. 2018) (describing this debate in the context of hypnosis).

[155] *See* Tim Bayne, *The Sense of Agency*, *in* THE SENSES: CLASSIC AND CONTEMPORARY PHILOSOPHICAL PERSPECTIVES 355, 368 (Fiona Macpherson ed., 2011) ("Many people are reluctant to regard physical or mental happenings that are unaccompanied by a basic 'experience of doing' as actions.").

[156] *See, e.g.*, Kenneth J. Weiss et al., *Parasomnias, Violence, and the Law*, 39 J. PSYCHIATRY & L. 249, 250–61 (2011) (discussing history of violence during sleepwalking). Sleepwalking is caused by partial arousal from stage 3–4 non-rapid eye movement (NREM) sleep. Sleepwalking "episodes typically take place during the first third of the night when slow-wave [or deep] sleep is predominant." Antonio Zadra et al., *Somnambulism: Clinical Aspects and Pathophysiological Hypotheses*, 12 LANCET NEUROLOGY 285, 285 (2013). "Sleepwalking," or "somnambulism," is distinguished from what's called "RBD," for "REM Sleep Behavior Disorder." *See* Naoko Tachibana, *REM Sleep Disorder*, 6 SLEEP MED. CLIN. 459 (2011). RBD is a "unique parasomnia characterized by dream enactment behavior during REM sleep." Ronald B. Postuma et al., *REM Sleep Behavior Disorder: From Dreams to Neurodegeneration*, 46 NEUROBIOLOGY DISEASE 553, 553 (2012). Judging someone's responsibility for criminal conduct while asleep is more complicated when the accused has used sleep aids, or alcohol. *See* Christopher Daley et al., *"I Did What?" Zolpidem and the Courts*, 39 J. AM. ACAD. PSYCHIATRY L. 535 (2011); Shreeya Popat & William Winslade, *While You Were Sleeping: Science and Neurobiology of Sleep Disorders and the Enigma of Legal Responsibility of Violence During Parasomnia*, 8 NEUROETHICS 203, 207–09 (2015).

of milk on her bed stand,[157] and then went to bed. She later "left her bed, fetched an axe from the woodheap, and struck two accurate blows on [Pat's] head with the blade of the axe, thus killing her."[158]

The year was 1950. The place was Australia, and the Korean War was waging not far away. Mrs. Cogdon had told Pat her worries about the war before going to sleep. When she awoke after the killing, Mrs. Cogdon reported having "dreamt that 'the war was all around the house,' that soldiers were in Pat's room, and that one soldier was on the bed attacking Pat."[159] She recalled nothing else. Tried for murder, she was acquitted.

Then there was Ken Parks. Parks had a gambling problem, which had strained his marriage. He got no sleep on May 22, 1987. On the following day, he went to sleep around 1:30 a.m., with much on his mind. The next thing Parks remembered was "looking down at his mother-in-law's face. Her mouth and eyes were open, and she had a 'frightened "help-me" look.'"[160]

As it turned out, after he'd fallen asleep, Parks had driven from his home to that of his in-laws, fourteen miles away. He stabbed his mother-in-law to death, and strangled his father-in-law unconscious. He then got back into his car and drove to a police station. He remembered bits and pieces of what happened, but only bits and pieces. The jury acquitted, believing he was asleep throughout.[161]

Sleepwalking, like hypnosis, is a state of altered or impaired consciousness.[162] Once again, the alien-self metaphor can help explain what happens, and why sleepwalkers, like the hypnotized, are kin to the insane. The consciousness of the insane and the somnambulist are altered insofar as the sense of agency is lost in both. Neither experiences himself as the author of what he does, and when agency is lost, the alien self materializes. The real (waking) self becomes dissociated from the alien (sleeping) self.[163] The alien

[157] *See* Norval Morris, *Somnambulistic Homicide: Ghosts, Spiders, and North Koreans*, 5 Res Judicatae 29 (1951). Another frequently cited case involving sleepwalking is *Fain v. Commonwealth*, 78 Ky. 183 (Ct. App. 1879).

[158] Morris, *supra* note 157, at 30.

[159] *Id.*

[160] Roger Broughton et al., *Homicidal Somnambulism: A Case Report*, 17 Sleep 253, 254–60 (1994) (detailed discussion of Parks's case).

[161] R. v. Parks, [1992] 2 S.R.C. 871.

[162] *See* Zadra et al., *supra* note 156, at 285 ("Somnambulism is defined as a series of complex behaviours that are usually initiated during arousals from slow-wave sleep and culminate in walking around with an altered state of consciousness and impaired judgment.") (internal quotations omitted).

[163] *See, e.g.*, Mark W. Mahowald et al., *State Dissociation: Implications for Sleep and Wakefulness, Consciousness, and Culpability*, 6 Sleep Med. Clinics 393, 395–96 (2011) ("Disorders of arousal are the most impressive and most frequent of the NREM sleep-state dissociation/admixture phenomena . . . . Disorders of arousal simply represent the simultaneous occurrence of [wakefulness]

self takes charge, and the real self becomes a passive bystander. The alien self may be acting out a dream, or something like a dream.[164] The alien self of sleepwalking isn't usually dangerous, but sometimes something happens to precipitate a crime.[165] Sleep crimes tend to be violent, but when awake, the sleepwalkers who commit them tend not to be.

Like the hypnotized, sleepwalkers aren't exactly like the insane. First, the loss of agency in sleepwalking is associated with the psychology of sleep, not constitutive of mental disease or defect. Second, unlike the hypnotic and the insane, the somnambulist may not be able to report what happened. Perhaps he doesn't remember, or perhaps he never forms memories about what happened in the first place. Still, the real self sometimes gets glimpses of what happened, and can recall fragments,[166] as did Parks when he recalled the look on his mother-in-law's face. Finally, when the actor wakes up, the lost sense of agency ends, the alien self disappears, and the self reintegrates. It takes more than waking up for the insane to reintegrate.[167]

Multiple Personality Disorder

In the popular imagination, the portrait of multiple personality disorder (now officially called dissociative identity disorder, or DID) is the character

and NREM sleep."); Dev Banerjee & Angus Nisbet, *Sleepwalking*, 6 SLEEP MED. CLINICS 401, 410 (2011) ("[S]leepwalking and other non-REM parasomnias might arise from a dissociation of sleep and wakefulness occurring across different brain regions . . . ").

164 *See, e.g.*, Zadra et al., *supra* note 156, at 288 ("[E]mpirical evidence suggests that sleep mentation is not only frequently part of the main experience of somnambulism, but also can modulate motor behaviour during an episode. . . . Furthermore, the mentation reported by patients was congruent with recorded nocturnal behaviour, suggesting that sleepwalking might be the acting out of dreamlike mentations."); Delphine Oudiette et al., *Dreamlike Mentations During Sleep and Sleep Terrors in Adults*, 32 SLEEP 1621, 1626 (2009) ("[D]reamlike mentations (mostly brief, frightening visual images) may occasionally exist during sleepwalking and sleep terrors, suggesting that a complex mental activity takes place during SWS [slow-wave sleep]. Sleepwalking may thus represent acting out of the corresponding dreamlike mentations.").

165 *See, e.g.*, Weiss et al., *supra* note 156, at 280 ("It appears that violent behavior can occur when NREM sleep is interrupted, during somnambulistic episodes, upon incomplete arousal from sleep.").

166 *See, e.g.*, Mark R. Pressman, *Sleepwalking, Amnesia, Comorbid Conditions and Triggers: Effects of Recall and Other Methodological Biases*, 36 SLEEP 1757, 1757 (2013) (noting that "recent reports of dream-like mentation associated with sleepwalking episodes and even the incorporation of elements of perceptual environment and behavior have suggested that amnesia for at least some patients and some episodes is not as complete as has been previously accepted"); Zadra et al., *supra* note 156, at 288 ("[M]any patients can and do recall at least portions of episodes upon awakening, and thus suggest that complete amnesia of the event is not standard for adult sleepwalkers.").

167 Sleepwalking cases raise the same doctrinal question as do hypnosis cases: Is the accused not guilty because he didn't act, or despite having acted? *See supra* note 154 and accompanying text.

Sybil, from the book and miniseries of the same name.[168] Alleged to have had sixteen different "alters" or personality states,[169] Sybil didn't commit any crimes, nor did any of her personalities. But some multiples do.

Bridget Denny-Shaffer was a delivery nurse at Rehoboth Hospital in Gallup, New Mexico. On May 10, 1992, Denny-Shaffer went to the Memorial General Hospital in Las Cruces, and identified herself as Linda, a medical student from the University of New Mexico. She then took one of the babies in the Hospital's nursery and headed for Texas. Charged with kidnapping, Denny-Shaffer, who was diagnosed with MPD, argued that she never kidnaped anyone; someone else did.[170]

When we talk about MPD, we need to be careful. We need to know, to the extent we can, what's going on in the MPD mind. One theory, at least compared to the next, is metaphysically extravagant.[171] Assuming a simple case of MPD, with one alter and one host, this account tells us we have two different people occupying the same body seriatim over time. If so, what should the verdict be when, in a case like Denny-Shaffer, the alter was in charge at the time of the crime?

Two possibilities pop out. One would be to judge the mind of the alter, who was, after all, the one in charge at the time of the crime. If the alter satisfies the elements of the crime charged, and has no defense, then the verdict should be guilty. That, of course, would mean the host goes to jail too, but assuming the host wasn't complicit in the alter's crime, the host was innocent. Sending an innocent person to jail doesn't seem fair.

Another possibility would be to judge the mind of the host (even though the alter was in charge at the time). If the host wasn't complicit, then the verdict should be not guilty. That, of course, would mean the guilty alter goes

[168] The character Sybil was based on Shirley Ardell Mason, who probably didn't actually suffer from MPD. *See* DEBBIE NATHAN, SYBIL EXPOSED: THE EXTRAORDINARY STORY BEHIND THE FAMOUS MULTIPLE PERSONALITY CASE (2011).

[169] MPD is thought to arise as a reaction to trauma: The self splits in order to manage a traumatic event, and an "alter" is thought to emerge in response to a particular emotional episode, which the alter can cope with better than the host.

[170] United States v. Denny-Shaffer, 2 F.3d 999, 1002–03 (10th Cir. 1993). Everyone agreed the accused's host personality ("Gidget") wasn't in charge at the time of the kidnapping; one of the alters, "Rina" or "Bridget," was. *See id.* at 1004. Whoever was in charge, Rina or Bridget, lied when she identified herself as "Linda."

Appellate opinions addressing the criminal liability of defendants diagnosed with MPD are rare. The reported cases, besides *Denny-Shaffer*, include Kirkland v. State, 304 S.E.2d 561 (Ga. Ct. App. 1983), Commonwealth v. Roman, 606 N.E.2d 1333 (Mass. 1993), State v. Grimsley, 444 N.E.2d 1071 (Ohio Ct. App. 1982), and State v. Greene, 136 Wash. App. 1002 (2006) (unpublished opinion).

[171] *See, e.g.*, ELYN R. SAKS, JEKYLL ON TRIAL 42–51 (1997) (describing this theory); Elyn R. Saks, *Multiple Personality Disorder and Criminal Responsibility*, 10 S. CAL. INTERDISC. L.J. 185, 189–90 (2001) (same).

free too, assuming the alter had no defense. Letting the guilty go free, even if sometimes necessary, isn't ideal. The metaphysically extravagant account, besides being extravagant, throws up hard choices.

The second theory avoids these conundrums, because it doesn't rely on the unlikely metaphysics of the first. It doesn't hypothesize two different people in the same body. Instead, it posits one body and one person.[172] What gets multiplied isn't the number of people in the body, but the number of selves in the person. When it comes to bodies and persons, the rule is "one to a customer."[173] One body, one person. Your person can handle multiple selves, but your body can only manage one person per lifetime. For present purposes, let's use Occam's razor and eliminate unnecessary persons. Assume, therefore, that the second theory is right. Someone with MPD is really one person with multiple selves.[174]

The second account and the alien-self metaphor are peas in a pod. In MPD-speak, the alter is the alien self, and the host is the real self. When the real self (host) loses its sense of agency,[175] the alien self (alter) emerges and takes control. The real self continues to experience a sense of ownership: He experiences the body the alter is occupying as his body, but he loses any sense of agency over it.[176] Agency and control are vested instead in the alter, with

[172] *See* Jeanette Kennett & Steve Matthews, *Delusion, Dissociation and Identity*, 6 PHIL. EXPLORATIONS 31, 33 (2003) ("[E]ach of the symptoms in the modern cases [of MPD] may be assimilated to other well recognized psychiatric conditions. . . . [W]hat we have [in cases of MPD] are single persons with a serious mental illness which, like other serious mental illnesses, impairs the development and exercise of unified autonomous agency."); *id.* at 34 ("The evidence suggests . . . that alter personalities are mere person-fragments, and not in the sense of being short-lived fully-fledged persons, but in the sense that alters are one-dimensional and lacking in character development."); Robert F. Schopp, *Multiple Personality Disorder, Accountable Agency, and Criminal Acts*, 10 S. CAL. INTERDISC. L.J. 297, 298 (2001) ("[T]o the extent that DID exculpates criminal defendants, it does so for the same reasons that support the exculpatory significance of impaired consciousness more generally.").

[173] DANIEL DENNETT, CONSCIOUSNESS EXPLAINED 422 (1991).

[174] The shift in the *Diagnostic and Statistical Manual of Mental Disorders* from "Multiple Personality Disorder" to "Dissociative Identity Disorder" reflects the shift in the psychiatric profession from the first theory to the second. As one of the psychiatrists behind the change put it: "Multiple personality carries with it the implication that [those with the disorder] . . . have more than one identity, . . . [but the real] problem is *fragmentation* of identity." Clyde Haberman, *Debate Persists Over Diagnosing Mental Health Disorders, Long After "Sybil,"* N.Y. TIMES, Nov. 23, 2014 (quoting Stanford psychiatrist David Spiegel) (emphasis added).

[175] *See* Kennett & Matthews, *supra* note 172, at 37–38 (noting that the experience of "depersonalization" is common to dissociative disorders and that depersonalization involves a "loss of feelings of agency"). Those who suffer from "depersonalization disorder" experience lost agency, but don't go on to form the delusions associated with MPD.

[176] *See id.* at 33 ("[T]here is co-consciousness (or the so-called 'looking-on' phenomenon). Some personalities claim they have phenomenological access to other personality states. It is not completely clear what this involves, but those patients' so-called alters who claim to experience it say they have an intimate and immediate observer-role in relation to other alters' thoughts and actions."); *id.*

the real self reduced to onlooker status. Sometimes the real self can recollect what the alien self did, but not always. Sometimes, like the sleepwalker, he catches and recalls snippets of what happened. Of course, an alien self doesn't really take control. That's what the first theory says: It takes the metaphor literally. The second theory, in contrast, takes the alien-self metaphor as just that: a metaphor used to make sense of the real self's lost sense of agency.

Compare Denny-Shaffer to Sarah. Sarah is schizophrenic, with delusions of alien control. Sarah's alien self kidnaps a baby, while Sarah's real self delusionally attributes her acts to the work of some force external to herself, though she doesn't give it a name and personality. All she knows for sure is that she wasn't the one in command when the baby was taken. Unlike Sarah, who doesn't give her alien overseer a name, Denny-Shaffer did. Indeed, she did more, delusionally investing it with an entire personality different (though perhaps not entirely different) from her own.[177] Still, Denny-Shaffer's alien self was arguably just a delusion, albeit an exceptionally elaborate one.[178]

MPD is sometimes thought to send the law of insanity into a tailspin, and indeed it does, but only if multiples are multiple people in one body (the first theory), and only if insanity is, as the traditional and Model Penal Code tests say, a matter of incapacity resulting from mental disease or defect. If the alter who commits the crime isn't incapacitated, and if the host, when back in charge, isn't incapacitated, then who was insane? In contrast, if MPD involves multiple selves in one person (the second theory), and if insanity is understood as consisting in lost agency, the problem goes away. In fact, far from being a problem case for insanity, MPD cases turn out to be paradigm cases of insanity. Sybil turns out to be insanity's poster child.

at 42 (suggesting "that amnesia with regard to important personal information in DID is often to be understood in terms of the difficulty of incorporating traumatic and depersonalized or delusional experiences into autobiographical memory").

177 Alters tend to be stock characters. "One study reports that in 85% of cases of DID there is a child alter, in 70% of cases there is a violent or destructive alter, in 53% of cases there is an opposite gender alter, in 52% there is a promiscuous alter. 22% of alters were judged to be hypomanic or manic and 38% were judged to be psychotic." *See id.* at 35.

178 Jeanette Kennett & Steve Matthews, *Identity, Control and Responsibility: The Case of Dissociative Personality Disorder*, 15 Phil. Pscyhol. 509, 511 (2002) ("[S]omeone with DID is an individual human person whose psychiatric symptoms . . . are akin to a species of *global self-delusion*. So-called alter personalities are not to be regarded as metaphysically separate entities from the person, but rather as altered states of that person.") (emphasis added).

Authority

Up to this point we've described and criticized the traditional and irrationality tests for insanity, and offered the lost agency theory as an alternative. We should now raise the question we've so far deferred, about the state's authority to punish those who are insane under the lost agency theory. We'll examine that question in light of the facts in M'Naghten.

We start with some stipulations. First, the United Kingdom, a parliamentary monarchy at the time of M'Naghten's trial, qualifies as a democracy vested with authority to ordain the rules comprising the criminal law. Second, the United Kingdom acted within its authority when it criminalized murder. Third, it acted within its authority when it mandated, as it did at the time, hanging as the punishment for murder, inasmuch as hanging wouldn't, at the time and for murder, have been grossly disproportionate.

That leaves culpability. The central question at M'Naghten's trial was whether he was, at the time, sane or insane, and thus culpable or not for his attempt on Drummond's life. The jury found he was insane, but suppose it found him sane. Moreover, suppose its judgment reflected a fair application of U.K. law at the time. If that's what U.K. law provided for, then M'Naghten's only chance to escape the gallows would be to claim the United Kingdom nonetheless lacked the authority to hang him pursuant to those laws, which would require showing that, at the time, he lacked either a guilty act or a guilty mind, or perhaps both.

Assuming for the moment that M'Naghten, when he killed Drummond, hadn't lost his sense of agency, assessing the guilt of his act and mind would require deciding if, at the moment he chose to kill, he realized he was committing a crime. If he did, the analysis goes in one direction. If he didn't, it goes in another. Although hardly free from doubt, let's keep things simple and assume M'Naghten did realize killing Drummond was a crime. That means we'd use the Stephen test to determine the guilt of his act (and thus if his choice to kill satisfied the *actus reus* requirement), and the Jekyll test to determine the guilt of his mind (and thus if his choice satisfied the *mens rea* requirement).

Applying those tests to M'Naghten isn't easy. We can imagine arguments both ways. We could run through some of those arguments, but instead, let's look instead at the tests themselves, for both invite inquiries about what M'Naghten could or would have done, had he known it was a crime to kill someone he believed was the prime minister. The Stephen test asks if M'Naghten had the capacity not to choose to kill Drummond. The Jekyll test asks if M'Naghten's choice to kill expressed insufficient concern for the law. Both questions presuppose, in other words, that M'Naghten was the one doing the choosing: They assume the act and mind we're putting to the test are M'Naghten's. But that might not have been so. As the lost agency theory teaches, the agent in question doesn't always experience himself as the agent in charge.

That being so, before we submit M'Naghten to the Stephen and Jekyll tests, he first needs to pass another test. There's little or no point in asking if M'Naghten satisfies the Stephen and Jekyll tests if M'Naghten didn't experience himself as the person in charge—as the person doing the choosing—at the time Drummond was killed. The sense-of-agency question thus becomes a threshold question or test precedent to any inquiry about the guilt of his act or mind.

Someone watching the events unfold on Parliament Street—seeing one man walk up to another and then shooting him—would probably think the man doing the walking and shooting was thoroughly in command of himself. Yet appearances can deceive. M'Naghten's body could well have acted with design and purpose even if M'Naghten wasn't at the helm. Indeed, though seldom remarked upon, M'Naghten's defense at trial was based almost entirely on the claim that (in some sense) he couldn't control himself.[179] Consider the following bits of uncontested testimony from the defense doctors:

> Dr. Monro: The act with which he is charged, coupled with the history of his past life, leaves not the remotest doubt on my mind of the presence of insanity sufficient to deprive the prisoner of all self-control.[180]
>
> Dr. Morison: [His delusions] deprived the prisoner of all restraint over his actions.[181]

179 For an exception, see Eigen, *supra* note 75, at 45 ("The most articulate pairing of delusion with loss of self-control was made only at the very end of the period under review, during the trial of Daniel McNaughtan."). In its summary of the "substance" of the medical testimony, the judges in *M'Naghten's Case* said: "[I]t was of the nature of the disease with which the prisoner was affected, to go on gradually until it had reached a climax, when it burst forth with irresistible intensity: that a man might go on for years quietly, though at the same time under its influence, but would all at once break out into the most extravagant and violent paroxysms." M'Naghten's Case, 8 Eng. Rep 718, 719 (1843).

180 SCHNEIDER, *supra* note 2, at 213. Dr. Monro was a physician with thirty years of experience practicing at Bethlem.

181 *Id.* at 220. Dr. Morison was "a physician at St. Luke's Hospital and also affiliated with Bethlem Hospital and the Surrey Asylum." *Id.* at 219.

> Dr. M'Clure: I consider when he fired at Mr. Drummond, at Charing Cross, he was suffering from an hallucination which deprived him of all ordinary restraint.[182]
>
> Dr. Hutcheson: The prisoner had lost all self-control at the moment he fired at Mr. Drummond. The act flowed immediately from the delusion. . . . [T]he act was the consequence of the delusion, which was irresistible.[183]

Someone versed in the history of the insanity defense, and especially the long-standing debate between cognitive and volitional tests, might think it's obvious what the doctors were saying: M'Naghten suffered from an "irresistible impulse;" he lacked the power to control himself; he couldn't have done otherwise; and so on. Simple as that. If so, then while the test ultimately to emerge from *M'Naghten's Case* rested on cognition, M'Naghten's defense at trial rested, ironically enough, on volition.

That's one way to interpret what the doctors were saying, but not the only way. Maybe all the talk about self-control and restraint wasn't really about M'Naghten's capacity to conform to the law. Instead, maybe it was about the sense of agency. What the doctors were trying to say, albeit using the language of self-control, was that M'Naghten wasn't in command at the time he killed Drummond. The language of self-control may, at the time, have seemed the most natural way to capture and express in language the phenomena they were really trying to describe, namely, a lost sense of agency. If so, if real M'Naghten lacked a sense of agency when Drummond was killed, then questions about the guilt of real M'Naghten's act or mind are beside the point.

Suppose M'Naghten was insane, under the lost agency theory, at the time he shot Drummond.[184] Suppose he was nonetheless found sane under prevailing positive law, and sent to the gallows. That would bring us at last to

[182] *Id.* Dr. M'Clure was a "London surgeon who had accompanied Monro and Morison in the prison examination of M'Naghten." *Id.*

[183] *Id.* Dr. Hutcheson was a "physician to the Royal Lunatic Asylum in Glasgow." *Id.*

[184] If insanity is indeed a matter of lost agency, it has an ironic upshot. Determinism tells us we're not really in control of what we do, at least not if being in control means having the contra-causal capacity to choose otherwise, and we lack that capacity. Be that as it may, our brains trick us into thinking that we do have such control. The only ones whose brains don't play this trick on them are those who lack a sense of agency, i.e., the insane. So, if it's insane to think we have contra-causal powers, then the only ones who aren't insane are the insane. *See* KEAN, *supra* note 95, at 264 ("[V]ictims of alien hand syndrome and other syndromes may have simply lost the illusion of free will for part of their bodies. In some sense, they might be closer to the reality of how the brain works than the rest of us. Makes you wonder who's really deluded.").

the question: If M'Naghten was sane, under whatever test of insanity positive law provided, would his punishment nonetheless have been illegitimate? Or, in other words, are those who act without a sense of agency immune to any effort a democratic state might make to assign culpability to their choices?

The answer depends on the reasonable doubt test. Framed in the first person, that test addresses itself to the reason of each citizen, asking, as applied here, if he believes, beyond reasonable doubt, that it would be unjust to ascribe culpability to someone who committed a crime, perhaps a ghastly one, but whose sense of agency had at the time and through no fault of his own abandoned him. Our sense of agency is tightly bound up with, if not constitutive of, our sense of ourselves as agents with free will, and the criminal law has long supposed that if we lack that sense, the criminal law should not call us to account. These facts, we believe, provide support for believing it would, beyond reasonable doubt, be unjust to ascribe culpability to anyone who committed a crime when his sense of agency had forsaken him.

M'Naghten wasn't a poor man. On the contrary, he had enough money to buy a very good defense. Not everyone in Victorian England was so lucky. The poorhouse was in vogue, and the birth of the modern English welfare state, dedicated to achieve some conception of distributive justice, was still over half a century away. Fast-forward to today. Imagine someone commits a crime, and imagine the state has failed him so badly, in terms of distributive justice, that we'd characterize him as having been excluded from the life of the polity or something along those lines. Does the state's dismal failure to live up to the demands of distributive justice jeopardize its authority to punish him?

That's our next question, on which Chapter 6 tries to provide some insight.

6
Injustice

On the night of June 4, 1968, five Marine Corps lieutenants were out on the town, celebrating in the nation's capital after having almost completed officer training at Quantico.[1] On their way back to the base, at around 3 a.m. on June 5, the five officers—all white, in dress-whites—stopped at the Little Tavern, a hamburger joint located at 3331 M Street, N.W.,[2] not far from Georgetown University.[3] Standing at the take-out counter, they noticed three black men, ranging in age from 20 to 27, sitting at the other end. The three men, Gordon Alexander, Cornelius Frazier, and Benjamin Murdock,[4] had arrived in Washington the night before to join the Poor People's Campaign, Dr. Martin Luther King's movement to win economic justice for the poor.[5]

According to prosecution witnesses, one of the officers, twenty-six-year-old Ellsworth Kramer, noticed Alexander staring at him. He returned the stare. No words were exchanged. Kramer soon turned away and faced the counter. A bit later, Alexander, Murdock, and Frazier got up to leave. As Murdock and Frazier left through a door behind the Marines, Alexander stopped. He tapped Kramer on the shoulder. When Kramer turned around, Alexander poked his name tag: "You want to talk about it more? You want to come outside and talk about it more?" When Kramer said he did, Alexander responded: "I am going to make you a Little Red Ridinghood."[6]

At that point, another officer, twenty-one-year-old William King, stepped beside Kramer. "What do you want, you n[*]gg[*]r?" King said.[7] Alexander

[1] United States v. Alexander, 471 F.2d 923, 928 (D.C. Cir. 1973) (per curiam). Chief Judge Bazelon wrote for the court on some of the issues presented; Judge McGowan wrote for the court on the others.

[2] *See* Thomas P. Lippman, *Machinist Convicted in Marines' Slaying*, WASH. POST, Feb. 27, 1969, at A23.

[3] *Alexander*, 471 F.2d at 957.

[4] Benjamin Murdock's name was actually Murdock Benjamin. *See id.* at 926 n.1. Alexander was twenty-seven; Murdock, a machinist, was twenty or twenty-one; and Frazier, a student at San Jose State College, was twenty-three. *See* Lippman, *supra* note 2, at A23.

[5] King had been assassinated just over two months before, on April 4, 1968.

[6] 471 F.2d at 928.

[7] Prosecution witnesses didn't agree on exactly what King said. *See id.*

Guilty Acts, Guilty Minds. Stephen P. Garvey, Oxford University Press (2020). © Oxford University Press.
DOI: 10.1093/oso/9780190924324.001.0001

then withdrew a long-barreled .38 caliber revolver, cocked it, and pointed it at the Marines. "I will show you what I want,"[8] he said. In the meantime, Murdock had re-entered the shop. According to his trial testimony, he then heard someone say, "Get out, you black bastards,"[9] at which point he withdrew a short-barreled .38 and began shooting. Murdock emptied his gun, leaving two of the Marines, including King, dead.[10] Alexander, Murdock, and Frazier fled in Alexander's car. As they drove off, Murdock fired three more shots, this time from Alexander's gun.[11]

Charged with two counts of second degree murder,[12] Murdock based his defense on three facts. First, when he heard one of the Marines call him a "black bastard," he flew into a rage. Second, he suffered from an "abnormal mental condition," which "substantially impaired his behavior controls," making it especially difficult, or maybe impossible, for him to control the rage.[13] Third, this abnormal mental condition resulted, as his lawyer put it, from a "'rotten social background,'"[14] which had molded Murdock into a "man whose bitterness and racial hostility [had] turned into blasting powder which [could] be touched off by a spark,"[15] including the spark of a racial epithet.

Upon that basic factual scaffold Murdock built two legal defenses: one, heat of passion, which would have mitigated the charge of murder to manslaughter; and two, insanity,[16] which would have resulted in acquittal (though

[8] *Id.*

[9] *Id.* at 929.

[10] Another Marine and a friend of one of the Marines, a woman named Barbara Kelly, were "seriously wounded." *See id.* at 926.

[11] *See id.* at 929.

[12] Murdock was also charged with carrying a dangerous weapon and four counts of assault with a dangerous weapon. *Id.* at 926–27.

[13] *Id.* at 958.

[14] *Id.* at 959 & n.100 (referring to Murdock's trial counsel's closing argument). The phrase "rotten social background" subsequently entered the criminal law literature, thanks mainly to Richard Delgado, *"Rotten Social Background": Should the Law Recognize a Defense of Severe Environmental Deprivation?*, 3 LAW & INEQ. 9 (1985). For Delgado's most recent thoughts on the subject, see Richard Delgado, *The Wretched of the Earth*, 2 ALA. C.R. & C.L. L. REV. 1 (2011). He now prefers the term "severe environmental deprivation."

[15] 471 F.2d at 962. Murdock's reaction might today be described as "black rage," a term attributed to WILLIAM H. GRIER & PRICE M. COBBS, BLACK RAGE (1968). *See* Patricia Falk, *Novel Theories of Criminal Defense Based upon the Toxicity of the Social Environment: Urban Psychosis, Television Intoxication, and Black Rage*, 74 N.C. L. REV. 731 (1996).

[16] At the time of Murdock's appeal, the D.C. Circuit adhered to the definition of insanity it had adopted in 1954 in *Durham v. United States*, 214 F.2d 862 (D.C. Cir. 1954). Murdock's appeal was decided on April 21, 1972 (though an amended opinion was filed on January 25, 1973), and the D.C. Circuit overruled *Durham* on June 23, 1972, in *Brawner v. United States*, 471 F.2d 969 (D.C. Cir. 1972) (en banc). *Durham* is briefly discussed in Chapter 5.

possible civil commitment). The trial court instructed the jury on both defenses,[17] but the jury returned a verdict of murder.

The verdict against Murdock, based on the law then prevailing in the federal courts of the District of Columbia, doesn't necessarily mean justice was served. Maybe the law was wrong, producing an unjust result. A philosophical anarchist might, for example, believe for one reason or another that it was unjust for the United States to lock Murdock up at all, or at least to lock him up for as long as it said it would, twenty-three years to life. For now, we'll focus on two explanations an anarchist might give to believe Murdock's punishment was unjust.

The first is based on the *revolutionary theory* and doesn't in the end depend on how rotten Murdock's background was. Nor does it depend on anything the state may have done to create or contribute to his background, nor on anything it failed to do to improve it. All it depends on is the historical fact that Murdock, like everyone else, had a background, rotten or not. According to the revolutionary, having a history and background means no one is morally responsible for anything he chooses to do, including crime. Moreover, because no one is morally responsible if he happens to commit a crime, punishing anyone who commits a crime would be unjust. Of course, if all that's true then justice requires doing away with punishment altogether. The revolutionary call to arms ends in penal abolition.

The second explanation is based on the *reform theory*. Unlike the revolutionary theory, according to which the justice of Murdock's punishment doesn't in the end depend on how rotten his background was, under the reform theory, it does. Unlike the revolutionary, the reformist doesn't come to bury punishment, but to place further limits on when the state, as a matter of justice, is permitted to impose it. According to some reformers, justice requires punishing someone with a rotten background less (if at all) than someone with a non-rotten background. According to other reformers, if the state bears blame for an offender's rotten background then it lacks the moral standing it needs to punish him, and if it lacks standing justice bans it from punishing him, unless and until the state regains its standing.

Revolution or reform. Those are two theories a philosophical anarchist might embrace, in the name of justice, when faced with the prospect

[17] Besides the heat of passion and insanity defenses, Murdock also sought an instruction on what's known as the "*mens rea* variant" of "diminished capacity." The Court of Appeals found that the trial judge, in accordance with existing circuit precedent, properly refused to give the requested instruction. *See* 471 F.2d at 967.

of the state punishing someone whose character was formed under rotten conditions. Concerned first and foremost about legitimacy, the statist would bracket questions about the justice of punishing the disadvantaged and instead ask if a democratic state has authority to punish the disadvantaged in the first place. Are the disadvantage somehow beyond a democratic state's authority altogether?

We'll eventually return to the statist and whether states with democratic authority retain the authority to punish those who, like Murdock, were the predictable product of a rotten social background. We won't get to that question until after a long detour investigating how an anarchist might respond to the justice of Murdock's punishment. We begin with the revolutionary, then turn to the reformer.

Revolution

The revolutionary's manifesto, declaring the injustice of punishing the disadvantaged, goes as follows. First, the state is morally permitted to punish a person for choosing to commit a crime only if he was morally responsible for his choice to commit it. Second, no one (including but not limited to the disadvantaged) is responsible for any choice he makes (including criminal choices). Therefore, the state is morally permitted, as a matter of justice, to punish no one (including the disadvantaged). Justice thus requires the state to abolish punishment altogether.

The Revolutionary Road

The revolutionary's conclusion is based on the skeptical premise that no one is morally responsible for what he does, no matter what he does, good or bad. The revolutionary argument's in favor of this skeptical premise unfolds in four steps, which we'll call "stops" along the revolutionary road.[18] For

[18] Philosophers refer to this argument as the "manipulation argument." The relevant literature would fill a small library. The most well-known manipulation argument, on which the Murdock hypotheticals described in the text are based, is Derk Pereboom's four-case argument. *See* Derk Pereboom, Living Without Free Will 112–17 (2001) [hereafter Pereboom, Living Without]; Derk Pereboom, Free Will, Agency, and Meaning in Life 71–103 (2014) [hereinafter Pereboom, Meaning]. In Pereboom's argument, Professor Plum plays the role of Murdock, and Mrs. White plays the role of Lieutenant King. For other versions of the manipulation argument, see, for example, Robert Kane, The Significance of Free Will 64–65 (1998) ("covert

our purposes, each stop along the way presents a hypothetical involving Murdock's choice to kill Lieutenant King.

The revolutionary road ends with the conclusion that no one, including Murdock, is morally responsible for any choice he makes. In order to enable the revolutionary to reach that conclusion for the reasons he wants to reach it we need to change the facts in the case of *U.S. v. Murdock*. We need to assume, contrary to the claims Murdock made at trial, that he wasn't at the time he killed King in the heat of passion, nor responding to any provocation the law would regard as adequate or reasonable. Suppose Murdock killed King just because he didn't like the way King was staring at him. The revolutionary believes Murdock, provoked or not, would bear no responsibility for King's murder.

Stop One

At Stop One, Murdock (Murdock-1) kills Lieutenant King, just as he did in the actual case, but with a twist. The Stop One hypothetical features a nefarious neuroscientist named Dr. Nefario. Nefario has developed a technique enabling him to implant beliefs and desires, thereby controlling a person's choices, minute-by-minute, second-by-second. The reasons motivating Murdock-1, and causing him to choose as he does, come directly from Nefario, which makes Murdock-1 a puppet and Nefario his puppeteer.[19]

If Nefario weren't pulling the strings, it would never have crossed Murdock-1's mind, when he saw King staring, to pull out his short-barreled .38 and start shooting. But it does cross the mind of Nefario, who decides he wants Murdock-1 to kill King. Nefario thus pulls his neuroscientific strings and implants in Murdock-1 a desire to kill. All works as planned. Murdock-1 forms the intent to kill, pulls out his .38, and starts shooting, leaving King dead on the Little Tavern floor.

nonconstraining control" cases); ALFRED MELE, AUTONOMOUS AGENTS 145–46 (1995) (Beth and Ann); ALFRED MELE, FREE WILL AND LUCK 189 (2006) (zygote argument) [hereinafter MELE, FREE WILL]. For an overview of the argument's basic structure, see Kristin Mickelson, *The Manipulation Argument*, *in* THE ROUTLEDGE COMPANION TO FREE WILL 166 (Kevin Timpe et al. eds., 2017); Neal A. Tognazzini, *The Structure of a Manipulation Argument*, 124 ETHICS 358 (2014); Kadri Vihvelin, *Arguments for Incompatibilism*, STAN. ENCYCLOPEDIA PHIL. § 3.2 (2018).

The revolutionary theory against moral responsibility described in the text assumes the truth of determinism. According to another line of thought, leading to the same conclusion, "it is not ontology [i.e., the truth of determinism] that rules out free will [and moral responsibility], it is *luck*." *See* NEIL LEVY, HARD LUCK: HOW LUCK UNDERMINES FREE WILL AND MORAL RESPONSIBILITY 2 (2011).

[19] Or, for Harry Potter fans, imagine Nefario is a wizard who's put Murdock-1 under the Imperius Curse.

Was Murdock-1 morally responsible for King's murder? The revolutionary tells you to pick your preferred theory of moral responsibility, so long as your theory somehow grounds an actor's moral responsibility in some fact about the actor at the time of choice, and put it to work. Maybe you're partial to what moral philosophers call a "reasons-responsive" theory of moral responsibility.[20] Or maybe you're partial to what they call a "quality of will" theory.[21] It doesn't matter. According to the revolutionary, whatever your theory of moral responsibility the verdict will be the same—namely, Murdock-1 was morally responsible when he choose to start shooting.

Suppose you go along. The revolutionary persuades you that whatever your theory of moral responsibility, it leads to Murdock-1's guilt. The revolutionary next invites you to bracket your theory and listen instead to your intuition. Theory aside, was Murdock-1 responsible for killing King? Surely, the revolutionary says, whatever your theory tells you, your gut would tell you Murdock-1 wasn't morally responsible for killing King. Nefario was. If it weren't for Nefario, Murdock-1 wouldn't have wanted to kill King in the first place. Finally, the revolutionary advises you to listen to your gut, not your theory. Of course, you might wonder why your gut is telling you Murdock-1 isn't to blame, especially when your theory is telling you he is. If your gut has it right, where did your theory go wrong?

In any event, whatever Murdock-1's moral responsibility, he probably wouldn't be found criminally responsible, not under existing doctrine. Criminal liability requires a voluntary act. That's black-letter law. If Murdock-1 didn't act voluntarily he isn't criminally responsible for King's death, even if Murdock-1's body figured in the chain of events causing King's death. Among the bodily movement the criminal law doesn't recognize as voluntary acts are those performed under hypnosis.[22] Of course, Nefario didn't hypnotize Murdock-1. He directly implanted beliefs and desires, but if a bodily movement under hypnosis isn't an act, then arguably neither is a bodily movement under neuro-manipulation. The only one who acted, and thereby caused Murdock-1's body to move, was Nefario, who'd likely be guilty of King's murder as a principal under the "innocent agency doctrine."[23]

[20] *See* Chapter 2, *supra* at p. 87, n.41.

[21] *See id.* at p. 97, n.61.

[22] *See, e.g.*, Model Penal Code § 2.01(2)(c) (Am. Law Inst. 1985) ("The following are not voluntary acts within the meaning of this Section: . . . (c) conduct during hypnosis or resulting from hypnotic suggestion.").

[23] *See, e.g.*, *id.*, § 2.06(2)(a).

Anyway, let's for now give the revolutionary what he wants. Let's agree Murdock-1, criminally liable or not, isn't morally responsible for killing King, any theory of moral responsibility to the contrary notwithstanding. That takes us to Stop Two.

Stop Two

At Stop One, Nefario's neuro-manipulations were local and hands-on. Second-by-second he would add or subtract beliefs and desires from Murdock-1's mind, such that when Murdock-1 saw King staring he started shooting. At Stop Two, Nefario takes a step back. His manipulations are hands-off. Rather than manipulate Murdock-2's mind in real time, he intervenes earlier, maybe before Murdock-2 is even born. He tinkers with Murdock-2's genetic makeup, such that when Murdock-2 sees King staring, he experiences the same desire to kill, which causes him to start shooting.

When Murdock-1 chose to kill, we gave the revolutionary our assent to the proposition that Murdock-1 was morally responsible under whatever theory of moral responsibility we preferred. We also gave him our intuition that, theory aside, Murdock-1 wasn't morally responsible. That brings us to what the revolutionary now wants: our assent to the proposition that no relevant difference exists between Murdock-1 and Murdock-2. Nefario's manipulations of Murdock-1 were local, whereas his manipulations of Murdock 2 are global. But that difference, the revolutionary wants you to agree, makes no difference. If so, and if Murdock-1 wasn't responsible, as your gut told you, then you should concede that Murdock-2 isn't responsible either, because no relevant difference exists between Murdock-2 and Murdock-1.

If the revolutionary's logic is sound, then Murdock-2, like Murdock-1, isn't morally responsible for King's death. His criminal liability, on the other hand, isn't so clear. One argument against criminal liability for Murdock-2 begins with an analogy between Nefario's genetic manipulations and "brainwashing."[24] Suppose Nefario hadn't played with Murdock-2's genetic

[24] Examples involving brainwashing don't fit neatly into any one of the four cases Pereboom describes. They might fit in Case 2 or Case 3, or maybe somewhere in-between. Pereboom's Case 2 describes someone who's "been programmed to weigh reasons for action" so as to be causally determined to act wrongly at a later time, whereas Case 3 describes someone who's been "determined by rigorous training practices" at an "early" age so as to be causally determined to act wrongly at a later time. *See* PEREBOOM, LIVING WITHOUT, *supra* note 18, at 113–14. Other have noted the indeterminacy in the phrase "rigorous training practices." *See* MELE, FREE WILL, *supra* note 18, at 143. Is "brainwashing" an instance of "programming" or "rigorous training"?

material, but had instead performed on him whatever coercive techniques brainwashers use to achieve their ends, with the same result. When Murdock-2 sees King staring, he experiences the same desire as when Nefario manipulated his genome, causing Murdock-2 to start shooting.

The term "brainwashing" entered popular discourse in the 1950s.[25] American POWs, returning home from North Korea, were accused of treason, having declared Communist allegiance. Their court-martials attracted considerable attention at the time,[26] but the most famous brainwashing case is probably that of Patty Hearst. Heir to a family fortune, Hearst was a nineteen-year-old student at Berkeley when members of the Symbionese Liberation Army (SLA), a left-wing terrorist group, kidnaped her from her apartment. Held in captivity, like the Korean POWs before her, Hearst was kept blindfolded in a small closet for several weeks, threatened with death. Two months later, Patty emerged as "Tania," joining the SLA in a series of criminal pursuits, including an armed robbery of the Hibernia Bank in San Francisco.

Suppose the SLA had indeed "brainwashed" Patty, turning her into Tania.[27] Tried in federal court, Hearst was convicted.[28] Having been brainwashed, would she have available any legal defense? She couldn't claim duress, because duress under federal law required an immediate threat, and no one

[25] Journalist (and former Office of Strategic Services Operative) Edward Hunter apparently coined the word, which he took from *xi-nao* (literally "wash brain"), the term Chinese Communists used to describe their techniques. *See* Kathleen Taylor, Brainwashing: The Science of Thought Control 3–4 (2004). Brainwashing looks, at least superficially, like it transforms the person whose brain has been washed into a different person. Injuries to, or tumors in, the brain can also sometimes "transform" a person. The most famous case involving brain injury is Phineas Gage, who suffered damage to his prefrontal lobe when a tamping rod penetrated his skull, allegedly transforming him from a gentle soul into an irascible one. *See* Sam Kean, The Tale of the Dueling Neurosurgeons Ch. 12 (2014); Malcolm MacMillan, An Odd Kind of Fame: Stories of Phineas Gage (2002). The most famous case involving a brain tumor is an unnamed forty-year-old man whose tumor turned him into a pedophile. *See* Jeffrey M. Burns & Russell H. Swerdlow, *Right Orbitofrontal Tumor with Pedophilia Symptoms and Constructional Apraxia Sign*, 60 Archives of Neurology 437 (2003). Of course, transformations resulting from brain injuries or tumors, unlike transformations resulting from washing, aren't due to the acts of any third party, unless a third party caused a brain injury or (somehow) implanted a tumor.

[26] *See* Elizabeth Lutes Hillman, *Disloyalty Among "Men in Arms": Korean War POWs at Court-Martial*, 82 N.C. L. Rev. 1629, 1631 (2004) (analyzing a "highly charged subset of Cold War courts-martial: the trials of repatriated POWs after a ceasefire ended the Korean War in 1953").

[27] What really happened to Patty? Did she simply change her mind about the SLA, or did the SLA change her mind for her? Was she persuaded, or was she brainwashed? No one can say for sure. For a recent account of the case, see Jeffrey Toobin, American Heiress: The Wild Saga of the Kidnapping, Crimes and Trial of Patty Hearst (2016).

[28] *See* United States v. Hearst, 563 F.2d 1331 (9th Cir. 1977) (upholding Hearst's conviction and seven-year sentence on two counts of armed bank robbery). Hearst was released from prison in 1979, after President Jimmy Carter commuted her sentence to time served. President Bill Clinton issued a full pardon in 2001.

threatened Tania with anything at the time she robbed the bank. (The M-1 carbine she was carrying throughout the robbery didn't help.) The federal law of duress isn't unique. The result would likely have been the same in most U.S. jurisdictions, then and now.[29]

The outcome under the Model Penal Code might have been different.[30] Quoting the Code's Commentaries: "The defense of duress may be appropriate in certain circumstances where a defendant was 'so far in the thrall of some power' that the choices he made were not really his."[31] If Murdock-2 was in Nefario's "thrall," then maybe he, like Murdock-1, would've been off the criminal law's hook, at least under the Model Penal Code. The only one left on it would be Nefario.

Anyhow, let's once again give the revolutionary what he wants. If Murdock-1 isn't morally responsible for killing King (and we've agreed he isn't), and if no material difference exists between Murdock-1 and Murdock-2 (as we'll also agree), then Murdock-2 isn't morally responsible for killing King either. That brings us to Stop Three.

Stop Three

At Stop Three, Nefario leaves the story altogether. In his place we substitute Murdock's rotten social background, which "implants" in Murdock-3 the desire causing him to kill King. Of course, Stop Three's story is the story of the real Murdock, insofar as the real Murdock, like Murdock-3, wouldn't have wanted to kill King had his background not been rotten.

[29] *See, e.g.*, Joshua Dressler, Understanding Criminal Law § 23.01[B], at 283–84 (8th ed. 2018) (noting prevalence of "imminence" requirement).

[30] Model Penal Code § 2.09 (Am. Law Inst. 1985). For a recent review of the literature, see Frances E. Chapman, *Implanted Choice: Is There Room for a Modern Criminal Defense of Brainwashing?*, 49 Crim. L. Bull. 1379 (2013). For the well-known debate between Richard Delgado and Joshua Dressler on the merits of incorporating a "brainwashing" defense into the criminal law, see Richard Delgado, *Ascription of Criminal States of Mind: Toward a Defense Theory for the Coercively Persuaded ("Brainwashed") Defendant*, 63 Minn. L. Rev. 1 (1978); Joshua Dressler, *Professor Delgado's "Brainwashing" Defense: Courting A Determinist Legal System*, 63 Minn. L. Rev. 335 (1979); Richard Delgado, *A Response to Professor Dressler*, 63 Minn. L. Rev. 361 (1979).

Paul Robinson has recently suggested that, in at least some cases, enduring a rotten social background might be analogized to brainwashing, such that if the latter excuses, then sometimes the former should too. *See* Paul Robinson, *Are We Responsible for Who We Are? The Challenge for Criminal Law Theory in the Defenses of Coercive Indoctrination and "Rotten Social Background,"* 2 Ala. C.R. & C.L. L. Rev. 53 (2011). Stephen Morse disagrees, arguing that "criminogenic values and beliefs" shouldn't excuse, even when they result from brainwashing, and thus neither should they excuse when they result from a rotten social background. *See* Stephen J. Morse, *Severe Environmental Deprivation (aka RSB): A Tragedy, Not a Defense*, 2 Ala. C.R. & C.L. L. Rev. 147, 161 (2011).

[31] Model Penal Code and Commentaries § 2.09, cmt. 3, at 376 n.40 (Am. Law Inst. 1985).

According to testimony presented at trial, the real Murdock was raised in the two-square-mile Los Angeles neighborhood known as Watts, which in the 1940s, when Murdock was a child, was predominantly black. Murdock's family was large, his father had deserted them, and Murdock "grew up . . . with little money and little love or attention."[32] Watts was racially and economically isolated. When, on August 11, 1965, the California Highway Patrol arrested a young black man on charges of DWI, Watts exploded in riots. Less than three years later, Murdock and King would meet in the Little Tavern. Murdock-3, like the real Murdock, wasn't the product of Nefario. He was the product of Watts.

The revolutionary sees no meaningful difference between Murdock-3 and Murdock-2, just as he saw no meaningful difference between Murdock 2 and Murdock-1. Nefario or Watts. The revolutionary believes it makes no difference. Either way, Murdock had no control over the forces causing him to become the person he was when he entered the Little Tavern and saw King staring: a person who at that moment wanted to and did start firing, intent on causing King's death. Because neither Murdock-2 nor Murdock-3 (nor the real Murdock) had any control over those forces, the revolutionary believes neither was morally responsible for killing King.

Whatever the revolutionary believes about Murdock-3's moral responsibility, we already know what the law would say about his criminal responsibility. The real Murdock was convicted (and Murdock-3 would have been convicted) of murder, and his conviction was (and would have been) upheld on appeal. Although the criminal law was on board at Stop One, and might have stayed aboard as far as Stop Two (at least in a Model Penal Code jurisdiction), it draws the line at Stop Three. Criminal responsibility won't be defeated just because the content of the accused's character was the product of a rotten social background—not under existing law anyway.

Then again, the revolutionary isn't interested in existing law. He wants justice, whatever the law says. According to the revolutionary, if Murdock-2 isn't morally responsible for killing King, and if Murdock-3 is really no different than Murdock-2, then Murdock-3 isn't morally responsible either, whatever the law says. If only for the sake of argument, let's go along. Let's agree with the revolutionary: Murdock-3 isn't morally responsible for killing King (and so neither was the real Murdock). That brings us to Stop Four, the end of the line.

[32] United States v. Alexander, 471 F.2d 923, 958 (D.C. Cir. 1972) (Bazelon, C.J., dissenting).

Stop Four

Stop Four take us to the revolutionary's final destination. Stop Four substitutes the real Murdock's rotten background with *any* background. Suppose Murdock-4 suffered, not from a rotten social background, but from a spoiled rotten social background.[33] His parents were rich. The world was his playground. However odd it might sound, however odd the causal pathway must have been, Murdock-4 somehow turned out just as the real Murdock did—wanting to kill King in the Little Tavern—not because of disadvantage, but because of privilege. But for his privileged life, he wouldn't have wanted to kill King, and the shooting would never have been.

Once again, the revolutionary sees, and wants us to see, no difference between Murdock-3 and Murdock-4. Both turned out as they did due to circumstances beyond their control. If Murdock-3 wasn't morally responsible, and if Murdock-4 is no different than Murdock-3, then neither is Murdock-4 morally responsible. It doesn't matter if Murdock-4's background or life history was rotten, spoiled rotten, or anything in between. All that matters is that he had a background: He had a history.

Of course, no one creates himself *ex nihilo.* Everyone has a history, and if having a history is all it takes to undermine moral responsibility for any choice, then we've at last reached the revolutionary's final destination. No one is morally responsible for any choice he makes. None of us is the ultimate source of who he is, but being such an ultimate source is, for the revolutionary, necessary for responsibility; ergo, none of us is responsible for our choices, no matter what we choose, good or bad. Murdock gets no blame for pulling the trigger on his .38 at the Little Tavern, nor does Mother Teresa get any praise for devoting her life to the poor in Calcutta.

After the Revolution

The state was supposed to wither away under Marxism. The revolutionary doesn't expect the state to wither away, but he does expect its criminal law to disappear. The post-revolutionary state would still respond when one person harms another, but the response wouldn't amount to punishment.

[33] *See, e.g.*, Erik Luna, *Spoiled Rotten Social Background*, 2 Ala. C.R. & C.L. L. Rev. 23, 29 (2011) (asking if the "SRSB [spoiled rotten social background] defendant should be deemed *more* culpable and should receive a *harsher* punishment than less affluent offenders").

That would require moral responsibility, belief in which the revolutionary has shown to be a dangerous fiction. The "system of moral responsibility"[34] on which the criminal law rests must therefore be overthrown.[35]

Outlawing an emotion. That's where the revolutionary effort to remake the world begins, and the main emotion to be purged is anger, along with all its cognates, like resentment and indignation. Imagine asking Lieutenant King's parents how they feel about Murdock once he's been convicted of their son's murder. Anger would probably top the list. But their anger, the revolutionary would tell them, is misplaced, if not irrational. Anger might make sense if Murdock was morally responsible for their son's death, but he wasn't (not if the revolutionary is right). Moreover, what goes for Murdock's parents goes for the state. Assuming King's murder was a wrong against the state, the state has no reason to be angry about it, unless Murdock was morally responsible for killing King, but he wasn't (not if the revolutionary is right). Besides anger, guilt too would have to go, insofar as guilt is nothing more than self-directed anger. Murdock might regret killing King, but it would be irrational for him to feel guilty about it.

If anger no longer makes sense, then how we talk about crime and punishment will need to change. Before the revolution, Murdock committed a "crime," called "murder." After the revolution, with anger nonsensical, we'd have to call it something else. A crime is whatever gets punished, and although not everyone agrees, we'll stipulate that punishment, roughly speaking, is a burden imposed on someone for violating a rule in order to express anger or some such reactive attitude or emotion.[36] Thus, if anger makes

[34] *See* Bruce N. Waller, The Stubborn System of Moral Responsibility (2015).

[35] The revolutionary arrives at penal abolition because he's committed to what's known in the philosophical literature as "source incompatibilism." Other abolitionists get there because they're committed to what's known as "leeway incompatibilism." *See, e.g.*, Derk Pereboom, *Source Incompatibilism and Alternative Possibilities*, *in* Moral Responsibility and Alternative Possibilities: Essays on the Importance of Alternative Possibilities 185, 185–86 (David Widerker & Michael McKenna eds., 2003) (discussing the distinction between leeway incompatibilism and source incompatibilism); Kevin Timpe, *Leeway vs. Sourcehood Conceptions of Free Will*, *in* The Routledge Companion to Free Will 213 (Kevin Timpe et al., eds. 2017) (same). Leeway incompatibilists believe moral responsibility requires alternative possibilities. If determinism is true, then alternative possibilities are impossible, and according to the leeway incompatibilist, determinism is true. Therefore, no one has alternative possibilities; therefore, no one is responsible; therefore, no one should be punished, at least not if responsibility is a necessary condition for just punishment.

[36] *See* Joel Feinberg, *The Expressive Function of Punishment*, *in* Doing and Deserving: Essays on the Theory of Responsibility 95, 98 (1970) (The "characteristic, or specific difference [that distinguishes punishments from penalties] . . . is a certain expressive function: punishment is a conventional device for the expression of attitudes of resentment and indignation, and of judgments of disapproval and reprobation, on the part either of the punishing authority himself or of those 'in whose name' the punishment is inflicted."). The state can, of course, express reactive attitudes without imposing a burden. For example, a criminal conviction, all by itself, can express the state's

no sense, then neither does talk of "punishment," and if talk of "punishment" no longer makes sense, then neither does talk of "crime." After the revolution, talk about crime and punishment would be odd, a relic of an unenlightened past. A different, anger-free language would be needed to describe the choice Murdock made (since it can't be a crime), as well as the state's response thereto (since it can't be punishment).

Begin with anger's replacement. Candidates include disappointment, sadness, sorrow—and fury. Take fury. According to one philosopher, we experience fury when we confront a threat, whatever its origin. That distinguishes it from anger, which we experience when we confront a responsible wrongdoer.[37] Among the possible replacements for anger, resentment, indignation and so forth, fury is probably as close to them as the revolutionary can get. If so, then in the post-revolutionary world we would need to replace anger with fury. As for "crimes," we might replace them with "violations"; as for "punishments," we might replace them with "penalties."[38] Before the revolution, a crime was that which the state punished. After the revolution, a "crime" is a violation, and a violation is that which the state penalizes. Penalties might look like punishments, but they're not, because no anger (nor any other forbidden emotion or attitude) attends their imposition.

Along with these conceptual changes would come practical ones. Before the revolution, Murdock would be, as he was, tried for murder, and if convicted, as he was, punished. He might be imprisoned, as he was. Pursuant to the applicable law, the judge might justify Murdock's sentence in the name of retribution, according to which Murdock's lost liberty is reckoned an intrinsic good. Or perhaps the judge cites the need to keep Murdock imprisoned as a warning to other would-be murderers (general deterrence), or to teach Murdock himself a lesson (specific deterrence). Or, believing Murdock to be especially dangerous, perhaps the judge sends him away long enough to

condemnation of the crime. The burden element is separate, and needs a separate justification, which is the work a "theory" of punishment is meant to perform. For a recent argument against Feinberg's thesis that punishment's expressive function is necessary to distinguish punishment from other kinds of non-punitive hard treatment, see Ambrose Y.K. Lee, *Arguing Against the Expressive Function of Punishment: Is the Standard Account That Insufficient?*, 38 Law & Phil. 359, 384 (2019).

[37] *See* Pereboom, Meaning, *supra* note 18, at 147 ("Fury, as I am understanding it, is an emotion we share with bears and wolves, and has no cognitive content or presupposition or associated belief that involves the notion of desert. If it has associated content, it's perhaps that there's a threat to be neutralized.").

[38] Feinberg, *supra* note 36, at 96 (distinguishing "punishments" from "penalties").

make sure he won't get out until he's an old man, and as such likely to be dangerous no more (incapacitation).

The revolution changes this familiar picture.[39] Assuming he contests the charge, Murdock would still get some process post-revolution, though not a full-blown trial to determine guilt beyond a reasonable doubt. (Remember: The revolution does away with guilt.) The post-revolutionary process, whatever its details, would instead be designed to determine "clutchability."[40] Someone found to have committed a violation would thereby find himself in the state's clutches. Once there, he'd be assessed for dangerousness, not punished.[41] If found safe (or safe enough), he'd get a good talking to, during which the state's disappointment, sadness, fury and so forth would presumably be expressed. Yet beyond that he'd be free to go, since the state would have no reason to detain him any further.

If found dangerous, and if monitoring on the outside would be enough to protect the rest of us against the risk of future depredations, then he'd be

[39] For accounts of what should replace the current criminal justice system, once we accept the truth of "free will skepticism," see, for example, Greg D. Caruso, *The Public Health-Quarantine Model*, *in* OXFORD HANDBOOK OF MORAL RESPONSIBILITY (Dana Nelkin & Derk Pereboom eds., forthcoming); Derk Pereboom, *Incapacitation, Reintegration, and Limited General Deterrence*, NEUROETHICS (forthcoming) [hereinafter Pereboom, *Incapacitation*]; Derk Pereboom, *A Defense of Free Will Skepticism*, 11 CRIM. L. & PHIL. 617, 624 (2017) [hereinafter Pereboom, *A Defense*]; Derk Pereboom, *Free Will Skepticism and Criminal Punishment*, *in* THE FUTURE OF PUNISHMENT 49 (Thomas A. Nadelhoffer ed., 2013).

[40] JOEL FEINBERG, *Crime, Clutchability, and Individuated Treatment*, *in* DOING AND DESERVING: ESSAYS ON THE THEORY OF RESPONSIBILITY 252, 267 (1970) ("[P]erhaps the words 'guilty' and 'innocent' might be expunged altogether, and defendants be found 'clutchable as charged' or 'unclutchable.'").

[41] Assessments of future dangerousness are notoriously unreliable, but set that aside, along with current controversies surrounding the fairness of using of algorithms to predict recidivism (on which see, for example, Deborah Hellman, *Measuring Algorithmic Fairness*, VA. L. REV. (forthcoming 2020). The revolutionary's focus on dangerousness raises another, more pressing question. If a violation is needed only because it provides evidence of dangerousness, why not cut to the chase? Why not let the state clutch anyone it has good reason to believe is dangerous, violation or no violation? *See, e.g.*, John Lemos, *Moral Concerns About Responsibility Denial and the Quarantine of Violent Criminals*, 35 LAW & PHIL. 461, 483 (2016) ("[W]hen one rejects belief in moral responsibility then one loses the resources to explain the inherent wrongness of punishing innocent persons and this is what makes responsibility deniers vulnerable to the problem of punishing the innocent.").

That's a fair question, but revolutionaries seldom address it so far as I can tell. Those who do usually say that a variety of considerations, like the right to liberty, or the concern against using people merely as means, prevents the state from detaining us until we've actually committed a violation. *See, e.g.*, Pereboom, *A Defense*, *supra* note 39, at 624. We enjoy, they say, a defeasible right to remain free from the state's clutches, at least until we commit a violation, though presumably a clutchable violation could be nothing more than forming an intent to hurt someone, with or without doing anything to follow through on that intention. *See, e.g.*, *id.* ("[A] demonstrable intention [to cause harm] standard is legally feasible."). Of course, if a democratic state decided through the democratic process to make the formation of a firm intent to commit a crime itself a crime, doing so would not run afoul of the *actus reus* requirement, whatever one might believe about that decision as a matter of justice. *See* Chapter 1, *infra* at pp. 84–85.

monitored. If monitoring wasn't enough, then but only then would he be sent to a decently accommodated "detention facility," where he'd be kept "quarantined" in the name of specific deterrence and incapacitation for purposes of public safety,[42] with general deterrence being an unintended but nonetheless inevitable side effect.[43] He would, as a matter of course, be offered rehabilitation services during any period of detention. When releasing him was safe, he'd be released. If releasing him was never safe, he'd never be released.[44] "No More Punishment! Quarantine Only, If Necessary, for Self-Defense!" So might go the revolution's banner slogan.

Resistance

Under the logic of revolutionary morality, if the United States were to lock Murdock up for twenty-five years for having caused King's death, ostensibly as "punishment" for his "crime," it would be guilty of having wronged him, not the other way around, since Murdock wasn't morally responsible for King's death. On second thought, of course, that can't be quite right. The state can't be guilty of wrongfully punishing Murdock, because it, like Murdock, presumably lacks responsibility for whatever it does. Guilt presupposes responsibility, but the revolutionary rejects the idea of moral responsibility altogether. If so, and if natural persons aren't morally responsible for anything, then neither presumably are states.[45]

[42] The idea of replacing punishment with quarantine is usually attributed to Ferdinand D. Schoeman, *On Incapacitating the Dangerous*, 16 AM. PHIL. Q. 27 (1979).

[43] Pereboom does allow "monetary penalties" and short-term detention to be imposed for the purpose of general deterrence, such that under limited conditions general deterrence would not merely be a side effect. *See* Pereboom, *Incapacitation*, *supra* note 39 (manuscript at 6–9).

[44] *See id.* (manuscript at 5) ("If a criminal cannot be reintegrated, and if protection of society demands his indefinite confinement, there would be no justification for making his life more miserable than is needed to guard against the danger he poses."). Criminal law theorists will recall Lady Barbara Wootten, whose well-known proposal along similar lines (over 50 years ago) prompted H.L.A. Hart's equally well-known response. *See* BARBARA WOOTTON, CRIME AND THE CRIMINAL LAW: REFLECTIONS OF A MAGISTRATE AND SOCIAL SCIENTIST (1963); H.L.A. HART, *Changing Conceptions of Criminal Responsibility*, *in* PUNISHMENT AND RESPONSIBILITY: ESSAYS ON THE PHILOSOPHY OF LAW 186, 206–09 (2d ed. 2008) (1968).

[45] In this connection, Larry Alexander argues that after the revolution, when we've all become free-will skeptics, "normativity completely disappears." *See* Larry Alexander, Hard Incompatibilism, and the Rejection of Moral Responsibility: A Skeptical Look at an Optimistic Account (Apr. 24, 2018) (unpublished manuscript at 5). Of course, the revolutionary disagrees, insisting that, whatever happens to "normativity," we can still find post-revolutionary meaning in life. *See, e.g.*, PEREBOOM, MEANING, *supra* note 18, at 175 (arguing that the "skeptical perspective does not threaten personal relationships, and that it holds out the promise of better relationships through release from reactive attitudes such as moral resentment and indignation").

Not all anarchists are prepared to join the revolutionary at the ramparts. On the contrary, some would oppose the revolution, joining the resistance against the revolutionary broadside on moral responsibility. We arrive at penal abolition, the resistance observes, only if we're prepared to travel the full length of the revolutionary road, all the way from Stop One to Stop Four.

The revolutionary road is meant to be a slippery slope. Take the first step, and you're supposed to have no way to stop the slide to the bottom.[46] Faced with an argument resting on slippery-slope logic, you can avoid its conclusion in at least two ways, and members of the resistance have pursued both. First, don't take the first step. If you don't take the first step, never arriving at Stop One, then you won't risk the long slide to Stop Four. This is the hard-line response to the revolutionary, which is hard inasmuch as it draws a hard line before Stop One.

Recall that at Stop One, Murdock was little more than Nefario's puppet, and the revolutionary wanted you to agree that Murdock-1, as a puppet, wasn't morally responsible for killing King. If you agreed, then you were on board and thus on the way to Stop Four. The hard-liner refuses to take the bait. He refuses to get on board because he doesn't agree: He believes Murdock-1 was responsible, puppet or not.

The second way to avoid a slippery-slope conclusion, even if you do take the first step, is to regain your footing before hitting bottom. This is the soft-line response to the revolutionary. Once you agree Murdock-1 wasn't morally responsible for killing King, the revolutionary wanted more. No principled difference, he invited you to agree, could be found between Murdock-1 and Murdock-4, so if Murdock-1 wasn't morally responsible, neither was Murdock-4. The soft-liner declines the invitation. The soft-liner believes, contra the hard-liner, that Murdock-1 wasn't responsible, but also believes, contra the revolutionary, that later versions of Murdock, at some point down the road, do bear responsibility for King's death. That being so, the revolutionary road leads somewhere, but not all the way to penal abolition.

Soft Resistance

Begin with the soft-line response. According to the revolutionary, Murdock-1 wasn't morally responsible when he killed Lieutenant King because he was subject to Dr. Nefario's ongoing neuro-manipulations. Soft-liners

[46] *See* Pereboom, Meaning, *supra* note 18, at 173–74 ("The core idea is that the right to harm in self-defense and defense of others justifies incapacitating the criminally dangerous with the minimum of harm required for adequate protection.").

happily agree: Murdock-1 wasn't responsible. If anyone was, it was Nefario. Nonetheless, soft-liners don't think the concession forces them to embrace penal abolition. A principled line, they believe, can be drawn somewhere between Stop One and Stop Four.

Some soft-liners draw the line between Stop One and Two. As they see it, Murdock-2 isn't like Murdock-1. Nefario micro-managed Murdock-1's beliefs and desires in real-time, whereas Nefario macro-managed Murdock-2's character in utero or altered it sometime thereafter, maybe through brainwashing. That difference, according to some soft-liners, makes a difference. As long as Murdock-2, despite Nefario's intervention, was otherwise morally responsible for killing King (on your preferred theory of moral responsibility), that's all it takes to hold him accountable. Nefario's machinations are rotten luck for Murdock-2, but that doesn't undermine his responsibility for pulling the trigger, because unlike Murdock-1-the-puppet, Murdock-2 isn't being manipulated on the fly.

Other soft-liners are prepared to travel further down the road. Compare Murdock-1, who Nefario manipulated from moment to moment, or Murdock-2, who Nefario manipulated through genetic preprogramming or brainwashing, with the Murdock-3, who became the person he was due to a rotten social background. One difference is obvious: Nefario is on the scene at Stops One and Two, but absent at Stop Three. Nefario manipulated Murdock at Stops One and Two, whereas no one manipulated him at Stop Three. If Murdock's choice to kill resulted from someone else's agency, like Nefario's, then he's not responsible, but if it didn't, then he is. Thus, according to this soft-line reply, a principled reason can be offered for staying on board through Stop Two, but taking an off-ramp before reaching Stop Three.[47]

Still other soft-liners stay aboard at Stop Three but get off before Stop Four. They see where the revolutionary's logic is intended to lead them, and they feel its force. Just the same, they can't quite bring themselves to follow the revolution through to the end. Someone who chooses to commit a crime when his character was forged in poverty and despair (Stop Three) is one thing. Someone who chooses to commit the same crime but suffered

[47] For soft-line replies of this sort, see, for example, ISHTIYAQUE HAJI, INCOMPATIBILISM'S ALLURE: PRINCIPAL ARGUMENTS FOR INCOMPATIBILISM 135 (2009) (emphasizing the difference between cases of indoctrination (not responsible) and those involving a "normal upbringing" (responsible)); MELE, FREE WILL, *supra* note 18, at 170 (emphasizing the difference between cases in which an actor's "capacity for control over his inner life" is "bypassed by processes that instill in him deliberative habits of certain kinds" (not responsible) and those in which his capacity for control over his inner life is not so bypassed (responsible)).

no disadvantage (Stop Four) is another.[48] Their instinct tells them non-disadvantaged Murdock-4 is responsible, but disadvantaged Murdock-3 isn't. Whether these reformers can persuasively hold the line at Stop Three is an open question. Whether one's luck is good or bad, it's still just luck. Murdock-3 wasn't the ultimate source of whatever springs of action caused him to kill King in the Little Tavern, but then again, neither was Murdock-4.

Needless to say, none of these soft-line resistance strategies will persuade the revolutionary. He'll soldier on, hoping to get the reformer to see the light, just as the reformer will try to persuade him to see the error of his ways. In a democratic state, the disagreement between them will be authoritatively resolved, as are all such disagreements, through the democratic process. Perhaps the revolutionary will someday prevail, in which case the state will dismantle its penal apparatus. Or perhaps the soft-liner will prevail, in which case the state's penal apparatus will remain, though it might range over fewer people than it otherwise would. All else being equal, either course of action is a legitimate course of action.

Hard Resistance

The soft-liner accepted the revolutionary's assessment of Murdock-1's responsibility. Someone who, like Murdock-1, kills while being manipulated like a puppet, the soft-liner concurred, isn't morally responsible. Hard-liners decline to take even that small step. They believe that Murdock-1, as long as he was otherwise responsible for killing King (according to your preferred theory of moral responsibility), would remain responsible, despite being neuro-manipulated. Now that really is taking a hard line.[49]

[48] For what might be construed as responses along these lines, see, for example, MARTHA KLEIN, DETERMINISM, BLAMEWORTHINESS, AND DEPRIVATION 173 (1990) (stating that "there can be no just blame or punishment . . . [but we cannot] give up reacting punitively and condemning when strong moral feelings are aroused," and suggesting that someone like Murdock-3 should be punished less, or not at all, because he, unlike Murdock-4, has due to his rotten social background "paid-in-advance"); Benjamin Ewing, *Recent Work on Punishment and Criminogenic Disadvantage*, 37 LAW & PHIL. 29, 65 (2018) (suggesting we might be able to "draw a morally principled distinction" between someone like Murdock-3 and someone like Murdock-4 inasmuch as Murdock-3, but not Murdock-4, lacked "a fair 'moral' opportunity" to avoid culpable wrongdoing); R. George Wright, *The Progressive Logic of Criminal Responsibility and the Circumstances of the Most Deprived*, 43 CATH. U.L. REV. 459, 489 (1994) ("Admittedly, no one, regardless of economic class position, is in control of all elements that may crucially affect her ability to comply with legal norms," but "it does not follow . . . that if we absolve some of the most deprived . . . , we should equally absolve those whose crimes . . . stemmed from wealth and advantage," because "we can point to dramatic asymmetries between the unchosen environments of the most privileged and the most deprived.").

[49] For the best-known hard-line reply to Pereboom's four-case argument, see Michael McKenna, *A Hard-line Reply to Pereboom's Four-Case Argument*, 77 PHIL. & PHENOMENOLOGICAL RES. 142 (2008); Michael McKenna, *Resisting the Manipulation Argument: A Hard-Liner Takes It on the Chin*, 89 PHIL. & PHENOMENOLOGICAL RES. 89 (2014); Michael McKenna, *Manipulation Arguments, Basic Desert,*

Indeed, the hard-line reply is so hard it requires a detour in our story. We've thus far been asking how a philosophical anarchist might respond when faced with the facts of the real Murdock's case, and one response was revolution, with the revolutionary believing it would be unjust for the United States to punish Murdock because it would be unjust for any state to punish anyone. We're now entertaining the hard-line reply to the revolutionary, but assessing that reply will, as we'll see, implicate the concerns motivating the statist, and in particular, the concern to identify some lines beyond which a democratic state cannot legitimately ascribe culpability.

Returning to the hard-line response, you might think that a statist would say the dispute between the hard-liner and the revolutionary should be settled in a democratic state through the democratic process, just like the dispute between the soft-liner and the revolutionary. Suppose the issue is joined and the hard-liner prevails in the democratic process. A vote is taken and the law is settled such that defendants like Murdock-1 are provided with no defense to criminal liability. When the state punishes neuro-manipulated Murdock-1, Murdock-1 could thus complain he's being punished unjustly, but he couldn't complain he's being punished illegitimately. The People have spoken.

Or could he complain? Could Murdock-1 complain his punishment was illegitimate, and not merely unjust? Answering that question would mean applying the reasonable doubt test, thereby drawing the line between legitimate and illegitimate state action. You'd have to ask yourself if you believe it would be unjust, beyond reasonable doubt, for a democratic state to punish someone like neuro-manipulated Murdock-1. If you believe it would not be unjust beyond reasonable doubt, then you should believe punishing Murdock-1 is within the state's authority. If you believe it would be unjust beyond reasonable doubt, then you should believe punishing him would exceed the state's authority.

Before offering the answer we'd give to that question, we need to know more about Murdock-1. Nefario changes or modifies Murdock-1's desires in real-time, thereby causing him to kill King. What we need to know is how Murdock-1 *experienced* those manipulations. Specifically, the question is

and Moral Responsibility: Assessing Derk Pereboom's Free Will, Agency, and Meaning in Life, 11 Crim. L. & Phil. 575 (2017). Victor Tadros offers a tempered hard-line reply. *See* Victor Tadros, Wrongs and Crimes 73 (2016) ("Hard-liners are . . . right to conclude that if compatibilist conditions of responsibility are fulfilled, agents have personal practical responsibility for their wrongdoing even if they are manipulated. Manipulation *weakens*, rather than destroys, responsibility.") (emphasis added).

whether Murdock-1, despite Nefario's manipulations, continues to experience himself as the author or agent of the beliefs and desires moving him to make the choice to kill King. In other words, we need to know whether Murdock-1 retained a sense of agency, despite Nefario's manipulations, as he pulled the trigger.

First, suppose Nefario not only implants, from moment-to-moment, the beliefs and desires causing Murdock-1 to kill King, but also does whatever he needs to do to make sure Murdock-1 retains his sense of agency. When Murdock-1 kills King, he experiences himself as its author: as the one in control. In that case, Murdock-1 would, according to some hard-liners, satisfy all the conditions anyone could ask for in order to hold him liable. He might be less responsible, due to Nefario's manipulations, but that doesn't mean he's not responsible at all. Unless we're prepared to say that this hard-line position—albeit one taken on a hypothetical set of facts wildly removed from any known reality—is unjust beyond reasonable doubt, which we're not, then we'd be obliged to say that Murdock-1's fate must be left to the democratic process to settle, assuming Nefario not only pulls Murdock-1's strings but implants in him a sense of agency as well.

Second, suppose Nefario's manipulations leave Murdock-1 without a sense of agency. He doesn't experience himself as the author of the beliefs and desires behind his choice. Maybe he comes to believe someone else is in control, or maybe he has no belief one way or the other about who's in control. All he knows is that it's not him. If so, then, as we saw in Chapter 5, Murdock-1 would be insane, for want of a sense of agency. Moreover, and if sanity is a necessary condition for legitimate punishment, as Chapter 5 proposed, then Murdock-1, like anyone who's lost his sense of agency, would be immune to state punishment.

For all their differences, the revolutionary, the soft-liner, and the hard-liner stand together as philosophical anarchists. The only authority they countenance—the only authority there is—is the authority of morality. They sharply disagree about what morality and justice require, but they all agree that's where the action is. We now turn to another anarchical response to Murdock's punishment, which comes from the reformer.

Reform

Like the revolutionary, the reformer is an anarchist, believing no state has authority. Unlike the revolutionary, however, the reformer doesn't believe responsibility is a myth or illusion. Nor does he call for penal abolition. Instead, he calls for reform, believing justice requires the state to respond to unjustly disadvantaged offenders one way, and everyone else (call them advantaged offenders) in a different way, all else being equal. That belief raises two immediate questions.

First, what makes someone "unjustly disadvantaged"? Different people may have different states of affairs in mind when they speak of unjust disadvantage, but for present purposes the following should suffice: A person is unjustly disadvantaged (poor, severely environmentally deprived, dispossessed, and so forth—choose your descriptor) when through the state's acts or omissions he's been denied what he's entitled to pursuant to some theory of distributive justice. Choose whichever theory of distributive justice you wish. The academic market offers an abundance of choices.[50] All we need for now is some theory by which to sort offenders into one category (disadvantaged, meaning hereafter unjustly disadvantaged) or the other (advantaged). Again, reformers might disagree among themselves. One might classify a person as disadvantaged; another might put him in the advantaged category. Again, that's by the by. All we need for now are the two categories.

Second, according to the reformer, the state should, as a matter of justice, respond to crimes of the disadvantaged differently compared to how it should respond to crimes of the advantaged. But how should its response differ? The answer, as we'll see, depends on why the reformer believes justice requires a differential response in the first place. We'll consider two theories: the culpability theory and the standing theory.

The culpability theory focuses on the disadvantaged offender. Insofar as the state has treated the disadvantaged unjustly, a disadvantaged offender is on this theory alleged to be somehow less culpable, morally speaking, than is his advantaged counterpart, all else being equal. Justice therefore requires the state to provide the disadvantaged offender with a partial defense, or fixed mitigation at sentencing, designed to reflect the difference

[50] For overviews of the many theories on offer, see, for example, Richard J. Arneson, *Justice*, *in* THE OXFORD HANDBOOK OF POLITICAL PHILOSOPHY 58 (David Estlund ed., 2012); Julian Lamont & Christi Ford, *Distributive Justice*, STAN. ENCYCLOPEDIA PHIL. (2017). For a recent discussion of distributive justice within the liberal tradition, see SAMUEL FREEMAN, LIBERALISM AND DISTRIBUTIVE JUSTICE (2018), and for a short history of distributive justice, from Aristotle to Rawls and beyond, see SAMUEL FLEISCHACKER, A SHORT HISTORY OF DISTRIBUTIVE JUSTICE (2004).

between his moral culpability and that of the advantaged offender, all else being equal.[51]

The standing theory focuses on the state. According to this theory, even if disadvantaged offenders are as morally culpable as advantaged offenders, justice nonetheless requires the state to treat them differently. Insofar as the state has treated the disadvantaged offender unjustly, justice strips the state of the moral standing it would otherwise have had to hold disadvantaged offenders criminally liable, and without standing it has no moral permission to punish. Justice therefore requires the state to provide a disadvantaged defendant with an estoppel defense forestalling any effort the state might make to call him to account. Because the state's hands are dirty vis-á-vis disadvantaged offenders, it would be unjust for the state to haul the disadvantaged into court and sit in judgment of them, at least until it washes clean its own hands.

Culpability

Reformers embracing the culpability theory believe the state should punish a disadvantage offender less than his advantaged twin, because the disadvantaged offender is, all else being equal, less morally culpable. Failing to give the disadvantaged a punishment discount, and so punishing him as much as the advantaged, would therefore be unjust. The reformer's burden is to offer a theory explaining how the state's failure to live up to the demands of distributive justice apropos the disadvantaged manages to render the disadvantaged less culpable when they commit the same crime an advantaged offender commits.[52]

[51] Is the moral culpability of the disadvantaged diminished, or is the moral culpability of the advantaged augmented? It depends on the baseline. Most discussions set the baseline in reference to the advantaged, such that the culpability of the disadvantaged is said to be diminished relative to the culpability of the advantaged.

[52] The culpability theory described in the text isn't the only theory a reformer might offer to explain why a disadvantaged offender should be punished less than his advantaged counterpart. At least four other theories worth noting, each focused somehow on the offender rather than on the state, can be found in the literature.

According to the first theory, insofar as the state has treated a disadvantaged offender unjustly, it should permit (or perhaps obligate) some state actor—judge, jury, chief executive—to impose less punishment, all else being equal, not as a matter of justice, but as a matter of compassion or mercy. *See, e.g.*, Andrew von Hirsch & Andrew Ashworth, Proportionate Sentencing: Exploring the Principles 65–70 (2005).

According to the second theory, insofar as the state has treated a disadvantaged offender unjustly, the unjust deprivation he suffered as a result should, as a matter of justice (and not simply as a matter compassion or mercy), be offset or be credited against whatever otherwise just deprivation

Consider a hypothetical, comparing the real Murdock with a fictional Durlock. Murdock, we know, grew up in Watts, "in a large family with little money and little love or attention."[53] His father deserted his mother. That's about all we know. For argument's sake, let's add: He never graduated from high school, dropping out in the 10th grade. He was also unemployed. The only jobs around, if he could have gotten one, paid minimum wage. His father was eventually imprisoned. His mother died of an overdose when he was twelve. He lives with his grandmother in a crime-ridden public housing project. They survive, just barely, on public assistance. All that, let's agree, puts Murdock in the "disadvantaged" category.

Like Murdock, Durlock is twenty years old. He goes to a local community college, living with his parents in a middle-class neighborhood in Glendale. He plans on going to a four-year college next year. He works at Walmart part-time. His mother teaches high school. His father is a police officer. His parents pay for college, as well as food, clothes, and so forth. When not in class or studying, he hangs out with friends, playing soccer and video games.

he would receive as punishment for his crime. *See, e.g.*, Peter Chau, *Poverty, Distributive Justice, and Punishment*, 25 CAN. J.L. & JURIS. 39, 42–44 (2012).

The third theory is related to the second but broader in scope. According to this theory, insofar as an offender (including but not limited to the disadvantaged) has suffered unjust deprivation, such unjust deprivation should, as a matter of justice, be offset or be credited against whatever otherwise just deprivation he would receive as punishment for his crime, *whether or not* the state is responsible for the prior unjust deprivation. *See, e.g.*, Larry Alexander, *Retributive Justice*, *in* THE OXFORD HANDBOOK OF DISTRIBUTIVE JUSTICE 177, 184–86 (Serene Olsaretti ed., 2018); Gertrude Ezorsky, *The Ethics of Punishment*, *in* PHILOSOPHICAL PERSPECTIVES ON PUNISHMENT xi, xxvi–xxv (Gertrude Ezorsky ed., 1972).

Perhaps the most popular theory is the fourth one. According to this theory, insofar as the average disadvantaged offender has, compared to the average advantaged offender, better reasons (judged against the same standard) to engage in criminal wrongdoing, the average disadvantaged offender is less culpable, all else being equal, than the average advantaged offender and should therefore be punished less. *See, e.g.*, RICHARD L. LIPPKE, RETHINKING IMPRISONMENT 84–88 (2007); Jules Holyrod, *Punishment and Justice*, 36 SOC. THEORY & PRAC. 78, 99–100 (2010); Christopher Lewis, *Inequality, Incentives, Criminality, and Blame*, 22 LEGAL THEORY 153, 169 (2016); Michael Tonry, *Can Deserts Be Just in an Unjust World?*, *in* LIBERAL CRIMINAL THEORY 141, 156 (A.P. Simester et al. eds., 2014). Because this fourth theory rests on claims about the average disadvantaged offender, compared to the average advantaged offender, it elides "difficulties in discerning the extent to which any given offender's actions have been affected by social deprivation [and] the magnitude of the sentence discount an offender warrants because of it," Richard L. Lippke, *Social Deprivation as Tempting Fate*, 5 CRIM. L. & PHIL. 277, 290 (2011), and so "does not seem to supply a *general* basis for reducing the punishments of deprived offenders." VON HIRSCH & ASHWORTH, *supra*, at 65 (emphasis added). Among those who criticize these reformist theories, Stephen Morse remains the most prominent. *See* Stephen J. Morse, *Deprivation and Desert*, *in* FROM SOCIAL JUSTICE TO CRIMINAL JUSTICE: POVERTY AND THE ADMINISTRATION OF CRIMINAL LAW 114 (William C. Heffernan & John Kleinig eds., 2000) [hereinafter Morse, *Deprivation*]; Morse, supra note 30, *passim*.

[53] United States v. Alexander, 471 F.2d 923, 958 (D.C. Cir. 1973).

He's not filthy rich, but neither is he poor. All that, let's agree, puts Durlock in the "advantaged" category.

Now for the crime. A year before his fateful encounter with Lieutenant King, imagine Murdock sold heroin to a sixteen-year-old high school student. Murdock realized he was committing a crime, but wanted the money to buy the latest iPhone. Likewise, at the same time, Durlock decides to sell the same amount of heroin to another sixteen-year-old high school student. He, too, realized he was committing a crime, but he, too, wanted the money for the latest iPhone. Both are charged with violating California Health and Safety Code § 11352(a), which criminalizes the sale of heroin. Each is convicted and receives a sentence of four years' imprisonment.

Reformers realize that Murdock's and Durlock's fate, based on those facts, is sealed, at least under existing law. Each satisfies the elements of the crime charged, and neither has any defense. No matter. The reformer isn't interested in existing law. He wants the law to change, to make it better conform to justice. That means the state should, in the name of justice, add to its penal code a partial defense or fixed mitigation for disadvantaged defendants like Murdock, such that in the end Murdock gets less punishment than Durlock. Maybe Durlock gets four years, and Murdock gets two or three.

Justice demands a shorter sentence for Murdock than for Durlock because, the reformer insists, Murdock is necessarily less culpable for violating § 11352(a) than is Durlock, all else being equal, and he's less culpable just in virtue of being disadvantaged. The hard question is why. Why is Murdock less culpable than Durlock, just because he falls into the disadvantaged category and Durlock falls into the advantaged category? The reformer's answer (or at least one answer) comes in three steps.

First, the reformer tells us, we need to determine the structure of Murdock's (conative) will at the time he chose to φ, i.e., to sell heroin in violation of § 11352(a). We find, of course, exactly what we'd expect. The force of Murdock's motivational reasons in favor of φ-ing (selling heroin) was greater than the motivational force of his reasons against φ-ing. In other words, $\Sigma MR_{\varphi} > \Sigma MR_{\sim\varphi}$, and because $\Sigma MR_{\varphi} > \Sigma MR_{\sim\varphi}$, Murdock chose to sell heroin. Selling heroin to the high school student was what he most wanted to do at the moment he did it. When we turn and look at Durlock's will, we naturally discover the same structure. He, too, wanted most to sell heroin to the high school student at the moment he sold it.

Now, at the time Murdock and Durlock sold the heroin, some measure of concern for the law and its ends—including the well-being of the high school student to whom they sold—may have been among their reasons not to sell. Let's assume it was, with x representing its motivational force.[54] Because Murdock and Durlock are meant to be the same, except for the fact that the former is disadvantaged and the latter isn't, we assume the value of x for both Murdock and Durlock is the same. For sure, x, combined with whatever other reasons Murdock and Durlock had not to sell heroin, was insufficient to defeat the motivational force of their reasons in favor of selling. Each chose to sell despite whatever concern they may have had for the law or the buyer's welfare.

Second, having determined the structure of Murdock's and Durlock's will, we need to judge its quality. For that we need some standard. Compared to what was the quality of their will either deficient (thereby making them culpable) or not (thereby making them non-culpable)? Suppose we take, as the relevant standard, the will of a law-abiding citizen. The will of a law-abiding citizen includes, among its motivational reasons, concern for the law and its ends, and moreover, the force of that reason is as strong as it should be: It has a force as strong as a democratic state can legitimately expect of its citizens. Say the strength of that reason is equal to y. Whatever value we assign to y, it has to be greater than 0. For a law-abiding citizen, the motivational force attached to conforming to the law must amount to something.

How does the value of y, the motivational force of a law-abiding citizen's concern for the law, compare to x, the motivational force of Murdock's and Durlock's concern for the law? It must be less, because if it had been as strong as that of a law-abiding citizen, they would have conformed to the law, but they didn't. Thus, $x < y$. The difference between x and y is the difference between the motivational force of Murdock's and Durlock's actual concern for the law and the concern they should have had, compared to a law-abiding citizen. Call this difference n, which tells us how much less concern Murdock and Durlock had compared to the concern they should have had. It thus represents a measure of their culpability. Because Murdock's actual concern and Durlock's actual concern is the same, their lack of concern or culpability must also be the same.

Now for the third step. If we judge the quality of Murdock's and Durlock's will against the same standard, i.e., that of a law-abiding citizen, then one is just as culpable as the other: They're equally culpable. But that's a mistake,

[54] This assumes neither Murdock nor Durlock disrespects the law, such that not conforming to it would have motivational force.

according to the reformer. We shouldn't, as a matter of justice, judge the quality of Murdock's will against the standard of a law-abiding citizen.

The reason why not is simple. Because the state has treated Murdock unjustly, Murdock, as a disadvantaged citizen, has less reason to conform to the law compared to a law-abiding citizen.[55] The state can't, as a matter of justice, expect disadvantaged citizens to care as much about the law, or the ends it serves and defends, as it does advantaged citizens. The state can, as a matter of justice, expect the advantaged to be law-abiding, but it can't expect the same measure of law-abidance from those it's treated unjustly. The quality of Murdock's will should therefore be judged against the standard, not of a law-abiding citizen, but against the standard of a disadvantaged citizen.

If the motivational force of a law-abiding citizen's concern for the law is y, then the motivational force of a disadvantaged citizen's concern for the law, call it z, must be less than y. Thus, $z < y$. Again, according to the reformer, we should, as a matter of justice, judge the quality of Murdock's will against z and the quality of Durlock's will against y.

Once more, let x represent the motivational force, if any, of Murdock's and Durlock's concern for the law. As the reformer would have it, the quality of Murdock's will should be judged in comparison to z (i.e., the concern for the law the state can legitimately demand of disadvantaged citizens), and the quality of Durlock's will should be judged in comparison to y (i.e., the concern for the law the state can legitimately demand of law-abiding citizens). Because $z < y$, the difference between z and x will be less than the difference between y and x. That means the quality of Durlock's will ends up being judged worse than the quality of Murdock's, which means Durlock is more culpable than Murdock, and Murdock less culpable than Durlock.[56]

The reformer then generalizes. All else being equal, when a disadvantaged citizen commits a crime, his culpability will be less than that of an advantaged citizen who commits the same crime, because the standard against which

[55] Jeffrey Reiman makes a similar claim when he writes: "[I]njustice reduces [disadvantaged criminals'] moral obligation to obey the law and thereby reduces the moral wrongness of their law-breaking." Jeffrey Reiman, *The Moral Ambivalence of Crime in an Unjust Society*, CRIM. JUST. ETHICS, at 3, 8 (Summer/Fall 2007). Whereas Reiman believes the disadvantaged are guilty of a lesser wrong when they commit a crime, the reformer described in the text believes they're less culpable.

[56] An example might help. Suppose x (the motivational force of Murdock's and Durlock's concern) equals 2; z (the motivational force of a disadvantaged citizen's concern) equals 5; and y (the motivational force of a law-abiding citizen's concern) equals 10. That means the quality of Murdock's will is $x - z$, or $2 - 5 = -3$, and the quality of Durlock's will is $x - y$, or $2 - 10 = -8$. Thus: Durlock's will is judged more ill than Murdock's, making him more culpable compared to Murdock, and Murdock less culpable compared to Durlock.

justice requires the quality of a disadvantaged citizen's will to be judged is less demanding (and more forgiving) than the standard against which an advantaged citizen's quality of the will should be judged. Justice therefore requires the state to punish disadvantaged citizens less, all else being equal, compared to advantaged citizens, because disadvantaged citizens are less culpable, all else being equal, compared to advantaged citizens. Moreover, they're less culpable just because they're disadvantaged. Consequently, the state should, as a matter of justice, enact a partial defense or fixed mitigation available only to the disadvantaged.

The reformer believes justice requires the culpability of the disadvantaged to be judged against a different and less demanding standard than the culpability of the advantaged. But that, one might object, is mistaken: Justice requires all citizens, disadvantaged or not, to be judged according to the same standard. The thought that the disadvantaged should be held to a lower standard rests on the misguided premise that the obligation to conform to the law is less demanding for the disadvantaged, when its force, according to the critic, is and should be the same for all. The force of the duty to abide by the law isn't diminished just because the state hasn't, for example, adhered to the difference principle.

Unless we're prepared to say, as the reformer might, that it would be unjust beyond reasonable doubt to punish the disadvantaged the same as the advantaged, all else being equal; or unless we're prepared to say, as the critic might, that it would be unjust beyond reasonable doubt to punish them differently, the disagreement between them should be resolved democratically. If so, the reformer must persuade his fellow citizens to adopt his vision of justice and translate it into law, and the critic must do the same. Nonetheless, whatever the outcome, neither the critic nor the reformer should wrap their complaint in the language of legitimacy, unless once again, we're prepared to say one or the other's beliefs about justice are true beyond reasonable doubt.

Standing

The next reform theory focuses, not on an accused's culpability for committing a crime, but on the state's standing to call him to account for it. When Murdock (or some other member of the disadvantaged class) commits a crime, this theory assumes he's culpable. Nor does it alleged any difference in culpability to explain why justice demands Murdock be treated one way and his advantaged counterpart another. Instead, justice demands different treatment because, whereas the state has standing to punish the advantaged, it lacks standing to punish the disadvantaged. Punishment is a two-way street. It requires an accused guilty of a crime, but it also requires a state with the standing to punish him.[57]

The standing theory assumes morality gives the state standing or permission to punish culpable wrongdoers,[58] but it also assumes said standing or permission can be forfeited. In Chapter 1, I offered two reasons a philosophical anarchist might give to believe a state has standing to punish in the first place.[59] According to one, morality gives the state standing to punish because, assuming the job has to go to someone, the state is most likely, among the possible candidates, to punish in the way justice requires. According to the other, morality gives the state standing insofar as the state "shares" the wrong the real victim suffered at the wrongdoer's hands. In any case, all we need for now is some plausible reason to believe morality gives the state standing or permission to punish.

Alas, what morality giveth, morality can taketh away. A state can, as a moral matter, forfeit its standing to punish. One reason morality might strip a state of its standing is grounded in the state's failure to do as morality requires outside the criminal law, in the domain of distributive justice.[60] According to the reformer, when a state fails to do as distributive justice requires, thereby creating or tolerating the continued existence of a disadvantaged class, it forfeits its standing to punish the disadvantaged. Reformers pursue two lines of thought to support this proposition.[61] According to one, the state loses its standing to punish when doing so would leave it vulnerable to a charge of hypocrisy.[62] According to the other, the state loses its standing

57 In law, standing is usually a matter of what it takes for a party to be in a position to ask for a judgment and remedy from a court. Here, in contrast, standing is a matter of what it takes for the state to sit in judgment of its citizens: to have permission to judge them.

58 Kyle G. Fritz, *Hypocrisy, Inconsistency, and the Moral Standing of the State*, 13 CRIM. L. & PHIL. 309, 312 (2019) ("[O]ne can think of standing as a privilege right [or permission].").

59 *See* Chapter 1, *supra* at pp. 33–34.

60 *See, e.g.*, Morse, *Deprivation, supra* note 52, at 152 ("The social forfeit theory, most closely associated with Judge David Bazelon, argues that if a society unduly deprives people of the opportunities and life chances justice demands, then that society forfeits its rights to punish deprived people when they offend.").

61 For an argument to the effect that the two lines of thought are really one, see Patrick Todd, *A Unified Account of the Moral Standing to Blame*, 53 NÔUS 347 (2019). Another theory, not discussed in the text, is based on an analogy to entrapment. *See, e.g.*, Jeffrey W. Howard, *Moral Subversion and Structural Entrapment*, 24 J. POL. PHIL. 24 (2016).

62 The literature discussing hypocrisy and moral standing to blame or punish includes G.A. COHEN, *Casting the First Stone: Who Can, and Who Can't Condemn the Terrorists?*, *in* FINDING

when it becomes complicit in (and thus itself responsible for) the accused's crime.[63]

Hypocrisy

Imagine Murdock is a teller at the First National Bank, but not a very loyal one. He embezzles $200. First National surely has standing to blame him for stealing the money, if anyone does. We might suppose that Joe, the squeaky clean teller next to Murdock, can blame him too, if only because they belong to the same bank "community."

Durlock, the teller on Murdock's other side, is another story. Just last week, he too embezzled $200. When Durlock tries to blame Murdock, Murdock tells him to shove off. "Who are *you* to blame *me*?," he asks. Murdock's question implicitly asserts that Durlock, in virtue of his own embezzlement, has forfeited whatever standing he'd otherwise have had as a member of the bank community to blame Murdock for his offense.

Durlock lacks standing because he's a hypocrite. He's happy to blame Murdock for embezzling, but exempts himself from the same treatment for

ONESELF IN THE OTHER 115, 121–23 (Michael Otsuka ed. 2013) (discussing "*tu quoque*" as a way of discrediting a condemner's standing) [hereinafter COHEN, *Casting*]; G.A. COHEN, *Ways of Silencing Critics*, *in* FINDING ONESELF IN THE OTHER at 134, 134–42 (Michael Otsuka ed. 2013) (same); T.M. SCANLON, MORAL DIMENSIONS: PERMISSIBILITY, MEANING, BLAME 175–76 (2008) (discussing hypocrisy); Macalester Bell, *The Standing to Blame*, *in* BLAME: ITS NATURE AND NORMS 262, 272–76 (D. Justin Coates & Neal A. Tognazzini eds., 2013) (rejecting the "nonhypocrisy condition" for standing to blame); Marilyn Friedman, *How to Blame People Responsibly*, 47 J. VALUE INQUIRY 271, 280 (2013) ("Anyone who blames other persons but not herself for violating particular moral norms is undermining her own standing to blame others for those violations because she exhibits inconsistent commitment to the norms in question."); Kyle G. Fritz & Daniel Miller, *Hypocrisy and the Standing to Blame*, 99 PAC. PHIL. Q. 118, 125 (2018) ("[H]ypocrisy involves at least an implicit rejection of the equality of person that grounds one's right to blame."); Angela M. Smith, *On Being Responsible and Holding Responsible*, 11 J. ETHICS 465, 479–80 (2007) (briefly discussing hypocrisy); R. Jay Wallace, *Hypocrisy, Moral Address, and the Equal Standing of Persons*, 38 PHIL. & PUB. AFF. 307, 308 (2010) ("[T]here is a form of hypocrisy that is worthy of serious censure, insofar as it offends against the commitment to the equality of persons that is constitutive of moral relations in the first place."); Victor Tadros, *Poverty and Criminal Responsibility*, 43 J. VALUE INQUIRY 391, 396–97 (2009) (discussing hypocrisy). For a more wide-ranging analysis of the morality of hypocrisy, see BÉLA SZABADOS & ELDON SOIFER, HYPOCRISY: ETHICAL INVESTIGATIONS (2004).

[63] The literature discussing complicity (or related ideas) and moral standing to blame or punish includes COHEN, *Casting*, *supra* note 62, at 125–31 (discussing "You're involved in it yourself" as a way of discrediting a condemner's standing); SCANLON, *supra* note 62, at 175 (briefly discussing complicity); Bell, *supra* note 62, at 276–77 (rejecting the "noncomplicity condition" for standing to blame); Tadros, *supra* note 62, at 398–400, 404–09 (discussing complicity); Patrick Todd, *Manipulation and Moral Standing: An Argument for Incompatibilism*, 12 PHIL. IMPRINT 1, 1–2 (2012) (arguing that "manipulators," who causally determine a wrongdoer's choices, lack moral standing to blame or punish); Gary Watson, *A Moral Predicament in the Criminal Law*, 58 INQUIRY 168, 178–80 (2015) (discussing the "claim of complicity" dispossessed offenders can make).

violating the same rule.[64] Durlock doesn't practice what he preaches, and his lack of integrity undermines whatever standing he'd otherwise have had to blame Murdock for committing the same wrong he committed. When the hypocrite condemns others who commit an equal or lesser wrong compared to the wrong he committed, it looks like he's declaring that only the little people follow the rules, and he's not a little person. On the contrary, he's better than the little people. Hypocrites are thus arrogant, and morality withdraws their standing to condemn others, at least if they refuse to repent their own wrongdoing.[65]

According to the reformer, the state is a hypocrite with respect to the crimes of the disadvantaged, such that morality withdraws its standing to punish them. A hypocrite loses standing when he's guilty of the same wrong, or a greater wrong, as the wrong he condemns. The victim of the hypocrite's wrongdoing might have been the same person he purports to condemn, or it might have been someone else. Who the hypocrite wrongs isn't critical, although it takes more *chutzpa* for a hypocrite to condemn someone when the person he condemns is the very same person he previously wronged. Anyway, what matters is that the wrong the hypocrite commits (call it β) is equal to or greater than the wrong he purports to condemn (call it φ).[66] If so, then hypocrisy requires that $\beta \geq \varphi$.

Murdock is disadvantaged because the state has treated him unjustly, according to some theory of distributive justice. The state nonetheless wants to prosecute him for embezzlement. Setting aside the specific embezzlement charge, let's instead generalize. Let's say Murdock commits crime φ, which can range from murder (or worse) to petty theft (or less), and let's say the

[64] *See* Szabados & Soifer, *supra* note 62, at 229 ("Hypocrites can be seen as displaying one set of standards in their preaching and another in their practice."); Fritz & Miller, *supra* note 62, at 122 ("The hypocrite is disposed to blame others for violations of *N*, but she is not disposed to blame herself for violations of *N*, and she has no justifiable reason for this difference."); Friedman, *supra* note 63, at 280 ("The key problem [with hypocrisy] consists of applying, in an arbitrarily discriminatory manner, moral norms that should be applied in the same way for a wider population."); Tadros, *supra* note 62, at 396 ("The moral significance of hypocrisy has to do with the way in which hypocrites imply that they are exempt from the moral standards that they apply to the people they accuse.").

[65] *See* R.A. Duff, *Moral and Criminal Responsibility: Answering and Refusing to Answer*, *in* 5 Oxford Studies in Agency and Responsibility 165, 186 (D. Justin Coates & Neal A. Tognazzini eds., 2019) ("What undermines my standing to call you to moral account for wronging me is not simply the fact that I have wronged you, or indeed that I am still wronging you, but the fact that I refuse to answer to you for those wrongs, whilst demanding that you answer to me for wronging me.").

[66] *See* Tadros, *supra* note 62, at 393 (One "explanation[] of how our standing to hold others responsible may be eroded . . . is grounded in hypocrisy: the fact that one person commits the *same kinds* of wrong as someone else deprives the one of the standing to hold the other person responsible for his wrongs.") (emphasis added); *id.* at 396 ("Hypocrisy can sometimes rest on a person's propensity to commit wrongs of a *similar or greater magnitude of seriousness*.") (emphasis added).

state has committed wrong β against Murdock. β might, for example, consist in the state's failure to provide adequate housing, medical care, education, protection from discrimination, and so forth, or some combination thereof, all of which are continuing wrongs of omission. The state hasn't lived up to its obligations, vis-á-vis Murdock, which makes it guilty of wronging him.

Now distinguish two theories of hypocrisy. According to the narrow theory, it makes little, if any, sense to compare whatever wrong the state has done to a disadvantaged citizen, with whatever crime a disadvantaged citizen has committed, just because they're different kinds of wrongs. The wrong Murdock committed (murder) wasn't just a moral wrong independent of the law (though it was); it was also a crime, however big or small. The difference is a difference in kind, not degree. In contrast, whatever the state failed to do for Murdock, its omission wasn't a crime. If morality denies hypocrites standing because they exempt themselves from rules they readily apply to others, then as long as the state doesn't exempt itself (or its agents) from the criminal law, it should retain its standing to punish criminal wrongdoers like Murdock, whatever its sins of omission.[67] The charge of hypocrisy against the state, on the narrow theory, misses its mark.

Not so, says the reformer, because the narrow theory misunderstands the morality of hypocrisy. According to the broad theory of hypocrisy, which the reformer embraces, it makes perfect sense to compare the state's wrong β with Murdock's crime φ. Contrary to the narrow theory, apples and oranges they're not. Some metric, surely, can be found by which to intelligibly compare the state's β and Murdock's φ. If so, then the possibility can't be ruled out that, at least sometimes, β is equal to or greater than φ, and when it is, the state is a hypocrite, without standing to punish.

Comparing β and φ won't always be easy. Were the state's wrongful omissions apropos the real Murdock equal to or greater than his murder of King? Or, what if Murdock hadn't killed King, but had instead robbed the Little Tavern?[68] Or, what if he'd just walked out without paying for his hamburger? When the state's β is intuitively big, and the accused's φ is intuitively small, or when the state's β is intuitively small, and the accused's φ is intuitively big, some measure of consensus on the comparative judgment might

[67] *See, e.g.*, Fritz, *supra* note 58, at 309 ("[T]he state is not disposed to make an unfair exception of itself for committing the *same sorts of crimes* as socially deprived offenders, so it is unclear that the state is truly *hypocritical*.") (emphasis added).

[68] *See Three "Poor Marchers" Held On Murder Charge*, New Pittsburgh Courier, June 22, 1968 ("Capital police believe the three youths . . . planned to hold up an all-night eatery and came upon five Marines in the restaurant.").

well be possible, but when they're not, the reformer has more work to do helping us see when one is bigger or smaller than the other.

The broad-theory reformer and his narrow-theory opponent, anarchists both, each believes he knows what justice requires when it comes to the morality of hypocrisy. One understands it one way; the other understands it another. Unless one or the other's reading is true, beyond reasonable doubt, the verdict on the true theory of the morality of hypocrisy, and thus on the state's moral standing to punish the disadvantaged, is one whose authoritative resolution should be left to the democratic process. If the reformer's broad theory prevails, the state will treat the disadvantaged and the advantaged differently, despite committing the same crime. If the narrow theory prevails, it will treat them the same. Within democratic politics, either result is fair game.

Complicity

In the story told so far, Murdock embezzled $200 from the First National, as did Durlock the week before. Both reached into their tills, and with *animus furandi*, took the money. In the doctrinal language of the criminal law, each acted as a principal. Each committed all the elements of the crime charged, all on his own.

Now suppose Durlock didn't actually take the $200 himself. Instead, he helped Murdock take it. Durlock wanted Murdock to steal, maybe because he'd get half the take. Toward that end, perhaps he distracted the manager while Murdock did the deed. In that case, Murdock and Durlock would, once again, both be guilty of embezzlement, only Durlock would be guilty as an accomplice, and Murdock would be guilty as principal. If for some reason Durlock were to turn around and start blaming Murdock for stealing, Murdock might fairly tell him to stand down. Accomplice Durlock, like hypocrite Durlock, has no standing to blame Murdock for his crime. Indeed, accomplice Durlock might have less standing than hypocrite Durlock, since he's guilty (thanks to his complicity) of the very crime for which he now has the audacity to condemn Murdock.

According to the reformer, the state loses its standing to condemn crimes of the disadvantaged insofar as the state is an accomplice to the crimes of the disadvantaged. Once again, we can distinguish a narrow theory and a broad one.

The narrow theory of complicity tracks existing law, and in particular, the law of complicity. Roughly speaking, it takes two things (beyond the principal committing the crime) to make one person another's accomplice.[69]

[69] The broad theory tracks what might be called the "common law of complicity." Many

First, the accomplice must do something amounting to aiding or encouraging the principal to commit the crime, or must fail to do something, which aids or assists the principal in the commission of the crime, when what the putative accomplice failed to do was something he was legally obligated to do. Even trivial aid—like saying "Go for it!" without saying or doing anything more—is enough for complicity under the law's theory of complicity.

Second, and more importantly, the accomplice must intend, as he provides his aid, or fails to act, to promote or facilitate the principal's commission of the crime.[70] On the narrow theory, complicity doesn't require causation. Durlock is Murdock's accomplice even if Durlock's help, by way of act or omission, didn't cause Murdock to reach into the till, either because Murdock would've reached into it anyway (no but-for cause), or because Murdock's decision to reach into the till breaks any causal chain linking his decision back to Durlock's help (no proximate cause).[71] Durlock's help might have caused Murdock's decision, but he's an accomplice even if it didn't, assuming Durlock wanted Murdock to take from the till.[72]

commentators dislike the common law of complicity, mainly because it can end up punishing an accomplice more than the commentator believes he should be punished. Proposals to reform complicity doctrine, as well as arguments to abolish it, abound. *See, e.g.*, Joshua Dressler, *Reforming Complicity Law: Trivial Assistance as a Lesser Offense?*, 5 OHIO ST. J. CRIM. L. 427, 429–30 (2008) (proposing a statutory distinction between causal and non-causal accomplices, with causal accomplices being liable for the principal's crime and non-causal accomplices being liable for a lesser offense); Douglas Husak, *Abetting a Crime*, 33 LAW & PHIL. 41, 64–65 (2014) ("[T]he best way to solve many of the problems in the law of abetting . . . is to replace a general complicity statute with myriad specific crimes."); Michael S. Moore, *Causing, Aiding, and the Superfluidity of Accomplice Liability*, 156 U. PA. L. REV. 395, 452 (2007) ("Eliminating the distinction [between principals and accomplices] would allow each of us to be judged as we should be judged: by what we individually contributed to some legally prohibited result, and by the state of mind we had when we did what we did.").

[70] *See, e.g.*, MODEL PENAL CODE § 2.06(3)(a) (AM. LAW INST. 1985) ("A person is an accomplice of another person in the commission of an offense if with the *purpose* of promoting or facilitating the commission of the offense" he aids such other person in committing it) (emphasis added); DRESSLER, *supra* note 29, § 30.05[A], at 447. The language used to describe the mental state required for accomplice liability varies from state to state. *See* John F. Decker, *The Mental State Requirement for Accomplice Liability in American Criminal Law*, 60 S.C. L. REV. 237 (2008). For recent efforts to say what the mental state requirement for complicity should be, see, for example, Heidi M. Hurd & Michael S. Moore, *Untying the Gordian Knot of* Mens Rea *Requirements for Accomplices*, 32 SOC. PHIL & POL'Y (Spring 2016), at 161; Alexander F. Sarch, *Condoning the Crime: The Elusive* Mens Rea *for Complicity*, 47 LOY. U. CHI. L.J. 131 (2015); Gideon Yaffe, *Intending to Aid*, 33 LAW & PHIL. 1 (2014); Sherif Girgis, Note, *The* Mens Rea *of Accomplice Liability*, 123 YALE L.J. 460 (2013).

[71] Moore, *supra* note 69, at 402–12. For the classic statement, according to which accomplice liability is necessarily non-causal because voluntary human agency necessarily cuts causal chains, see Sanford Kadish, *Complicity, Cause and Blame: A Study in the Interpretation of Doctrine*, 73 CALIF. L. REV. 323, 405 (1985).

[72] *See, e.g.*, DRESSLER, *supra* note 29, § 30.04[B][2][a], at 445 ("A secondary party is accountable for the conduct of the primary party even if his assistance was causally unnecessary to the commission of the offense.") (emphasis omitted).

Under the narrow theory, the state probably isn't an accomplice to the crimes of the disadvantaged. Even if the state's sins of omission vis-á-vis the disadvantaged amount to "encouraging" their crimes, it would be far-fetched to say the state, as it fails to live up to its obligations of distributive justice, wants the disadvantaged to commit whatever crimes they commit.[73] The state doubtless realizes, or at least should realize, its failures apropos the poor will or might lead them to crimes they otherwise wouldn't have committed. The injustices the disadvantaged endure are "criminogenic." Nonetheless, realizing a causal link exists between its injustice and crime, or culpably failing to realize one exists, isn't enough to establish complicity, not on the narrow theory, which requires intent.

Not so fast, says the reformer. The narrow theory misunderstands the morality of complicity. Once again, the reformer prefers a broad theory, which sweeps well beyond the narrow theory and the criminal-law complicity doctrines to which it adheres.[74] The broad theory takes the narrow theory's two basic elements and enlarges them. First, it doesn't limit complicity to aiding or encouraging. Any act or omission inconsistent with the requirements of distributive justice is sufficient, as long as it causes a disadvantaged citizen to commit a crime. Second, it doesn't limit complicity to intent. If the state fails to provide the disadvantaged their distributive due, if that failure causes the disadvantaged to commit crimes, and if the state realizes, or should have realized, its failure will or might cause the disadvantaged to commit crimes, then that's enough to make the state complicit, according to the broad theory.

As you might have noticed, expanding the narrow theory's basic elements entails adding a third. On the narrow theory, Durlock is an accomplice, all else being equal, even if he doesn't cause Murdock to embezzle. The broad theory, in contrast, would require causation: It would require Durlock's act

[73] *See, e.g.*, Tadros, *supra* note 62, at 405 ("Only conspiracy theorists believe that our political leaders, in perpetrating economic injustices against the poor, intend that the poor will commit crimes.").

[74] The broad theory is similar to another criminal law doctrine, often called the "innocent agency" doctrine. As set forth in the Model Penal Code, the innocent agency doctrine provides that one person is guilty as a principal if, "acting with the kind of culpability that is sufficient for the commission of the offense, he causes an innocent or irresponsible person to engage in . . . conduct [constituting the crime]." MODEL PENAL CODE § 2.06(2)(a) (AM. LAW INST. 1985) (emphasis added). The broad theory and the innocent agency doctrine are similar insofar as one person's responsibility for another person's crime depends on the first person causing the second to commit a crime. They differ insofar as the innocent agency doctrine applies only when the person who commits the crime is "innocent" or "irresponsible," like a child or someone who's insane, whereas the broad theory applies whether or not the person who commits the crime is "innocent" or "irresponsible."

or omission to cause Murdock's crime. Whereas the narrow theory links Durlock to Murdock's crime through intention—on Durlock wanting Murdock to embezzle—the broad theory links Durlock to Murdock's crime through causation—on causing him to embezzle.[75] The broad theory expands complicity's reach, but only so far as causation will allow. If Durlock's help didn't cause Murdock's crime, then the broad theory won't call him an accomplice.

The state's status as an accomplice to the crimes of the disadvantaged thus depends, pursuant to the broad theory, on causation. Imagine the real Murdock, as he stands in the dock for King's murder, proclaims: "You cannot punish me: You have no standing. And you have no standing because you're complicit, and you're complicit because you—the state—caused me to kill Lieutenant King." Now imagine the prosecutor's response: "Mr. Murdock, with all due respect, the state didn't cause you to kill Lieutenant King. You did that all on your own." According to the prosecutor, Murdock's decision to pull the trigger was enough to break any causal chain linking the state's omission to King's death. According to Murdock, however, his decision to pull the trigger wasn't enough. The state's standing, on the broad theory, hangs in the balance.

Once again, the broad-theory reformer and his narrow-theory opponent, anarchists both, each believes he knows what justice requires, this time when it comes to the morality of complicity. Once again, one understands it one way; the other understands it another. Once again, unless you believe one or the other's insight into the morality of complicity is true, beyond reasonable doubt, then you should also believe the authoritative resolution of their disagreement should be left to the democratic process. Once again, within democratic politics, either theory is fair game. If the broad theory prevails, the state will deny itself standing to punish Murdock; if the narrow theory prevails, it won't.

Of course, even if the reformer prevails in the democratic arena and manages to get enacted into law his broad theory of hypocrisy or complicity, his job isn't over. He still needs to say what morality says the state should do, as a matter of justice, assuming it has no standing to punish the disadvantaged. Should the disadvantaged get a pass for any crime they commit, at least until

[75] *See, e.g.*, Watson, *supra* note 63, at 179 ("[T]he key to implicating the dominant society in . . . crimes" committed by the disadvantaged is that "conditions of severe deprivation and inequality foreseeably promote [i.e., cause] criminal behavior.").

the state treats the disadvantaged as justice requires? Only for some crimes, like "victimless" crimes or victimless crimes "which have impact primarily" on the advantaged?[76] Or perhaps the state can regain its standing to *sua culpa* if it does a *mea culpa*, such that it regains its permission to punish the disadvantaged, but only if it takes responsibility for its own wrongdoing.[77] If so, how would that work? Should AUSAs and district attorneys file formal written apologies (on the state's behalf)? Should the sentencing judge apologize? Or would such apology rituals let the state off too easily, as little more than cheap talk? Should a "Social Justice Commission" be created to deal with the problem, as one thoughtful observer has recommended?[78]

Different reformers give different answers. If the reformer manages to prevail in the democratic process, then internecine disagreements over the practical consequences will, like the question of standing itself, need to get sorted out in the democratic process. Whatever answers emerge will be authoritatively binding. Whatever changes to the law are needed to implement the reformist solution to the state's standing problem will legitimately oblige everyone they touch—police, prosecutors, judges, jurors—to conform.

Authority

For revolutionaries, Murdock shouldn't be punished at all, because punishment presupposes responsibility, and justice requires overthrowing responsibility. That goes for the advantaged and disadvantaged alike: Neither bears responsibility for what, before the revolution, would have been called crimes. Reformers don't go so far. For some, a disadvantaged citizen like Murdock should be punished less than his advantaged counterpart, because he's less

[76] *See, e.g.*, Tadros, *supra* note 62, at 413 ("In some cases . . . while failing to prosecute and convict the offender will cause some injustice to the victim or to other citizens, the injustice is insufficiently grave to outweigh the injustice of holding the offender responsible for what he has done. This will particularly be true with respect to victimless crimes which have impact primarily on the security of the well off."). Tommie Shelby argues that states lack the "authority to punish disobedience to law and [the] moral standing to condemn" and punish those among the excluded who commit violent crimes, but that the state nonetheless has an enforcement right to penalize such acts in order to "deter and contain" them. *See* Tommie Shelby, Dark Ghettos: Injustice, Dissent, and Reform 248 (2016).

[77] *See, e.g.*, *id.* at 410 ("[A]n ideal practice of responsibility might involve complicit parties holding their partners in crime *and themselves* responsible for the crimes they commit.") (emphasis added); Watson, *supra* note 63, at 183 ("The conclusion is that, speaking collectively, we have no business punishing the dispossessed *without taking responsibility for our part in the crimes*.") (emphasis added).

[78] *See* Duff, *supra* note 65, at 187.

culpable. For others, the state has no standing to punish the disadvantaged, in which case the reformer needs to figure out what happens next.

For all their differences, revolutionaries and reformers, being philosophical anarchists, speak for morality. For them, the authority of the United States to punish Murdock (or anyone for that matter) is derivative, piggybacking on morality's authority. They deny the United States (or any state) can be a legitimate authority unto itself, since no state has the power to morally obligate its citizens to conform to its laws, criminal laws included. Thus, insofar as the rules the United States followed to send Murdock to prison—from his arrest on the streets of Georgetown to his confinement in federal prison—didn't conform to morality's rules, Murdock's punishment was unjust, which for an anarchist is all it takes for it to be illegitimate as well.

The statist takes a different view. Democracies are, he believes, authorities unto themselves, with the power to morally obligate conformity to the rules the democratic process produces. As for the changes in law the revolutionary and the reformer propose, advanced in the name of justice, the statist is agnostic. Justice is important, but more pressing to the statist is legitimacy. When the statist witnesses Murdock being carted off to prison, foremost in his mind is the question of legitimacy. The statist would frame the question thusly: When a democratic state fails to abide the demands of distributive justice, what happens to its authority over the casualties of its failure?

As we saw in Chapter 1, the authority of a democratic state has limits. It has no authority to criminalize conduct falling within what we've vaguely been calling traditional liberal rights, such as freedom of speech, press, association, and so forth. Nor does it have authority to inflict what we've been calling, once again vaguely, grossly disproportionate punishments. These rights, however spelled out, limit the state's authority to define crimes and impose punishments. We've also seen, in Chapters 2 through 5, how the requirements of a guilty act and guilty mind limit the state's authority to define the conditions of culpability. All these limits establish immunities disabling the state's moral power to enact rules defining crimes, defining culpability, and prescribing punishments.

Now comes Benjamin Murdock, arrested in the District of Columbia for the murder of Lieutenant King. Assume Murdock is willing to accept the following. First, the United States, as a democratic state, is a legitimate authority, all else being equal. Second, its authority is limited, and these limits are embodied in immunities Murdock can assert to disable the state's power. Third, punishing Murdock for murdering King would violate none of the rights discussed thus far: Murdock had no right to kill King; his act and mind were guilty when he did; and his punishment, if he's convicted, wouldn't be grossly disproportionate.

Murdock nonetheless believes the United States has no authority over him, not because any of his rights have been violated, but because its authority over him (and all the disadvantaged like him) has been lost altogether. So, when Murdock is asked to plead to the charge of murder, he proclaims:

> I refuse to recognize the authority of this court, nor the authority of the United States, which has treated me, a citizen, abysmally. It has failed to afford me the security, opportunities, and material well-being to which I, as a citizen, am entitled as a matter of justice. Because its failure has been so profound, persistent, and pervasive, it no longer has any authority over me: It no longer has any moral power to impose on me an obligation to conform to its laws. Consequently, my failure to conform cannot, and does not, constitute a wrong against the state, and because I've committed no wrong against the state, the state has no moral permission to punish me.[79]

Powerful words. The statist's reply unfolds in three steps.

The State of Exclusion

Step 1 begins with a distinction, between a state of nature and a state of exclusion. Murdock was seriously disadvantaged. He experienced severe environmental deprivation. His life in Watts was precarious. He lived on the edge, and so on. Moreover, none of that, we're supposing, would have been true if only the state had lived up to its obligation to treat Murdock as justice required. The conditions under which Murdock made his way through life were, as his lawyer put it, rotten, and they wouldn't have been rotten if the state had done its job and conformed to the demands of justice.

Still, as rotten as Murdock's life was, the state presumably hadn't abandoned him altogether. Police presumably remained on duty, ready to enforce

[79] Murdock's declaration assumes the federal government is solely responsible for his plight. In reality, of course, the City of Los Angeles, not to mention the State of California, must bear some responsibility as well. Their acts and omissions, as well as those of the federal government, influence how well or badly Murdock's life goes. In order to keep the discussion manageable, however, let's assume we have only one state, the United States, with jurisdiction over Murdock.

criminal laws protecting life, limb, and property. Maybe the police were too few, insufficient to maintain good order; or maybe too many, causing Murdock to believe he was living in a police state. Still, the police hadn't gone completely AWOL. So, too, prosecutors remained on the job, ready to charge and try accused offenders, and the courts likewise remained open, ready to offer judgment. Yes, Murdock's situation was one of destitution and despair, but that's not yet a state of nature. The state hadn't, after all, walled off Watts from the rest of the world, as in some post-apocalyptic movie, leaving its inhabitants to fend for themselves.[80]

The state of nature is a state without a state. However "nasty, brutish, or short" his life may have been, Murdock wasn't in a state without a state. If you believe otherwise, if you believe the state had completely abandoned Murdock, returning him de facto to a state of nature, then the statist really has nothing to say. Statism presupposes a state. If the state genuinely had left the building, leaving Murdock completely in the cold, then Murdock's proclamation in the dock is true. The state doesn't have any authority over him. Then again, if no state existed, Murdock wouldn't have been in the dock in the first place. There would have been no dock.[81]

Even if the United States didn't return Murdock to the state of nature, its sins nonetheless left him in a state inconsistent with his status as a citizen. This state needs a name: Call it a state of exclusion. A state of exclusion is one

[80] It's hard to imagine a large-scale state of nature, but we can imagine localized and fleeting states of nature. For example, when you're about to suffer some harm—the harm is imminent—and you don't have any time to turn to the state for help, it looks like you're in a localized state of nature. *See, e.g.*, Whitley R.P. Kaufman, *Self-Defense, Imminence, and the Battered Woman*, 10 New Crim. L. Rev. 342, 360 2007) ("[A] threat is imminent when there is insufficient time to enlist the aid of the authorities to protect oneself."); Dennis Klimchuck, *Excuses and Excusing Conditions*, *in* Rethinking Criminal Law Theory 161, 166 (François Tanguay-Renaud & James Stribopoulos eds., 2012) (noting the maxim "*necessita habet non legem*—necessity knows no law"). As you might expect, existing law provides affirmative defenses, such as self-defense, defense of others, and necessity, permitting a person, under the circumstances the defense identifies, to do what would otherwise be a crime in order to protect himself, provided his response to the imminent harm was proportional, and provided he's not at fault for being in the predicament.

We can also imagine harder cases, in which the threatened harm isn't strictly imminent, but in which the state has, for one reason or another, repeatedly and egregiously failed to provide protection, either to a particular person (as when the police fail to respond to the repeated pleas of a battered spouse) or perhaps to an entire neighborhood. If you take the law into your own hands, is the state permitted to punish you? For an engrossing exploration of this question, see Paul H. Robinson & Sarah M. Robinson, Shadow Vigilantes: How Distrust in the Justice System Breeds a New Kind of Lawlessness (2018).

[81] *See* Matt Matravers, "*Who's Still Standing?*" *A Comment on Antony Duff's Preconditions of Criminal Liability*, 3 J. Moral Phil. 320, 327 (2006) ("[T]here is a point at which the state fails to function to such a degree that its citizens can properly think of themselves as having returned to a state of nature. At that point, all legal (and, I think, moral) bets are off (that is, no legal [and, I think moral] obligations obtain).").

in which we say of a citizen living there such things as: He has effectively been excluded from the polity, he's a second-class citizen, he's not a member of the political community, even in some minimal sense of community, he's a serf in a "quasi-feudal" regime,[82] and so forth. Describing a citizen as not only disadvantaged (according to some theory of justice), but so disadvantaged as to be excluded, is meant to convey the thought that excluded citizens don't see themselves, for good reason, as full-fledged citizens, and thus don't see themselves as authors of the laws under which they live. Moreover, excluded citizens may well have formal access to the franchise, but that alone isn't enough to count them among the included.

Reasonable minds can disagree on whether the real Murdock was or wasn't in a state of exclusion. For now, we proceed conditionally. A statist who believes Murdock was not excluded will dismiss out of hand his declaration rejecting the state's authority.[83] If he wasn't excluded, he was, like it or not, obligated to conform to the law, just like everyone else. On the other hand, a statist who believes Murdock was excluded won't dismiss his claim, at least not out of hand. Instead, he'll proceed to Step 2.

Core Crimes

Step 2 invokes another distinction, introduced in Chapter 1, between core crimes and non-core crimes. Assuming Murdock is an excluded citizen, the question at this step can be framed as follows: Is the state morally permitted to punish excluded citizens, like Murdock, who culpably commit core crimes?

Recall from Chapter 1 the story of Leviathan and the islanders on Anarchia. When the islanders first arrived, the state of nature prevailed. Their lives and limbs, not to mention the things they gathered for their own, were insecure. They attacked one another, stole from one another, and generally lived a dicey and dangerous existence. When Leviathan came on the scene, he promulgated his Code, setting forth a short lineup of core prohibitions, and threatened to throw non-conformists into the Cage. Consequently, the islanders began to conform, and once they did, fairness to their fellow conforming islanders placed them all under a moral obligation to conform,

82 Tommie Shelbie, *Justice, Deviance, and the Dark Ghetto*, 35 PHIL. & PUB. AFF. 125, 134 (2007).

83 *See, e.g.*, Morse, *Deprivation*, *supra* note 52, at 153 ("In a working democracy, the majority of citizens will not believe that the society is sufficiently unjust to compromise its legitimacy.").

an obligation owing to one another and to Leviathan, in his capacity as the Code's author.

The story yielded the following lesson. A person is morally obligated to conform to those prohibitions constituting the criminal law's core insofar as everyone else, or most everyone else, is likewise conforming. Conforming to core prohibitions enables everyone to escape the state of nature. These core crimes might be described as *malum in se* crimes. That's harmless enough, but potentially misleading. If the phrase "*malum in se*" encompasses all moral wrongs that are wrong independent of the law, then core crimes aren't equivalent to *malum in se* crimes. Lots of things are morally wrong independent of law, like lying to a friend for no good reason, but that doesn't make them core crimes. Instead, core crimes resemble the standard litany of common law crimes: murder, rape, manslaughter, robbery, larceny, ason, mayhem and burglary, to which one might add assault.

A person is morally obligated to conform to the prohibitions embodied in core crimes because that's only fair. Insofar as the mass of one's fellow citizens is conforming—refraining from murder, rape, robbery, burglary, and so forth—thereby securing the collective good of social peace, their conformity generates an obligation to conform, which none can escape. That obligation runs not only to everyone who's conforming, but to the state as well. If so, then when Murdock murders King, he morally wrongs King because he intentionally, with guilty act and mind, and without justification, caused his death; he morally wrongs those who, unlike him, chose to conform to the law prohibiting core crimes, including murder; and he wrongs the United States, as author of the prohibition against murder. Insofar as Murdock's choice not to conform constitutes a wrong against the United States, his choice confers on the United States a moral permission to punish him for that choice.

Nor is Murdock released from his obligation to conform insofar as he's an excluded citizen. Murdock's duty to conform to the core rules, and the state's moral permission to punish him for failing to conform, doesn't depend on the state having authority over him. His obligation arises from the existence of the rules, owing to the state having promulgated them, together with the brute fact that most everyone else is conforming. It doesn't depend on the state having earned the moral power to impose obligations on him. If so, then so long as the state hasn't abandoned him to a state of nature, Murdock remains duty-bound to conform to the criminal law's core. His status as an excluded citizen is deplorable, but it doesn't grant him a license him to kill.

When Murdock, standing in the dock, repudiates the state's authority over him, he's right. The state has no moral power to create moral obligations, levied on anyone, excluded and non-excluded alike, running to the state. But that, once again, doesn't mean the state isn't permitted to punish Murdock for killing King. Having excluded Murdock qua citizen, the state has no authority qua moral power over him, but its moral permission to punish him for committing a core crime doesn't depend on its having authority over him, or over anyone for that matter.[84]

Non-Core Crimes

Now suppose Murdock didn't commit a core crime, like murder. Suppose instead he committed a crime outside the core. The line between core and non-core crimes isn't bright, but that needn't prevent us from making progress. For now, stipulate that cocaine possession for personal use is a non-core crime. Suppose, then, that Murdock is arrested for possessing cocaine, in violation of 18 U.S.C. § 844, which criminalizes simple possession of a controlled substance. Once again, standing in the dock, Murdock refuses to enter a plea. He repeats what he said before: Neither the United States, nor its courts, have any authority over him.

What now does the statist have to say?

For starters, he can't, as he did when Murdock was charged with murder, claim that the state, despite lacking authority over Murdock, is morally permitted to punish him all the same. That only works when most everyone is conforming to rules prohibiting core crimes and when such conformity is necessary to secure social peace, thereby fending off the state of nature. Cocaine possession, we've stipulated, is a non-core crime, which means people can live without fear of being killed, or of having their possessions purloined, and so forth, even if no rule prohibiting cocaine possession is on the books. Someone high on coke might be more inclined to commit a core

[84] If a state lacks authority qua moral power over a person, and if a relationship of authority between punisher and punished is a necessary condition for punishment (as the classical analysis of punishment says), then a state without authority over a person can't punish him, conceptually speaking. It can, of course, impose on him a burden or deprivation in response to culpable wrongdoing, and it can do so with the intent to condemn. But whatever we call such a burden or deprivation, we make a conceptual mistake if we call it "punishment." If one nonetheless insists on calling it "punishment," it should at least be understood as a non-paradigmatic form of punishment, i.e., "punishment" occurring outside a relationship of authority.

crime, like assault or robbery, which might be a good reason for a state with authority to prohibit coke possession. Or it might not be a good reason, or not good enough. That would depend on your theory of justice in criminalization. Nonetheless, possessing cocaine isn't itself a core crime.

If Murdock hadn't been excluded, the statist could have turned once again to Leviathan and the Anarchian islanders for help responding to Murdock when, now charged with cocaine possession, he denies the state has authority over him. A state's authority to define non-core crimes was, we learned in Chapter 1, based on the need to resolve reasonable disagreement among the islanders over which acts and omissions outside the core, if any, should be criminalized, not to mention resolving disagreements over the rules defining culpability and prescribing punishments. When those disagreements are resolved democratically, through a process in which all citizens are treated as equally free, all citizens are, as citizens, morally obligated to conform to the resulting rules. A democratic state, in other words, has authority over its citizens.

Alas, that authority doesn't extend to excluded citizens. Charged with murder, Murdock spoke the truth when, standing in the dock, he declared the state had no authority over him. Likewise, now charged with cocaine possession, he again speaks the truth when he declares the same. When the charge was murder, a crime within the core, the state was nonetheless morally permitted to punish him, despite having no authority over him. This time, however, when Murdock is charged with the non-core crime of cocaine possession, that gambit won't work.

If a state's moral permission to punish excluded citizens for non-core crimes can't come from its own authority, it can only come from morality itself. Whether or not morality gives the state such permission depends on morality. Does morality permit a democratic state to criminalize non-core crimes at all? If so, which ones? Does it permit a democratic state to ascribe culpability to an excluded citizen when he commits a non-core crime? If so, under what conditions? Does it grant a democratic state standing to punish an excluded citizen when he culpably commits a non-core crime? If so, how much punishment does it permit the state to impose for committing the non-core crime in question?

All those questions ask what morality requires or permits when it comes to punishing excluded citizens for non-core crimes, and reasonable citizens of democratic states will disagree on how to answer them. The usual way to resolve such questions, and to resolve them authoritatively, is through the democratic process, and that, of course, is how they will, as a matter of fact, be resolved. Having emerged from the democratic process, the resulting rules will authoritative for, and will morally bind, non-excluded citizens. But they won't be authoritative for, nor will they morally bind, excluded citizens, or at least they won't be morally binding just because they're been democratically enacted and don't infringe any immunity all citizens possess against the exercise of democratic authority.

Any moral permission a democratic state has to punish excluded citizens for non-core crimes must come from morality's authority. It can't come from the state's authority, insofar as a democratic state has no authority over the excluded. In other words, when it comes to the state's moral permission to punish the excluded, the statist finds himself in the same boat with the anarchist.[85] If the United States punishes Murdock for cocaine possession, and if Murdock is an excluded citizen, his punishment will be morally permissible only if morality itself grants the United States permission to punish him. But whether or not morality does indeed grant such permission is among the many questions about justice on which Murdock and his fellow citizens disagree. The democratic process exists to resolve such disagreements, and its resolution will be authoritative for non-excluded citizens. Its resolution will have no authority, however, over excluded citizens like Murdock.

[85] *See* Göran Duss-Otterström & Erin I. Kelly, *Injustice and the Right to Punish*, 14 Phil. Compass 1, 7 (2019):

> Since . . . unjust states' right to punish flows directly from morality, and not from a claim to citizens' legal compliance with the law *qua* law, it is necessary to think about how extensive the criminal law of an unjust state should be. An intuitive answer is that unjust states are permitted to punish core crimes against persons . . . but not crimes like drug dealing, benefits fraud, or tax evasion. However, the viability of this answer ultimately depends on the extent to which punishment of lesser offenses is necessary to furnish a social order in which people's basic rights are secure. Until we know this, it will simply be unclear how different the criminal law of just and unjust states should be.

Conclusion

Justice, it's famously been said, is the first virtue of social institutions.[1] The institution through which the state punishes those found guilty of crime is presumably a social institution, and thus presumably justice is its first virtue, too. Yet perhaps we should instead say, as some have,[2] that justice is the supreme virtue of social institutions, but not the first. Faced with disagreement over what justice requires, perhaps legitimacy, understood as a virtue distinct from justice, is the first virtue, and legitimate social institutions are first insofar as we can within them peaceably pursue our disagreements over the demands of justice.

"Legitimacy" means different things to different people. As a property of state action, we've defined legitimacy in terms of "authority." "Authority" likewise means different things to different people. As a property of states, we've defined authority as the moral power to change the normative status of those subject to its jurisdiction. A state with authority is thus a state with the moral power to announce new moral obligations, or recognize preexisting ones, where the duty to conform to the obligations announced or recognized runs to the state. A state endowed with the power in which authority consists is in turn a legitimate state, and action taken within the scope of its authority is legitimate action. If all that's so, then the legitimacy of state action depends on what it takes for a state to become blessed with the power in which authority consists.

A state vested with this power is, I've proposed, practically necessary to secure political peace, at least in states whose citizens believe their beliefs about justice are subject to no authority beyond the authority of their own conscience, and who disagree about which rules should, as a matter of justice, govern their collective life. The rules governing how their disagreements

[1] *See* John Rawls, A Theory of Justice 3 (1971) ("Justice is the first virtue of social institutions, as truth is to systems of thought.").

[2] Charles Larmore, *The Truth in Political Realism*, *in* Politics Recovered: Realist Thought in Theory and Practice 27, 32 (Matt Sleat ed., 2018). Bernard Williams "identif[ies] the 'first' political question in Hobbesian terms as the securing of order, protection, safety, trust and the conditions of cooperation. It is 'first' because solving it is the condition of solving, indeed posing, any others." Bernard Williams, In the Beginning was the Deed: Realism and Moralism in Political Argument 3 (2005).

Guilty Acts, Guilty Minds. Stephen P. Garvey, Oxford University Press (2020). © Oxford University Press.
DOI: 10.1093/oso/9780190924324.001.0001

are provisionally resolved must respect or be consistent with the pre-political status each citizen is assumed to have as free and equal. The provenance of those rules must respect each citizen as free insofar as each citizen is assumed to be endowed with the capacity to discover for himself what morality demands of him, and as equal insofar as all of his fellow citizens are assumed likewise to be so endowed. The only state capable of meeting these demands will, we've averred, be one instantiating the characteristics of a democratic state.

Nothing has been said here about the specific features or range of features a state must exhibit, nor about the conditions or range of conditions it must satisfy, in order to qualify as a democratic state and thus as a state endowed with authority. Much of that, but presumably not all of it, will involve matters on which citizens disagree and will thus itself be fodder for democratic politics. Yet whatever shape or form a democratic state must take, within some permissible range of such shapes or forms, in order to acquire authority, we're hard pressed to see how a non-democratic state whose citizens disagree about justice could legitimately exercise coercion against them, outside the rules constituting what we've called the core crimes of the criminal law, especially when the coercion comes in the form of punishment.

That brings us to the question of limits. If a democratic state is legitimate and thus equipped with the moral power in which authority consists, perhaps its authority is unlimited. If so, then any democratically pedigreed rule would acquire the force of a moral obligation binding on all those subject to the state's jurisdiction. Citizens would have no rights limiting the scope of the state's authority over them. That tempting possibility has forceful proponents, for whom democracy goes all the way down. We nonetheless declined that option, electing instead to search for some way to ground legitimate limits, expressed as immunity rights, on the authority of an otherwise legitimate democratic state.

Working with an over-simplified example, suppose two people disagree about a proposed rule governing some aspect of their life together, like the conditions under which someone is culpable for having committed a crime. One believes justice requires adopting one rule or set of rules; the other believes it requires a different rule or set of rules. Their disagreement persists, even after long discussion. We might want to believe they will, after more talk, succeed in finding an accord. But while they carry on that quest, they must as a practical matter settle on some rules enabling them to carry on living together in peace. Real people can't wait for the Godot of some hoped-for philosophical consensus. Some resolution is needed, in order to get on with the practical need of getting on.

Now suppose each of our interlocutors imagines himself in the role, not of a legislator, but of a constitution-maker, tasked with setting the second-order ground rules for resolving their first-order disagreements. If each begins with a commitment to treat the other as an epistemic equal, each will need to ask himself what he believes justice requires in light of their disagreement. One possibility is that, as constitution-makers, each believes, having listened to the other, that justice could go either way on the rule in question. Each sees the other's point. They therefore agree to disagree, in which case they agree their disagreement should be allocated to a democratic process for resolution, with each recognizing that he'll be morally bound to conform to the result.

Yet suppose the first interlocutor qua constitution-maker has another belief. He believes his interlocutor's proposed rule not only doesn't comport with justice, but will perpetrate an injustice—and he believes this beyond reasonable doubt, even after having carefully and respectfully listened to all the second interlocutor has to say. If so, he will have identified what is, for him, a limit on otherwise legitimate democratic authority. Of course, the second interlocutor, applying the same standard to his own beliefs, might not agree. Now they disagree at the second order. That's a problem left unresolved, indeed, unaddressed, in these pages. Still, one can perhaps look forward to at least some measure of agreement, now and around here, when the agreed-upon aim is to settle on limits to democratic authority, and where each citizen believes he should embrace a proposed limit only if he believes the state, should it breach the limit, would be guilty of an injustice. The limits thus identified would form a "benchmark of minimal legitimacy,"[3] a safeguard against tyranny and fear.

I've proposed two broad limits on a democratic state's otherwise legitimate authority to ascribe culpability or guilt to those accused of criminal wrongdoing, in addition to a separate limit grounded on an accused's loss of a sense of agency. Those limits have been expressed using the criminal law's traditional vocabulary of *actus reus* and *mens rea*, construed, in contrast to their conventional reading, as limits on democratic authority: as immunity rights disabling the exercise of any state authority inconsistent with them.

[3] John Gray, Two Faces of Liberalism 22 (2000).

The *actus reus* requirement, roughly speaking, disables a democratic state from ascribing culpability to those who, through no fault of their own, didn't and couldn't have realized their conduct failed to conform to the law; or, if they did realize, nonetheless lacked, again through no fault of their own, the capacity to conform. The *mens rea* requirement, roughly speaking, disables a democratic state from ascribing culpability to those who, through no fault of their own, didn't realize their conduct failed to conform to the law, provided their ignorance reflected sufficient concern for the law and its ends; or, if they did realize, their failure to conform nonetheless reflected no lack of sufficient concern for the law. In either case, the concern a law-abiding citizen has for the law sets the admittedly indeterminate benchmark against which to judge the accused's beliefs and choices.

We imagine two reactions to these proposed limits: disappointment and disbelief.

First, disappointment. Start with the proposed right (part of the *actus reus* requirement) disabling the state from assigning culpability to those who realized they were committing a crime, but were unable to conform their conduct to the law. That right might seldom need to be invoked. In some places, existing law, through volitional formulations of the defense of insanity and involuntary intoxication, will already protect those the proposed right would protect. Thus: disappointment. The right would have little work to do, so what's the big deal? (That doesn't mean the proposed right would be entirely idle. Many jurisdictions reject volitional incapacity as a form of insanity, nor is the proposed right limited to volitional incapacities arising from particular sources, like mental diseases or defects, or involuntary intoxication.)

Much the same could be said about the proposed right (part of the *mens rea* requirement) disabling the state from assigning culpability to those who realized they were committing a crime, but whose failure to conform nonetheless manifested no lack of sufficient concern for the law. That right too might seldom need to be invoked. In some places, existing law, through a broad formulation of the duress defense, will already protect those the proposed right would protect. Thus again: disappointment. The right would have little work to do. (Again, that doesn't mean it would be entirely idle. The proposed right would immunize defendants who might otherwise be liable under narrower formulations of the duress defense, and unlike current formulations of duress, it extends not only to external threats from third parties, but to internal threats arising from the accused's own psychology as well.)

Where a state already has on the books laws doing the work the proposed *actus reus* and *mens rea* requirements would otherwise do, the state has exercised its authority to obligate judges and juries to honor rights that, we submit, exist independently of the state's exercise of its authority. The state, in other words, has to that extent already exercised its authority to ensure it doesn't punish in excess of its authority. That might be disappointing to some, since it leaves the *actus reus* and *mens rea* requirements with less work to do than they otherwise would have had. But to others it might be reassuring, evidence that self-government can be self-disciplined.

Now to disbelief. This reaction comes into view when we move from defendants who realized they were committing a crime to those who didn't. The *actus reus* and *mens rea* requirements, applied to unwitting wrongdoers, present a direct challenge to the *ignorantia* maxim, which is widely regarded as among the most deeply entrenched rules of the substantive criminal law. The fact that the *actus reus* and *mens rea* requirements present a direct challenge to the *ignorantia* maxim might thus engender disbelief. If punishing someone who's ignorant is illegitimate, and not (merely) unjust, surely something has gone wrong. How can democratic states have been punishing illegitimately for so long? Why would the people have stood for it?

One reply begins with the observation that the state hasn't in fact been punishing illegitimately, because it generally doesn't, as a matter of fact, punish the ignorant. Indeed, when on occasion the state does punish the unwitting its action arguably arouses indignation precisely because, in the grand scheme of things, such action is an outlier: So far as one can tell the state doesn't very often punish the ignorant, or at least it punishes them less often than one might imagine if one looks only at the law on the books. For a variety of reasons, the risk that the ignorant will be prosecuted, convicted and punished is smaller than one might imagine it to be,[4] which isn't to say the risk is zero.

First, a defendant who commits a core crime will usually realize he was doing something criminal, even if he doesn't know exactly what. Second, prosecutors may be reluctant to charge defendants who they believe truly, and through no fault of their own, didn't even suspect they were doing anything

[4] *See* Douglas Husak, Ignorance of Law: A Philosophical Inquiry 73 (2016) (noting that it is "probably correct" to say that the "dearth of appellate cases on *ignorantia juris* may be due to the fact that exculpation 'is often accommodated in other ways'") (citing Andrew Ashworth, Principles of Criminal Law 236 (5th ed. 2006)); *id.* at 129 ("[I]gnorance of law exculpates far more frequently in positive law than many theorists concede.").

criminal, so those cases don't even make it into court. Third, courts sometimes interpret an existing criminal offense to make it unlikely the statute can be used to convict the reasonably ignorant. Finally, of course, the state itself has already, in the exercise of its authority, carved out limited exceptions to the *ignorantia* maxim, including an exception for those who would qualify as insane or involuntarily intoxicated under a cognitive formulation of those affirmative defenses.

With all that in mind, perhaps what started out as disbelief will turn, once again, into disappointment. If the state doesn't routinely punish the ignorant, then it won't routinely run afoul of the *actus reus* and *mens rea* requirements, meaning those requirements will have less work to do than one might otherwise have thought. But again, that's arguably cause for satisfaction, not disappointment. Which isn't to say the requirements would never be called upon. In some cases, they will be called into action, especially when lawmakers enact new crimes or eliminate old defenses with the intent to nudge or shove countervailing social norms in new directions; when they push the criminal law ever deeper into inchoate territory in an effort to identify and preemptively incapacitate the dangerous; or when prosecutors deploy existing crimes with vague elements in a bid to punish conduct widely believed to be unethical though not yet widely believed to be criminal.

In order for a democratic state to remain within the bounds of its authority, any punishment it imposes must be imposed pursuant to democratically enacted rules, emerging from a democratic process capable of generating an obligation to conform, and those rules must themselves conform to a range of immunity rights democratic citizens have against the imposition of state punishment. Those rights disable the state from enacting rules criminalizing some indefinite range of acts and omissions, punishing in gross disproportion to the crimes committed, and ascribing culpability absent a guilty act and guilty mind. We've explored here only the last of these rights, leaving largely unexplored the first and second, whose contours we invite others to investigate more fully. But plumbing the depths of the guilty act and guilty mind is a start.

Index

For the benefit of digital users, indexed terms that span two pages (e.g., 52–53) may, on occasion, appear on only one of those pages.

abstraction, moral propositions, 69
accomplice liability, 291–95
actus reus, 7–9, 71, 307. *See also* *specific topics*
  conventional theory, 7–8, 76, 78–87, 94
  criminal statutes, 8
  definition, 75–76
  insanity and *M'Naghten*, 214–15
  Morissette v. United States, Jackson on, 77
  murder, 7–8
  Powell v. Texas, 73
  power (capacity), 180 (*see also* Stephen test)
  reasonable doubt test, conventional theory, 78–79, 81–87
  voluntary act requirement, 79–80
actus reus, ignorance, 180–86
  insanity, 183–86
  Lex test, 181–83
  rights theory, 90–94
actus reus, knowledge, 121–34
  capacity to choose otherwise, 121–26
  insanity, 132–34
  Stephen test, 127–31, 180
actus reus, rights, 77–94
actus reus, rights theory, 8–9, 87–94
  ignorance, 90–94
  knowledge, 87–90
  reasonable doubt test, 88–90, 91–92
actus reus non facit reum nisi mens sit rea, 75–76, 95–96
addiction. *See also* knowledge
  United States v. Moore, 118–20
  United States v. Moore, dysphoric duress, 140–42
  United States v. Moore, insanity, 133
  thin ice principle, 158–60
  willing addict, 153–56
agency, 207–59. *See also* delusion; insanity
  authority, 256–59
  definition, 233
  Durham Rule, 220–22, 232–33
  irrationality, 222–33
  irrationality, delusion, 228–33
  irrationality, fundamentals, 222–24
  irrationality, unintelligibility, 223–28
  M'Naghten Rule, 133–34, 208, 210
  M'Naghten's Case, 132, 207–9
  M'Naghten test, 208–9
  Model Penal Code, § 4.01, 217–18
  theory, 233–35
  tradition, 210–21
agency, lost, 233–55
  defects of consciousness, 247–55
  defects of consciousness, hypnosis, 247–50
  defects of consciousness, multiple personality disorder, 252–55
  defects of consciousness, sleepwalking, 250–52
  demon within, 236–46
  reasonable doubt test, 259
  theory, 233–35
alien control, delusions of, 238–40, 242–43, 244, 245, 255
alien hand syndrome, 233–34
alien-self metaphor, 236, 251–52, 254–55
anarchism
  legitimacy, 22–24
  vs. philosophical anarchism, 22–23
anarchism, philosophical, 1–2
  vs. anarchism, 22–23
  criminal law theorists, 9
  legitimacy, 2
  vs. statism, example, 3–6

anarchism–Rex's dilemma, 24–35
  criminalization, 26–29
  culpability, 29–30, 38
  laws Rex, 24–35
  punishment, 30–35
anger, 37–38, 40, 49, 271–72
arrest rates, 58
Article 477, Texas Penal Code, 20, 73, 78, 80, 87, 89, 90–91
auditory verbal hallucination, 240–41
Augustine, Saint, *actus reus non facit reum nisi mens sit rea,* 75–76, 95–96
authority, 20–71, 295–303. *See also specific topics*
  agency, 256–59
  anarchism–Rex's dilemma, 24–35 (*see also* anarchism–Rex's dilemma)
  crimes, core, 299–301
  crimes, non-core, 301–3
  democratic (*see* democratic authority)
  legitimacy, 304
  rights, 60–71
  state of exclusion, 297–99
  statism–Leviathan's peace, 35–46
  United States v. Campbell, 20–24
authority, state
  legitimate action, 2
  limits, 81
  moral power, 2
awareness
  dispositional, 177–78, 192
  occurrent, 175–76, 177

belief
  dispositional, 175–76
  vs. knowledge, 174–75
  unconscious, 175–76
Blackstone, William, 96–97
brainwashing, 266–68, 276
brute desires, 120, 146–47
brute self-control, 143–44, 147
Bryan v. United States, 178–79
burglary, common law
  definition, 94
  mens rea, 95

capacity requirement, 88–90, 91–93
  Stephen test, 127–31
capacity to choose otherwise, 121–26
  compatibilism, 124–25
  hard determinism, 122–25
  libertarianism, 122–23
Capgras delusion, 228, 244
character theory, 114–16
clutchability, 273
cognition
  incapacity, 93
  motivated, 187–88
  unconscious cognitive attitudes, 175–76
command hallucination, 240–41
compatibilism, 124–25
complicity
  common law of, 291–92
  standing theory, 291–95
conative will
  Jekyll test, 186–87
  knowledge, 121, 122–23, 130–31, 137
  Lex test, 182
  motivating reasons, 121
  rights, 97–99, 102, 103, 104, 113
conduct rules, 40–41, 42–43, 44–45. *See also* criminalization
  authority, 62
  vs. decision rules, 45–46, 51
confidence, 174–75, 176
conform, duty to, 38–39, 47–48
  democratic skeptic on, 56–57, 59
  democratic state, 51–56
  morally wronging, 39–40
  political peace, 42, 43–46
  social peace, 36–40
conform, right to, 53
conformity
  anarchist, 23–24
  coercing, moral permission, 47
  state's right to, 47–50
consciousness, 175, 176, 177
consciousness, defects of, 247–55
  hypnosis, 247–50
  multiple personality disorder, 252–55
  sleepwalking, 250–52
consequentialism, 32
conventional theory
  actus reus, 7–8, 76, 78–87, 94
  actus reus, reasonable doubt test, 78–79, 81–87
  mens rea, 7–8, 76, 94–95
  Morissette v. United States, 76, 77

Powell v. Texas, 76
rights, 76
conviction rates, 58
core crimes, 299–301
crime. *See also specific topics and cases*
core, 299–301
definition, 7
non–core, 301–3
crime rates, 58
criminalization, 27–28. *See also* conduct rules
anarchism, 26–29
anarchist *vs.* statist on, 62–65
legal moralism, 27, 28–29
Mill's theory, 26–27, 28
rights, 62–65
rules: crimes, conditions, and punishments, 6–7
theories, 4–5
criminal justice system. *See also specific topics*
on criminal law, 58–59
criticism, more and better justice, 1
criminal law
criminal justice system *vs.* People on, 58–59
malum in se, 26, 27–28, 50–51, 300
non-core rules, 50–51
criminal law theory, 9–12
as moral theory, 9–10
philosophical anarchists, 9
as political theory, 10
purpose, 9, 10–11
criminal statutes, *actus reus,* 8
cruel and unusual punishment, 6–7, 68, 72–73
culpability, 29–30, 38
anarchism, 29–30, 71
M'Naghten's Case, 256–59
rights, 70–71
statism, 71
culpability theory, 281–86

decision-making, democratic, 41–43, 44
decision rules, 45–46. *See also* punishment
authority, 65–70
vs. conduct rules, 45–46
"deific-decree" doctrine, 240–41
delusion, 182. *See also* agency; insanity
alien control, 238–40, 242–43, 244, 245, 255
Capgras, 228, 244
irrationality, 228–33
M'Naghten's Case, 132, 207–9
M'Naghten test, 208–9
of persecution, 243
of reference, 242–43
thought insertion, 239–40, 242, 244
democratic authority, 5–6, 10–12, 46–59, 304–5
actus reus, 11–12
democratic state's authority, 50–59
free and equal, 60
mens rea, 11–12
state, 50–59
state's right to conformity, 47–50
democratic authority, rights, 60–61
disabling, 61
recognition and application, 61
democratic decision-making, 41–43, 44
democratic state, 304–5
limits, 305–9 (see also *actus reus; mens rea*)
limits, disappointment in, 307–8
limits, disbelief in, 308–9
demon within, 236–46
desire
brute, 143–44, 146–47
occurrent, 97, 141
determinism, 122
hard, 122–25
dignity principle, 62
diminished capacity defense. *See* incapacity
disadvantaged
offenders (*see* injustice)
unjustly, 279–80
disappointment, limits of democratic state, 307–8
disbelief, limits of democratic state, 308–9
dispositional awareness, 177–78, 192
dispositional belief (attitude), 175–76
dissociative identity disorder, 252–55
duress, 135–49
defense of, 266–68
dysphoric, 140–49
Model Penal Code, 231, 268
sacrificial, 101, 135–40

Durham Rule, 220–22, 232–33
dysphoric duress, 140–49

Eighth Amendment, cruel and unusual punishment, 6–7, 68, 72–73
electio nocens, 90
endorsement theory, 114, 115–16
epistemic reason, 103–5, 111–12
exclusion, state of, 297–99
executive will, 187
  knowledge, 121, 122–23, 141, 154
  motivating reasons, 103, 121
  rights, knowledge, 97–98

fair play, 47–48
forgetting, Jekyll test, 191–94
freedoms, rights-defining, 63
free speech, right to, 63, 69
fury, 272, 273

greatest punishment law permits, 127, 129, 131
guilty act. See *actus reus; specific topics*
guilty choice, 90
guilty ignorance, 187–91. *See also* Jekyll test
guilty mind. See *mens rea; specific topics*
guilty will, 96–97

Hadfield, James, 231–32
Hall, Jerome, 172
hallucination
  auditory verbal, 240–41
  command, 240–41
  schizophrenia, 225
hard determinism, 122–25
hard resistance, 277–79
harm principle, Mill's, 28, 62
heat of passion defense, 261–62
Hogwarts effect, 130–31, 137
Holmes, Olive Wendell, 29–30, 172
hypnosis, 247–50
hypocrisy, standing theory, 288–91

ignorance, 162–206. See also *ignorantia juris neminem excusat*
  Bryan v. United States, 178–79
  confidence, 174–75, 176
  consciousness, 175, 176, 177
  definition, 174–78
  guilty, 187–91 (*see also* Jekyll test)
  Lambert v. California, 162–65
  tracing, 202–6
  willfully, 176–77, 178–80
ignorance, *actus reus,* 180–86
  insanity, 183–86
  Lex test, 181–83
  rights theory, 90–94
ignorance, *mens rea,* 186–202
  Jekyll test, 186–91
  Jekyll test, applying, 191–202
  Jekyll test, forgetting, 191–94
  Jekyll test, imaginary crimes, 196–99
  Jekyll test, loophole, 194–96
  Jekyll test, stand your ground, 199–202
  rights theory, 103–8
ignorantia juris neminem excusat (ignorance of law does not excuse), 29–30, 70, 92–93, 107. *See also* ignorance
  actus reus and *mens rea* challenge, 308–9
  state exceptions, 169–70
ignorantia juris neminem excusat, Lambert, 166–80
  defending the maxim, 170–73
  ignorance of law defined, 173–80
  ignorance of law defined, "ignorance," 174–78
  ignorance of law defined, "law," 178–80
  maxim's scope, 166–70
  meaning, 166
  notice, 169–70
  Staples v. United States, 168–69
imaginary crimes, Jekyll test, 196–99
immunity right, 91–92, 305
incapacity, 129–30, 183–84. *See also* insanity
  cognitive, 93
  Stephen test, 127–31 (*see also* Stephen test)
inclusive theory, will, 113–14, 116
injustice, 260–303. *See also specific theories*
  authority, 295–303

reform theory, 262, 279–95
revolutionary theory, 262, 263–79
United States v. Alexander, 260–63
United States v. Murdock, 260–63
innocent agency doctrine, 293
insanity. *See also* agency
alien-self metaphor, 236, 251–52, 254–55
hallucination, auditory verbal, 240–41
ignorance, 183–86
irrationality, 222–33 (*see also* irrationality [test])
knowledge, 132–34
knowledge, *United States v. Moore,* 133
M'Naghten, actus reus, 214–15
M'Naghten's Case, 132, 207–9
M'Naghten test, 208–9
normative status, 183–84
traditional test, 210–21
United States v. Durham, 220–21
irrationality
motivated, 104
as unintelligibility, 223–28
irrationality (test), 222–33
delusion, 228–33
fundamentals, 222–24
unintelligibility, 223–28
irresistible impulse, 125–26, 213–14, 220–21
irresistible impulse test, 134, 183, 238

Jekyll test, 108–13, 186
dysphoric duress, 147–49
provocation, 151
sacrificial duress, 137–38, 139
willing addict, 154–55
Jekyll test, ignorance and *mens rea,* 186–91
applying, 191–202
applying, forgetting, 191–94
applying, imaginary crimes, 196–99
applying, loophole, 194–96
applying, stand your ground, 199–202
justice
lack of, 260–303 (*see also* injustice)
legitimacy and, anarchism, 35
requirements, democratic disagreement, 81
social institutions, 304
justice, moral wrongs, 26–28, 36–40
anarchism and Rex's dilemma, 33–34
duty to conform, 39–40
Leviathan's peace, 37–38

Kant, Immanuel, 125–26
knowledge, 118–61
vs. belief, 174–75
United States v. Moore, 118–20
vs. suspicion, 174–75
thin ice principle, 158–60, 202
tracing, 157–61
knowledge, *actus reus,* 121–34
insanity, 132–34
rights theory, 87–90
Stephen test, 127–31, 180
knowledge, capacity to choose otherwise, 121–26
compatibilism, 124–25
hard determinism, 122–25
libertarianism, 122–23
knowledge, *mens rea,* 135–56
duress, 135–49
duress, dysphoric, 140–49
duress, sacrificial, 135–40
provocation, 149–53
rights theory, 97–103
willing addict, 153–56

lack of capacity defense. *See* incapacity
Lambert v. California, 162–65. *See also* ignorance
law, defined, 100, 178–80
law-abiding citizen, Jekyll test, 109, 192–93
legal moralism, 27, 28–29, 62
legitimacy, 1, 22
anarchism, 22–24
authority, 304
philosophical anarchism, 2
statism, 3, 22
Leviathan's peace, 35–46
political, 40–46
social, 36–40
Lex test, 181–83, 215–16
libertarianism, 122–23

limits
authority, state, 81
democratic state, 305–9 (see also *actus reus*; *mens rea*)
democratic state, disappointment in, 307–8
democratic state, disbelief in, 308–9
loophole, Jekyll test, 194–96
lost agency, 233–55
defects of consciousness, 247–55
defects of consciousness, hypnosis, 247–50
defects of consciousness, multiple personality disorder, 252–55
defects of consciousness, sleepwalking, 250–52
demon within, 236–46
reasonable doubt test, 259
theory, 233–35

malum in se, 26, 27–28, 50–51, 300
manipulation argument, 210–11
mar, 27, 28
mens rea, 7–9, 71, 307. *See also specific topics*
burglary, 95
conventional theory, 7–8, 76, 94–95
criminal statutes, 8
definition, 75–76
democratic authority, 11–12
guilty will, 96–97
mental state, 7
Morissette v. United States, 75
Morissette v. United States, Jackson on, 77
murder, 7–8
nature of, 108
reasonable doubt test, 108, 112–13, 115–16
mens rea, ignorance, 186–202
Jekyll test, 186–91
Jekyll test, applying, 191–202
Jekyll test, forgetting, 191–94
Jekyll test, imaginary crimes, 196–99
Jekyll test, loophole, 194–96
Jekyll test, stand your ground, 199–202
rights theory, 103–8
mens rea, knowledge, 135–56
duress, 135–49
duress, dysphoric, 140–49
duress, sacrificial, 135–40
provocation, 149–53
willing addict, 153–56
mens rea, rights theory, 8–9, 87, 95–117
boundaries of will, 113–17
ignorance, 103–8
Jekyll test, 108–13
knowledge, 97–103
mental disease/defect. *See also* insanity; *specific topics and types*
addiction as, 133–34
definition lacking, 133–34
irresistible impulse test, 134, 183, 238
Mill, John Stuart, 28
harm principle, 28, 62
M'Naghten litmus test, 213, 216–17, 218, 226, 228
M'Naghten Rule, 133–34, 208, 210
M'Naghten's Case
agency, 132, 207–9 (*see also* agency; insanity)
culpability, 256–59
M'Naghten test
criticisms, 213–14
new, 212, 213–14
old, 208–9, 210–11
Model Penal Code
§ 4.01, 217–18
necessity and duress, 231, 268
monetary transaction, 20
money laundering. *See also* authority
definition, 26
United States v. Campbell, 12, 20–22, 64 (see also *United States v. Campbell*)
moral agent, 9–10, 54–55, 224–25
moral innocence, 168–69
morality. *See also specific topics*
agent of, 33, 34–35
defying authority of, 33
moral obligation to obey, 48, 80–81
moral permission, 23–24
moral power, 22
authority, state, 2
definition, 2
moral reasoning, 81–82
moral responsibility. *See* revolutionary theory
moral theory, 9–10

moral wrongs justice, 26–28, 36–40
  anarchism and Rex's dilemma, 33–34
  duty to conform, 39–40
  Leviathan's peace, 37–38
Morissette v. United States, 73–75
  conventional theory, 76, 77
  executive will and conative will, 98
  Jackson, *actus reus* and *mens rea,* 77
  Jackson, Court opinion, 77
  motivating reason, 98
  rights theory, 76–77
motivated cognition (reasoning), 187–88
motivated irrationality, 104
motivating reason
  capacity to choose otherwise, 121–23, 125
  competing, 97–98
  conative will, 97–98, 103, 121
  definition, 103
  desire, 130–31
  duress, dysphoric, 141–46, 149
  duress, sacrificial, 137–38
  executive will, 103, 121
  Jekyll test, 108, 109, 112–13
  mens rea, 108
  provocation, 151
  Stephen test, 127–28, 131
  will, boundaries of, 113–16
  willing addict, 154
multiple personality disorder, 252–55
murder. *See also* agency; insanity
  actus reus, 7–8
  core crime, 12, 299–301
  Jekyll test, 191–202
  malum in se, 26
  mens rea, 7–8
  M'Naghten, 207–9 (see also *M'Naghten's Case*)
  moral wrong, 26
  provocation and dysphoric stress, 150–53
  sleepwalking, 250–52
  stand your ground, 199–202
  United States v. Alexander, 260–63 (*see also* injustice)

non–core crimes, 301–3
normative status, 22

occurrent awareness, 175–76, 177
occurrent desire, 97, 141

partial capacity defense. *See* incapacity
peace
  political, 304–5
  political, good of, 51
  political, Leviathan's, 40–46
  social, Leviathan's, 36–40
penalty *vs.* punishment, 37–38
persecution, delusions of, 243
philosophical anarchism, 1–2
  vs. anarchism, 22–23
  criminal law theorists, 9
  legitimacy, 2
  vs. statism, example, 3–6
political obligation, 47–48
political peace, 40–46, 304–5
  good of, 51
political theory, 10
Powell v. Texas, 72–73
  actus reus, 73
  actus reus, rights theory, 87–89
  actus reus, rights theory, ignorance, 90–91
  actus reus, rights theory, knowledge, 87–94
  capacity requirement, 88–90, 91–93
  conventional theory, 76
  rights theory, 76–77
  voluntary act requirement, 32–88
power (capacity), *actus reus,* 180
private property, right to, 63
product test (*Durham* Rule), 220–22, 232–33
proportionality, punishment, 66–68
provocation, 149–53
public wrong, 34
punishment. *See also* decision rules
  anarchist, 30–35
  anarchist *vs.* statist on, 65–66
  cruel and unusual, 6–7, 68, 72–73
  greatest punishment law permits, 127, 129, 131
  vs. penalty, 37–38
  proportionality, 66–68
  rights, 65–70
  rules: crimes, conditions, and punishments, 6–7

reasonable doubt test
  actus reus, conventional theory, 78–79, 81–87
  actus reus, rights theory, 88–90, 91–92
  lost agency, 259
  mens rea, 108, 112–13, 115–16
  voluntary act requirement, 80–87
  willing addict, 156
reasonable person, 109
reasoning
  epistemic, 103–5, 111–12
  moral, 81–82
  motivated, 187–88
reference, delusions of, 242–43
reform theory, 262, 279–95
  culpability theory, 281–86
  standing theory, 281, 286–95
  standing theory, complicity, 291–95
  standing theory, hypocrisy, 288–91
resistance, revolutionary theory, 274–79
  hard, 277–79
  soft, 275–77
retribution, 31–32
retributivism, 31–32
revolutionary theory, 262, 263–79
  after the revolution, 270–74
  argument, 263
  resistance, 274–79
  resistance, hard, 277–79
  resistance, soft, 275–77
  revolutionary road, 263–70
  revolutionary road, fundamentals, 263–64
  revolutionary road, stop 1, 264–66
  revolutionary road, stop 2, 266–68
  revolutionary road, stop 3, 268–69
  revolutionary road, stop 4, 270
Rex's dilemma, 24–35. *See also* anarchism–Rex's dilemma
rights, 60–71. *See also specific types and topics*
  conventional theory, 76
  crimes and conditions, limiting, 6–7
  criminalization, 62–65
  culpability, 70–71
  democratic authority, 60–61
  democratic authority, disabling, 61
  democratic authority, recognition and application, 61
  free speech, 63, 69
  fundamentals, 60–71
  Morissette v. United States, 73–75
  Powell v. Texas, 72–73
  private property, 63
  punishment, 65–70
rights, *actus reus,* 77–94
  conventional theory, 76, 78–87, 94
  reasonable doubt test, conventional theory, 78–79, 81–87
rights, *mens rea,* 94–117
  conventional theory, 76, 94–95
  reasonable doubt test, 108, 112–13, 115–16
rights-defining freedoms, 63
rights theory, 8–9, 76–77
  Morissette v. United States, 76–77
  Powell v. Texas, 76–77
rights theory, *actus reus,* 8–9, 87–94
  ignorance, 90–94
  knowledge, 87–90
  reasonable doubt test, 88–90, 91–92
rights theory, *mens rea,* 95–117
  boundaries of will, 113–17
  ignorance, 103–8
  Jekyll test, 108–13
  knowledge, 97–103

sacrificial duress, 101, 135–40
schizophrenia, 245
self
  character theory, 114–16
  conative will, 97–99, 102, 103, 104, 113
  endorsement theory, 114, 115–16
  inclusive theory of will, 113–14, 116
self-control
  brute, 143–44, 147
  brute desires, 120
  dysphoric duress, 141–45, 147, 148–49, 151
  Jekyll test, 149, 151, 154
  provocation, 153
  skilled, 142–44, 146–47
  synchronic, 142
self-deception, 104, 187–91, 239
skilled self-control, 142–44, 146–47
sleepwalking, 250–52

social peace, 36–40
soft resistance, 275–77
specific-intent crimes, 95
standing theory, 281, 286–95
  complicity, 291–95
  hypocrisy, 288–91
stand your ground, Jekyll test and ignorance, 199–202
Staples v. United States, 168–69
state of exclusion, 297–99
United States v. Moore, 118–20
  dysphoric duress, 140–42
  insanity, 133
State v. King, 194–96
statism, 1, 2–3
  legitimacy, 22
  vs. philosophical anarchism, example, 3–6
statism–Leviathan's peace, 35–46
  political peace, 40–46
  social peace, 36–40
Stephen, James Fitzjames, 127
Stephen test, 127–31, 180, 215–16
  willing addict, 154, 155
suspicion, *vs.* knowledge, 174–75
synchronic self-control, 142

theoretical reason. *See also specific theories*
  failure and its causes, 186–87
  stress test (*see* Lex test)
thin ice principle, 158–60, 202
  ignorant defendant, 202–3
thought insertion, 239–40, 242, 244
tracing
  ignorance, 202–6
  knowledge, 157–61

unconscious belief, 175–76
unconscious cognitive attitudes, 175–76
unintelligibility theory, irrationality, 223–28
United States v. Alexander, 260–63. *See also* injustice
United States v. Campbell, 20–24, 64
  court of justice appeal, 21–22
  facts of case, 20
  response, anarchist, 22–24
  response, legitimacy, 22
  response, statist, 22
United States v. Contento-Pachon, 135–39
United States v. Durham, 220–21
United States v. Peterson, 199–202
unjustly disadvantaged, 279–80

vicious will, 96, 97, 98–99
voluntary act requirement
  actus reus, 79–80
  executive will, 97–98
  reasonable doubt test, 80–87
voluntary movement, 73

will
  boundaries, 113–17
  conative, 97–99, 102, 103, 104, 113
  executive (*see* executive will)
  guilty, 96–97
  inclusive theory, 113–14, 116
  quality of, 98–100, 103, 108, 113–15
  on reason, 187
  stress test for (*see* Stephen test)
  vicious, 96, 97, 98–99
  weakness, 239
willfully ignorant, 176–77, 178–80
willing addict, 153–56
willpower, 144–45
wishful thinking, 104, 187–91
writ large, 100
wrong, public, 34